Sunset
Western Garden
Annual

2000 EDITION

By the Editors of *Sunset Magazine* and Sunset Books

Flowering dogwood in a Portland garden *(page 126)*

Sunset Publishing Corporation ■ **Menlo Park, California**

NORMAN A. PLATE

SUNSET BOOKS

VP and General Manager
Richard A. Smeby
VP, Editorial Director
Bob Doyle
Production Director
Lory Day
Art Director
Vasken Guiragossian

STAFF FOR THIS BOOK

Managing Editor
Suzanne Normand Eyre
Contributing Editors
Philip Edinger
Helen Sweetland
Production Assistance
Linda Bouchard
Indexer
Pamela Evans
Production Coordinator
Patricia S. Williams

SUNSET PUBLISHING CORPORATION

President/Chief Executive Officer
Steve Seabolt
VP, Consumer Marketing Director
Robert I. Gursha
VP, Manufacturing Director
Lorinda Reichert
VP, Editor-in-Chief, Sunset Magazine
Rosalie Muller Wright
Managing Editor
Carol Hoffman
Art Director
James H. McCann
Senior Editor, Gardening
Kathleen Norris Brenzel
Designers
Dennis W. Leong
Laura H. Martin
Keith Whitney

Annual Inspiration

Now in its seventh year of publication, the *Western Garden Annual* contains the entire body of gardening and outdoor living material from the prior year's issues of *Sunset Magazine*. In each of its 12 chapters—one for each month of 1999—you will find not only the articles that appeared that month in your own region, but also those from the other regional editions of the magazine.

Each month's chapter begins with the Garden Guide's mini-articles: brief descriptions of gardening events, plants, tools, innovations, and landscaping relevant to that month or to one just ahead. Some of these bulletins appear in a recurrent format, such as the Back to Basics boxes, in which elementary techniques are reviewed. Following that section, separate Checklists for each region serve as reminders for garden tasks advisable to complete that month. Concluding each chapter are the illustrated feature-length articles that appeared in all of that month's editions.

As you peruse these chapters, you'll notice that plant performance and gardening activities are keyed to numbered climate zones. Those 24 zones, covering the entire West, are described and mapped in the sixth edition (1995) of the *Sunset Western Garden Book*.

Front cover: A hardy water lily, 'Comanche' has pale peach petals brushed with rose. Cover design: Vasken Guiragossian. Photographer: Norman A. Plate.

Back cover: *Rhynchelytrum nerviglume* 'Pink Crystals' (see page 68). Photographer: Allan Mandell.

Endpapers (hardcover edition): Tulips. Photographer: Norman A. Plate.

All material in this book originally appeared in the 1999 issues of *Sunset Magazine*.

Sunset Western Garden Annual was produced by Sunset Books. If you have comments or suggestions, please let us hear from you. Write us at:

Sunset Books
Garden Book Editorial
80 Willow Road
Menlo Park, CA 94025
or visit our website at
www.sunsetbooks.com

Contents

This garden of greens achieves distinction through an artful mingling of foliage textures and variations on the theme color. The Sonoma fieldstone and weathered wood deck merge seamlessly into clumps of blue fescue (see page 255).

Sunset and the West: Partners in Progress

The West has long been a meeting ground for peoples and traditions from far-flung parts of the globe. And from this dynamic mingling has come a distinctly Western viewpoint on, and approach to, gardening. Here in the West, with no sense of culture shock, we observe effervescent cottage-style plantings next door to spare Zen-inspired gardens. Down the street we see endless variations on amalgams of Mediterranean, Mexican, and postmodern motifs. Now that one century has closed and a new one opens before us, *Sunset* can reflect with pride on its role in developing this wide-ranging blend of styles throughout the 1900s. For over 70 years of that era, in fact, Westerners—both native born and eager new arrivals—turned to *Sunset Magazine* for dependable, cogent, up-to-the-minute advice on all aspects of gardening and outdoor living in their privileged Western climates.

The year 1999 offers a perfect sampling of that certain *je ne sais quois* that is Western gardening. Stylistic innovations received major play. February's issue covered the second biennial Western Garden Design Awards, showcasing creative gardens that perfectly illustrate Western panache and variety. Then, in May, a photo essay premiered the all-new *Sunset* "Idea Gardens" established at the Los Angeles Arboretum, where gardeners can gain design inspiration to take home and adapt. Acknowledging the yen for serenity in contemporary life, September's issue featured a planting scheme composed totally of green. And throughout, to satisfy the typically Western do-it-yourself spirit, readers were invited to design their own hanging basket "gardens," wreaths of all sorts, elaborate raised-bed plots, and "instant" ponds and pathways.

If design furnishes a garden's bones, it is plants that flesh them out. Featured in 1999 among others were colorful callas, foolproof daylilies, lush hydrangeas, lavish Sasanqua camellias, and mild-climate tulips. New and worthy plants brought to readers' attention included 'Peaches 'n' Dreams' hollyhock, hybrid penstemons, the Fiesta series of double impatiens, *Callibrachoa,* and 'Pink Crystals' ruby grass. Regional tips promoted perennials for desert gardens, cold-hardy climbing roses for mountain states, and showy Australian shrubs for mild-winter California zones.

Devotees of homegrown edibles digested a feast of information: choosing and growing strawberries, how and when to harvest vegetables, starting seeds indoors, growing year-round salad greens, and more. Techniques ranged from protecting and caging tomatoes to transplanting seedlings to sowing a cover crop for natural fertilizer. For the ultimate start-from-scratchers, "The Best Seeds in the West" and similar features guided readers to innovative suppliers.

Does this sound like Nirvana . . . or Paradise? It may be close, but it's also just another typical Western gardening year.

GARDENERS who plant these humble brown root crowns and tubers are rewarded with delicious perennial vegetables that are handsome as well. Advice on growing bare-root vegetables begins on page 16.

January

gardenguide

A jewel of a rose

■ Velvety-textured red flowers and handsome, disease-resistant foliage make 'Raven' a rose to treasure. This new introduction from Weeks Roses doesn't fit neatly into any category. Its 1- to 2-inch-wide flowers and small leaves would make 'Raven' perfect for the miniature category, but its 4-foot height makes it too tall to qualify. It's actually a small shrub rose.

No matter. 'Raven' is just the right size for the garden. It looks good in front of taller roses, combined with perennials and shrubs in a flower border, or as a solo act in a container. In our test gardens, we found it a generous producer and nearly maintenance-free. It's nice for cutting, too; all the flowers in a cluster tend to open together, and the blossoms last a long time.

If you can't find 'Raven' at your nursery, ask to have it ordered from Weeks Roses, the wholesale grower. Or mail-order it from Regan Nursery in Fremont, California; (510) 797-3222.

— *Sharon Coboon*

GARNET-COLORED 'Raven' sparkles in garden beds.

Gold-medal zinnias and a "zuke" in the round

■ What if you combined the best traits of two garden-worthy zinnias in a single plant? Breeders at Sakata Seed America in Morgan Hill, California, did just that by crossing heavy-blooming *Zinnia angustifolia* with large-flowered *Z. elegans* to create the new Profusion series. This "breeding breakthrough" so impressed judges for the 1999 All-America Selections, they awarded the AAS Gold Medal—the first in 10 years—to 'Profusion Cherry' and 'Profusion Orange' (shown at far right).

Profusion zinnias bear masses of 1½- to 3-inch, daisylike flowers over a long season. The deep cherry red or reddish orange blooms are borne among supple, deep green leaves on 12- to 18-inch-tall plants. In *Sunset*'s gardens, they performed equally well in sunny beds and in containers. Another big plus: Profusion zinnias resist powdery mildew, a trait they inherited from *Z. angustifolia*.

Also on this year's AAS honor roll is 'Eight Ball'—a perfectly round squash with the dark green skin of zucchini. Its mild-tasting fruits mature early on plants compact enough to grow in

containers. They're best if harvested when they're 2 to 3 inches across. If you let them reach softball size, seeds start to form and the flesh becomes pithy, but you can still hollow them out to stuff and bake. Like other squash, 'Eight Ball' is susceptible to powdery mildew; to discourage it, avoid overhead water.

Look for seedlings of both plants in nurseries this spring, or order seed from Park Seed Co.; (800) 845-3369. — *Dick Bushnell*

QUICK TIP

Shape-up time for roses

■ Unlike hybrid tea roses, which benefit from heavy pruning in winter, shrub and ground cover roses need only shaping or light shearing. Their casual, unstructured form is part of their appeal in home gardens.

FOR SHRUB ROSES:

Remove dead growth and prune old, weak, or diseased canes. Then cut back wayward stems.

If you want to reduce the plant's height and create a bushier form, shear it back by a third to a half.

FOR GROUND COVER ROSES:

Cut back stems of Flower Carpet and other ground cover roses by about a third of their length. To develop a more prostrate form, cut vertical stems back to the plant's main stem.

NORMAN A. PLATE (3)

DEBRA LAMBERT (3)

Three-in-one orchard is a space-saver

■ If you have room for just one stone fruit tree, you can squeeze in three. With space for two, you can shoehorn in six. How? Plant three trees in a triangular space not much bigger than you'd use for one.

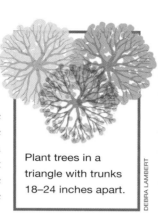

Plant trees in a triangle with trunks 18–24 inches apart.

DEBRA LAMBERT

This age-old technique triples your options. You can stretch the harvest of one fruit crop by planting early-, mid-, and late-season varieties—'Snow Queen', 'Heavenly White', and 'Arctic Queen' nectarines, for instance. Or plant two or three different fruit trees—a peach, a nectarine, and a self-fruiting plum.

Most stone fruit trees can be planted three-to-one. Just make sure the trees have comparable rootstocks—a tree with a standard rootstock will rapidly outgrow companions grafted onto dwarf or semidwarf stock. Find out whether the trees you want are self-fruiting or need second pollinators. And determine whether the area where you live can provide the necessary chill hours for the trees you want to grow.

Once you've decided on your triplets, here's how to plant:

1 Select a sunny, well-draining site where you can plant three trees in a triangle with the trunks spaced 18 to 24 inches apart.

2 For each tree, dig a hole that's broad and deep enough to accommodate the roots easily. (Cut off broken roots and shorten long, stringy ones first.)

3 Make a firm cone of soil in the bottom of the first hole. Spread the roots of one tree over the cone, positioning the plant so that the bud union is slightly aboveground and

MARION BRENNER

tilting the tree slightly outward. Repeat in the next two holes.

4 Backfill each hole with soil (mixed with organic amendments if desired), firming with your fingers as you fill. Water well. When the soil settles, check plant height. If necessary, pull the tree up slightly so the bud union is aboveground again.

5 On each tree, prune off any limbs that cross its center or reach out to cross the center of the neighboring tree. Cut each tree's main stem back to about 4 feet aboveground to force scaffold limbs to develop. Remove all but three or four well-spaced branches per tree, and shorten the remaining branches to two buds. In subsequent years, never allow any one tree to dominate and shade out the others. — *S. C.*

NORMAN A. PLATE

Sharp pruner with a long reach

■ The Pruning Stik has features that make it more versatile than a conventional pole pruner. Weighing just 2 pounds, the device consists of a 4½-foot-long aluminum pole topped by a pruning head that rotates in a 240° arc. By turning the head, you select the best angle for cutting overhead branches or plants at ground level. The steel bypass pruning blades cut wood up to 1¼ inches in diameter. To activate the cord-operated blades, you pull a handle in the middle of the pole or a ball at the bottom. The Pruning Stik costs $65 to $80. To find a dealer near you, call Fiskars (800/500-4849 or 608/643-4389); or order by mail from Improvements (800/642-2112). — *Lauren Bonar Swezey*

Pacific Northwest Checklist

PLANTING

☑ **BARE-ROOT STOCK.** Zones 4–7: Shop for bare-root berries, grapes, fruit and shade trees, and ornamental shrubs and roses, as well as perennial vegetables (see page 16). Get them into the ground any time the soil can be worked.

☑ **HARDY PERENNIALS.** Sow seed in coldframes or greenhouses for hardy perennials like delphiniums, hellebores, veronicas, and violas. About a month before the last frost is expected, plant seedlings with one or two sets of true leaves in beds outdoors.

☑ **WINTER-BLOOMING SHRUBS.** Zones 4–7: An amazing group of shrubs bloom this month, including Chinese witch hazels, hybrid camellias, and wintersweet. You'll find them in nurseries in full bloom, ready to plant.

MAINTENANCE

☑ **CARE FOR HOUSE PLANTS.** When dust accumulates on leaves, set plants in the shower and rinse them with tepid water. Water carefully, but fertilize only those plants that bloom or set fruit this time of year. Otherwise, wait until April to begin a feeding program. Groom plants, snipping off dead or yellow foliage. If soil at the top of the pot is crusty, use a spoon to scoop off an inch or two, or enough to expose roots. Then add a fresh layer of sterile potting mix.

DEBRA LAMBERT

☑ **CHECK STORED BULBS.** One rotten bulb or tuber can spoil the whole batch. Throw out ones with soft spots. Dahlia tubers are the exception; cut out any bad spots, dust tubers with sulfur, and store away from others. If bulbs are shriveled, sprinkle on a little water to rehydrate them.

☑ **FERTILIZE ASPARAGUS.** Top-dress rows with well-rotted manure, or sprinkle a complete granular fertilizer over plantings.

☑ **PRUNE FRUIT TREES.** Zones 4–7: Prune on a day when temperatures are well above freezing. First, cut out dead, diseased, and closely parallel or crossing branches. Then prune for shape. In zones 1–3, hold off pruning until spring.

PEST CONTROL

☑ **APPLY DORMANT OIL.** Spray dormant oil on deciduous fruit and ornamental trees and shrubs to kill larvae, eggs, and overwintering insects.

☑ **FIGHT SLUGS.** Each time there's a warm spell, slugs awaken and nibble. Scatter bait under rocks, through ground covers, and under decks, patios, and shrubs. Keep children and pets away from the poison bait. Scatter bait on a still, dry day. ◆

Northern California Checklist

PLANTING

☑ **CHOOSE NEW SHRUBS WISELY.** Zones 7–9, 14–17: Before you buy a shrub, consider the height and spread it will reach at maturity. Otherwise, it might grow too large for the space where you want it. Plant only shrubs that will fit.

☑ **DECORATE WITH ORCHIDS.** Nurseries and florists stock a number of blooming orchids this month. Liven up your living room with a corsage orchid (*Cattleya*), miniature cymbidium, moth orchid (*Phalaenopsis*), *Oncidium,* or pansy orchid (*Miltonia*). All of these orchids need bright light indoors. Cool temperatures prolong bloom. Move cymbidiums outdoors when bloom is over (protect them from frost).

☑ **PERK UP FLOWER BEDS.** Zones 7–9, 14–17: Ornamental vegetables add an interesting new dimension to flower beds. Some cool-season choices include cabbage, chard, kale, and red and green lettuces. Mix them with Iceland poppies, Johnny-jump-ups, pansies, and violas.

Sunset
CLIMATE ZONES

Mountain (1-2)
Valley (7-9)
Inland (14)
Coastal (15-17)

DEBRA LAMBERT

☑ **PLANT BARE-ROOT.** Zones 7–9, 14–17: This is the prime month to buy and plant dormant roses, shrubs, fruit and shade trees, and vines. Bare-root plants cost less and adapt more quickly than those sold in containers. Plant immediately. Or if necessary, temporarily lay the plants on their sides in a shallow trench and cover them with moist sawdust or soil (a process called "heeling in"). For tips on planting bare-root perennial vegetables, see page 16.

☑ **SHOP FOR AZALEAS AND CAMELLIAS.** Zones 7–9, 14–17: Now, while plants are blooming, is a good time to shop for azaleas and camellias. But don't be swayed by the flower color alone. Before buying, make sure the plants are healthy and lushly green. Avoid plants that are potbound, with circling roots protruding through the drain holes.

☑ **SOW VEGETABLE SEEDS.** Zones 7–9, 14–17: Sow seeds of cool-season vegetables such as chard, lettuce, and spinach for planting out in February. For a change of color, try 'Bacardi' or 'Merveille des Quatre Saisons' red butterhead lettuce, or 'Rouge d'Hiver' red romaine. All are available from Ornamental Edibles (408/946-7333).

MAINTENANCE

☑ **CUT BACK HYDRANGEAS.** Zones 7–9, 14–17: Cut stems that have bloomed back to 12 inches. To produce fewer, larger flowers next spring, also reduce the number of stems by cutting some of them back to the base of the plant. For more numerous, medium-size blooms, retain more stems.

PEST CONTROL

☑ **APPLY DORMANT SPRAY.** Zones 7–9, 14–17. To control overwintering insects, such as woolly aphids on apples and bud moths on plums, spray fruit trees with horticultural (dormant) oil. Hold off spraying if freezing weather or rain is predicted. ◆

Southern California Checklist

PLANTING

✔ **BUY BARE-ROOT PLANTS.** They cost less than leafed-out ones, and they take hold more quickly. Shop for bare-root artichokes, asparagus and other perennial vegetables, cane berries, deciduous shade trees, roses, stone fruit trees, and strawberries. Plant all immediately. Or, if the soil is too wet, cover roots with loose soil or plant temporarily in containers. (For more on bare-root plants, see page 16.)

✔ **PLANT COOL-SEASON COLOR.** If the soil isn't soggy from rain, there's still time to plant Iceland poppies, pansies, primula, snapdragons, stock, and other winter annuals, especially along the coast. Low-desert gardeners (zone 13) can also plant petunias.

✔ **PLANT WINTER CROPS.** It's not too late to start winter crops from seed, especially if you're patient (cooler temperatures slow germination). Greens—chard, endive, kale, lettuce, mustard, and spinach—are the best bets. Beets, peas, radishes, and turnips can also go in the ground now. Sow dill, fennel, and flat-leafed parsley in bare spots.

Sunset
CLIMATE ZONES
1-3 7-9 11 13 14-24

DEBRA LAMBERT

✔ **SHOP FOR SUCCULENTS.** Winter-blooming succulents add splashes of color to winter plantings. They look especially at home in Mediterranean-style gardens. Look for aloes, echeveria, kalanchoe, and other flowering succulents at your nursery.

MAINTENANCE

✔ **CARE FOR ROSES.** On hybrid tea and climbing roses, cut out all dead wood, crossing branches, and twiggy growth. (For shrub and ground cover roses, see tip on page 9.) Also remove some of the oldest, woodiest canes, leaving three to five strong, vigorous canes on young plants, five to seven on older ones. Prune remaining canes back by a third, making cuts about $1/4$ inch above an outward-facing bud. Strip off remaining leaves. Rake up and dispose of leaves and litter to prevent spread of disease. Spray bare canes with horticulture oil to smother overwintering insects.

✔ **CUT BACK HYDRANGEAS.** Prune stems that have already bloomed to 12 inches tall (make the cuts just above a leaf node). For the largest flowers next spring, reduce the number of stems; if you want more numerous but smaller blooms, keep more stems. To prevent blue hydrangeas from turning pink next spring, irrigate the pruned plant with 1 tablespoon aluminum sulfate per gallon of water.

✔ **DIVIDE PERENNIALS.** If the soil isn't too wet, this is a good month to dig, divide, and replant overcrowded perennials such as agapanthus, African daisies, chrysanthemums, coreopsis, daylilies, delphiniums, dianthus, gazanias, rudbeckia, and Shasta daisies.

✔ **WATER NATIVES.** If rains have been light or nonexistent, water drought-tolerant plants. Irrigate young, unestablished native plants as well. Plants set out in fall also need regular deep soaking. ◆

Mountain Checklist

PLANTING

☑ **ORDER SEEDS.** Seed dealers who specialize in plants for high-elevation gardens are listed in the story beginning on page 22. Early orders are most likely to be filled quickly and with no substitutions. To calculate when to start seeds indoors, find out the average date of the last frost in your area, then count backward about five weeks.

☑ **HARDY PERENNIALS.** In milder parts of the intermountain West, start perennials such as delphinium, hellebore, pansy, primula, veronica, and viola in a coldframe or greenhouse for transplanting when at least two sets of true leaves appear. In the coldest areas, transplant when the soil can be worked.

MAINTENANCE

☑ **CARE FOR LIVING CHRISTMAS TREES.** Move them outside to a place that's protected from hard freezing and from midday and afternoon sun. A cool, bright porch is ideal, but a spot on the patio or under a large tree can work well, too, if outside temperatures aren't so low that the tree's rootball will freeze. If it's too cold, sink the rootball into the ground, container and all, and cover it with mulch. After two weeks in a shaded location, move the tree into full sun.

Sunset
CLIMATE ZONES
☐ 1-3   ☐ 10-11

DEBRA LAMBERT

Water whenever the top 2 inches of soil are dry.

☑ **CHECK STORED BULBS, PRODUCE.** Look over any tender bulbs, corms, tubers, and produce you have stored away to check for shriveling and rot. You can usually rehydrate shriveled bulbs by sprinkling them with water. Remove anything that shows signs of decay. Dahlia tubers are the exception: cut out the bad spots, dust tubers with sulfur, and store separately.

☑ **FERTILIZE ASPARAGUS.** After the ground thaws, top-dress asparagus with rotted manure or organic mulch mixed with a complete fertilizer.

☑ **TEND HOUSE PLANTS.** During the winter, low humidity combined with indoor heat can cause plants to dry out quickly. Check soil often, and water when the top ½-inch has dried out. Also, inspect plants regularly for aphids, scale insects, spider mites, and mealybugs. Sometimes the first sign is sticky honeydew on pot rims and leaves; it's exuded by feeding insects. Rinse infested plants with lukewarm water from the shower, then spray with insecticidal soap to kill the insects and wash off the honeydew.

☑ **TUNE UP TOOLS.** Sharpen shovels and hoes, rub down wood handles with linseed oil, and replace or hone dull blades on pruning shears and knives. Now is also a good time to order new tools for spring work.

☑ **PRUNE TREES, SHRUBS.** In the mildest parts of the intermountain West, you can prune when daytime temperatures are well above freezing. Cut out dead, diseased, crossing, and closely parallel branches first, then prune for shape. ◆

Southwest Checklist

PLANTING

✔ **BARE-ROOT STOCK. Zones 10–13:** In mild-winter areas, shop for bare-root berries, fruit trees, roses, vines, and shade and flowering trees in nurseries; in cooler zones, they'll show up in a month or two. Ask the nursery staff to pack the bare roots in damp peat moss or sawdust for the trip home, then plant immediately.

✔ **PRE-CHILLED BULBS. Zones 12–13:** After six weeks of refrigeration, tulips and other spring-flowering bulbs are ready to plant. Set them out in amended soil and water well.

✔ **VEGETABLES. Zones 12–13:** Sow eggplant, melons, peppers, and tomatoes indoors now for transplanting in the garden when the weather warms up. Hurry to plant seedlings of cool-season vegetables, including salad crops and cabbage family members.

✔ **WINTER COLOR. Zones 11–13:** Set out nursery plants of bachelor's button, calendula, cineraria, cyclamen, English daisy, pansy, primrose, snapdragon, sweet alyssum, and wallflower.

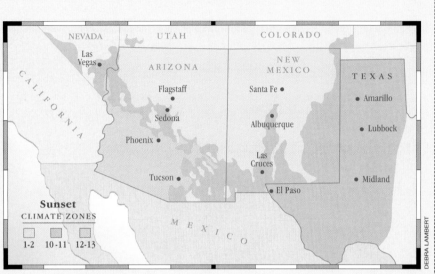

Sunset CLIMATE ZONES ☐ 1-2 ☐ 10-11 ☐ 12-13

DEBRA LAMBERT

MAINTENANCE

✔ **FEED CITRUS TREES.** Thoroughly irrigate the root zones, then apply ammonium sulfate a day later at the following rates for mature trees (five years or older): 2½ pounds for grapefruit, 4 pounds for orange and tangerine, and 5 pounds for lemon. Water again after feeding.

✔ **PROTECT CITRUS FRUIT.** When temperatures below 28° are forecast, cover trees at night with a cloth (old sheets will do); remove the cover in the morning. If fruit is damaged, as it often is when temperatures drop below 25° for more than two hours, pick and juice it within a day.

✔ **PRUNE ROSES.** Cut hybrid tea roses back to three to five of the strongest canes. Prune about a third of the top growth on each remaining cane.

✔ **SPRAY DORMANT TREES AND SHRUBS.** Spray dormant oil on deciduous trees and shrubs to kill overwintering insects, eggs, and larvae.

✔ **SPREAD MULCH.** Keep winter weeds down by spreading a thick layer of mulch around shrubs, trees, vegetables, and flowers.

✔ **WATER LANDSCAPE PLANTS.** During dry spells, deeply water evergreens, including conifers. ◆

Artichoke

That most civilized of thistles, the artichoke, grows on a sturdy stem amid deeply cut, silver-green leaves that arch gracefully to give the plant a fountainlike appearance. It's the unopened flower buds you cook to eat. Rinse them, snip off their thorny tips, then boil them. Serve hot with melted garlic butter or hollandaise sauce, or cold with mayonnaise seasoned with tarragon, mustard, or dill. If you leave the buds on the plant, they open into sumptuous, purple thistle flowers that are handsome in fresh or dried arrangements.

Bare-Root Bounty

Start these perennial vegetables for beauty in spring and flavorful harvests for years to come

At first glance, those humble brown roots of perennial vegetables that fill nursery bins in winter may not seem to promise much. But once they start growing, artichokes, asparagus, horseradish, Jerusalem artichokes, and rhubarb are well worth having on two counts: they're wonderful food plants, and most are unabashedly beautiful. ▲ In the garden, rhubarb stalks have all the architectural grace of Greek columns, red-and-green pillars holding up handsome, heart-shaped leaves. Lush artichoke leaves are equally impressive, along with the airy, cloudlike ferns of asparagus and the sunflowers that cover Jerusalem artichokes. A mature horseradish plant, on the other hand, may look homely, but a single plant is all you need to yield a generous supply of the zesty root. ▲ Plant artichokes, asparagus, rhubarb, and horseradish from root divisions or crowns any time during winter bare-root season—now in mild-winter areas and spring in cold-winter climates. Start Jerusalem artichokes from potato-like tubers in spring. ▲ All of these crops have a decided advantage over annual vegetables: you prepare the soil once, then reap the harvest for years or even decades. Give perennial vegetables full sun and good garden loam (dig a 3-inch layer of compost or rotted manure into the top foot of soil before you plant). If your soil is sand or clay, plant in raised beds filled with imported garden loam.

BY JIM McCAUSLAND • HARVEST PHOTOGRAPHS BY JAMES CARRIER

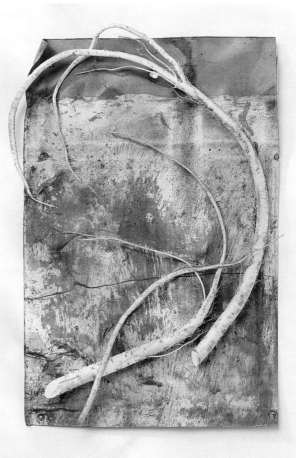

Asparagus

ABOVE LEFT: Asparagus makes a permanent and dependable crop. Choose a spot in the garden where the plants can stay for years—along a sunny fence, for instance. The tall, feathery, graceful ferns are highly ornamental behind other vegetables. Tender spears are one of dinner's great luxuries; they're tasty when steamed whole and served with creamy hollandaise sauce.

Horseradish

ABOVE: More condiment than spice or herb, horseradish is easy to grow; it has adapted well to the West from its native southeastern Europe. In the garden, this perennial forms a large clump of long, narrow, ragged-edged green leaves that feel like chard. It does best in rich, moist soil in cool regions. You peel and grate its white roots to make the spicy-hot sauce (see page 21).

Jerusalem artichoke

LEFT: Jerusalem artichoke (*Helianthus tuberosus*), also known as sunchoke, is not from Jerusalem and not an artichoke. Instead, it takes its first name from *girasole,* Italian for "turn toward the sun," which is something this plant and other sunflowers do from dawn to dusk. In late summer, beneath the 7-foot, bright yellow sunflowers lie rough, tuberous roots with a nutty flavor. They're tasty fresh or cooked like potatoes (see page 21).

Rhubarb

Cooks and gardeners love to argue about the difference between fruits and vegetables (all the trouble stems from differing definitions). But both sides get tongue-tied when it comes to rhubarb. Although it is a vegetable, its tart stalks are cooked, sugared, and used as a fruit. Rinse rhubarb, trim off leaves and dried ends, then cut stalks into pieces for cooking in pies, cobblers, and tarts. Enjoy it, but don't eat too much or you may be reminded of one of the plant's early medicinal uses: its roots were harvested as a powerful laxative. Rhubarb's poisonous leaves, of course, must be avoided; they are toxic if eaten. (Plant out of reach of children.)

Bare-Root Vegetables
Growing Tips

VEGETABLES IN THE RAW: 1. Asparagus root crowns 2. Rhubarb root crowns 3. Artichoke from root division 4. Jerusalem artichoke tubers 5. Horseradish root crowns. 1 and 2 are available by mail from Territorial Seed Company (541/942-9547); and 4 and 5 from Johnny's Selected Seeds (207/437-4301).

Artichoke

Artichokes need mild winters and summers. They thrive in coastal gardens, particularly in central California—the epicenter of Western artichoke culture—where they grow into leafy mounds 5 feet tall. (In hot interior climates, they may grow only half that tall.)

They're propagated in winter or spring from root divisions; these are sold bare-root or, more often, potted up.

WHERE IT GROWS: A dependable perennial crop in *Sunset* climate zones 8, 9, and 14 through 24. Elsewhere, plant in spring when divisions become available at nurseries, and hope for the best. In the desert, grow plants in filtered light, out of direct afternoon sun.

PLANTING AND CARE: Space divisions 4 to 6 feet apart, with growth buds or shoots just above the soil surface. Bait for snails and slugs.

Mulch plants well to keep roots cool and moist in summer. Feed in spring or fall; water whenever the soil surface beneath the mulch dries out. In cold-winter climates, cut plants down to the ground after harvest in fall (unnecessary in mild-winter climates). Replace them every five years or so.

HARVESTING: Pick buds when they're small by cutting stalks 2 to 3 inches below buds with a knife. You can eat buds whole when they're smaller than an apricot. As buds mature and grow, there's more to eat, but also more to discard, as scales become hard and stringy.

Along the central California coast, plants can produce two crops a year. After you harvest the first buds in June, cut the plants down almost to the ground, and they will regrow, giving you a second harvest in autumn. Elsewhere, expect one crop, usually in early summer.

BEST VARIETIES: 'Green Globe' is the standard California artichoke, but there are hardy varieties like 'Imperial Star'. The purple, egg-size 'Violetto' is also becoming popular.

Asparagus

Buy bare-root crowns (clumps of roots and dormant buds). Asparagus plants are either male or female. Look for all-male varieties: instead of wasting energy producing seeds, males grow bigger spears (and more of them) and spare you the task of weeding out inferior seedlings. If you grow a variety that contains both male and female plants, cut the seed capsules off the females to eliminate seedlings later.

Plants take two to three years to come into full production.

WHERE IT GROWS: All zones.

PLANTING AND CARE: Dig a trench about 6 inches deep in well-amended soil. Set the crowns in the trench at 15-inch intervals, and cover them with 2 inches of soil. As the spears grow, add 2 inches of soil for every 2 inches of growth, barely covering the tips of the new spears. Keep doing this until the soil is mounded 4 inches above ground level.

At planting time, add 1 pound of 5-10-10 fertilizer per 12½ feet of row. In following years, mix a high-nitrogen

NORMAN A. PLATE (6)

fertilizer into the soil just before new spears appear, then again after harvest.

HARVESTING: To strengthen their roots and ensure good harvests in the years to come, let asparagus shoots develop into ferns the first season. Wait until the second spring to harvest a few spears. From the third spring onward, you can harvest spears over a two-month period, or until new spears start to become thinner. When they're just $^3/_8$ inch in diameter, stop picking.

Harvest by snapping or cutting 5- to 10-inch spears off at ground level. In fall in mild regions, cut ferns to the ground. In snowy-winter areas, leave them until late winter so the ferns can help hold the snow mulch in place and protect the roots below from freezing (they can tolerate temperatures to −40° with no damage).

BEST VARIETIES: 'UC 157' (about 70 percent male); 'Jersey Giant', 'Jersey King', and 'Jersey Knight' (all male). Purple varieties like 'Purple Passion' are also gaining popularity for flavor and color.

Horseradish

WHERE IT GROWS: All zones except the low desert (zone 13).

PLANTING, CARE: Plant the fleshy roots in the ground 2 to 3 feet apart, or in a horseradish container like the one pictured here. Either way, horseradish that's rooted in spring will be ready to harvest after you cut the tops off in fall; it yields about 1 pound of roots per plant. Unless your soil is poor, horseradish needs no fertilizing, since nitrogen encourages forked roots. Horseradish does need regular water; grown drier, it produces smaller, more pungent roots.

HARVESTING: For horseradish in the ground, you can harvest either the lateral roots, leaving the center taproot to renew the plant, or harvest the main taproot itself.

If you're going to try the second method, carefully remove the soil from around the top two-thirds of the root when the plant is a foot tall. Nip off the lateral roots you've exposed, then gently repack the soil around the taproot. Repeat the process six weeks later. This directs the plant's energy into the main taproot, allowing it to grow fat for fall harvest; it's far easier to peel and prepare one large root than several small ones. After you've dug the taproot, replant one of the lateral roots growing off the bottom of the taproot to make next year's plant. Don't leave other bits of root in the soil, since they too will grow new plants and you'll have a hard-to-harvest colony instead of a single plant.

BEST VARIETIES: There are few named varieties of horseradish.

HORSERADISH SAUCE: Put $1^1/_2$ cups peeled and diced horseradish root in a food processor. Whirl it with 1 small peeled, diced turnip, 1 teaspoon salt, and $^1/_2$ teaspoon sugar; slowly pour in 1 cup white vinegar. Yield: 3 cups prepared horseradish, which keeps about three months in the refrigerator.

Jerusalem artichoke

WHERE IT GROWS: All zones.

PLANTING, CARE: Plant tubers on the north side of the garden, where they won't shade shorter plants, or in a space you can contain (in the narrow strip between the sidewalk and garage, for example). Four to six weeks before the last spring frost, plant the tubers whole or in two-eyed chunks (eyes up) 5 inches deep. If you have to plant in open garden, surround the plants with the kind of plastic root barrier that's often sold to contain bamboo. If you don't, they'll spread and become pests.

HARVESTING: Start digging tubers for harvest after the first frost, which sweet-

ens them. You can leave some tubers in the ground for winter harvest and for next year's plants, or dig all the tubers and refrigerate them. Any tuber you leave in the ground will regrow and spread.

Scrub or peel the tubers; submerge them in water with a little lemon juice added to prevent browning, then dice them to use like water chestnuts in salads or stir-fries. Or steam them until tender (about 15 minutes if whole, 5 to 10 minutes for slices) and season with butter, tarragon, or lemon juice.

BEST VARIETIES: For smooth tubers (easier to clean), try 'Red Fuseau', which doesn't bloom readily. For lots of rather rough tubers, try 'Stampede'.

Rhubarb

WHERE IT GROWS: Best in zones 1 through 11 (in cold-winter areas it can produce for decades), but it can handle mild winters (zones 14–24) too, if summers aren't too hot. In the desert, grow rhubarb as a fall-planted annual for harvest in winter and spring; it stops growing and starts rotting when daytime temperatures average above 90°.

PLANTING AND CARE: Plant rhubarb with the top of the crown at the soil surface, and mulch with manure in fall and spring. Rhubarb is virtually pest-free, but it is vulnerable to drought. Cut out flower stalks when they appear.

HARVESTING: You can harvest in spring of the second year, but you won't get a full crop until the third or fourth spring. To harvest, pull stalks back from the base of the plant and twist. Don't cut them off—the remaining stalk will rot. You can take up to a third of the stalks from a mature plant over a 10-week period every year without hurting the plant.

BEST VARIETIES: 'Victoria', with its greenish red stalk, is a standard. Heavy-producing 'Cherry Red' is excellent-flavored. 'MacDonald', 'Valentine', and 'Crimson Red' are all very red. ◆

The best seeds in the West

Regional seed dealers round up an amazing variety of flowers, herbs, vegetables, and native plants

BY SHARON COHOON

■ Kids know: Planting a seed in the ground and pulling up a radish a few weeks later is magic. Some Westerners never outgrow their fascination with it. So they put their wonder to work by becoming seed dealers. "You start with a handful of seeds, turn it into a bushelful, and then into a truckload. And it never stops being amazing," says Howard Shapiro, vice president of agriculture at Seeds of Change in Santa Fe.

Climatic diversity is one reason there are so many seed dealers in the West. In coastal areas, the weather is mild enough that crops can be grown year-round. But in the mountains and the deserts, conditions such as short growing seasons or sparse rainfall are so challenging that regional varieties are bred to cope with them.

Idealism also plays a part. Individuals with a mission—whether it's perpetuating native flora, growing seeds organically, or helping preserve genetic biodiversity—have turned their passions into livelihoods. Multiculturalism contributes, too. Exposed to Asian and Latin American produce well before the rest of the country, Western-

ers have developed adventurous palates and a penchant for growing exotic crops.

Thanks to the collective efforts of these Western seedsmen and -women, home gardeners here have one of the world's richest seed banks at their disposal. Request the catalogs (free unless noted) of the seed firms listed here and curl up with them on a chilly night. Then order some plant you've never tried, perhaps one of the growers' picks, and experience that magic all over again.

Abundant Life Seed Foundation

This nonprofit organization is dedicated to preserving rare heirloom vegetables, medicinal herbs, and Pacific Northwest natives.

SPECIALTIES: About 140 tomato varieties, including 'Slava', an heirloom tomato from the Czech Republic.

GROWER'S PICK: Jake's melon, an heirloom cantaloupe that bears exceptionally sweet fruit.

Catalog $2 donation. Box 772, Port Townsend, WA 98368; (360) 385-5660 or abundant@olypen.com.

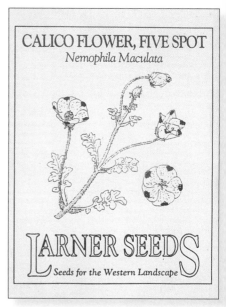

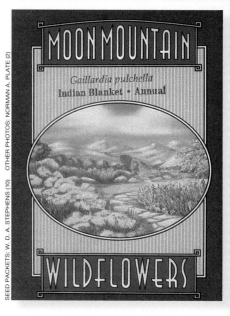

The Golden Poppy
State Flower of California

Theodore Payne Foundation
10459 Tuxford Street
Sun Valley, CA 91352

Seeds of Change®
ORGANICALLY GROWN SEEDS

Net Wt.
3 gm

TARAHUMARA WHITE SHELLED
SUNFLOWER

CANARY BIRD VINE
Tropaeolum peregrinum

$1.09
NET WT.
1.25 g

FAST
GROWING
CLIMBER

Hints enclosed-See back

Ed Hume Seeds

Ornamental
Edibles
SPECIALTY SEEDS BY MAIL

HERB
PUPRLE PASSION BASIL

Garden Seeds

SWEET
PEAS
Winter Flowering Mix
LATHYRUS ODORATUS (A)
FL3297
Sampler / 3 grams
Packed for 1998 - $2.75

Territorial Seed Company
P.O. Box 157, Cottage Grove, Oregon 97424

GROWERS & IMPORTERS OF QUALITY SEEDS
NICHOLS GARDEN NURSERY

HERB SWEET BASIL

H012 GENOVESE SELECT

1190 North Pacific Hwy. Albany, OR 97321

WHERE & WHEN TO PLANT: Plant seed indoors in
boxes for transplanting to the open later when weather
is thoroughly settled.
HOW TO PLANT: As seed is very fine, should be barely
covered with finely sifted soil & well pressed down.
HOW TO THIN OR TRANSPLANT: When plants are
2" tall to their outdoor location spacing plants 12" apart
in rows, 18" apart.
REMARKS: Foliage should be gathered by mid-sum-
mer when in blossom, cutting to within a few inches of
ground. Stumps will develop a second and sometimes
a third crop.

150 MG

Net Wt.

Oriental Vegetable Seeds
Chinese Kale (Kailaan)

NET WT.
2 G

芥 藍 Cái Ró

EVERGREEN Y.H. ENTERPRISES

4 g
$1.50
HALLOWEEN PUMPKIN
Organically grown
MONTANA JACK

A great carving pumpkin with thick flesh
for tasty pies. Bred by Garden City
Seeds to mature in cool northern
summers. Round, 8-10 pounds.
READY IN 95 DAYS

Garden City Seeds
for an Early Harvest

Buton runner beans
(Abundant Life)

Bountiful Gardens

This is the seed production arm of a larger nonprofit organization called Ecology Action, which promotes bio-intensive vegetable gardening.

SPECIALTIES: Open-pollinated, untreated seeds of rare vegetable and herb varieties.

GROWER'S PICK: 'Madras', a podding radish that is grown not for its roots but for the sweet edible pods it bears.

18001 Shafer Ranch Rd., Willits, CA 95490; (707) 459-6410 or bountiful@ zapcom.net.

Ed Hume Seeds

If you garden in the Northwest, chances are you know of Ed Hume; his television show, *Gardening in America,* is seen by millions. His family-owned seed company has been around since 1977.

SPECIALTIES: Flowers and vegetables with a proven record in the Northwest.

GROWER'S PICK: 'Sugar Lace', a stringless snap pea.

Catalog $1. Box 1450, Kent, WA 98035; fax (253) 859-0694; www.humeseeds.com.

Evergreen Y. H. Enterprises

As the West's taste for Oriental vegetables grows, so do the entries in owner Wen Hwang's catalog.

SPECIALTIES: Asian vegetables of all sorts, from winged beans to pickling melons.

GROWER'S PICK: 'Chin Gu', a variety of yu choy (also known as edible rape) that bears leaves and flowering stalks to use in stir-fry dishes.

Box 17538, Anaheim, CA 92817; (714) 637-5769 or eeseeds@aol.com.

Garden City Seeds

Begun in 1982, this outfit concentrates on sustainable vegetable varieties for areas with short growing seasons.

SPECIALTIES: Early-harvest vegetables with a focus on corn, squash, melons, peppers, and tomatoes.

GROWER'S PICK: 'Yukon Chief', a dwarf corn (3 feet tall) bred in Alaska that bears 5- to 6-inch-long ears in only 55 days.

Catalog $1. 778 Hwy. 93 N., Hamilton, MT 59840; (406) 961-4837 or www. gardencityseeds.com.

J. L. Hudson, Seedsman

"If your phone doesn't ring, it's me," jokes J. L. Hudson. His office—in the midst of a wild biological preserve in La Honda, California—is phoneless and faxless, so when he says *mail* order, he means it. The nearly 100-page catalog full of exotic plants is worth the wait.

SPECIALTIES: Heirloom vegetables and unusual plants.

GROWER'S PICK: 'Purple Calabash' tomato ("the ugliest but tastiest tomato around," according to Hudson).

Catalog $1. Star Route 2, Box 337, La Honda, CA 94020.

Larner Seeds

Owner Judith Lowry doesn't just sell seeds of California native plants. In addition to offering everything from wildflowers to trees, her 22-year-old company has an on-site nursery and demonstration garden.

SPECIALTIES: Annual and perennial wildflowers.

GROWER'S PICK: Coast lotus (*Lotus formosissimus*), a perennial with clover-like foliage that bears yellow and pink flowers.

Catalog $2.50. Box 407, Bolinas, CA 94924; (415) 868-9407.

Moon Mountain Wildflowers

Becky Schaff offers seeds of annual and perennial wildflowers, individually or mixed, in packets or small bulk amounts.

SPECIALTY: Wildflower mixtures, including 16 regional mixes.

GROWER'S PICK: Bird and butterfly mix, a collection of 17 wildflowers designed to provide larval food and nectar.

Catalog $3. Box 725, Carpinteria, CA 93014; (805) 684-2565 or www. ss-seeds.com.

Native Seeds/Search

When volunteers working on the Tohono O'odham reservation near Tucson discovered that seeds for traditional corn, beans, and squash were rapidly disappearing, they formed a nonprofit foundation to safeguard the plants' future. Sixteen years later, Native Seeds

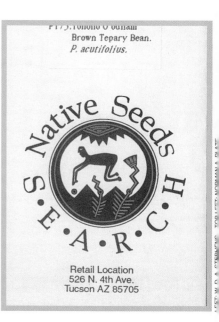

Native Seeds
S·E·A·R·C·H

Retail Location
526 N. 4th Ave.
Tucson AZ 85705

has 1,900 varieties in its seed bank.

SPECIALTIES: Native American varieties of beans, chilies, corn, melons, gourds, and squash.

GROWER'S PICK: Hopi purple string bean, a black-striped bean that can be eaten green or dried.

Catalog $1. 526 N. Fourth Ave., Tucson, AZ 85705; (520) 622-5561 or desert. net/seeds/home.htm.

Nichols Garden Nursery

Forty-nine years ago N. P. Nichols got a few elephant garlic cloves from a friend, grew a surplus crop, and started a mail-order business. Today, his daughter Rose Marie Nichols McGee continues her father's propagation of culinary herbs, and she stays on the lookout for superior vegetables, too.

SPECIALTIES: Culinary and medicinal herbs, gourmet and specialty vegetables.

GROWER'S PICK: 'Catalina', an all-purpose potato with brown skin and white flesh.

1190 N. Pacific Hwy. N.E., Albany, OR 97321; (541) 928-9280 or www. gardennursery.com.

Ornamental Edibles

Beautiful vegetables with great flavors fill the catalog of this 10-year-old company owned by Joyce McClellan.

'Rainbow Inca' sweet corn
(Seeds of Change)

SPECIALTIES: Salad greens, including baby lettuce and mesclun, and braising greens such as chard and bok choy.
GROWER'S PICK: 'Bull's Blood', a beet grown for its sweet, red-purple leaves to eat in salads.
Catalog $2. 3622 Weedin Court, San Jose, CA 95132; (408) 946-7333 or www.ornamentaledibles.com.

Plants of the Southwest

Gail Haggard started this business in 1977 because she was angry: There she was in Santa Fe amid one of the richest veins of flora in the world, and she couldn't find native plants because no one was producing seed. Now, thanks to Haggard, someone is.
SPECIALTIES: Southwest native wildflowers, grasses, and shrubs.
GROWER'S PICK: Blackfoot daisy (*Melampodium leucanthum*), a summer perennial that bears white flowers with yellow centers.
Catalog $3.50. Agua Fria Rd., Route 6, Box 11A, Santa Fe, NM 87501; (505) 438-8888 or www.plantsofthesouthwest.com.

Redwood City Seed Company

"Herb and vegetable varieties are the basis of regional cuisines. Lose these varieties and you lose part of the culture," says Craig Dremann. His firm, which concentrates on endangered cultivated plants, is in the business of seeing that that doesn't happen.
SPECIALTIES: Chilies—60 to 70 varieties, including 'Tepin', reputedly the world's hottest pepper.
GROWER'S PICK: 'California Valley Yokuts Indian' sunflower bears 100 or more 2- to 3-inch flowers on each plant.
Box 361, Redwood City, CA 94064; (650) 325-7333 or www.ecoseeds.com.

Seeds Blüm

Everybody warned Jan Blüm, "A seed company that spends half its time encouraging home gardeners to save their own seeds is doomed to fail." But 18 years later, Seeds Blüm is still around, and its list of offerings continues to mushroom.

SPECIALTIES: Amaranth, beans, lettuces, potatoes, pumpkins, tomatoes, old-fashioned flowers.
GROWER'S PICK: 'Super Italian Paste' tomato, which bears fruits four times larger than the standard market variety.
Catalog $3. 27 Idaho City Stage Rd., Boise, ID 83716; fax (208) 338-5658; www.seedsblum.com.

Seeds of Change

Organic gardening and business success are not mutually exclusive, as this 10-year-old company has proved. Seeds of Change sells only certified organically grown seeds, and its business is thriving.
SPECIALTIES: Beans, chilies, corn, sunflowers.
GROWER'S PICK: 'Jack in the Beanstalk Bean', a European heirloom you can pick early as a snap bean or let dry to be a soup bean.
Box 15700, Santa Fe, NM 87506; (888) 762-7333 or www.seedsofchange.com.

Seeds West Garden Seeds

New owners Ron Jacob and Leslie Campbell continue founder Jane Winslow's commitment to vegetables that perform in the high elevations of the West.
SPECIALTIES: Beans, Indian corn, and chilies.
GROWER'S PICK: 'Valencia Orange'—a tomato with brilliant orange color.

Catalog $2 (seed list free). 317 14th St. N.W., Albuquerque, NM 87104; (505) 843-9713 or www.seedswestgardenseeds.com.

Territorial Seed Company

"If it doesn't grow well in the Pacific Northwest, it doesn't get in our catalog," says Tom Johns, president of this 20-year-old Oregon company. Vegetable varieties that can handle the Northwest's cool, moist weather often perform as well or better in warmer regions.
SPECIALTIES: Vegetables and flowers for the year-round garden.
GROWER'S PICK: 'Marketmore 97', a slicing cucumber that resists plant diseases.
Box 157, Cottage Grove, OR 97424; (541) 942-9547 or www.territorial-seed.com.

Theodore Payne Foundation

English horticulturist Theodore Payne came to California in 1893 and soon fell in love with its native plants. He developed a seed business to make native flora available to the public. Payne passed away in 1963, but this nonprofit organization continues his work.
SPECIALTIES: California native wildflowers and landscape plants.
GROWER'S PICK: Wildflowers-in-a-Pot Mixture (short-stemmed types).
Catalog $3.50. 10459 Tuxford St., Sun Valley, CA 91352; (818) 768-1802 or theodorepayne@juno.com. ◆

HEART OF IDAHO
WILDFLOWER MIX
(Covers approx. 400 sq. ft.)

Wildflower Seeds
from HIGH ALTITUDE GARDENS

Seeds Trust/ High Altitude Gardens

This family-owned outfit concentrates on open-pollinated vegetable, herb, wildflower, and native grass seeds that can survive the cold climate and short growing season of Hailey, Idaho. But gardeners in milder climates have great luck with their seeds, too.
SPECIALTIES: Bulk wildflower seeds, native grasses, Siberian tomatoes.
GROWER'S PICK: 'Sasha's Altai', a very early tomato with sweet, juicy fruit.
Box 1048, Hailey, ID 83333; (208) 788-4363 or www.seedsave.org.

The wild, wonderful tillandsias

These plants are shapely and
thrive without roots or soil

BY LAUREN BONAR SWEZEY

ROCK VASES show off tillandsias' natural beauty. From top: *Tillandsia stricta*, *T. harrisii*, and *T. ionantha* 'Rosita'.

If plants grew on Mars, they might look like tillandsias. "They're other-worldly," Barb Owens, co-owner with her husband, Rick, of Owens Gardens in Washington, says of these curious-looking bromeliad cousins.

Tillandsias form rosettes of spidery or knifelike gray or green leaves that are sometimes wiry and contorted, as though ready to crawl. They don't grow in soil or absorb nutrients and water through roots the way most plants do. Instead, their leaves are covered with trichomes—tiny plant hairs that trap moisture and dissolve minerals for nutrients. (In their native Central and South America, these plants are epiphytes that grow in trees and live on captured rain and dew.) Their roots are strictly for support.

They range from *Tillandsia ionantha*, reminiscent of a pineapple top, to *T. juncea*, which shoots out long grassy leaves to look like a broom. *T. bulbosa*, which has contorted, rubbery leaves, is the most alien-looking of them all. "But people can't keep their hands off it," says Owens.

The odd nature of tillandsias is one reason gardeners are attracted to them. Their flowers are another: depending on species, they can range from blazing orange to brilliant purple and bloom up to four months.

Because they don't need soil to live, tillandsias may seem carefree. But like any plant, they do require regular watering and periodic fertilizing to thrive (see box at far right). They also need bright light.

Of all the tillandsias the Owenses grow, 10 (listed below) are clear winners. "These are the ones customers select over and over again," Barb explains. "They have definite eye-appeal."

TEN FAVORITE TILLANDSIAS

- **T. aeranthos.** Leaves form a rosette 3 inches wide. Deep, rosy flower bract with blue flowers.
- **T. bulbosa.** Smooth, shiny, deep green recurved leaves, 6 to 8 inches long. Red flower spike lasts up to 4 months.

- **T. butzii.** Thin, 10-inch-long, twisted tubular leaves with purple freckles. Muted red flower spike with blue flowers.
- **T. caput-medusae.** Fuzzy, grayish 8-inch-long recurved leaves are contorted. Flat red flower spike with blue flowers.
- **T. harrisii.** Whitish leaves on a broad, 4- to 5-inch-wide plant. Thick, bright red flower spike with blue flowers.
- **T. ionantha.** Dark green, 2-inch-long foliage looks like a pineapple top. Foliage may blush red at bloom time. Clusters of tubular purple flowers.
- **T. ionantha 'Rosita'.** Grayish foliage blushes bright pink at bloom time. Tubular flowers are violet blue.
- **T. juncea.** Thin, grassy leaves up to 2 feet long. Grown for its foliage; flowers aren't common.
- **T. magnusiana.** Very fuzzy, 5-inch-long whitish leaves give it the appearance of a giant sea anemone. Short, fat, red flower spike fills the center of the plant. Blue flowers.
- **T. stricta.** Bushy green rosette with thin 6-inch-long leaves. Fat, bright pink spike with blue flowers. One of the most dramatic blooms.

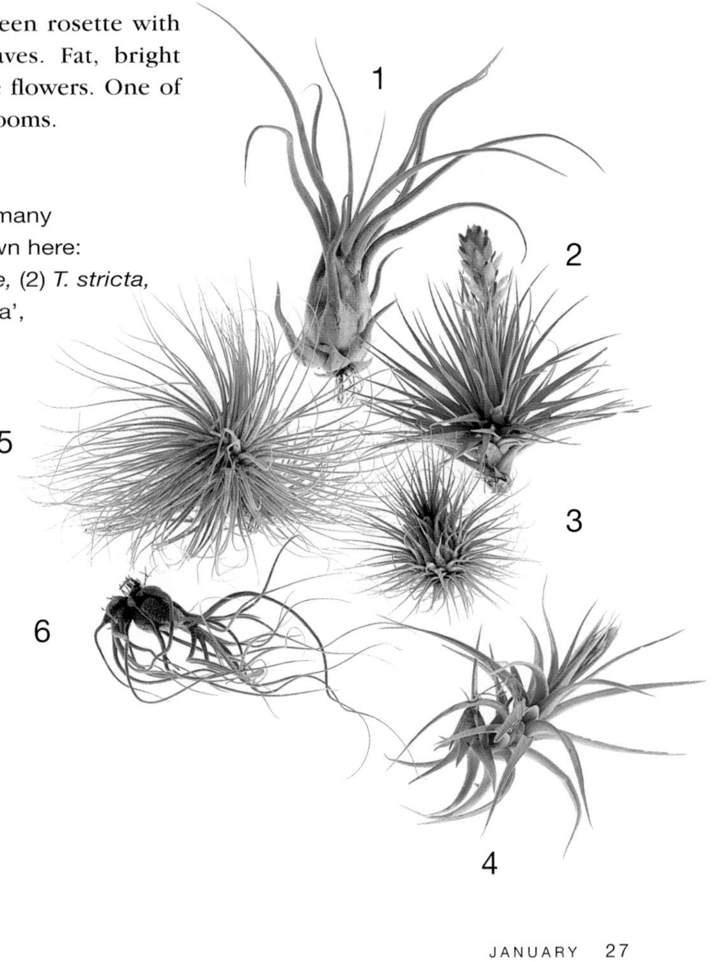

Tillandsias come in many unusual forms. Shown here:
(1) *T. caput-medusae*, (2) *T. stricta*,
(3) *T. ionantha* 'Rosita',
(4) *T. aeranthos*,
(5) *T. magnusiana*,
(6) *T. butzii*.

Tillandsia care

- **GROW** these plants indoors in bright, indirect light. They also grow outdoors in *Sunset* climate zones 22–24.
- **SOAK OR MIST** heavily one to three times a week, depending on the temperature and humidity. Let plants dry between waterings.
- **FERTILIZE** once or twice a month spring through summer by spraying or soaking plants in a $\frac{1}{4}$-strength solution of a water-soluble fertilizer high in phosphorus.

Where to order

Holladay Jungle; (559) 229-9858. More than 200 tillandsias. Free price list. Information at home.earthlink.net/~tillandsia. *Owens Gardens;* (360) 794-6422. About 100 kinds, with about 50 available at any one time. ◆

1

2

5

3

6

4

WATER TUMBLES from a terra-cotta jug in this Mediterranean-style garden in Saratoga, California. This and 16 other winners of Sunset's second biennial Western Garden Design Awards are featured on pages 42–53.

February

gardenguide

ASIATIC LILIES and a Giant Pacific delphinium reach toward the sun in Lynn Nichols's garden in Basalt, Colorado.

ROB PROCTOR

A fresh look at Colorado's garden scene

■ Anyone who's ever complained that Colorado is too windy, hot, dry, or cold to create glorious landscapes needs to see *Colorado's Great Gardens: Plains, Mountains, & Plateaus,* by Georgia Garnsey (Westcliffe Publishers, Englewood, CO, 1998; $45). Illustrated with exquisite photographs by Rob Proctor, this book proves just how far savvy gardeners have taken horticulture in Colorado.

It shows several gardens from each of the state's three regions. As you travel from Inez Busig's garden in Sterling to David Alford's Blue Lake Ranch in Hesperus, you'll see plenty of landscaping ideas and great plant combinations like these:

• Birches underplanted with a border of blue delphiniums and red and yellow columbines.
• 'Peace' roses surrounded by adobe-pink yarrow and white daisies.
• Pots of summer flowers floating in a sea of bishop's weed.
• Pink Japanese anemones lighting up the dappled shade beneath an aspen.
• An island of purple asters ringed by golden and rose-pink chrysanthemums.

Unfortunately, most of the photos aren't captioned, and the text too often gives no clue to the identity of the plants shown in the pictures. Even so, *Colorado's Great Gardens* is a beautiful book that's loaded with more good ideas than any garden can hold. Look for it in bookstores; or order directly from the publisher (800/523-3692).

— *Jim McCausland*

An irresistible hollyhock

■ Visitors to *Sunset's* headquarters in Menlo Park last summer couldn't resist reaching out to touch the soft, fluffy blossoms of 'Peaches 'n' Dreams' hollyhock. Its fully double flowers in shades of creamy peach to raspberry pink appear on 4- to 6-foot-tall stalks, with the lower buds opening first and bloom continuing up the stalk for eight weeks or longer.

Unfortunately, the foliage wasn't so dreamy. In *Sunset's* garden, the leaves were severely disfigured by rust (a disease that produces orange pustules on the undersides of leaves). Place the hollyhocks at the back of the border so other plants in front will mask any unsightly foliage. Also, to reduce the spread of rust, avoid overhead watering and pick off any infected leaves. If you prefer a chemical control, at the first sign of infection, spray with a fungicide specified for rust.

'Peaches 'n' Dreams' should bloom its first summer if seeds are started in late winter; sow them in pots this month in mild-winter areas (in cold-winter areas, wait until spring). Order seeds from Thompson & Morgan (800/274-7333).

— *Lauren Bonar Swezey*

NORMAN A. PLATE   BELOW: W. D. A. STEPHENS

Find Renee's Garden on nursery racks or the Internet

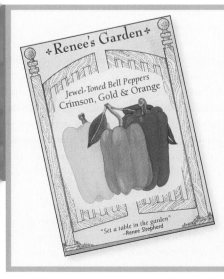

■ Always an avid vegetable gardener, Renee Shepherd got started in the seed business in 1984, when she founded Shepherd's Garden Seeds. After that company was bought by White Flower Farm, Shepherd missed her personal connection with growers. So a year later, she launched Renee's Garden, based in Felton, California.

She offers an excellent selection of herbs and vegetables (Monet's Garden mesclun, with beautiful, very succulent leaves, is one of her favorites), plus annual flowers, including a Music Box mixture of knee-high sunflowers. Shepherd likes "rainbow gardening"—growing several colors of vegetables (tomatoes, squash, peppers, and pole beans) side by side—so she packages special "Rainbow Seed" collections.

Renee's Garden seeds are sold at selected nurseries and garden centers; call (888) 880-7228 for retail outlets. You can also order her seeds directly via the Internet: www.garden.com/reneesgarden.

— *Sharon Cohoon*

Feather grass catches the sunlight

■ Landscape architect Sydney Baumgartner of Santa Barbara didn't invite Mexican feather grass (*Stipa tenuissima*) to share a pot occupied by a variegated ivy geranium. The intrepid blond-maned grass grew there on its own. Years ago, Baumgartner bought one plant of this freely self-sowing grass, and its offspring have been popping up in her garden ever since. Usually she rogues out the upstarts. But this seedling escaped her notice until it was well established. Baumgartner liked the serendipitous pairing so well she put it on a pedestal—a ceramic dragon salvaged from an old building. Then she framed the scene with aeoniums and a chartreuse-leafed geranium.

With their soft textures and flowing lines, some ornamental grasses make ideal pot plants, says Baumgartner. "To show them off, try to situate them where they'll be backlit by morning or late-afternoon light," she advises. Keep plantings simple. Grasses look better solo or paired with a plain foliage plant that has a contrasting shape, like a geranium, ivy, or vinca.

Other grasses with showy seed heads that shine in the sun include *Miscanthus sinensis,* Moor grass (*Molinia caerulea*), palm grass (*Setaria palmifolia*), and *Pennisetum.* These grasses are becoming more readily available in nurseries. A good mail-order source with a wide selection is Digging Dog Nursery, Box 471, Albion, CA 95410; (707) 937-1130.— *S.C.*

IN BLOOM, Mexican feather grass is as showy as any flower. Giving the grass its own container and raising it on a pedestal makes the most of its blond beauty.

Dreamy pots for collectors

■After running a medical office for most of her adult life, Lynda Ann Nielson thought up a plot for a children's book. Full of woodlands and wizards, the story made her wonder what kind of pot a fairy would make. The notion took on a life of its own, and pottery designs filled Nielson's mind. Finally (to the dismay of her friends), she quit her job, bought 100 pounds of clay, and started making extraordinary sculptural flowerpots.

Adorned with everything from perfect daffodils to coneflowers to dogwoods, all in three dimensions, each piece is completely hand-built (none has ever ridden a potter's wheel). All are high-fired; they have that characteristic bell-like stoneware ring when you tap them. Colors include Vashon orange, Klamath red, and crystal white. "I like Klamath red the best," says Nielson, "because it's like working in chocolate. It has that same feel, and some of the same color."

The high-relief floral themes are so sculptural that sometimes Nielson works them into free-hanging wall ornaments sans containers. But usually they embellish vases, wall pots, and planters.

These containers don't absorb water, so they don't flake when temperatures plunge to freezing. They'll break, however, if the soil inside them is saturated when it freezes, so it expands. You can't argue with physics.

Visit Nielson's studio, Woodlands Garden Pottery, by appointment or call for a brochure; (206) 362-5424. Prices start at $50 for a 10-inch vase; flower containers range from $75 for an 8-inch-diameter, 11-inch-tall pot to $250 for a 16-inch-wide, 20-inch-tall pot. Saucers are included (drain holes are standard unless you specify otherwise). Orders take about a month to complete, and they average $25 for shipping. —*J.M.*

DAFFODILS AND OTHER FLOWERS adorn the pottery of Lynda Ann Nielson.

BEN WOOLSEY

Get tomatoes started right

■Start your own tomatoes from seeds, or purchase seedlings from a garden center. The seedlings should be sturdy, but not overmature. If you grow your own seedlings, start them indoors 5 to 7 weeks before you plan to set them out (at least 10 days after the last frost date in spring). Expose tender seedlings, including purchased tomato plants, to cool outdoor air gradually. This is called "hardening off" the plants before setting them out in the garden, and it will decrease transplant shock.

When tomato seedlings are ready to go into the ground, they will develop into much sturdier plants if their stems are set deep in the soil. Dig a hole to accommodate the rootball and part of the stem. Then pinch off the lower leaves, leaving only the top two or three sets. Set the plant in the hole so the bottom set of leaves is above the soil surface. Fill in the hole, firm down the soil, and water thoroughly. Soon the root hairs along the buried portion of the stem will develop into roots. — *L. B. S.*

Parking plants in the driveway

■ Plant collectors are constantly seeking out vacant plots where they can plant their latest acquisitions. Landscape designer Peggy Quaid of Fort Bragg found spare ground in an unlikely spot—between the concrete tracks of her driveway. She removed a thirsty strip of lawn that struggled there and replaced it with a lush planting of blooming ground covers and rock garden plants.

After Quaid removed the lawn, she amended the soil with compost, rock phosphate, and slow-release fertilizer. Then she started planting the 50-foot-long strip, using low-growing plants so they wouldn't get shaved by vehicles. Sun lovers compose most of the palette. These include *Achillea wilczekii*, *Artemisia assoana*, *Dianthus* 'Crimson Treasure', *Erodium alba*, snow-in-summer, *Thymus* 'Pink Ripple', and wall rockcress. Where her house shades the driveway, Quaid used some plants that take partial shade—*Campanula* 'Birch Hybrid', for instance.

During warm summer weather, she waters about once week. Otherwise, plants get a good soaking every 10 days or so.

— *Lauren Bonar Swezey*

A blend of East and West

■ Harry Carle's garden in Edmonds, Washington, is a subtle blend of elements from Japan and the Northwest.

Along its winding paths are plants and materials that look as if they were lifted directly out of our majestic wild landscape. Billowy shrubs and trees borrow the native timber beyond the garden's boundaries for a backdrop. Ground covers hug the earth in sweeps. Rocks—many of them encrusted with moss—anchor the plantings, edge a stream, and form stony piles that look as though they were deposited by ancient glaciers and left to age gracefully.

The Japanese influence is hard to miss. A weathered cedar-plank bridge leads across a small, shimmering pond fringed with Siberian irises and sword ferns. Here and there, lone conifers rise like living sculptures behind boulders and low, mounding shrubs.

A natural union of East and West, the garden is as rugged and rocky as the Cascades. Yet it is also as simple and elegant as a Japanese garden. And that suits Harry Carle, a longtime fan of Japanese culture and art, just fine.

— *Steven R. Lorton*

ALLAN MANDELL

Sonoran Desert style in Scottsdale

■ The keys to creating a natural-looking landscape are selecting the right plants and arranging them as they might grow in the wild. In the planting shown here, for example, native and well-adapted non-native plants were deftly combined in a landscape that reflects the essence the Sonoran Desert. The planting is part of a garden remodel designed by the firm Landscaping by André for John and Carol Durham's vacation home in Scottsdale.

Near the house the designers planted clusters of saguaro (*Carnegiea gigantea*)—the Sonoran Desert's signature plant—where its bold columnar forms provide a visual balance to the mass of the adobe house and the surrounding low walls. To complement the saguaros, other cactus with strong sculptural qualities were used, including the prickly pear cactus called bunny ears (*Opuntia microdasys*) in the left foreground and fishhook barrel cactus (*Ferocactus wislizenii*) in the center next to purple prickly pear (*Opuntia santa-rita*), whose purplish pads bring out the mauve tones in the wall behind.

STEVEN GUNTHER

NATURALISTIC GARDEN features red-flowered autumn sage (center) and bunny ears cactus (left foreground), plus a visiting bunny.

Flowering plants provide bursts of seasonal color. The red-flowered plants blooming here in early spring include autumn sage (*Salvia greggii*) at left center, spiky *Aloe saponaria* at right, and ocotillo (*Fouquieria splendens*) in the background. Woven throughout the planting is turpentine brush (*Ericameria laricifolia*), a scrappy native shrub whose bright green, aromatic leaves hang on through cold, heat, and drought and whose golden flowers appear in fall.

In this landscape the spaces between the plants recall the intervals of open ground that occur naturally in the desert, where plants compete for limited moisture. To complete the naturalistic effect, the designers spread crushed granite to replicate the texture of the desert floor, and carefully placed granite boulders among gentle mounds and shallow swales.

—*Judy Mielke*

A FRUITFUL FENCE

ALLAN MANDELL

A lattice of espaliered dwarf apples

■ No space for an apple orchard? Try a 6-foot-tall lattice "wall" of espaliered dwarf apple trees as shown above.

The espalier style we chose is a modified form of the Belgian fence, in which branches, or cordons, cross to form diamonds. To create the support grid, we tied bamboo poles with twine in a diamond pattern. The diamonds measure about 2 feet on each side, allowing plenty of air circulation.

Next, we ordered bare-root dwarf trees from Northwoods Nursery (503/266-5432) and Raintree Nursery (360/496-6400). (Take care to select varieties that are recommended by the nurseries for your particular *Sunset* climate zone.) In February, we planted the dormant trees 2½ feet apart, slanted at 45°, to line up with thediagonal grid. We loosely tied the trunks to the poles (we'll remove the poles in a few years when the tree trunks are larger).

By the second year, our trees were dotted with delicious full-size apples. Periodic pruning maintains the pattern and encourages fruit production.

— *Lisa Shara Hall*

Warm-season start-ups

■ Starting tomatoes, peppers, and eggplants from seed is easy if you follow these steps. Figure on six to eight weeks of indoor growing time before the seedlings will be ready to transplant outdoors.

Fill 4-inch pots to just below the rim with a light, porous seed-starting or potting mix. Moisten the mix and let it drain.

1. Scatter a dozen seeds over the soil surface of each container and cover with ½ inch of potting mix. Moisten lightly again. Set containers on a water heater or use a heating mat to keep the soil between 75° and 90°. Keep the soil surface damp. When the seeds germinate, move the pots into an area with bright light and temperatures between 60° and 75°.

When the seedlings develop their first set of leaves, transplant them. To remove seedlings from the pot, gently squeeze the sides of the pot and turn it upside down, keeping one hand around the soil ball.

2. With both hands, carefully pull the soil ball apart and set it down on a flat surface.

3. Separate the fragile rootballs with a toothpick or skewer.

4. Carefully lift each plant and its rootball, keeping your finger under it for support. Place each seedling in a 4-inch pot filled with soil mix, cover the roots with mix, and water. Set pots in bright light and let seedlings grow until they're sturdy enough (at about 4 inches tall) to transplant into the garden. — *L. B. S.*

Pacific Northwest Checklist

PLANTING

✔ **BARE-ROOT STOCK.** Zones 4–7: Trees, shrubs, vines, and cane berries can all be planted this month. If you can't plant immediately, protect the roots from drying out by packing them in damp sawdust or compost; keep them out of direct sun. In zones 1–3, bare-root planting comes later in spring.

✔ **FLOWERING SHRUBS, TREES.** The Pacific Northwest is blessed with a variety of landscape plants that bloom in late winter or early spring, including early-flowering rhododendrons, Chinese witch hazel, Cornelian cherry, corylopsis, daphne, sasanqua camellias, and wintersweet. Shop for blooming plants, slip nursery cans into decorative containers for temporary display, then plant them as soon as flowers fade.

✔ **HARDY ANNUALS.** Direct-sow seeds of calendula, clarkia, English daisies, Iceland poppies, and snapdragons.

✔ **PEAS.** Zones 4–7: Plant edible peas around midmonth. Give them a head start by sprouting them indoors. Soak the seeds in water overnight, then place them between damp paper towels on a cookie sheet and set it in a warm place until seeds germinate. Once they've sprouted, plant them in the ground. Protect plants from slugs.

✔ **PRIMROSES.** Two kinds of English primroses will be widely sold this month: acaulis types (usually one large flower per stem) and polyanthus types (multiple blooms on longer stems). In zones 1–3, choose acaulis types for indoor display. In zones 4–7, group shorter acaulis primroses in outdoor containers and plant taller polyanthus types in garden beds.

MAINTENANCE

✔ **FUSS WITH HOUSE PLANTS.** Plants that bloom or set fruit this time of year should be fed with a complete liquid fertilizer. For other plants, wait until April to begin a feeding program. Trim off yellowed or damaged foliage. If leaves are dusty, set plants in a bathtub or shower, rinse them off with tepid water, and let them drip dry. If the potting soil surface is crusted with salts, use a spoon to scoop off an inch or so of old soil and replace it with fresh mix.

✔ **PRUNE ROSES.** Zones 4–7: After removing dead or injured canes, select the three to five strongest canes and cut them back to 6 to 8 inches (each cane should have one robust, outward-facing bud). The remaining canes should form a vase shape. In zones 1–3, wait until April to prune. ◆

Northern California Checklist

PLANTING

☑ **FLOWERING CHERRIES.** Zones 7–9, 14–17: For staggered bloom, plant several kinds. *Early-blooming varieties:* 'Akebono' (pink single blossoms), 'Royal Burgundy' (dark pink double; purplish foliage), 'Taiwan' (rosy pink single). *Midseason:* 'Beni Hoshi' (bright pink single), 'Kwanzan' (rosy pink double). *Late:* 'Mt. Fuji-Shogetsu' (light pink semidouble).

☑ **LIVING VALENTINES.** Give your sweetheart a valentine that will live on long after February 14. Blooming pots of azaleas, camellias, and daffodils can be planted outdoors after flowering. Or wrap up a bare-root rose.

☑ **SPRING COLOR.** Zones 7–9, 14–17: Choices include calendula, candytuft, cineraria, dianthus, English daisy, pansy, Iceland poppy, English and fairy primroses, forget-me-not, *Primula obconica,* snapdragon, stock, sweet William, and viola.

Sunset
CLIMATE ZONES
- Mountain (1-2)
- Valley (7-9)
- Inland (14)
- Coastal (15-17)

☑ **SUMMER BULBS.** Zones 7–9, 14–17: Set out summer-flowering bulbs, including tuberous begonias, cannas, crocosmias, dahlias, gladiolus, tigridias, and tuberoses.

MAINTENANCE

☑ **FERTILIZE.** Zones 7–9, 14–17: Feed fall-planted annuals and perennials and established trees and shrubs. Wait to feed azaleas, camellias, and rhododendrons until after bloom. Later this month, feed lawns.

☑ **PRUNE TREES AND SHRUBS.** Zones 7–9, 14–17: If you haven't yet pruned deciduous ornamental and fruit trees, grapes, roses, and wisteria, do so by midmonth, before plants break dormancy. Wait to prune spring-flowering plants until after they bloom.

☑ **REPOT CYMBIDIUMS.** If your cymbidium orchids are bulging out of their containers or the bark has decomposed, repot them between mid-February and early July. Remove old bark, cut off dead roots, and discard soft or rotted bulbs. Transfer the entire plant to a larger container filled with a medium-size bark or cymbidium mix; or divide the plant into groups of three to five pseudobulbs (with leaves) and repot each division individually.

Southern California Checklist

PLANTING & SHOPPING

☑ **BARE-ROOT PLANTS.** Shop soon for bare-root berries, fruit and shade trees, grapes, roses, plus perennial vegetables, including artichokes, asparagus, and horseradish.

☑ **COOL-SEASON CROPS.** In coastal (zones 22–24) and inland (zones 18–21) areas and the high desert (zone 11), continue to sow beets, carrots, celery, chard, kale, lettuce, mustards, onions, peas, potatoes, radishes, spinach, and turnips, plus herbs like cilantro, chervil, and dill. Set out seedlings of cabbage-family vegetables, including broccoli and cauliflower.

☑ **WARM-SEASON VEGETABLES.** In the low desert (zone 13) after mid-month, set out seedlings of eggplant, peppers, tomatoes, and other warm-season crops, but be prepared to protect them with hot caps or row covers if a late frost threatens. In other areas, start seeds indoors for transplanting into the garden in six to eight weeks.

☑ **SPRING COLOR.** Set out bedding plants, including calendulas, dianthus, Iceland poppies, lobelia, snapdragons, stock, and sweet alyssum.

Sunset CLIMATE ZONES

1-3 7-9 11 13 14-24

DEBRA LAMBERT

☑ **SUMMER BULBS.** Gladiolus corms are in good supply this month at nurseries. In coastal and inland gardens, get glads in the ground now so they'll bloom before thrips attack. Other summer-blooming bulbs to plant now include crocosmia, dahlia, tigridia, tuberose, and tuberous begonia.

MAINTENANCE

☑ **DORMANT PRUNING.** Before new growth emerges, prune deciduous fruit and ornamental trees, grape and wisteria vines, roses, and summer-blooming shrubs. Wait to prune spring-flowering shrubs until after bloom. Also hold off on tropicals like hibiscus; it's too early to encourage growth.

☑ **START SPRING FEEDING.** Feed ground covers, shrubs, roses, perennials, and trees with a complete granular fertilizer or apply organic fertilizer such as well-rotted manure.

☑ **WATER.** If rains are light or sporadic, irrigate plants deeply. Keep seedbeds moist to encourage good germination, and water seedlings regularly until they get established.

WEED CONTROL

☑ **CONTROL LAWN WEEDS.** To prevent crabgrass and other annual weed seeds from germinating later this spring, apply a preemergent herbicide to lawns early this spring. If you prefer not to use a chemical herbicide, consider one of the corn gluten–based products such as Wow! (order from Gardens Alive; 812/537-8650). ◆

Mountain Checklist

PLANTING

☑ **BARE-ROOT PLANTS.** If the soil can be worked, plant bare-root berries, fruit and shade trees, grapes, and perennial vegetables, including asparagus, horseradish, and rhubarb.

☑ **ORDER SEEDS.** Although it's too soon to plant your summer garden, order seeds right away, before new or scarce varieties are sold out.

☑ **HARDY PERENNIALS.** In milder parts of the intermountain West, start delphinium, hellebore, pansy, primrose, veronica, viola, and wallflower in a coldframe or greenhouse for transplanting when at least two sets of true leaves appear (and, in coldest areas, when the ground can be worked).

☑ **VEGETABLES.** Start seeds of cool-season vegetables like broccoli, cabbage, cauliflower, kale, and lettuce indoors about six weeks before planting time in your area.

☑ **WILDFLOWERS.** Sow seeds of hardy wildflowers in cultivated, weed-free soil. Most will bloom this season, but some biennials and perennials won't flower until their second season.

Sunset
CLIMATE ZONES
☐ 1-3 ☐ 10-11

DEBRA LAMBERT

MAINTENANCE

☑ **AMEND PLANTING BEDS.** As soon as the ground can be worked, dig compost or other organic matter into the soil to prepare flower and vegetable beds for spring planting. In areas where spring comes late, you can even dig in manure that's not fully rotted yet; by planting time, it will be mellowed enough so that it won't burn plants.

☑ **CHECK STORED BULBS, PRODUCE.** Inspect stored bulbs, corms, tubers, and produce for shriveling and rot. Rehydrate shriveled bulbs by sprinkling on a little water. Remove any that show signs of decay, except dahlia tubers: cut the bad spots out of these, dust tubers with sulfur, and store apart from the rest until planting time.

☑ **GET FROST PROTECTORS READY.** Order cloches or row covers now so you'll have them on hand to protect warm-season plants against late frosts after you set them outdoors.

☑ **PRUNE TREES, SHRUBS.** Prune when daytime temperatures are above freezing. First remove dead, diseased, crossing, and closely parallel branches, then prune for shape.

☑ **STERILIZE FLATS, POTS.** Before you sow seeds in flats or pots, wash containers with a weak solution of household bleach and water. Also use a sterile potting mix to reduce the risk of damping off and other diseases.

PEST CONTROL

☑ **MONITOR HOUSE PLANTS.** Examine leaves for aphids, spider mite webs, and the sticky honeydew that signals the presence of many kinds of insects. Spray pests off leaves with lukewarm water, then treat the plants with insecticidal soap. Scrape off scale insects if necessary. ◆

Southwest Checklist

PLANTING

✔ **BARE-ROOT PLANTS.** Set out bare-root berries, grapes, fruit and shade trees, and perennial vegetables, including asparagus and Jerusalem artichoke.

✔ **GROUND COVERS, VINES.** Zone 11 (Las Vegas): Set out Hall's honeysuckle, *Vinca major,* or *V. minor.* Zones 12–13: Set out these plus star jasmine, trailing indigo bush (*Dalea greggii*), and perennial verbena.

✔ **PERENNIAL WILDFLOWERS.** Zones 1–2, 10–11: You can still scatter wildflower mixes now for bloom this summer. Zones 12–13: Set out spring bloomers such as desert marigold, evening primrose, paperflower (*Psilostrophe cooperi*), penstemon, and salvia.

✔ **VEGETABLES.** Zones 1–2: Order seed now for sowing when the weather warms up. Zones 10–11: Start seeds of cool-season crops (broccoli, cabbage, cauliflower, and lettuce) indoors after midmonth. Zones 12–13: Set tomatoes outdoors, but have row covers ready to protect seedlings from frost. Start bush and lima beans, beets, corn (after midmonth), cucumbers, eggplant, melons, peas (zone 13—Phoenix only), peppers (zone 12—Tucson only), potatoes, radishes, summer squash, tomatoes, and watermelons.

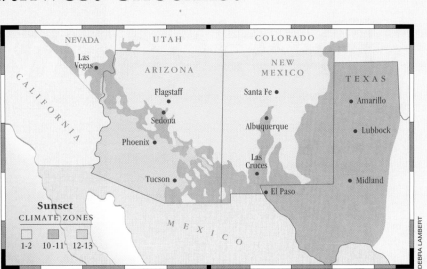

MAINTENANCE

✔ **AMEND PLANTING BEDS.** Get flower and vegetable beds ready for spring planting by digging compost or other organic matter into the soil. If the soil is very alkaline in your garden, you can adjust its pH and increase fertility by adding 2 pounds of ammonium phosphate and 3 pounds of soil sulfur per 100 square feet.

✔ **FEED ROSES.** On a late-February day when night temperatures are forecast to remain above freezing, water established plants, let the soil drain, apply a complete fertilizer, and water again.

✔ **MAINTAIN DRIP SYSTEMS.** Clean or replace drip system filters. Then turn on the system and check each emitter. When you find one that can't be unclogged, install a new emitter next to it.

PEST CONTROL

✔ **CONTROL APHIDS.** Zones 12–13: Check tender new growth for aphids. When you see them, blast them off with a jet of water and, if necessary, follow up with a spray of insecticidal soap. ◆

Western Garden Design Awards

17 winning gardens celebrate outdoor living in the West

BY LAUREN BONAR SWEZEY

SCULPTURED STEEL gate mimics ocean waves in a Southern California garden, left (for details, see page 48). Center: A "keyhole" of Spanish lavender thrives with little care in this rural Northern California garden (page 50).

LARGE BOULDERS shape a hillside that encircles a rock firepit in this Washington garden (page 49). Perennials, grasses, and flowers grow between the rocks.

Here they are: the 17 winners of *Sunset's* second biennial Western Garden Design Awards—gardens remarkable for their innovation and creativity. Out of scores of entries submitted by landscape architects and designers, the winners represent the best in each of six categories— Garden Decoration, Garden Renovation, Outdoor Living, Problem Solving, Regional, and Small Space. They were selected by four jurors (distinguished landscape professionals and a *Sunset* garden editor). And they're filled with ideas for handsome plant combinations, paving, materials, and water features that you can use no matter where in the West you live.

GARDEN DECORATION:
SCOTTSDALE, ARIZONA

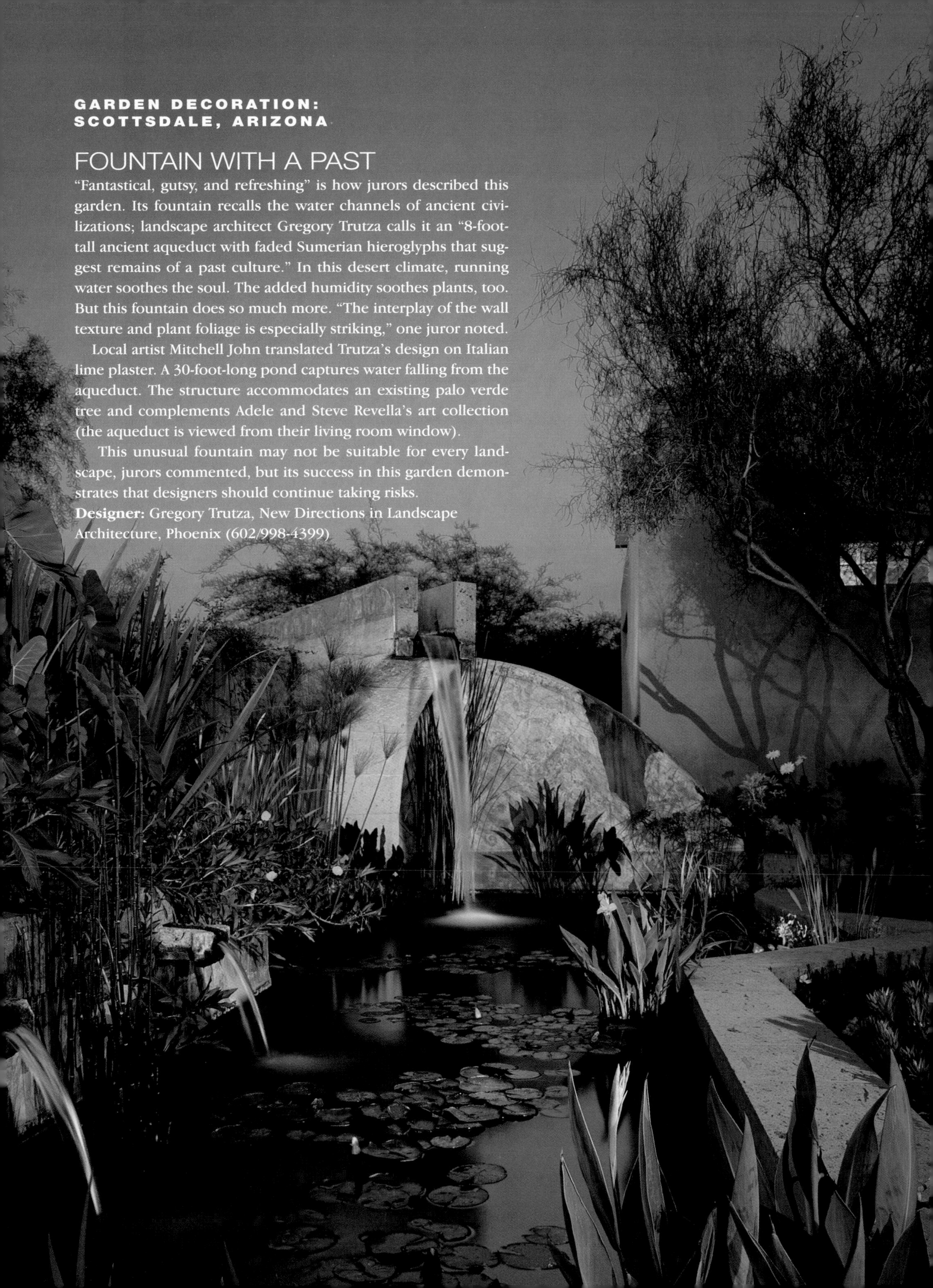

FOUNTAIN WITH A PAST

"Fantastical, gutsy, and refreshing" is how jurors described this garden. Its fountain recalls the water channels of ancient civilizations; landscape architect Gregory Trutza calls it an "8-foot-tall ancient aqueduct with faded Sumerian hieroglyphs that suggest remains of a past culture." In this desert climate, running water soothes the soul. The added humidity soothes plants, too. But this fountain does so much more. "The interplay of the wall texture and plant foliage is especially striking," one juror noted.

Local artist Mitchell John translated Trutza's design on Italian lime plaster. A 30-foot-long pond captures water falling from the aqueduct. The structure accommodates an existing palo verde tree and complements Adele and Steve Revella's art collection (the aqueduct is viewed from their living room window).

This unusual fountain may not be suitable for every landscape, jurors commented, but its success in this garden demonstrates that designers should continue taking risks.

Designer: Gregory Trutza, New Directions in Landscape Architecture, Phoenix (602/998-4399)

WGDA

STAGE SET

Marlene Dietrich would have felt right at home in this desert garden. Dramatic lines, an elegant pool, and exquisite stone paving make a setting fit for a movie star. But in spite of its refined appearance, the garden has a practical side too: it's wheelchair accessible.

Sliding glass doors open the house directly onto a level, covered patio-pavilion. "The open pavilion is like an extension of the interior," said one juror. Wide paths lead around the garden.

Landscape architect Gregory Trutza designed the garden to complement the house's contemporary adobe style. A graduated rear wall frames the pool and the mountain view; higher sections block out nearby development. Night lighting is an important feature, since the owners enjoy entertaining; lighting on the trees, in the wall, and inside the pavilion sets the garden aglow by night. This space, like Dietrich, is charming at any hour of the day.

Designer: Gregory Trutza, New Directions in Landscape Architecture, Phoenix (602/998-4399)

A LARGE, ANGULAR POOL (above) and detached spa (right) offer plenty of opportunities for dipping, no matter what the weather. Elegant patio pavers are Pietra travertine. A gas firepit (left), set in black Mexican beach pebbles, adds a sense of drama at night.

PATCHWORK IN CONCRETE

Turn an old concrete driveway upside down and what do you get? "A soft solution to a hard problem," said an enthusiastic juror. Other jurors agreed: this is a very creative solution to a perennial challenge—the driveway. "It's hard to mask all of that glaring concrete," explained a juror. "Yet this designer did it with flair."

The driveway was part of a front yard remodel for Brian and Kathy Paterson. Designer Cevan Forristt framed it with blocks of granite, then used flat pieces to form patterns in the center. In between the granite sections he laid chunks of concrete—recycled from the old driveway—upside down. To finish, Forristt filled in the cracks with gravel and planted the edges.

Designer: Cevan Forristt Landscape Design, San Jose (408/297-8538)

SMALL SPACE: SAN JOSE, CALIFORNIA

A GARDEN FOR ALL PLEASURES

Compact gardens, where every inch must count, are often more of a design challenge than grand ones with space to spare. So while this garden is intimate—just 1,250 square feet— its efficient use of space, as well as its colors and textures, particularly impressed the jurors. "It makes wonderful use of the outdoor areas," one noted.

Before the remodel, owners Maureen Cornelia and Peter Sheremeta rarely used the garden. The expansive brick patio was hot and unappealing, and it felt hemmed in by the glaring whitewashed studio and house. Designer Cynthia Hayes cleverly toned down the walls by painting the house a putty color and the studio a rich dark green to blend it into landscape. Then she added arbors, seat walls, and planters to create separate rooms and interesting vistas. Different paving materials—including gravel and flagstone—define the individual garden areas. Much of the brick paving was reused throughout the garden.

Plants were chosen for their all-seasons good looks. Pink angel's trumpet provides a dramatic focal point from the bedroom. Bamboo, Japanese ferns, lamium, loropetalum, and nandina were selected for their handsome foliage and delicate textures.

Designer: Cynthia Hayes, Mosaic Landscape Design Group, San Jose (408/377-5680)

TRELLISES, RAISED BEDS, and walls designed for seating add new dimension to a garden that once featured only brick paving. At the back of the garden, a rock waterfall and pond add the pleasure of running water.

GARDEN RENOVATION: LOS ANGELES, CALIFORNIA

L.A. STORY

The spectacular makeover of this Bel Air property stopped jurors in their tracks. "It's a bold house and a bold garden," declared one juror. "When the design of the house and garden work this well together," said another, "the whole is greater than the sum of its parts."

The garden's strength comes from creative use of materials and prominent shapes—the result of collaboration between landscape designers Mia Lehrer, Alan Bernstein, and Tim Parker and the house's owner. A stone path interplanted with creeping thyme leads visitors to the front door through a dramatic curved wall that extends from the house's interior. Large, sculptural blue-gray and yellow agaves saved from the old garden echo the building's colors. A low-maintenance blue fescue lawn is surrounded by agaves, artemisia, feathery cassia, woolly grevillea, and other unthirsty plants.

In the back garden, where views of the city dominate, the infinity-edge pool and paving keep the design stark and clean. "This is a marriage that worked," concluded one juror.

Designer: Mia Lehrer and Associates, Los Angeles (213/892-0009)

JAY GRAHAM LEFT: STEVEN GUNTHER

OUTDOOR LIVING: SOUTHERN CALIFORNIA

SAILS BY THE SEA

Ocean waves and coastal breezes inspired this whimsical garden in Southern California, designed by landscape architect Jana Ruzicka. "It's an extraordinary marriage of art and the natural landscape," commented one juror. "Playful, yet appropriate." Another called it "a garden for relaxation and reflection."

Two lots make up the property—one developed, the other left natural to protect ocean views. Before the remodel, an unattractive chain-link fence separated the pool from the open lot, hampering views and limiting patio space. Ruzicka removed the old fence and situated a new sculptural steel fence where it would enhance the scenery. On the patio, free-form walls hug the chairs and chaises. Overhead, giant sail-like patio covers gently flutter in the breeze. Fruit trees and pool-friendly plants, such as *Asteriscus maritimus* and ligularia, grow around the patio. Beyond them, grasses, native plants, and wildflowers maintain the natural look.
Designer: Jana Ruzicka, Laguna Beach, CA (949/494-8871)

OUTDOOR LIVING: PHOENIX, ARIZONA

EMBRACING THE DESERT

When designing a garden in the desert, you have two options: welcome its plants and animals into the garden or fence them out. Landscape architect Christy Ten Eyck chose the former, embracing the desert in this Phoenix garden. The site's alluring beauty set

the stage for generous outdoor living areas full of colorful native plants, with the Phoenix Mountains Preserve as a backdrop. The garden's lines "are both elegant and comforting," said a juror.

In the front courtyard, graceful curved planters and steps form concentric circles around a patio of recycled concrete. Palo verdes provide light shade; penstemon, desert milkweed, and other natives attract butterflies and hummingbirds.

In the backyard, low, curved retaining walls shore up the sloping hillside. An outcropping of boulders bisects the walls, spilling water into a swimming hole and pond. "This garden could melt your cares away," concluded one juror.
Designer: Christy Ten Eyck, Ten Eyck Landscape Architects, Phoenix (602/468-0505)

GALLERY ON THE GREEN

Historic architecture surrounded by a contemporary garden may seem an uncomfortable pairing at first. But for Art Berliner and Laura Werlin's garden, designed by landscape architect Randy Thueme, the partnership works beautifully. Judges praised the design for its simple, direct, modern approach, and for the way it uses outdoor sculptures as accents. "Garden art should harmonize with its surroundings," noted a juror. "The designer accomplished this superbly."

Thueme made a concerted effort to reuse and recycle as many elements as possible. He reduced the front lawn and relocated camellias, ferns, and Japanese anemones to fill in the enlarged planting beds. At the rear, one of three original concrete pads was retained and recut for a slate patio. A second slate patio leads to a deck, which was modified and refinished. In spring, bulbs, flowering cherry, and wisteria bloom in concert. Sculptures are carefully placed to provide focal points.

Old and new mesh elegantly here, said the jurors.
Designer: Randy Thueme Design, San Francisco (415/495-1178)

ROLLING STONES

"With a view like this, there's no mistaking the garden's Northwest location," noted a juror of this hilltop garden that overlooks Puget Sound, designed and built by Hendrikus Schraven. "Other gardens might be overwhelmed by the view. This garden enhances it beautifully," the juror said.

All the jurors noted that superb stonework is one reason the garden looks so natural. More than 330 tons of rock were hoisted by crane up a 75-foot cliff to form the waterfall, pond, and curved rock wall. A rock firepit provides warmth on cool evenings.

Because the soil is rocky, Schraven had to bring in about 225 yards of topsoil before planting. Ferns, grasses, irises, and ground covers grow in the crevices and tumble over the rocks.
Designer: Hendrikus Schraven Landscape Construction & Design, Issaquah, WA (425/392-9977)

WGDA

LAWNLESS IN MALIBU

The impressive transformation of Robert and Ann Hyland's Malibu garden from lawn to a haven for outdoor living and gardening caught the eye of the judges. "The old garden was very plain and not very considerate of the California environment," stated a juror. "The change is remarkable."

A raised, cloister-inspired garden replaced the old lawn. A fountain with insets of California Arts and Crafts–style tile is the focal point; it's surrounded by eight planting beds set in decomposed granite and filled with a variety of fruit trees, herbs, perennials, spring-flowering bulbs, and vegetables. A casual arbor creates a sense of privacy.

Two steps down from the raised garden is a cozy outdoor living and entertaining area with a built-in barbecue, fireplace, and dining table. The garden's soft colors blend with the home. "This garden is designed for living," said a juror. "And it's probably used 100 times more than the lawn ever was."

Designer: Nancy Goslee Power, Nancy Goslee Power & Associates, Santa Monica (310/264-0266)

REGIONAL: PHILO, CALIFORNIA

SPLENDOR IN THE GRASSES

Taking a hands-off approach to their rural property in Mendocino County, landscape architects Patrick and Jane Miller created a stunningly simple garden to surround their barnlike home and work studio. "It's very brave, very original, and very accommodating to the site," said a juror.

Although all jurors agreed that the property is unique and the design specific to the site, they found it worthy of commendation for its genius. "The designers really understood their site and the local environment," a juror noted.

From the start, the Millers knew they didn't want their garden to compete with the surrounding natural landscape. So they added native plants—oaks, manzanitas, and incense cedars that would thrive on minimum water and care. Their one nod to a more refined landscape was the lavender drift—a formal arrangement of Spanish lavender in a keyhole shape.

Two open 60-foot raked gravel circles (called "infinity spirals") around the house serve as entry court, casual patio for socializing and games, and fire protection. This garden is in harmony with its surroundings.

Designers: Patrick and Jane Miller, 2M Associates, Berkeley (510/524-8132)

MEDITERRANEAN ODYSSEY

Designer Chris Jacobson took cues from Spain for the remodel of this Saratoga garden. Judges immediately appreciated his climate-appropriate design. Grasses, lavenders, rosemary, and other Mediterranean plants are particularly suited to Northern California's dry summers. And the stacked-rock walls, casual paths of decomposed granite and flagstone, and subtle use of water give the garden a soft and earthy look.

Before the redesign, a wide concrete path bisected the garden but led nowhere, plants hadn't been maintained, and the aqua-colored in-ground spa was deserted. Jacobson reconfigured the land into berms and turned the spa into a black-bottomed pond; water circulates from an urn fountain through a water course to the pond. Some of the existing plants were retained or relocated. Offering the ultimate compliment, one judge said, "Wouldn't you just love to be sitting there?"
Designer: Chris Jacobson, Gardenart, San Francisco and Los Gatos, CA (415/664-5913)

WATER TUMBLES from a terra-cotta jug embedded in a rock wall. Lush ferns surround it.

SAXON HOLT

GRAND ENTRANCE

Even royalty would feel welcome ascending the vast new walkway to John and Joyce Wilson's Cameron Park home. "The steps seem to sweep visitors right up to the front door," remarked a juror. "It's very gracious," said another.

Before the redesign, visitors had to ascend an 11-foot grade of multilevel wood decks to reach the front door—if they could find the entrance, that is, since the door wasn't visible from the driveway and the decks didn't look as if they led to an entry. To hide the magnitude of the grade, landscape architect Gary Orr offset the walk and created patio-size pads with low steps. Handsome stone retaining walls line one side of the walk and a grove of 30 birch trees softens the 20-foot-tall house wall. At the top of the walk, an impressive arbor covered with lush vines directs visitors to the front door. When does the prince arrive?
Designer: Gary Orr, Orr Design Office, Sacramento (916/441-4500)

JAY GRAHAM (2)

WGDA

FOREST FANTASY

Picture this: You're hiking through a forest when you come upon an isolated natural hot spring surrounded by boulders and lush greenery. You step in, letting the hot water envelop you and soothe your aching muscles. Just a dream, you say? Not to Mike and Brandy Galos, who built their fantasy hot spring right in their own garden with the help of landscape designer and contractor Hendrikus Schraven. Jurors were bowled over by the substantial rock work and the spa's very natural appearance. "Most spas are sterile-looking," noted a juror. "This one feels very secluded and natural."

Secluded it may look, but secluded it isn't: this 12- to 16-foot-wide spa is tucked into the Galoses' front yard below a grove of Douglas fir trees. To screen the spa from the street, existing woodland vegetation was enhanced with cedars, enkianthus, hemlocks, and tall rhododendrons. An angled granite path leads to the spa; large, flat rocks stair-step down into it. This is the ultimate spa, jurors agreed.

Designer: Hendrikus Schraven Landscape Construction & Design, Issaquah, WA (425/392-9977)

RANCH DRESSING

This Tucson garden, shaded by mesquite trees and a eucalyptus and planted with desert-adapted shrubs and grasses, has the look and feel of a historic Southwest rancho. "The plan has the look of the southern Sonoran Desert, all in an urban setting," said an impressed juror. "The ocotillo fencing, ramada, and lush plantings feel very original."

Though the garden looks mellowed by time, landscape designer Jeffrey Trent completed the work just three years ago. He removed old sheds, crumbling walls, railroad ties, paving, and most shrubs, replacing them with a stone ramada (designed by Robert Bailey) and entry arbor to resemble a 1930s WPA structure.

A preexisting fountain encircled by brick paving became the garden's focal point, connected by a flagstone patio to the house. Low seat walls define the patio's perimeter. Behind them are beds of lush-looking desert plants. Ocotillo fencing protects the pool area at the rear of the property.

"This designer had a real sensitivity to the color and feel of the desert," summed up one juror.

Designer: Jeffrey Trent, Tucson (520/792-9274)

SMALL SPACE: LOS ALTOS, CALIFORNIA

GRIDS GALORE

Elegant simplicity made jurors take note of this 1,500-square-foot front garden in Los Altos, California, designed for Bill Truxell by his brother, Robert.

Before the remodel, trees and shrubs camouflaged the entry. Now, a new gate and fence make it easy for visitors to find their way to the front door. "The clever grid design of the fence and gate provides privacy and a sense of openness at the same time," remarked one juror. "It's very welcoming." The design also created an outdoor room. Here, a pathway that leads to the gate jogs under the canopy of crape myrtles. The trees provide four seasons of drama: bronzy red-tinged leaves in spring, flowers in summer, brightly colored leaves in fall, and a sculptural branch structure in winter.
Designer: Truxell & Valentino Landscape Development, Clovis, CA (559/292-2871)

GARDEN RENOVATION: SACRAMENTO, CALIFORNIA

THE '60s REVISITED

To perfect rather than update the 1960s-era garden and home of Loretta Landers was landscape architect Gary Orr's goal when he took on this garden remodel. "This renovation was so subtle and successful we almost overlooked it," noted a juror. "This is a wonderful expression of how to maintain a style while greatly improving on it."

The successful transformation included a facelift for the house (enlarged column, fresh paint, new door) and a complete remodel of the garden. Offset platforms of pebbled concrete replaced the original straight concrete walkway. Black stucco retaining walls with randomly placed square insets cut across the garden. A similar wall, 5 feet tall with square cutouts, screens the living room window from passersby and serves as a handsome backdrop for plants. Large sculptural boulders decorate the porch and planting bed under the existing birches.

The '60s style may not appeal to everyone, noted one juror, but here it is exceptionally well done.
Designer: Gary Orr, Orr Design Office, Sacramento (916/441-4500) ◆

in the ground

•

in terra-cotta pots

•

in hanging baskets

Strawberries, like many fruits and vegetables, taste much better homegrown than store-bought. When freshly picked, they are nature's most perfect dessert—sweet, juicy, tender. They're also low in calories (about 50 per cup) and high in vitamin C. They're a snap to grow; you probably won't need the fumigants and pesticides that most commercial growers use. And unlike most fruits, they can yield a crop just months after planting. • To get started, pick up bare-root strawberry plants as soon as they're available (now in most areas, as late as April in the mountains), or those in 4-inch containers anytime. Strawberries can thrive almost everywhere—note the West's strawberry festivals, staged annually in Utah, Colorado, California, Oregon, and Washington. • You can plant strawberries three ways: in the ground, in strawberry pots, and in hanging baskets. Plant certain varieties now and you can be slicing the juicy fruits over shortcake by June, and dropping whole, fresh berries into smoothies through autumn.

Strawberries
How to grow and harvest your best crop ever

BY JIM McCAUSLAND

WHICH STRAWBERRY?

Though people have been eating Europe's tiny wild strawberries—*fraises de bois*—for centuries, big strawberry-pie fruits are newer hybrids between an eastern North America native and another species native to Chile. These hybrids fall into two classes:

June-bearing (also called spring-bearing) strawberries bloom in spring and bear fruit, depending on variety, beginning in April in Southern California and in June in Northwest and mountain states. In cold-winter climates, that one-crop habit is unchanging. But in mild California climates, June bearers have a less pronounced one-crop habit, and many kinds extend their harvest over months, acting like everbearers. June bearers produce the highest-quality fruits, but they're ready to harvest all at once. That's great if you juice or freeze the fruit. Plant them in February (when they're easiest to find at retail nurs-

eries) or in fall; either way, you'll get your first crop after plants have been through their first winter.

Everbearing strawberries (including day-neutral varieties, which flower and fruit with little regard for day length) bear their crops over a long season, beginning the spring after planting. Their biggest crop comes in late spring and early summer (about the same time as for June bearers); the smaller crops appear, often in cycles, through fall.

NORMAN A. PLATE (7)

place the exhausted mother plants.

To discourage weeds and hold in moisture, mulch the soil with black plastic before planting, as shown at bottom left. Plant strawberries through holes cut in the plastic, then mulch with a 3-inch layer of straw. Water with a soaker hose, drip irrigation, or flooding, or by overhead sprinkling.

Grown in good, healthy soil, disease-free strawberries can live and bear fruit for a long time; five years isn't unusual in a home garden (most commercial fields replace their strawberries every year, though some wait two years).

A matted row 10 feet long and 20 inches wide should yield 5 to 10 quarts of strawberries a year.

THE STRAWBERRY POT

Strawberry pots were originally designed to accommodate one to three plants in the top; as their runners developed, their offspring could be rooted in the little pockets protruding from the container's sides.

These days, impatient gardeners plug small strawberry plants into all the openings to guarantee a fast harvest and to fill the pot out quickly. Use a big strawberry jar (at least 16 inches tall); the little ones dry out too quickly.

Follow these guidelines to make a strawberry pot that will bear all season long for three to five years. These tips also apply to plants in baskets.

•Plant an everbearing variety like 'Quinault' or 'Seascape' so that you get as many months of harvest as possible. In mild parts of California, where June bearers act like everbearers, 'Sequoia' is another popular choice.

•Keep plants in as much sun as they'll tolerate without drying out too rapidly, especially when berries are ripening.

•Before planting, fortify the potting mix with controlled-release fertilizer.

•Feed monthly with liquid fertilizer.

•Water whenever the top inch of soil dries out—daily in hot weather. To apply water evenly, install a homemade irrigation tube, like the one pictured at right at planting time.

Approximate yield for a pot 16 inches tall: up to 2 quarts a year.

WHERE TO BUY PLANTS
You can find strawberries at most retail nurseries. Mail-order suppliers also carry them. One that has everything on our list (see page 59) except 'Sequoia', plus dozens of other varieties, is Lassen Canyon Nursery. Lassen is generally wholesale, but you can order plants from it (530/223-1075). For details, visit its Web site (www.snowcrest.net/ lcninc); bare-root plants cost $20 per 100 plus shipping and a small patent fee if it applies.

IN THE GROUND

To grow strawberries in rows, prepare the soil by digging in composted manure or other organic matter (in heavy or wet soil, plant in 8-inch-high mounds or raised beds). If salinity is a problem where you garden (mostly in the Southwest), saturate the top 6 inches of soil with water three times before you plant, allowing it to drain between waterings. Then amend the soil with peat or garden compost (not manure, which is often salty).

If you buy bare-root plants, trim their roots back to about 6 inches and soak them for 30 minutes. Set out plants in a diamond pattern; space them 12 to 18 inches apart in rows 20 to 30 inches wide. Leave 18 inches between the rows for a path—you'll need it for weeding and harvesting. Set plants in the soil with their roots spread out and down and their crowns just above ground level. Keep runners picked off the first year, but the second year let some grow to fill in for the mother plants you'll remove the third or fourth year.

To grow strawberries ground-cover-style, space plants in rows as described above, but allow their runners to grow, root, and fill the gaps between the mother plants. When the bed is filled (matted), pinch off new runners—unless you need them in later years to re-

How to plant a strawberry pot

1. To make a watering tube, cut a piece of PVC pipe so one end will be even with the pot's rim when it is placed vertically inside. Cap it on one end. Drill ⅛-inch-diameter holes about 1 inch apart along alternate sides of the pipe.

2. Partially fill the pot with soil, then insert the watering tube, capped end down, near the center. Add more potting mix, loosely filling up to the rim.

3. Working from the bottom up, plant each pocket, adding soil around the roots as needed. Soak the soil well.

4. To irrigate through the growing season, slip a funnel into the PVC pipe and pour water into it; the pipe's holes will distribute water evenly.

How to care for strawberries

FEEDING. For maximum production in garden beds, use a complete fertilizer (10-10-10 is a good formula). Fertilize strawberries twice a year: apply 2 pounds per 100 square feet of bed when new growth begins in spring, and 2 more pounds per 100 square feet of bed after the main spring or summer crop. If you're just feeding a few individual plants, apply a flat tablespoon of complete fertilizer per plant. In the Northwest, you may want to dig superphosphate into the soil when you plant. In California and the Southwest, you can substitute high-nitrogen fertilizer for complete fertilizer, but at half the rate (1 pound per 100 square feet) at each feeding.

If your soil is rich and well amended, plants can also thrive on a simpler regime we used at *Sunset:* apply dilute fish emulsion every two weeks until flowering, then stop.

To feed plants in pots and baskets, see instructions on page 57.

PEST CONTROLS. In the short run, pests usually cause strawberries the most grief.

•Birds have an uncanny ability to find ripe fruits before gardeners do. Cover crops with bird netting.

•Sow bugs and pill bugs eat little hollows in the sides of the fruit. Lay a board flat on the ground next to the plants and periodically handpick the sow bugs and pill bugs that collect under it during the day.

DISEASE PREVENTION. A combination of viruses and soil-borne funguses usually takes out strawberries in the long run. You can keep these problems at bay by starting your strawberry patch with certified disease-free plants (instead of using runners that are given away by your neighbor).

•To avoid root rot, plant in soil with good drainage.

HANGING BASKETS

Strawberry baskets may just be the ultimate fruit baskets. They can hang anywhere you have sun. Suspended off the ground, they stay out of reach of slugs, snails, and sow bugs. It takes longer to plant in a basket than in the ground or in a jar, but patient gardeners are rewarded with a beautiful eye-level crop.

The basket pictured above, planted by Ted Mayeda of M & M Nursery in Orange, California, contains a heavenly feast of strawberries. To make one like it, buy a 16-inch wire basket and about 24 strawberry plants. To line the basket, use damp sphagnum moss or coconut fiber. Or you can purchase a green polyester-and-plastic basket liner called E-Z Liner ($8.49 per liner, or $21.49 for a liner with a 16-inch wire basket and hanger; to order, call 800/644-8042 or 714/538-8042).

Set 18 plants into the basket's sides, inserting them through the sphagnum moss or through 3-inch slits in the liner. Fill the basket with potting soil. Plant the remaining six plants in the top of the basket.

With good care (follow the guidelines for the strawberry pot, page 57), the basket should bear fruit and look good for about three years. As the plants die, you can just replace them.

Eight Great Strawberries for Western Gardens

Variety	Type; flavor	Where it grows best	Resistance?	
'Benton'	June-bearing. Produces a good crop of firm berries that have a sweet, fruity flavor with peach overtones.	Great in Northern California, the Northwest, and mountain and intermountain areas.	Virus-tolerant and mildew-resistant.	
'Camarosa'	June-bearing. A little earlier than 'Chandler', maintains huge berry size through the season. Flavorful, favored by restaurants.	Most widely grown California commercial strawberry. In Northern California, bears January-April; in Southern California, December-June.	Susceptible to mites.	
'Chandler'	Everbearing. Large berries, excellent flavor, good texture, juicy. Sweeter than 'Camarosa'. Good for freezing.	Good performance in California. Bears January-April or May in Northern California, January-June in Southern California.	Some resistance to leaf spot.	
'Quinault'	Everbearing. Fruit has large, gourdlike shape; it's tasty, rather soft. Good producer of runners, so lends itself to growing in matted rows.	At its best from Oregon through Alaska, where long days push production. Acceptable in Northern California.	Resists virus and red stele (a root rot), but it's susceptible to botrytis.	
'Seascape'	Everbearing. Good size and firmness. Somewhat sweet; the best-tasting of commercial everbearers (but most people would rate the noncommercial 'Quinault' and 'Tristar' higher).	Best in California, but also did well in Oregon trials. Flowers first in February, then again three times through fall. Stops fruiting in high summer heat, but rebounds in fall.	First crop is often so early that it gets botrytis from central California north. Later crops fine.	
'Sequoia'	June-bearing, but can act like an everbearer. Produces extremely tasty berries over many months.	At its best in California, but with wide climate adaptability, even in coldest winters. Not widely grown in the Northwest.	Resistant to alkalinity, yellows (a virus), and most leaf diseases.	
'Totem'	June-bearing. Productive, juicy. Perky sweet-tart fruit is on the soft side. This is the Northwest's major processing berry (great in strawberry jam).	A fine choice for western Oregon and Washington, but since it flowers early, late frosts can impair fruit set.	Resists red stele, viruses. Holds berries off ground, so fruit rot is rarely a problem.	
'Tristar'	Everbearing. Flowers almost constantly and produces very flavorful fruit. Even bears well the first year. Very prolific, adaptable, but a little soft. Seedy.	Good throughout the West.	Resists red stele and mildew, but moderately susceptible to viruses.	

IF YOU LOVE DAFFODILS, March isn't just a great month to admire the blooms in fields and gardens throughout the West. it's also an ideal time to select bulbs for fall planting. For more on these golden beauties, see page 66.

March

gardenguide

CORAL BELLS (lower left) and red Jupiter's beard edge the brick walk.

Rebirth of a Denver garden

■ Three years ago, this color-packed perennial garden was home to a lonely Colorado blue spruce growing in an empty lot. Owner/landscape architect Charles Randolph of Lifescape Associates, who lives on the property, transformed the space into an urban retreat as well as a living showroom of plants that perform well in Denver's climate. "I wanted an outdoor room in a beautiful garden, a natural space in the center of the city with privacy, birds, and butterflies," he explains.

In Randolph's garden, red Jupiter's beard (*Centranthus ruber*) and coral bells border the brick path. Beds of fragrant roses and lavender fill sunny spaces. Dense, dry shade under the spruce goaded Randolph to install a "bulletproof shade garden," as he calls it. Plants that thrive there—astilbe, bleeding heart, hosta, Japanese spurge, meadow rue, and spiderwort—hold their own against shade, cold, and the spruce's fibrous root system.

There are also tree peonies, Korean lilac, and fruitless crabapples for spring bloom; red-leaf plums and climbing hydrangeas for summer color; sweet autumn clematis and gink-

goes for fall flowers and foliage; and mugho pine and contorted filbert for winter interest.

Around paved areas, Randolph spreads "spot" color with pots of miniature roses, vinca, dwarf eulalia grass, nicotiana, and other ornamentals.

If you're considering a garden remodel, this is time to firm up your plans. In the Denver area, you can set out most perennials and deciduous trees and shrubs in March, which is the month Randolph's crews start work on his clients' landscapes.

— *Jim McCausland*

Aussies among us

■ Shrubs from Down Under, such as New Zealand tea tree, are at their blooming best late winter through early spring. Tailor-made for vases, they have wispy but not floppy stems; tiny, often needlelike foliage; and small but abundant flowers that last. They're useful fillers between pricey florist flowers. Or they can be harvested more generously to go solo in bouquets. Now's the time to buy and plant them for future winter-into-spring harvests.

• New Zealand tea tree (*Leptospermum scoparium*) has needlelike foliage. From winter into early spring, it bears white, pink, or red flowers all along the stems. The most popular hybrids range from 5 to 10 feet. This evergreen shrub prefers full sun and grows best in *Sunset* climate zones 14–24.

• Geraldton waxflower (*Chamelaucium uncinatum*). Airy evergreen shrub to 10

WINTER BLOOMS in strawberry sundae colors come from tea tree and Geraldton waxflower.

DEIDRA WALPOLE

feet with bright green, needlelike foliage and showy sprays of white, pink, rose, or violet flowers at branch ends. Needs good drainage and full sun. Once established (second summer), needs infrequent but deep summer watering. Zones 8–9, 12–24.

Harvesting stems for indoor use keeps plants tidy and ensures a good flower crop the following year. Cut stems 18 to 24 inches long. Leave some foliage below your cut; never cut into hardwood. If you prefer the blooms on the plant, do all major pruning by midsummer.

If you can't find these shrubs, ask your garden center to order them from Monterey Bay Nursery in Watsonville (wholesale only). — *Sharon Cohoon*

Orchid indulgence

CHUCK PLACE

■ Whether you like your orchids rare and strange, or simply staggeringly beautiful, here's your opportunity to indulge. The 54th Annual Santa Barbara International Orchid Show took place in mid-March 1999. The 55th annual show will be held on March 31, April 1 and 2, 2000. More than 65 commercial and amateur orchid growers from the West and the Pacific Rim will have their most luscious, exotic blooms on exhibit. Many growers will also have plants for sale. Orchid-growing supplies— as well as opportunities to discuss problems with experts—will be available. If your taste for orchids isn't sated, visit up to a half-dozen commercial orchid nurseries in the area, such as Santa Barbara Orchid Estate, pictured at left. Most of these nurseries are not open to the public except during this event.

The orchid show is at the Earl Warren Showgrounds, at U.S. 101 and Las Positas Rd. in Santa Barbara. Check for times and prices by contacting the show organization at 1096 North Patterson Avenue, Santa Barbara, CA 9311. Maps showing the locations of host nurseries will be available at the show or at www.SBOrchidShow.com. Or call (805) 967-6331. — *S.C.*

JANET LOUGHREY

Penstemons kissed with color

■ Six new members of the penstemon family were recently born in the Pacific Northwest. Bred by Joy Creek Nursery in Scappoose, Oregon, these hybrids vie for your attention with their delicious flower colors and long bloom season.

There are four sisters in the Kissed series, all with pure white throats and colored lips: 'Cerise Kissed' (vivid rosy pink); 'Coral Kissed' (soft coral pink); 'Violet Kissed'; and 'Wine Kissed' (deep burgundy). The tubular flowers measure 1½ inches long and 1 inch across on plants that grow about 2 feet tall and equally wide.

In addition to this series, there are two kissing cousins: 'Purple Tiger' has purple blooms with white-striped throats, and 'Raspberry Flair' (shown at left) has extra-large flowers with cerise lips and raspberry-red streaks in the throats.

These penstemons are hardy perennials in *Sunset* climate zones 4–9 and 14–17. In cold-winter areas (zones 1–3), you can grow them as annuals. Penstemons do best in full sun and require well-drained soil. To encourage continuous bloom from summer to frost, deadhead spent flower spikes just above the first set of true leaves. Water them once or twice a week, if rain doesn't do it for you.

Joy Creek Nursery sells all six varieties by mail order. In spring, plants in 4-inch containers cost $6 each. After June 1, plants in 1-gallon containers sell for $9.50 each, plus shipping. To order plants or a catalog ($2), call the nursery at (503) 543-7474.

— Janet Loughrey

The queen of cornflowers

■ The most spectacular member of the cornflower family has to be *Centaurea rothrockii*. When this Southwest native recently appeared in seed catalogs, we ordered a packet and started seeds in early spring for transplanting in *Sunset's* summer garden. As soon as the blooms began to unfurl, the admiring stares they drew from visitors told us we'd found a winner.

The flowers resemble Scottish thistles, but their frilled petals are as soft as feathers. The iridescent purplish pink petals spread 5 inches wide around creamy white centers with a sweet fragrance that is attractive to bees. In *Sunset's* garden, blooms kept coming on foot-long stems from midsummer to late November. They make exquisite cut flowers if you remove the buds *before* they have started to open.

Grow this frost-tender biennial as an annual. In cold-winter areas, start seed indoors in 4-inch pots and transplant seedlings into the garden after danger of frost is past. Reaching 4 to 6 feet tall, the sturdy, upright plant looks best at the rear of a border. Give it full sun, well-drained soil, and moderate water. In windy areas, it's wise to stake the main stalk, which supports 20 or more flowers at one time. Clip off faded blooms.

Seeds of *C. rothrockii* are available from two mail-order sources: Plants of the Southwest (Aqua Fria St., Route 6, Box 11A, Santa Fe, NM 87501; 800/788-7333) and Thompson & Morgan (Box 1308, Jackson, NJ 08527; 800/274-7333). *— Dick Bushnell*

FOR THIS ARRANGEMENT, plant (clockwise from top left) 'Limemound' spiraea, *Acorus gramineus,* columbine, thyme, *Helichrysum,* chrysanthemum, and phlomis (center).

MARION BRENNER

Divine lime, in a pot

■ Plants with colored foliage are playing an increasingly important role in the garden—even in containers. In a new twist on the classic flowerpot, *Sunset* head gardener Rick LaFrentz featured yellow, green, gray, and variegated foliage with a smattering of yellow flowers. Planted last March, the sophisticated arrangements looked attractive throughout the summer and needed only minor shaping as plants filled in. Here's a recipe for making your own foliage pot. Start with 1-gallon or 4-inch plants.

WHAT TO BUY

- *Acorus gramineus* 'Variegatus'
- *Chrysanthemum multicaule* 'Moonlight' (from Thompson & Morgan; 800/274-7333), or use a whiteflowered variety
- *Helichrysum petiolare* 'Limelight'
- *Phlomis fruticosa*
- *Spiraea bumalda* 'Limemound'

- Variegated columbine (*Aquilegia vervaeneana*) 'Woodside Variegated Mixed' (from Thompson & Morgan), or use a green-foliaged variety
- Variegated thyme (*Thymus citriodorus* 'Aureus')
- 2-cubic-foot bag potting mix
- 24-inch-wide container — *L.B.S.*

QUICK TIP

Roses from seed

■ When you're hankering for a new rose, most likely you head for the bare-root or container section of your nursery. But that's not the only place you'll find a beautiful rose. Next time, try the seed rack instead.

New this year from Renee's Garden Seeds is a lovely miniature rose called 'Angel Wings' that blooms in just 10 to 12 weeks from transplant. Plants produce clusters of precious-looking single and semidouble pink or white flowers that appear throughout the season. Plants eventually reach $1\frac{1}{2}$ to 2 feet tall, making them perfect for containers or the front of a border.

Sow one or two seeds in a 4-inch pot. When seeds germinate, set the pot in bright light; water to keep the soil moist. Thin out all but the strongest plant. When plants have several sets of leaves, fertilize with fish emulsion or a $\frac{1}{4}$ dilution of a liquid fertilizer. Transplant to larger containers or the ground when roots have filled the pots. Purchase seeds at a nursery (call 888/880-7228 for a source) or order on-line from www.garden.com/reneesgarden.

— *Lauren Bonar Swezey*

NORMAN A. PLATE

'ANGEL WINGS' ROSE—a miniature that grows up to 2 feet tall—produces dainty pink and white flowers just three months after sowing.

How to plant a straight row

NORMAN A. PLATE

■ To plant seeds or seedlings in straight rows, follow one of the two techniques pictured here. Use them when annual vegetable crops such as lettuce, peas,or beans **1.** Insert stakes at both ends of the bed, making sure they align. Tie a piece of string to one stake, stretch it to the other, and tie it, keeping it taut. Plant beneath it. **2.** Cut a 1-by-2 board to the desired length of the row, place it on the soil surface, then plant along its edge.

How to prune frost-damaged plants

■ Inspect the upper stems for the first sign of new growth.

If you see new growth: Prune out dead wood, cutting well into live tissue. Make the cut just above a node where new growth emerges.

If you're uncertain whether the plant is still alive, carefully scratch the surface of the bark to see if the stem is still greenish. If the stem is succulent and tender, wait to prune until new growth appears. Keep in mind that some plants may die back to the ground and reemerge from the roots. Look for new growth in the crown (center) of the plant too. — *L.B.S.*

DEBRA LAMBERT

A Southwest classic is back in print

■ After its initial publication in 1981, *Plants for Dry Climates: How to Select, Grow and Enjoy,* by Mary Rose Duffield and Warren D. Jones, was widely acclaimed by Southwest gardeners. Now, thanks to Arizona publisher Bill Fisher, this once out-of-print classic is back as a softbound.

Whether you're a beginner or an old hand at gardening in the Southwest, this comprehensive 192-page guide belongs in your library. The heart of the book is an encyclopedia of more than 300 species with information on their care, planting, and use in landscaping. Although the accompanying photographs haven't been updated since the book was first published, most are still helpful.

Look for *Plants for Dry Climates* (Fisher Books, Tucson, 1998; $17.95) at bookstores, or order from the publisher (800/255-1514; $5 shipping). — *L.B.S.*

Daffodil days

■ If you love daffodils, this is the season you wait for all year. In fields and gardens throughout the West, these beauties are blooming in shades of gold, orange, and apricot. It's an ideal time to select the ones you like for fall planting. Public gardens and nursery demonstration beds are good places to see blooming daffodils. Or make a pilgrimage to the Northwest's daffodil mecca—the Puyallup Valley near Tacoma. Growers here cultivate vast fields for the bulb and cut-flower markets.

One grower, VanLierop Bulb Farm, welcomes visitors to tour its display garden when it's in bloom and order bulbs for fall delivery. Or shop for bulbs in the catalog ($3). The VanLierop family has been raising daffodils here since 1934. Today they grow about 150 varieties, from big, yellow 'Dutch Master' to tiny, orange-cupped 'Matador' (both are shown on page 60 in the arms of Anne VanLierop-Johnson). A rising star is 'Mrs. R.O. Backhouse', whose ruffled soft apricot cups are surrounded by white petals. Write or call VanLierop Bulb Farm, 13407 80th St. E., Puyallup, WA 98372; (253) 848-7272. You can also visit the farm's Web site: www.flower-movers.com.

Daffodils grow in any climate, tolerating cold and heat, and they're one bulb that gophers will not eat. They naturalize in the garden, increasing every year. Enjoy the flowers, then let foliage ripen to nourish the bulbs for next season's show. After the flowers fade and the leaves wither, you can dig and divide crowded clumps. Replant the bulbs immediately so you won't miss a bloom next spring. — *Steven R. Lorton*

Flower gardening, desert-style

Yes, you can have a true perennial garden—with all the flowers and seasonal interest that term implies—in the desert. Southern California is rich with native perennials that are perfectly adapted to arid climates and eminently gardenworthy. That's the premise behind the new Wortz Demonstration Garden at the Living Desert in Palm Desert. And it succeeds brilliantly. The plants in the garden island shown are all sun-loving Southwest native perennials. Black-

foot daisy, coreopsis, and poppies (golden flowers); daleas; Indian blanket flower; monkey flower; penstemon and salvias (crimson flowers); wild petunias (*Ruellia*); and zinnias bloom here at different times. The stone fountain, with its hidden water source, adds a cooling touch—as if you'd stumbled across a desert spring. In another section of the garden, under the filtered shade of acacias and

THE LIVING DESERT is at 47-900 Portola Ave., Palm Desert; (760) 346-5694.

desert willows, is an equally colorful shade border, planted with coral bells, Mexican lobelia, columbine, and other desert perennials.

The new garden adds another dimension to the Living Desert, a combination zoo and botanical park in the Palm Springs area. You'll get lots of ideas, and if you like, you can buy the plants in the adjoining nursery. — *S. C.*

'Pink Crystals', a grass that glows

■ As I admired the borders in Denver Botanic Gardens last summer, one ornamental grass really grabbed my attention. 'Pink Crystals' ruby grass (*Rhynchelytrum nerviglume*), with its shimmering pink-and-silver flower, glows like a beacon.

This grass was recently introduced through Plant Select, a program administered by Denver Botanic Gardens and Colorado State University that features new or unknown plants that thrive in local climates.

In cold-winter areas, 'Pink Crystals' is grown as an annual. In areas with milder winters like Pueblo, Colorado, this grass is a perennial. Give it full sun and loamy soil. Water regularly to keep the soil moderately moist but not wet. Planted in spring, young plants develop into 1-foot mounds of spiky blue-green foliage. Then in late summer, masses of 2-foot-tall flower spikes spring from the base of the clump.

Small potted plants of 'Pink Crystals' are available from High Country Gardens (800/925-9387 or www.highcountrygardens.com). — *L.B.S.*

Pacific Northwest Checklist

PLANTING

✔ **CAMELLIAS.** Zones 4–7: Blooming plants will be in ample supply at nurseries this month. Enjoy them up close before you plant them out. Slip them into decorative containers to enjoy near a window or out on a deck while in flower. When blooms fade, plant them in the garden.

✔ **COOL-SEASON CROPS.** Zones 4–7: Start seeds of beets, carrots, chard, lettuce, peas, radishes, spinach, and most members of the cabbage family.

✔ **LAWNS.** In all zones, you can start a new lawn this month. Spade and rake the top 6 to 12 inches of soil to a fine consistency and amend it with organic matter. Next, lay sod or rake in a seed mix. There are dozens of blends on the market. Knowledgeable nursery employees can help you choose the right mix for your garden. Water your new lawn regularly.

✔ **SUMMER BULBS.** Zones 4–7: Summer-blooming bulbs of acidanthera, calla, crocosmia, gladiolus, ranunculus, and tigridia can go in the ground from midmonth on. If a late hard frost is predicted, cover bulb beds with 1 inch of organic mulch.

✔ **WARM-SEASON CROPS.** In all zones, start seeds of basil, eggplant, peppers, tomatoes, and other summer crops indoors for transplanting outside after the weather begins to warm up.

MAINTENANCE

✔ **DIVIDE PERENNIALS.** Zones 4–7: Dig, divide, and replant summer- and fall-blooming perennials early this month so you won't lose any bloom this season. In zones 1–3, wait until April. In all zones, wait until autumn to divide spring-flowering perennials.

✔ **FEED LAWNS.** Start a lawn feeding program this month. Use a fertilizer with a 3-1-2 ratio of N-P-K (nitrogen, phosphorus, potassium). Apply ½ pound of actual nitrogen per 1,000 square feet of turf.

✔ **PRUNE CLEMATIS.** In zones 4–7: Cut back summer-flowering clematis now and apply a handful of complete fertilizer (10-10-10 is a good choice) at the base of each plant. In zones 1–3, do this after the danger of a hard freeze is past. In all zones, prune back spring-flowering varieties as soon as they finish blooming.

PEST CONTROL

✔ **FIGHT SLUGS.** You'll understand the meaning of rage if you put a blooming primrose in a bed without slug protection. Overnight the gastropods will chew it down to a stub, leaving nothing but a trail of slime. Whatever your weapon (bait, handpicking, or beer traps), attack them now. ◆

Northern California Checklist

PLANTING

☑ **PLANT POTATOES.** Zones 7–9, 14–17: Just for fun, try growing potatoes in different colors and flavors— yellow 'Bintje' or 'Yukon Gold'; 'All Red' or 'Red Dale'; or 'All Blue' or 'Caribe'. (You can choose from 96 varieties and order from Irish Eyes with a Hint of Garlic, formerly Ronniger's Seed & Potato Co., Box 307, Ellensburg, WA 98926; 509/925-6025. Catalog $2).

☑ **PLANT TUBEROUS BEGONIAS.** Zones 7–9, 14–17: When pink buds appear in the concave part of a tuber, plant tubers concave side up in a container filled with potting soil. Barely cover with soil mix, then soak with water. Set the pot in filtered shade. Don't water again until the top of the soil feels dry. Zones 1–2: Start tubers in a greenhouse or indoors in a cool, dry place. When first leaves appear, place in bright, indirect light and keep at 65° to 70°. Move outdoors after frosts.

☑ **SET OUT SCENTED GERANIUMS.** Zones 7–9, 14–17. Dozens of scented geraniums (*Pelargonium,* not true geraniums) are available at nurseries or by mail (from Geraniaceae in Kentfield, 415/461-4168; catalog $4). Scents to try include apple, apricot, ginger, peppermint, and nutmeg.

Sunset
CLIMATE ZONES

☐ Mountain (1-2)
☐ Valley (7-9)
☐ Inland (14)
☐ Coastal (15-17)

DEBRA LAMBERT

☑ **SHOP FOR CITRUS.** Zones 7–9, 14–17: Buy young trees in 5-gallon cans; they'll get established faster. Look for the new dwarf citrus on Flying Dragon rootstock from Monrovia Nursery (and others). Try 'Lisbon' lemon, 'Melogold' grapefruit-pummelo hybrid, 'MidKnight' and 'Valencia' orange, 'Star Ruby' grapefruit (requires less summer heat to ripen than most grapefruit), or 'Washington' navel orange. In zones 7–9, wait to plant until the end of the month.

MAINTENANCE

☑ **AMEND SOIL.** Zones 7–9, 14–17: Before planting, amend fast-draining or heavy clay soils with compost, ground bark, or other organic material to improve soil texture and water retention. If you use ground bark or another wood product, make sure it has been nitrogen stabilized (read the label or ask the supplier). Otherwise, the mulch will retard plant growth. If it hasn't been, add a nitrogen fertilizer.

☑ **CARE FOR HERBS.** Zones 7–9, 14–17: To rejuvenate perennial herbs such as mint and sage, cut back old or dead growth on established plants, then fertilize and water to stimulate new growth. Plant new herbs such as mint, oregano, parsley, rosemary, sage, and thyme in loose, well-drained soil. One good mail-order source is Mountain Valley Growers (559/338-2775).

PEST CONTROL

☑ **SPRAY DORMANT OIL.** Zones 7–9, 14–17: The best time to spray dormant oil to control overwintering insects is before buds appear. But a new all-season oil made from soybeans, called Bug Oil, is lighter than petroleum-based oils and can be used all year long. It's also environmentally friendly. To order Bug Oil, call the Natural Gardening Company (707/766-9303). An 8-ounce pouch costs $4.95 plus shipping. ◆

Southern California Checklist

PLANTING

☑ **PLANT AZALEAS AND CAMELLIAS.** Select plants while they're in flower, and plant them as soon as possible. Amend the soil well with organic material and a soil acidifier such as oak leaf mold or peat moss. Plant azaleas and camellias so that the tops of the rootballs are an inch or so aboveground after the soil settles.

☑ **PLANT PERENNIALS.** Nurseries are well stocked with blooming perennials. And, second only to fall, early spring is the best time for planting them. Choices include campanula, columbine, coral bells, delphinium, digitalis, diascia, pelargonium, penstemon, salvia, scabiosa, Stokes aster, true geraniums, and yarrow.

☑ **REPLACE BEDDING PLANTS.** As the weather warms and cool-season annuals start to fade, replace them with heat-loving bedding plants. Choices include amaranth, celosia, coleus, dahlias, dianthus, linaria, lobelia, marigolds, nicotiana, petunias, salvia, scaevola, and verbena. In the high desert (zone 11), set out marigolds, petunias, and zinnias late this month.

☑ **PLANT HERBS.** Plant young chives, parsley, rosemary, sage, savory, sorrel, tarragon, and thyme. Sow seeds of arugula, chervil, cilantro, and dill.

Bishop

NEVADA

CALIFORNIA

San Luis Obispo

Bakersfield

Tehachapi

Santa Barbara

Lancaster

Los Angeles

Palm Springs

Sunset
CLIMATE ZONES

San Diego

1-3 7-9 11 13 14-24

MEXICO

DEBRA LAMBERT

☑ **SOW SEEDS FOR CUT FLOWERS.** Cleome, cosmos, nicotiana, and sunflowers all make great cut flowers and germinate easily. Sow directly in the garden where you want them to grow.

MAINTENANCE

☑ **START SPRING FEEDING.** Feed ground covers, shrubs, roses, perennials, and trees with a controlled-release fertilizer such as bonemeal, cottonseed meal, or blood meal to provide gradual nutrition throughout the season. Or, if you prefer, use a faster-acting complete fertilizer. Don't feed azaleas and camellias until they finish blooming. Don't feed California natives or drought-tolerant Mediterraneans; their growth slows before summer dormancy.

☑ **THIN FRUIT TREES.** Thin apples, pears, and stone fruit when they are about ½ inch. Space fruit 4 to 6 inches apart or leave one fruit per spur. In general, the earlier the variety, the more it needs to be thinned.

PEST AND WEED CONTROL

☑ **CONTROL APHIDS.** These sucking pests go for tender new growth. Dislodge them with a blast of water from a hose. On more delicate blossoms, mist with insecticidal soap. Or strip aphids off stems with your fingers; wear rubber gloves if you're squeamish.

☑ **WATCH FOR AFRICANIZED HONEY BEES.** The so-called "killer bees"—the more aggressive cousins of the European honey bees—have entered Southern California. Stinging has been reported in Imperial, Riverside, San Bernardino, and San Diego counties. For tips on bee-proofing your home and other general precautions, call your county extension or agricultural commission and ask for the "Bee Alert" brochure. ◆

Mountain Checklist

PLANTING

☑ **BARE-ROOT PLANTS. Zones 2–3:** Set out bare-root plants of berries, grapes, all kinds of fruit and shade trees, and perennial vegetables including asparagus, horseradish, and rhubarb. Zone 1: Plant bare-root stock after the snow has melted and the soil has thawed. If you can't plant immediately, wrap the bare roots in damp cloth or sawdust and keep them moist until you can get them in the ground.

☑ **LAWNS.** Overseed an old lawn or plant a new one late this month in milder zones. For overseeding, rough up the soil and sow it with the same kind of grass that is growing there. Otherwise the texture and color of the new grass will contrast with the old. For a new lawn, till 2 inches of organic matter into the top 8 inches of soil before you sow. For drought tolerance, consider planting a native like blue grama or buffalo grass (or a blend of the two). Keep newly sown areas well watered until the grass is tall enough to mow.

MONTANA
• Helena

• Boise

IDAHO

WYOMING

Cheyenne •

NEVADA

• Reno

Salt Lake City

Denver •

UTAH

COLORADO

Las Vegas

Sunset
CLIMATE ZONES
☐ 1-3   ☐ 10-11

DEBRA LAMBERT

MAINTENANCE

☑ **PREPARE BEDS.** Dig composted manure or compost into beds to prepare them for spring planting. For bad soil, till 4 to 6 inches of organic matter into the top foot of soil. Rake amended beds, water, and let settle for a week before planting.

☑ **FEED EVERGREENS.** Sprinkle high-nitrogen fertilizer over the root zones of plants and water well.

☑ **FEED SHRUBS.** On a mild day when temperatures are well above freezing, apply high-nitrogen fertilizer to early-flowering shrubs as soon as they've finished blooming.

☑ **FERTILIZE BERRIES.** Blackberries, blueberries, and raspberries benefit from feeding this month. Use high-nitrogen fertilizer or well-aged manure.

☑ **FEED ROSES.** Fertilize on a day when night temperatures are expected to remain above freezing. Water established plants, let the soil drain, apply a complete fertilizer, and water again.

☑ **INSTALL IRRIGATION SYSTEMS.** It's easier to put in drip-irrigation systems early, before root and top growth get in the way.

☑ **MAKE COMPOST.** Use last fall's rotted leaves to start a compost pile. Alternate layers of green matter with dry leaves, straw, or sawdust. Turn the pile and keep it damp; you should have finished compost in a few weeks.

PEST & WEED CONTROL

☑ **BLAST APHIDS.** Aphids show up first on tender new growth. If an infestation starts, blast them off with hose water or spray with insecticidal soap.

☑ **HOE WEEDS.** Get them now, while they're young and shallow-rooted. If you wait until they form deep taproots, they'll grow back. If weeds germinate between the time you prepare a flower bed and plant, hoe them off lightly without disturbing more than the top ½ inch of soil. If you hoe more deeply or till, you'll bring up a fresh batch of weed seeds. ◆

Southwest Checklist

PLANTING

✔ ANNUALS. Zones 12–13: Set out warm-season flowers such as black-foot daisy (*Melampodium leucanthum*), celosia, gomphrena, lisianthus, Madagascar periwinkle, marigold, portulaca, and salvia.

✔ CITRUS TREES. Zone 12 (Tucson): Plant kumquats and mandarins like 'Fairchild', 'Fortune', and 'Fremont'. Zone 13 (Phoenix): Plant lemons, grapefruits, and oranges including 'Trovita', 'Valencia', and those sold as Arizona Sweets ('Diller', 'Hamlin', 'Marrs', 'Pineapple').

✔ GROUND COVERS. Zones 12–13: Start ground covers such as aptenia, calylophus, dwarf rosemary, lantana, Mexican evening primrose, verbena, and vinca to give their roots a chance to get established before hot weather arrives.

✔ HERBS. Perennial culinary herbs like chives, rosemary, sage, and thyme can go in the ground now.

✔ PERENNIALS. Zones 10–13: Set out aster, autumn sage (*Salvia greggii*), chrysanthemum, coreopsis, feverfew, gerbera, helianthus, hollyhock, penstemon, and Shasta daisy.

✔ SUMMER BULBS. Set out dahlia tubers and gladiolus corms after danger of frost is past. In zones 10–13, shop for caladium, canna, and crinum now but wait until the soil warms to 65° before planting.

✔ VEGETABLES. Zones 10–11: Plant broccoli, cabbage, carrots, cauliflower, kohlrabi, lettuce, potatoes, radishes, and spinach immediately. Start tomatoes by midmonth. Zones 12–13: Sow asparagus, beans, black-eyed peas, cucumbers, melons, summer squash, and sweet corn. Set out pepper and tomato seedlings now but cover plants if frost threatens.

✔ VINES. Zones 10–13: Plant Boston ivy, Carolina jessamine, Japanese honeysuckle, Lady Banks' rose, silver lace vine, trumpet creeper (*Campsis radicans*), Virginia creeper, and wisteria.

MAINTENANCE

✔ CARE FOR HERBS. Zones 10–13: Cut back old growth of perennial herbs like mint and sage, then fertilize and water.

✔ DIVIDE PERENNIALS. Zones 10–13: Dig and divide bearded irises, chrysanthemums, and daylilies right away.

✔ TRIM ORNAMENTAL GRASSES. When new growth appears, cut back the old grass to keep the clump neat. ◆

DEBRA LAMBERT

Color champions of the West

■ Color draws the eye and lifts the spirit—it's no wonder most gardeners can't get enough. They dream of vibrant flowers and foliage that last a season or longer but are still easy to grow and, if possible, easy on the West's precious water supply.

We found 95 real-life examples of those dreamy plants after asking horticultural experts in each region of the West to list the most outstanding color-makers—annuals, perennials, shrubs, and vines. The top vote-getters are the plants the panelists recommend to nursery shoppers, install in clients' landscapes, or grow in their own gardens. Many are familiar, but a few are so new to the nursery trade that they aren't yet in the *Sunset Western Garden Book*.

Shop for these plants at well-stocked nurseries. Depending on your garden's climate and soil conditions, you can set out the plants from this month through May. Remember, even unthirsty or drought-tolerant perennials and shrubs need extra water during their first summer.

Use these richly hued beauties to brighten your garden's bare spots. And consider this: If you find space for just some of the plants listed here, you'll enjoy the most colorful summer ever.

PACIFIC NORTHWEST HORTICULTURAL PANELISTS

- Tina Dixon, garden designer, Plants à la Cart, Bothell, Washington
- Alice Doyle, grower, Log House Plants, Cottage Grove, Oregon
- Paul Sansone, grower, Here & Now Garden, Gales Creek, Oregon
- Karen Steeb, landscape designer, Woodinville, Washington

Selections for the Pacific Northwest

22 choice plants for your most spectacular summer garden ever

BY JIM McCAUSLAND

ANNUALS AND TENDER PERENNIALS

***Cerinthe major purpurascens* 'Kiwi Blue'.** Tender perennial. Covered

with succulent leaves, this Mediterranean native bears bell-shaped purple flowers with soft blue to violet bracts spring through fall. Easily grown from seed, plants reach 1½ feet tall in poor soil, 2½ feet in rich soil. Sun. Moderate water.

Creeping zinnia (*Sanvitalia procumbens*). Annual. Button-size yellow daisies with large dark centers adorn this creeper. Tina Dixon lets it cascade over the rims of big pots. "You can just ignore it, and it flowers all summer long," she says. Full sun. Little water.

ABOVE LEFT: The Bartels Stek series of summer phlox has fluffy, 4-inch-wide flower clusters. LEFT: *Gaillardia grandiflora* 'Goblin' has 3- to 4-inch blooms.

NORMAN A. PLATE (3)

BIG AND SMALL
black-eyed
Susans:
Rudbeckia hirta
'Indian Summer'
(above) has 6-
to 9-inch-wide
flowers;
R. fulgida
'Goldsturm'
(below) has
3-inch blooms.

Lady Washington pelargonium
(*P. domesticum*). Tender perennial. Often called Martha Washington geranium or regal geranium, it puts on a nonstop spring and summer show of 2-inch blooms in shades of purple, lavender, red, pink, or white. Plants usually stay under 2 feet tall in containers (miniature Japanese varieties stay under a foot). Full sun or partial shade. Regular water.

Mealy-cup sage (*Salvia farinacea*). Tender perennial. A prolific producer of intense blue flowers that keep coming all summer. "This is the best of all the salvias," says Karen Steeb. 'Victoria' grows 18 inches tall, perfect for containers. Full sun. Light water.

Nasturtium (*Tropaeolum majus*). Tender perennial. 'Hermine Grasshof' (orange-red) and 'Margaret Long' (pale apricot) bear frilly double flowers all summer long. The plants ramble about 2 feet in a growing season. Give them well-drained soil. If black aphids attack, spray with insecticidal soap. Sun or light shade. Regular water.

Twinspur (*Diascia barberae*). Annual. Small, delicate spurs of rosy pink flowers come all summer long on foot-tall plants; they look great under roses or in mixed container plantings. Sow plants in pots or directly in the ground. Full sun on the coast; partial shade in hot-summer areas. Light water.

PERENNIALS

Bishop's weed (*Aegopodium podagraria* 'Variegatum'). Green-and-white variegated leaves light up shady spots from spring to frost. It grows densely enough to outcompete most weeds but can be invasive if you don't cut it back or hem in the roots with plastic barriers.

Goes deciduous in winter. Deep or partial shade. Moderate water.

Black-eyed Susan (*Rudbeckia* species). These bulletproof perennials produce abundant daisies with dark centers over a long season. Among the best is *R. fulgida* 'Goldsturm', which bears 3-inch flowers from June through November on plants up to 3 feet tall. *R. hirta* 'Indian Summer' (6- to 9-inch flowers) goes from seed to bloom its first summer. Full sun. Moderate water.

Blanket flower (*Gaillardia grandiflora*). The offspring of two American natives, this thigh-high plant is a prolific producer of flowers in blends of maroon, red, orange, and yellow. 'Goblin' grows into a 1-foot mound of red flowers with yellow rims. Full sun. Light water.

Hardy geraniums. These true geraniums are near-perfect plants for woodland gardens. Their delicate, five-petaled flowers are borne over divided leaves. 'Claridge Druce' bears pink flowers over a 1- to 2-foot mound of evergreen leaves. 'Johnson's Blue' carries violet-blue blooms over a 1-foot mound. Partial shade. Ample water.

Joe Pye weed (*Eupatorium maculatum* 'Atropurpureum'). Topping out at 6 to 8 feet, its towering presence makes a great back-of-the-border plant. Huge domes of purple flowers over striped, burgundy-green foliage bloom from late July through September. Full sun or partial shade. Ample water.

Jupiter's beard (*Centranthus ruber*). For showy bloom in areas with poor soil or dry shade, this unthirsty plant is hard to beat. It bears clusters of red, pink, or white ('Albus') flowers from early spring to midsummer. The plant perennializes only in *Sunset* climate zone 7 (Oregon's Rogue River Valley); grow it as an annual elsewhere. Sun or shade. Little water.

***Ligularia stenocephala* 'The Rocket'.** Stand back and watch the blastoff: 5- to 6-foot-tall spikes of yellow flowers keep coming for three or four weeks in midsummer. Partial shade. Ample water.

Penstemon hybrids. They produce 2- to 4-foot spikes of tubular flowers in

PURPLE CONEFLOWER carries 3- to 4-inch-wide flowers with drooping purple rays on tall stems.

MICHAEL S. THOMPSON

LEFT: *Ligularia stenocephala* 'The Rocket' has tiny flowers that burst from 5-foot spires. RIGHT: *Clematis jackmanii* can cover a fence with 4- to 5-inch-wide blossoms.

marked and blotched shades of pink, red, burgundy, and violet from June through October. The new Kissed series bred by Oregon's Joy Creek Nursery (503/543-7474) includes 'Cerise Kissed', 'Violet Kissed', and 'Wine Kissed'. Give them well-drained soil. Full sun. Light to moderate water.

Purple coneflower (*Echinacea purpurea*). Long-lasting, 3- to 4-inch purple blooms come in midsummer. There are also pink and white varieties, all with puffed-up purple centers. Full sun. Regular water.

Sedum telephium **'Autumn Joy'.** Dome-shaped clusters of flowers start out as chartreuse buds in summer and open to coppery rose blooms in late summer or fall. Succulent leaves cover the lower stalks of this 2½-foot-tall plant. Full sun or partial shade. Average water.

Summer phlox (*P. paniculata*). It bears fluffy clusters of flowers in shades of lavender, red, rose, pink, or white on 3- to 5-foot stems. The Bartels Stek series resists mildew, the bane of other summer phlox. "Cut it back after the first round of bloom and it'll bloom again in October," advises Paul Sansone. Full sun. Moderate water.

Windflower (*Anemone sylvestris*). For about six weeks in May and June, it bears 1- to 3-inch white flowers. Native to northern Europe, this woodland plant grows to 18 inches tall. Light shade. Ample water.

SHRUBS

Roses. *Rosa rugosa* varieties are tough and trouble-free, beautiful and fragrant. Flowers come in red, pink, purple, yellow, or white, followed by attractive orange hips. Among the best are 'Blanc Double de Coubert' (white double blossoms), 'Frau Dagmar Hartopp' (pink single), and 'Hansa' (purple-red double with a clove scent).

Among shrub roses, 'Champlain' is a recurrent bloomer, bearing clusters of deep red, 2-inch double blossoms from spring to fall. One of the Canadian Explorer series, this 3- to 4-foot plant is not only extremely cold-hardy but also resistant to diseases and most insects (even aphids). Full sun. Regular water.

VINES

Clematis jackmanii. A 10-foot vine that bears deep purple, 4- to 5-inch flowers during July and August. An improved form called *C.j.* 'Superba' has bigger flowers with a bit more red along the midribs. Keep the roots shaded, let the top grow in the sun. Regular water.

Clematis montana **'Rubens'.** A 15- to 25-foot vine, it cloaks itself with masses of rose pink, 2-inch flowers with a delicious vanilla scent in late spring and early summer. Same needs as *C. jackmanii* (see above).

Sweet autumn clematis (*C. dioscoreifolia;* also sold as *C. maximowiczina, C. paniculata,* or *C. terniflora*). Covered with glossy leaves, this 20-foot vine produces a cascade of fragrant white 1-inch flowers in late summer and fall. In mild-winter areas, where the vine may stay evergreen, give it a warm, sunny spot. Same needs as *C. jackmanii* (see above).

Bidens bipinnata 'Goldie' wears a mass of ½-inch blooms.

NORTHERN CALIFORNIA HORTICULTURAL PANELISTS

- **Kathy Crane,** California native-plant specialist, Yerba Buena Nursery, Woodside
- **Don Ellis,** horticultural director, Elizabeth F. Gamble Garden Center, Palo Alto
- **Rick LaFrentz,** head gardener, *Sunset,* Menlo Park
- **Jeff Rosendale,** owner, Sierra Azul Nursery & Gardens, Watsonville
- **Renee Shepherd,** owner, Renee's Garden Seeds, Felton
- **Lance Walheim,** horticulturist, Exeter
- **Deborah Whigham,** owner, Digging Dog Nursery, Albion
- **Tom Wilhite,** landscape designer, San Francisco

SOUTHERN CALIFORNIA HORTICULTURAL PANELISTS

- **Ken Andersen,** owner, Walter Andersen's Nursery, Poway
- **Matt Hamilton,** nursery manager, Roger's Gardens, Corona del Mar
- **Wade Roberts,** garden director, Sherman Library and Gardens, Corona del Mar
- **Scott Spencer,** garden designer, Fallbrook
- **Judy Wigand,** owner, Judy's Perennials, San Marcos
- **Chris Wotruba,** owner, Perennial Adventure, La Mesa

Selections for California

29 choice plants for your most spectacular summer garden ever

BY DAMON HEDGEPETH

ANNUALS AND PERENNIALS

Aster frikartii. Perennial. Daisylike flowers 2 to 3 inches across with lavender-blue petals and yellow centers bloom nonstop from summer to fall. 'Mönch' is one of the most widely sold varieties. This 2- to 3-foot-tall plant adds sparkle to the middle or back of a border, but needs staking to look its best. Full sun. Regular water.

Bidens bipinnata 'Goldie'. Perennial. "One of the longest-blooming small perennials," says Jeff Rosendale. It's aglow with small gold flowers resembling single marigolds from May through October. Compact (10 inches high, 2 feet across) and relatively pest-free, 'Goldie' combines well in a low border or hanging basket. Full sun. Moderate water.

Catmint (*Nepeta faassenii*). Perennial. Its low, billowy mounds of aromatic gray-green foliage look soft and cool all season at the edge of a border. Lavender-blue flower spikes erupt in spring and early summer; shear off spent ones to bring on repeat bloom. Full sun. Little to moderate water.

Cosmos bipinnatus. Annual. "One of the best annuals for California, it makes a big color statement," says Renee Shepherd. Flowers in shades of lavender, crimson, pink, or white appear from early summer to late fall. Ranging in height from 3 to 8 feet tall, cosmos blend well in mixed beds. Or use them as backdrops at the rear of a border. Full sun. Little water.

■ **Daylily** (*Hemerocallis* hybrids). Perennial. Rusty red, orange, yellow, buff, and bicolor flowers are borne over sword-shaped leaves. Each blossom lasts only a day, but they come in quick succession. Two of the best long-bloom-

LEFT: 'Pink Joey' kangaroo paw has fuzzy ½- to 1-inch-long flowers.
RIGHT: *Lantana montevidensis* 'Radiation' has flower clusters 1 to 1½ inches across.

■ Selected for Northern California only   ■ Selected for Southern California only

Rosa chinensis 'Mutabilis' has silky blossoms that open yellow, then fade to pink and crimson.

BELOW: *Aster frikartii* forms a lavender cloud of 2½-inch-wide flowers.

LEFT: *Lavatera thuringiaca* has 3-inch-wide flowers resembling hollyhocks.
RIGHT: Matilija poppy blossoms reach 6 to 9 inches across.

ing varieties are 'Bitsy' (yellow) and 'Black Eyed Stella' (yellow with reddish eye). Full sun (light shade in hottest areas). Light water during bloom.

■ **Ivy geranium** (*Pelargonium peltatum*). Perennial. Clusters of single or double flowers, in shades of lavender, magenta, red, pink, or white, appear most of the year along with glossy ivy-like leaves. Balcon is a choice series. Use this trailing plant (2 to 3 feet or longer) as a ground cover or border edging. Full sun on coast; light shade inland. Regular water.

■ *Erysimum* **'Bowles Mauve'.** Perennial. It's no wonder this plant remains so popular: its clusters of distinctive mauve flowers bloom almost continuously year-round, and its attractive gray-green foliage looks good in mixed perennial beds or cottage gardens. The mannerly plants grow 3 feet tall and spread to 6 feet. Sun or light shade. Little to moderate water.

Jupiter's beard (*Centranthus ruber*). Perennial. For showy bloom in areas with poor soil or dry shade, this unthirsty plant is hard to beat. It bears clusters of red, pink, or white ('Albus') flowers from early spring to midsummer. But watch out: it spreads easily and may pop up where you don't want it. Sun or shade. Little water.

■ **Kangaroo paw** (*Anigozanthos flavidus*). Perennial. Native to western Australia, this clumping plant bears striking tubular flowers that, with their curved tips, resemble kangaroo paws. Named varieties include 'Big Red', 'Pink Joey', and 'Harmony' (yellow). The hairy flowers are borne on 5-foot spikes from spring through fall (cut spent flower spikes to the ground to keep blooms coming). Full sun. Regular water during bloom.

■ **Matilija poppy** (*Romneya coulteri*). Perennial. This California native bears spectacular 6- to 9-inch flowers with white crepe-papery petals and fuzzy golden stamens from May to July. Reaching 8 feet or taller, "Matilija poppy has a stateliness all its own, and a big stand in bloom is an incredible sight," says Kathy Crane. It can be invasive if given too much summer water. Full sun. Little water.

Mexican bush sage (*Salvia leucantha*). Perennial. Long, arching velvety purple spikes studded with tiny white flowers bloom in cycles from spring to fall. A bushy plant with gray-green foliage, it grows 3 to 4 feet tall. Cut old stems to the ground. Sun or light shade. Little water.

Penstemon hybrids. Perennial. Hummingbirds love its tubular flowers, which dangle on 2- to 4-foot spikes. It blooms heavily in spring, intermittently in summer, with another flush in fall (remove faded flower spikes after each cycle). Named varieties come in shades of purple, lavender, red, pink, or white; 'Apple Blossom' (pink), 'Firebird' (red), and 'Royal Beauty' (deep burgundy) are

particularly long-blooming ones. Give them well-drained soil. Sun or partial shade. Little water.

■ **Russian sage** (*Perovskia* 'Blue Spire'). Perennial. Spikes of rich violet-blue flowers are borne over lacy, gray-green leaves. A plant in full bloom is a 3-foot-tall haze of color. Combines well with unthirsty Mediterranean and native plants. Full sun. Little water.

■ **Pincushion flower** (*Scabiosa columbaria*). Perennial. Our panelists praised the variety 'Butterfly Blue', which bears lavender-blue, 2-inch flowers that resemble pincushions from June to frost. Its cousins 'Butterfly Pink' and 'Pink Mist' are nearly as good. Full sun. Moderate water.

■ *Rehmannia elata* (sometimes sold as Chinese foxglove). Perennial. Tubular flowers resembling foxgloves are borne on 2- to 3-foot-tall stalks from spring through fall. The common form has rose-purple flowers with yellow, red-dotted throats; the form with white-and-cream blooms is harder to find. Partial or light shade. Moderate to regular water.

Santa Barbara daisy (*Erigeron karvinskianus*). Perennial. In the mildest areas, this compact mounding plant is almost always in bloom from spring to frost. Masses of dainty 3/4-inch daisies in white to pink cover plants that spread 3 feet or more. It can be invasive unless cut back periodically. Full sun or light shade. Moderate water.

Mexican bush sage carries velvety flower spikes on 3- to 4-foot stems.

SANTA BARBARA DAISY bears ¾-inch flowers in white and pink on the same plant.

■ **Star clusters** (*Pentas lanceolata*). Perennial. Star-shaped flowers in lavender, red, pink, or white open in 4-inch clusters over a long season—April through October is typical. "The red form seems especially hearty and long-blooming," says Wade Roberts. Plants reach 2 to 3 feet tall with a 2-foot spread. Full sun. Regular water.

■ *Verbena bonariensis.* Perennial. All summer, spikes of lilac purple flowers appear on airy branching stems 3 to 6 feet tall. The blooms are a magnet for bees and butterflies. "In the border, *Verbena bonariensis* gives height but not mass, and its flowers go well with every other color," says Tom Wilhite. Full sun. Little water.

ORNAMENTAL GRASSES

■ **Eulalia grass** (*Miscanthus sinensis*). Perennial. One of the tall grasses (5 to 6 feet), it forms clumps of slender, weeping leaves topped by feathery silver to beige flower clusters in summer and fall. The variety 'Yaku Jima' grows to 3 to 4 feet. Sun or shade. Ample water.

Purple fountain grass (*Pennisetum setaceum* 'Rubrum'). Perennial. From summer through fall, this clumping grass (to 4 feet) sends up arching, purplish pink flower plumes that fade to pale brown seed heads. Tolerant of any soil, it works well in beds, borders, and containers. The noninvasive form 'Rubrum' (also sold as 'Cupreum') does not set seed. Full sun. Little water.

SHRUBS AND VINES

Bougainvillea. Shrubby vine. Flower-like bracts in vibrant shades of purple, magenta, red, pink, orange, or white open all summer. The thorny vines range in size from low shrubby types suitable for containers to monsters that can reach 40 feet. Full sun (light shade in hottest areas). Little water.

Butterfly bush (*Buddleia davidii*). Shrubby perennial. "One of the showiest big perennials there is," says Rosendale. It delivers bloom from May through midsummer, sometimes on into fall. Fluffy clusters of fragrant flowers, in shades of purple, blue, lilac, pink, yellow, or white, attract butterflies and hummingbirds. Plants typically reach 10 to 12 feet tall. Full sun or light shade. Water enough to maintain growth.

■ **Giant Burmese honeysuckle** (*Lonicera hildebrandiana*). Evergreen vine. "A really tough but spectacular vine," says Andersen. In cycles from fall to spring, this big twiner (to 40 feet) bears fragrant, 6- to 7-inch-long tubular flowers that open white and fade to yellow and gold. Large, shiny emerald green leaves look good all year long. Sun; light shade inland. Moderate summer water.

'Iceberg' rose. Creamy white clusters of semidouble flowers bloom in flushes from spring to fall. "One of the best roses I know," says Don Ellis. "It easily gives six or seven months of bloom, and the contrast between the white flowers and shiny leaves is cool and elegant." A floribunda, this rose is sold as a bush (to 4 feet) or climber ('Cl. Iceberg'; to 10 feet). Pest-resistant. Full sun. Regular water.

■ *Lantana montevidensis* (*L. sellowiana*). Evergreen shrub or ground cover. Clusters of flowers in shades from rosy lilac to golden yellow appear almost year-round on trailing branches clad with leathery dark green leaves. (This vigorous plant is invasive in parts of Hawaii.) Varieties such as 'Confetti' (yellow, pink, and purple flowers) and 'Radiation' (orange-red) range from 2 to 5 feet tall and from 3 to 8 feet wide. Shear to shape plants and encourage new flowers. Full sun. Infrequent, deep water.

Lavandula intermedia '**Provence**'. Evergreen shrub. Prized in French perfumery, this lavender produces dense spikes of intensely fragrant violet flowers in late spring and early summer; its gray-green foliage is aromatic, too. "It has a long-season bloom and stays more orderly looking than many other lavenders," says Ellis. The plant typically reaches 1½ feet tall with an equal spread. Shear off the flower spikes for harvest and to stimulate repeat bloom. Sun or light shade. Little water.

■ *Lavatera thuringiaca.* Evergreen shrub. Almost everblooming, it sports maplelike leaves and 3-inch flowers resembling single hollyhocks. The variety 'Barnsley' has light pink flowers that pale to white centers; 'Rosea' has pink flowers. The plant grows quickly to 6 to 8 feet tall; cut it back to keep it compact. Full sun. Little to regular water.

Oleander (*Nerium oleander*). Shrub or small tree. Ubiquitous along freeways, oleander is unsurpassed for providing color in tough conditions, including drought and poor soil. In bloom from May through October, single or double flowers come in shades of red, pink, or white; some are fragrant. Out of bloom, oleander resembles an olive tree. Reaching 8 to 12 feet tall, it can be grown as a multitrunked shrub or can be trained into a single-trunk tree. Smaller varieties (3 to 4 feet) are also available. Full sun. Little or no water.

Rosa chinensis '**Mutabilis**'. Old China rose. "The whole plant is a color show," says Wilhite. Flowers resembling silky butterflies pass through three color phases, opening yellow, turning pink, then crimson; even the handsome leaves fade to orange or gold as they age. Arching to 12 feet, the plant is an "all-around garden warhorse—tough, drought-tolerant, and pest-resistant," adds Wilhite. Full sun. Moderate water. ◆

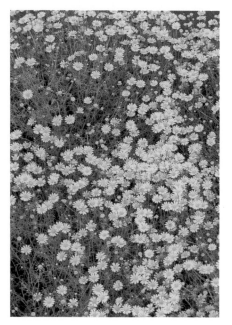

Selections for the mountain West

22 choice plants for your most
spectacular summer garden ever

BY JIM McCAUSLAND

**MOUNTAIN WEST
HORTICULTURAL PANELISTS**

- Kelly Grummons, part-owner,
  Timberline Gardens, Arvada, Colorado
- Dick Hildreth, horticulturist, Red Butte
  Garden & Arboretum, Salt Lake City
- Panayoti Kelaidis, plant evaluation coordi-
  nator, Denver Botanic Gardens, Denver
- James Klett, professor of ornamental
  horticulture, Colorado State University,
  Fort Collins
- Lauren Springer, garden designer and
  writer, Masonville, Colorado

ANNUALS AND TENDER PERENNIALS

California poppy (*Eschscholzia cali-fornica*). Tender perennial. Scatter its seed in a sunny area and this unthirsty native of California will give you a great show of 2-inch blooms on foot-tall plants in late spring and early summer. Orange is the classic color, but red, yellow, pastel, and bicolor varieties are now available. Plants often self-sow. Full

sun. Summer water extends bloom.

Dahlberg daisy (*Dyssodia tenui-loba*). Tender perennial. This Southwest native is covered with golden daisies for most of summer. A compact plant (3 to 6 inches tall, 6 to 12 inches wide), "it can fit as easily into a formal design as a naturalistic one," says Panayoti Kelaidis. Full sun. Little water.

Dwarf cup flower (*Nierembergia hippomanica violacea*). Tender perennial. Bell-like floral cups 1 to 1½ inches across cover this mounding 6- to 12-inch-tall plant throughout summer. The species bears blue to violet flowers; the best variety, 'Mont Blanc', has white blossoms. Full sun. Regular water.

ABOVE LEFT:
Dahlberg daisy
forms a carpet of
golden flowers.
LEFT: *Phlox nana*
has 1-inch-wide
blooms.

Common trumpet creeper bears
3-inch-long tubular
flowers on vigorous vines.

BELOW: Ice plant *Delosperma
floribundum* blankets the ground
with 1½-inch-wide flowers and
succulent leaves.

SCAEVOLA 'Purple Fanfare' has fan-shaped flower clusters 1½ inches across. Try this tender perennial in hanging baskets or other containers.

Jupiter's beard (*Centranthus ruber*). Tender perennial. For showy bloom in areas with poor soil or dry shade, this unthirsty plant is hard to beat. It bears clusters of red, pink, or white ('Albus') flowers from early spring to midsummer. Sun or shade. Little water.

Scaevola. Tender perennial. This Australian native is a champ in Salt Lake City, where it is grown as an annual. Blue or purple flowers form in fan-shaped clusters through most of summer. The varieties 'Blue Wonder' and 'Purple Fanfare' do well in containers; 'Mauve Clusters' works best as a bedding plant. Full sun. Moderate water.

Verbena bonariensis. Tender perennial in coldest areas; comes back in milder mountain regions. Spikes of purple flowers—magnets for butterflies—are borne on branching 3- to 6-foot stems all summer. Full sun. Little water.

Zinnia angustifolia. Annual. Small, tough, and mildew-resistant, this zinnia can hold its own in any mixed bed or container. It bears orange flowers summer to fall. Full sun. Light to moderate water.

PERENNIALS AND BIENNIALS

Black-eyed Susan (*Rudbeckia* species). Abundant daisies with dark centers bloom over a long season. Among the best is *R. fulgida* 'Goldsturm', which bears 3-inch flowers from June to frost on 2-foot plants. *R. hirta* 'Indian Summer' (6- to 9-inch flowers) goes from seed to bloom its first summer. Full sun. Moderate water.

Common sneezeweed (*Helenium hoopesii*). Masses of golden yellow daisies on 3- to 4-foot plants appear for several weeks between July and September. Native to the Rockies, it does fine on hot, dry sites. Full sun. Little water.

Crocosmia 'Lucifer'. A hybrid form of montbretia, it grows from a corm and produces masses of bright red blooms that open on branched spikes for as long as a month in late summer. The plants reach 3 to 4 feet tall and have sword-shaped leaves. The corms need a heavy blanket of mulch to protect them in winter. Partial shade in hot-summer climates. Light water.

Gaura lindheimeri. Throughout the summer, this Southwest native bears dainty white or pink blossoms on wispy stems. Plants reach 2 to 4 feet. 'Siskiyou Pink' is widely available. Full sun. Little water.

Ice plant (*Delosperma cooperi*). Spring through fall, it bursts with hot rose-purple flowers. This ground cover is so hardy it can easily tolerate 0° if it's insulated by mulch or snow. Lauren Springer favors *D. floribundum*, a newly introduced species. Both need good drainage. Full sun. Little water.

Penstemons. There are many species and varieties, all with tubular flowers that appear throughout summer. Springer grows the dainty *P. pinifolius* 'Mersea Yellow'; it forms a low mat of heatherlike leaves and large, daffodil-yellow flowers. Kelly Grummons prefers 'Prairie Jewel' hybrids, which come in shades of blue, lavender, burgundy, plum, wine, pink, or white; they make quite a show on 3- to 4-foot plants. James Klett suggests 'Mexicali' hybrids

GAURA bears 1-inch-long flowers resembling shooting stars.

(many colors) for gardens with alkaline soils. Give them all well-drained soil. Sun or partial shade. Little water.

Phlox nana (also sold as Santa Fe phlox). A Southwest native, it produces hot pink, 1-inch flowers from May through frost. The plant grows 8 inches tall and 12 inches wide. "The greatest phlox ever," as Springer calls it, is quite hard to find. One mail-order source is Plants of the Southwest (800/788-7333; catalog $3.50). Full sun. No extra water once established.

Pincushion flower (*Scabiosa*). One of the best perennial forms is 'Butterfly Blue', which bears pale blue, 2-inch flowers resembling pincushions from June to frost. Its cousins 'Butterfly Pink' and 'Pink Mist' are nearly as good. Full sun. Moderate water.

Scarlet hedge nettle (*Stachys coccinea*). This is a big hit with humming-

RIGHT: Apache plume has 1½-inch white flowers followed by feathery fruits that cloak the plant in a pinkish haze.

BELOW: Pincushion flower bears 2-inch-wide blooms on foot-tall stems. Here, it grows over ageratum (bottom left) and sweet William.

CHARLES MANN

birds, who draw nectar from the tubular flowers that open on 2-foot spikes over a long season. But don't put this plant in the hottest spot in your garden or its red flowers will fade to light pink, warns Grummons. Although not hardy in the coldest areas (Denver may be its limit), it's easily grown from seed and blooms its first year. Full sun. Light water.

Silver sage (*Salvia argentea*). This biennial has first-year rosettes of white leaves that are as big and bold as rabbit ears. The second year, a 4-foot candelabra of white-hooded flowers rises up for a grand finale. Grow it in a dry spot. Sun. Little water.

Sunset hyssop (*Agastache rupestris*). A Southwestern member of the mint family, it sends up spikes of fragrant, orange-and-lavender flowers over 2-foot plants. Hummingbirds are drawn to the nectar-filled blooms that start in late July and continue through summer's end. Full sun to partial shade. Regular water.

SHRUB

Apache plume (*Fallugia paradoxa*). It is "absolutely lovely in flower and fruit," says Dick Hildreth. The flowers, resembling single white roses, come in spring, followed by feathery fruits that cloak the plant with a soft pink haze in summer. It grows to 3 to 8 feet tall. Give it well-drained soil. Full sun. No water once established.

VINES

Common trumpet creeper (*Campsis radicans*). Lush, tubular orange-and-scarlet flowers pop from a vine that can grow to 40 feet. Springer prefers the species, which blooms heavily in late July, then sporadically until frost. It's hardy in most places; even when it freezes to the ground, it usually bounces back. Full sun or partial shade. Moderate water.

Sweet autumn clematis (*C. dioscoreifolia*; sold as *C. paniculata*, *C. maximowiczina*, or *C. terniflora*). In late summer and fall, it produces a cascade of fragrant white flowers on a 20-foot vine covered with glossy leaves. It's hardy enough for Denver and Salt Lake City but won't take it much colder. Keep the roots shaded; let the top grow in sun. Regular water.

Trumpet honeysuckle (*Lonicera sempervirens*). Scarlet, trumpet-shaped flowers bloom all summer long on a vine that can reach 12 feet. It's semi-evergreen in cold-winter climates and needs protection to survive in the coldest areas. Full sun or light shade. Moderate summer water. ◆

Selections for the Southwest

22 choice plants for your most spectacular summer garden ever

BY DAMON HEDGEPETH

SOUTHWEST HORTICULTURAL PANELISTS

- Tom Brodt, nurseryman, Baker's Nursery, Phoenix
- Chris Broughton, plant specialist, Mesquite Valley Growers, Tucson
- Judy Mielke, landscape designer, Scottsdale, Arizona
- Carrie Nimmer, landscape designer, Phoenix
- Kenny Ostrand, nurseryman, Desert Tree Nursery, Phoenix
- Judith Phillips, landscape designer, Albuquerque

PERENNIALS

Catmint (*Nepeta faassenii*). Its low, billowy mounds of aromatic gray-green foliage look soft and cool all season at the edge of a border. Lavender-blue flower spikes erupt in spring and early summer; shear off spent ones to bring on repeat bloom. Full sun. Little to moderate water.

Daylily (*Hemerocallis* hybrids). Rusty red, orange, yellow, buff, and bicolor flowers are borne on long stems over sword-shaped leaves. Each blossom lasts only a day, but they come in quick succession. Choose repeat-blooming types or plant early, midseason, and late varieties for color from spring to fall. Full sun (light shade in hottest desert areas). Light water during bloom.

Firecracker penstemon (*P. eatonii*). Its shiny gray-green foliage is handsome, but the tubular scarlet flowers are absolutely stunning when they appear from late spring to early sum-

ABOVE: Trumpet honeysuckle bears 1½- to 2-inch blooms on twining vines. RIGHT: Russian sage forms a 3-foot mound of cool color.

CHARLES MANN (2)

YELLOW BELLS forms clusters of 2-inch-wide flowers. It thrives on heat and little water.

HESPERALOE PARVIFLORA shows off its flowers on airy spikes that can reach 8 to 9 feet tall on mature plants.

foliage. It thrives in heavy clay soil and midsummer heat. Full sun. Little water.

Pincushion flower (*Scabiosa columbaria*). 'Butterfly Blue' bears lavender-blue, 2-inch flowers resembling pincushions from June to frost. Cousins 'Butterfly Pink' and 'Pink Mist' are nearly as good. Full sun. Moderate water.

Russian sage (*Perovskia* 'Blue Spire'). Spikes of rich violet-blue flowers are borne over lacy, gray-green leaves. A plant in full bloom is a 3-foot-tall haze of color. Combines well with unthirsty Mediterranean and native plants. Full sun. Little water.

Verbena rigida. Small clusters of lilac to purple flowers open steadily from summer to fall on stiff 10- to 20-inch stems. A spreading plant, it works well alone as a ground cover but is somewhat invasive in mixed beds. Full sun. Little water.

SHRUBS AND VINES

Bougainvillea. Shrubby vine. Flowerlike bracts in vibrant shades of purple, magenta, red, pink, orange, or white open all summer. The thorny vines range in size from low shrubby types suitable for containers to monsters that can reach 40 feet. Full sun (light shade in hottest desert areas). Widely grown outdoors in *Sunset* climate zones 12–13. Little water.

Butterfly bush (*Buddleia davidii*). Shrubby perennial. Fluffy clusters of fragrant flowers, in shades of purple, blue, lilac, pink, yellow, or white, attract butterflies and hummingbirds. It delivers bloom from May through midsummer, sometimes into fall. Plants typically reach 10 to 12 feet tall. Full sun or light shade. Water enough to maintain growth.

Cape plumbago (*P. auriculata*). Shrub or vine. Phloxlike clusters of blue to white flowers appear from March through December in the low desert. "The variety 'Royal Cape' has the deepest blue flowers and looks great under Arizona skies," says Carrie Nimmer. Grown as a shrub, it reaches 6 feet high by 8 to 10 feet across. Given support, it can also be grown as a billowy vine to

mer. It reaches 1½ to 3 feet tall. Give it perfect drainage. Full sun. Little water.

Gaura lindheimeri. Spring and summer, this Southwest native bears dainty white or pink blossoms on wispy stems that wave in the slightest breeze. Plants reach 2 to 4 feet. 'Siskiyou Pink' is widely available. Full sun. Little water.

Hesperaloe parviflora. Clusters of pink to rose red nodding flowers open on tall, slim stems in spring and early summer, with repeat bloom in mild desert areas. Native to Mexico and Texas, this succulent forms yuccalike clumps of 3- to 4-foot rapier-shaped leaves. Its bold form combines well with other sculptural desert plants. Full sun. No dry-season water.

Jupiter's beard (*Centranthus ruber*). For showy bloom in areas with poor soil or dry shade, this unthirsty plant is hard to beat. It bears clusters of red, pink, or white ('Albus') flowers in late spring and early summer. But watch out: it spreads easily and may pop up where you don't want it. Sun or shade. Little water.

Madagascar periwinkle (*Catharan-*

thus roseus). One of the showiest flowers for hot-summer climates, it's in bloom from May to November. Phlox-like flowers come in shades from hot pink to pure white with a rosy eye. Clad with glossy leaves, the bushy plant reaches 2 feet tall (compact and creeping strains are shorter). This tender perennial overwinters in the low and intermediate deserts. Full sun or light shade. Light to moderate water.

Mexican evening primrose (*Oenothera berlandieri;* also sold as *O. speciosa childsii*). Neither poor soil, baking heat, nor drought can keep this daytime bloomer from putting out carpets of pink flowers 1½ inches across from spring to fall. 'Rosea' is nearly everblooming; 'Siskiyou' has light pink blooms. Be forewarned: It spreads rapidly and can be invasive. Plant it where pavement will hem in the roots. Full sun. Little water.

Orange globe mallow (*Sphaeralcea incana*). Native to northern New Mexico, it bears orange flowers resembling tiny hollyhocks all summer. The blooms appear on 3- to 5-foot stems over rich green

LEFT: *Lantana montevidensis* 'Radiation' bears flower clusters 1 to 1½ inches across.
RIGHT: *Caesalpinia pulcherrima* 'Phoenix Bird' (front) is a new yellow-flowered poinciana; standard red bird of paradise (rear) has red or orange blooms.

12 feet. Hardy only in zones 12–13. Full sun. Little water.

'Iceberg' rose. Creamy white clusters of semidouble flowers come in flushes from spring to fall. The shiny leaves look cool and elegant. A floribunda rose, it's sold as a bush (to 4 feet) or climber ('Cl. Iceberg'; to 10 feet). Pest-resistant. Sun to partial shade. Moderate to regular water.

Lantana montevidensis (*L. sellowiana*). Shrub or ground cover. Clusters of flowers in shades from rosy lilac to golden yellow appear almost year-round on trailing branches clad with leathery dark green leaves. Varieties such as 'Confetti' (yellow, pink, and purple flowers), 'Irene' (magenta and lemon yellow), and 'Radiation' (orange-red) range from 2 to 5 feet tall and from 3 to 8 feet wide. Full sun. Infrequent, deep water.

***Lavandula intermedia* 'Provence'.** Evergreen shrub. Prized in French perfumery, this lavender produces dense spikes of intensely fragrant violet flowers in spring and summer (longer in zones 12–13). Its gray-green foliage is aromatic, too. The plant typically reaches 1½ feet tall with an equal spread. Shear off flower spikes for harvest and to stimulate repeat bloom. Sun or light shade. Little water.

Oleander (*Nerium oleander*). Shrub or small tree. Oleander is unsurpassed for providing showy color in tough conditions, including drought and poor soil. In bloom from early May through October, single or double flowers come in shades of red, pink, or white; some are fragrant. Most varieties reach 8 to 12 feet tall. Full sun. Little or no water.

Poinciana (*Caesalpinia pulcherrima*). Shrub. Airy clusters of red, orange, or yellow flowers bloom throughout warm weather. The flowers stand out against lacy, fernlike foliage. "'Phoenix Bird' is the most spectacular variety. It has clear lemon yellow flowers and easily outperforms the other poincianas," says Tom Brodt. A fast-growing shrub (to 10 feet by 10 feet), it quickly makes a colorful screen. Hardy only in zones 12–13. Full sun. Infrequent, deep water.

Trumpet honeysuckle (*Lonicera sempervirens*). Vine. Showy orange-yellow to scarlet, trumpet-shaped flowers bloom all summer on this twining vine that reaches 12 feet. Semi-evergreen in cold-winter climates, it needs protection to survive in the coldest areas. Full sun or light shade. Moderate summer water.

Yellow bells (*Tecoma stans*). Shrub or small tree. Large clusters of clear yellow bells bloom summer through fall, and into winter. Even when the plant is out of bloom, its toothed, dark green leaves look handsome. Reaching 12 feet, "it is tall enough to make a good stand-alone shrub or a hedge," says Kenny Ostrand. Full sun. Little water. ◆

Callas in fresh new colors

BY JIM McCAUSLAND

Elegant as they are, the white flowers of the common calla pale in comparison with the new breeds making their way into Western nurseries. Now callas come in a range of soft pastel hues as well as hotter shades that glow like candle flames. Resembling fluted cups, the colored flowers are 3 to 5 inches long—about half to two-thirds the size of the common calla (*Zantedeschia aethiopica*). These beauties grow from rhizomes you plant now for bloom in spring and lush, lance-shaped leaves that last into fall. They thrive in well-drained garden soil and containers.

CALLA COLOR SPECTRUM

The plants described here range in height from 1 to 2 feet.

Giant yellow calla (*Zantedeschia pentlandii*) has golden yellow flowers and unspotted leaves.

Golden calla (*Z. elliottiana*) has golden yellow flowers and white-spotted leaves.

Pink callas with unspotted leaves are mostly descended from *Z. rehman-*

PLANT rhizomes with bumpy "eyes" facing up. In containers, place rhizomes close together and cover with 2 inches of potting soil.

THE RAINBOW of calla colors includes hybrid yellow (left), 'Rubylite Rose' (front), 'Flame' (rear), and spotted calla.

nii. *Z.r.* 'Superba' has deep pink blooms; *Z.r. violaceae* has deep rose flowers.

Spotted calla (*Z. albomaculata*) has creamy yellow or white flowers with crimson to purple throats and white-spotted leaves.

The most heavily flowering colored varieties are sold as Callafornia Callas but are often renamed by retailers. They include 'Crystal Blush' (white with rose blush), 'Lavender Gem', 'Rose Gem', 'Rubylite Pink Ice', and 'Rubylite Rose'. In *Sunset's* test garden, the favorite was 'Flame', whose flowers resemble yellow-orange candle flames, then darken to red as they age.

Look for calla rhizomes or potted plants in well-stocked nurseries and garden centers. Rhizomes are sold by species, named variety, or color alone. Mail-order sources for rhizomes are Dutch Gardens (800/818-3861) and Van Bourgondien Bros. (800/622-9997).

GROWING TIPS

Plant rhizomes, rounded side down, 1 foot apart and 2 inches deep in rich, well-drained soil. Callas like full sun near the coast and partial shade in hotter inland climates. Or in wide, shallow containers (we used 16-inch-wide, 7-inch-deep pots), plant rhizomes 2 inches deep but space them more closely (1 to 6 inches apart) for a concentrated show. Plant the same colors together. Mixtures don't work as well because different-colored callas bloom at slightly different times.

Drench the rhizomes once at planting, then water sparingly until leaves emerge. After that, water regularly and feed occasionally until the leaves die down.

In mild-winter areas, calla rhizomes can overwinter in the ground if drainage is good. Mulch plants if hard frost is a possibility in your garden. In cold-winter areas where the ground freezes, dig up rhizomes in fall, dry them, place in flats covered with dry peat moss, and store in a frost-free place for the winter. ◆

A garden on wheels

Weathered wagon displays cargo of smaller containers— including a watering can and an aged bucket— all stuffed with blooming plants such as tulips, freesias, hyacinths, and daffodils. In front, a wood box comes alive with tulips, pansies, and ranunculus. Copper umbrella holder behind rear wheel is stuffed with hyacinths, freesias, and pink polka-dot plant (*Hypoestes*).

Spring bouquets…instantly

Blooming bulbs in nursery pots make gorgeous arrangements

BY KATHLEEN N. BRENZEL

On a sunny day last March, *Sunset* test garden coordinator Bud Stuckey and friends gathered at floral designer Linda Arietta's ranch in Watsonville, California, to make quick arrangements out of blooming bulbs and other spring flowers. They brought old containers— baskets, boxes, and buckets they'd gathered from their garages or from junk shops. They brought potted spring bulbs in Easter egg colors, purchased from nurseries or grocery stores. Arietta picked seasonal flowers such as sweet peas in her garden and put them in water-filled vases.

Then the fun began. Serenaded by a mockingbird that seemed as delighted by this glorious day as they were, the bouquet makers worked at patio tables pairing blooming bulbs with annuals and cut flowers in interesting containers. Then they dined on moose burritos and wine as they admired the fresh-as-spring, mostly living bouquets they could take home to their own gardens. The event was "a celebration of spring and good friends," says Stuckey. And the bouquets, "beautiful if temporary reminders of the occasion."

Whether you make arrangements like these by yourself or gather friends to help, you'll find them quick and easy to put together. Nurseries and florists are well stocked with blooming daffodils, tulips, hyacinths, and freesias in 6-inch plastic pots; pansies, violas, and other spring annuals are available at nurseries in 4-inch pots.

Choose any container that's large enough to hold several nursery pots: rustic baskets, wood wine boxes (stain them green or gray), buckets, old copper watering cans. Line the container with a plastic garbage bag, then arrange the potted plants and vases of cut flowers directly in the large container. Cover pots and vases with sphagnum moss or Spanish moss.

Use the bouquets to dress up your entry, garden steps, and deck, or to bring a bit of spring indoors. Water the nursery containers regularly.

(Continued on next page)

Jug of bulbs

Antique ash can holds hyacinths and tulips in 6-inch pots. Ivy and trailing lobelia in
4-inch pots (well hidden beneath sphagnum moss) soften the can's edges.

Easter egg pastels

White hyacinths are lacy counterpoints to yellow and purple freesias. Antique Shades pansies (in sixpacks) fill in spaces between them. Sweet pea clippings—with flowers in white and shades of pink—tumble from a water-filled vase hidden inside the basket.

A few tips

- Have a container in mind when you shop for the plants. Measure it, so you can easily figure out how many plants you need to buy.

- If some of the nursery pots don't quite fit together in a big container, remove them from the pots and slip rootballs into plastic sandwich bags.

- Once bloom is through, take apart the arrangements, allow bulbs to die back, and save all but the tulips for planting out next year. ◆

Meadow in a basket

Spring blooms and grasses give the arrangement above the look of a flower-strewn meadow. Fescue (three plants, in 4-inch pots) creates the wispy backdrop. Flowers include red ranunculus (one, in a 4-inch pot) and pansies (from sixpacks). Sprays of cut flowers—forget-me-nots and daffodils—fill a bud vase nestled in the basket's center.

ORANGE CALIFORNIA POPPIES and red Shirley poppies pepper this front yard in Phoenix, replacing a boring carpet of Bermuda grass. For details on this landscape renovation, see page 103.

April

gardenguide

SPIKY GOLD-FRINGED LEAVES of *Cordyline australis* 'Albertii' burst over a mosaic of ground covers such as *Senecio mandraliscae* (below it), purple-flowered *Origanum* 'Rosenkuppel', and purple-foliaged *Trifolium repens* 'Wheatfen'.

MARION BRENNER

Foliage for all seasons

■ The new entry garden at Strybing Arboretum & Botanical Gardens in Golden Gate Park beautifully demonstrates the power of foliage to create a landscape with year-round eye appeal. Visitors stroll along paths that meander through a living tapestry of plants chosen for their striking foliage textures and colors. The leafy planting scheme fulfills the vision of designers Roger Raiche and David McCrory of Planet Horticulture.

"The old garden was a California version of an English perennial garden," explains Raiche. "We wanted the [new] garden to be less seasonal and to feature unusual plants that grow well in San Francisco's unique microclimate." To make the entry a preview of what was to come in the arboretum, the designers repeated some of the plants that are found elsewhere (for example, *Cordyline australis* 'Albertii', shown above, is also in the New Zealand collection).

Now the small botanical garden contains nearly 500 plants set on low mounds to create variations in topography. The plants are arranged around "rock outcroppings" created from 16th-century monastery stones, bottomless urns, and industrial clay pipes. There's also a bubbling spring among the flowers and foliage. "We wanted to draw people off the main walkway and completely immerse them in a world of new plants," says Raiche. "They're irresistible." — *Lauren Bonar Swezey*

Tulip look-alike from Thailand

■ When is a tulip not a tulip? When it's a Siam tulip—a ginger (*Curcuma alistnatifolia*) introduced several years ago from Thailand. This beauty has long, narrow, stiff leaves and a flower (actually a bract) of pink, rose, or white that lasts up to four weeks on the plant or eight days as a cut flower. Each 2-foot-tall plant blooms only once, but a new plant develops and forms a new flower every 20 to 30 days. The cycle runs from June to around October.

After the soil has warmed to about 60°, plant rhizomes in full sun either in pots or in the ground. Place pointed end up and cover with an inch of soil. Water regularly; flowers will appear in 8 to 12 weeks. In mild climates (*Sunset* zones 14–24), rhizomes can be left in the ground through winter if the soil is well drained. In colder climates, dig up the rhizomes (do not damage the food-storing "milk tanks" on the end of the roots) and store them in a cool, dry place. Dust them with sulfur to prevent decay.

Rhizomes cost $5 plus shipping from Stokes Tropicals, Box 9868, New Iberia, LA 70562; (800) 624-9706 or www. stokestropicals.com. Siam tulips are most readily available in pink. — *L.B.S.*

NORMAN A. PLATE

CONNIE COLEMAN

The slam-dunk clematis

■ After budding basketball players grow up and leave home, their parents often retire the family's old backboard over the driveway. But John and Susan Ebel still had hoop dreams after their children departed, so they used the backboard to train a rising star: *Clematis montana* 'Rubens'.

A vigorous vine reaching 15 to 25 feet, *C.m.* 'Rubens' grows in all *Sunset* climate zones but does best in zones 1–6 and 15–17. The Ebels trained their plant to climb up the post and over the basket. In early spring, fragrant 2- to 2½-inch flowers cover the whole vine.

When the time comes for their visiting grandchildren to reclaim the basketball court, the Ebels plan to build a real trellis for the clematis next to the backboard, cut the plant back, and let it grow up anew. — *Steven R. Lorton*

IN THIS FORMER PLANTER, water proves more soothing than flowers once were.

Just add a little water

■ Santa Barbara landscape architect Sydney Baumgartner inherited a garden with a good design—one of the last projects of the late, well-known landscape architect Ralph Stevens. She liked the grand scale of Stevens's double staircase leading to the upper garden and left it alone. But the circular planter between the two stairs was a puzzle. "I tried annuals, I tried perennials, I tried everything," she says. "Nothing worked. It all looked silly." Finally, Baumgartner decided she liked the planter best when empty. So she turned it into a simple reflecting pool—no koi, no plants. "Negative space is just what was needed," says Baumgartner with satisfaction.

The bones of the garden may have come from Stevens, but the plants are pure Baumgartner. The 'Yankee Point' ceanothus spilling over the retaining wall was selected for its black-green foliage, and its medium blue flowers also pair beautifully with white rockrose. Clumps of tropical-looking palm grass (*Setaria palmifolia*) flank the pool. Around its edge, potted geraniums and succulents are joined by a changing cast of plants that vary with the season and Baumgartner's mood.

— *Sharon Cohoon*

FIELD OF DREAMS:
Skagit Valley Bulb
Farm opens its
"Tulip Town"
to visitors.

Tulipomania: Now blooming in the Skagit Valley

■ Gardeners looking for the perfect excuse to play hooky can find it in the Skagit Valley of northwest Washington this month as more than 1,500 acres of tulips and daffodils burst into bloom in fields near the town of Mt. Vernon. A million visitors are expected to flock here during this year's Skagit Valley Tulip Festival (for information, call 360/428-5959). If you go on a weekend,

expect roads through the fields to be clogged with traffic. But if you treat yourself to a weekday outing, you can mosey along to take in the myriad colors, pausing to snap photos and perhaps enjoy a leisurely lunch at one of the local restaurants.

Three Mt. Vernon bulb farms with superb display gardens are not to be missed: Roozengaarde (15867 Beaver

Marsh Rd., 800/732-3266); Skagit Valley Bulb Farm, "Tulip Town" (15002 Bradshaw Rd., 360/424-8152); and Lefeber Bulb Company (1335 Memorial Hwy., 360/424-6234). As you walk through their display gardens, jot down the names of the tulip varieties you like, then pick up the free catalogs so you can order bulbs for fall planting.

— S.R.L.

Petroglyph pottery

I nspired by the rock inscriptions left behind by the Anasazi, career potter Dick Masterson puts renderings of those ancient petroglyphs on the containers he makes in his studio in Santa Fe. "There are places along the Santa Fe River," Masterson says, "where petroglyphs have been accumulating for a thousand years. And to my eye, the earlier ones are better." Although he's modified the images to his own taste, the pre-pueblo influence underlies his work.

Masterson's adaptations of petroglyphs include images of birds, deer, mountain sheep, and humanoid figures like the ones on the pot shown above. All of the pieces he incises with petroglyphs are high-fired stoneware. Beyond that, every order is customized for the buyers, who choose colors, proportions, and sizes that work best with the plants they want to show off. The planters look especially good with cactus, succulents, and foliage plants. You can order containers with or without drainage holes, and with or without saucers. Sizes range from 8 to 24 inches in diameter and up to a yard tall.

Prices for planters run from $80 to $300, and the time between ordering and shipping is usually around two months. For more information, including locations where you can view his work, call Masterson at (505) 424-3718. — *Jim McCausland*

A happy balance of blue grama and buffalo grass

■ On Western prairies, blue grama grass and buffalo grass have coexisted for ages. Increasingly, these warm-season grasses are being grown together to form drought-tolerant lawns. But if you start them at the same time, the fast-germinating blue grama quickly grows over the slower-sprouting buffalo grass and shades it out.

The trick to getting these grasses to grow in harmony is to mow the blue grama to 2 inches as soon as it reaches 3 or 4 inches tall. Keep it mowed at that height for the first two summers to give the buffalo grass a chance to fill in. After that, you can continue mowing for a fine-textured lawn or let it grow into a foot-tall meadow. Both these grasses fade to brown during winter dormancy, then green up again when warm weather arrives.

As a mowed lawn, a blue grama–buffalo blend needs 3 inches of water per month and 2 pounds actual nitrogen per 1,000 square feet each year.

As an uncut meadow, this blend does fine with about 2 inches of water per month during summer. It needs only $\frac{1}{2}$ pound actual nitrogen per 1,000 square feet each year. Leave it uncut during winter to catch the snow and take advantage of the moisture it supplies. Before new growth starts in spring, mow it once at 1 to 2 inches to clear away the dead grass. — *J.M.*

Cover tomatoes to beat the blight

■ For the past two summers, late blight (*Phytophthora infestans*) has devastated tomatoes in the Pacific Northwest. This disease is worst in cool, wet summers and least troublesome in hot, dry years. When late blight strikes, the symptoms first appear on leaf veins, stems, and green fruit as water-soaked spots that quickly enlarge into dark or purplish black areas that kill the affected plant parts. On ripening fruit, cream-colored concentric areas grow and merge over the whole fruit. Late blight can affect potatoes as well; it's the same disease that caused the Irish potato famine of 1845–'46.

One way to protect tomatoes against this disease is to erect plastic-covered shelters over plants, as shown below. The shelters keep tomato leaves dry—and spores of late blight must land on wet leaves to infect the plant. However, shelters like this aren't effective in areas that get soaking fogs. Also, overhead watering defeats the shelter's purpose.

These shelters, built by Chuck and Mona Pinches on Thetis Island, British Columbia, use 2-by-2 stakes to support gables covered with 6-mil, ultraviolet-resistant plastic. The tops can be lifted off to make it easier to harvest fruit in the center of the 3- to 4-foot-wide rows. The Pincheses found that besides saving their crop from blight, the shelters also prevented cherry tomatoes from splitting after late summer rains.

—J.M.

Lessons from a "guerrilla" garden

■ The official mission of the Pitzer College Arboretum in Claremont, California, is to create "more mutually supportive relationships between humans and natural systems." The unofficial mission, admits director John Rodman, is "guerrilla gardening." Rodman's goal is "liberating" lawn and asphalt and turning it back into native-plant communities. He has already liberated a third (10 acres) of the campus by planting such natural beauties as bluebells, California poppies, and rockrose.

Spring, when the Eunice Pitzer Wildflower Garden (shown above) is at its peak, is an excellent time to visit. Pick up a map of the arboretum at the Public Information Office (Avery Hall 105). Parking for the arboretum is at Claremont Boulevard and Ninth Street in Claremont. Walk half a block north on Pitzer Service Road. — *S.C.*

Catch the show in Salt Lake City

■ One of the West's most dazzling displays of spring bulbs starts this month in Salt Lake City. In 30 acres of beds around Temple Square, headquarters of the Church of Jesus Christ of Latter-day Saints, about 5,000 crocus, 10,000 daffodils, and 15,000 tulips flower over a six-week period.

But that's only a small part of the show. Head gardener Peter Lassig mingles the bulbs among colorful drifts of cold-hardy perennials and biennials, including aubrieta, candytuft, English daisy, forget-me-not, Iceland poppy, pansy, primrose, stock, viola, and yellow wallflower.

Bloom comes in three bursts. The first flush (about April 6–12) is a beautiful blend of hyacinths, daffodils, and early tulips such as *Tulipa kaufmanniana*. The main surge (around April 20) includes cottage and Darwin tulips. The final flush (around Mother's Day) features late daffodils like 'Cheerfulness' and 'Thalia' along with parrot tulips and Darwin hybrids. You can stroll among the beds anytime on your own, or join one of the free 30- to 60-minute guided garden tours that run daily by calling Christena Gates at (801) 240-5916 for an appointment.

—*J.M.*

CHARLES MANN

Brilliant poppies replace a Phoenix lawn

■ When Bill and Barbara Loutos of Phoenix hired landscape designer Carrie Nimmer to renovate their front yard, they didn't expect instant gratification. Nimmer removed a boring carpet of Bermuda grass, added a gentle grade to the yard, laid a meandering path of flagstone, installed some privacy walls, and planted palo verde and mesquite trees, several varieties of Texas ranger, and ornamental grasses like *Muhlenbergia capillaris* 'Regal Mist'.

Yet when Nimmer had finished installing the new landscape, the yard looked pretty sparse (see photo above). One reason is that Nimmer gave each plant sufficient space to grow to its full size and show off its natural shape. She used 1-gallon plants because they are less expensive and because smaller specimens get established more easily. Plus she allowed plenty of space for wildflowers.

The Loutoses' landscaping investment and patience paid off in a big way: two springs later (photo on page 94) the yard is adrift with California and Shirley poppies. The wildflowers care for themselves, spreading seed each spring to sustain the next year's show. — *S.C.*

A honey of a bee house

■ Honeybees don't have it easy. On their pollen-collecting rounds, bees are vulnerable to chemical pesticides. Back in the hive, they're threatened by two parasitic enemies—tracheal and varroa mites. One way to give bees a boost is to create safe housing for them on your property, as Madeleine McLendon has done in her garden.

McLendon bought her bee box unassembled and unpainted from a local source, then put her own artistic stamp on it by adding a mural. The bees must like it: she harvests 45 to 50 pounds of honey from her hives up to twice a year. A three-tiered bee box like the one below costs about $90 unassembled, $125 assembled. One source is Los Angeles Honey Co. (323/264-2383) which also sells beekeeping accessories, including protective gear for honey collection. McClendon ordered her bees from Allen's Bee Ranch (530/221-1458).

Collecting honey is hard work, says McLendon, but otherwise beekeeping is easy. The only other chores are treating the bee box with a mite preventive once a year and monitoring the hive periodically.

Want to learn more? McLendon suggests reading the book *Keeping Bees,* by John Vivian (Williamson Publishing, Charlotte, VT, 1986: $10.95; 800/234-8791). — *S.C.*

BACK TO BASICS

How to stake a tree

■ Stake a tree only if it can't stand well on its own or if the site is very windy. Find the proper height to place ties by sliding your hand up the trunk until the treetop straightens. Set two stakes on opposite sides of the trunk, lining them up perpendicular to the prevailing wind and beyond the rootball. Tie the tree to the stakes using wire or rope covered with trunk-protecting hose or rubber tubing scraps, or buy rubberized tree ties. The tree should be allowed to sway some in the wind, which encourages it to develop a strong trunk. Remove ties as soon as the tree can support itself (after a year or so).

NORMAN A. PLATE

DEIDRA WALPOLE

Woodland in a vase

■ San Diego garden consultant Laurie Connable's spring bouquets look like woodland gardens in miniature. Her daffodils, irises, and gladiolus appear to rise from a mossy patch of earth instead of a water-filled vase. The smaller blooms and greenery at their base add to the garden look.

The best flowers for woodland arrangements thrust upward, says Connable. "They're not bush flowers, like roses." Whether you use cuttings from your garden or blooms from a florist, they make perfect centerpieces for spring tables.

— *Debra Lee Baldwin*

CREATE SIMILAR SPRING DRAMA in a teacup. Be bold; let flowering bulbs tower above their containers.

MATERIALS

- Shallow oval container, approximately 12 inches long by 3 inches deep
- Florist's foam, trimmed to fit container and soaked until moist throughout
- 12 (or so) 4-inch pieces of fern and/or small-leafed ivy
- Sphagnum moss
- Flowers: two gladiolus, about 2 feet tall; three irises, about 18 inches tall; three daffodils, about 12 inches tall; 12 (or so) filler flowers

such as freesia, narcissus, nemesia, linaria, or stock
- Foliage: several bunches of lemon thyme and/or additional strands of ivy
- Scissors or clipping shears

DIRECTIONS

1. Insert ferns and ivy horizontally into the foam above the container's rim. Cover the foam top with moist sphagnum moss.
2. Insert gladiolus on one side of the foam block and

irises on the other, forming two flower clusters. Trim stems to vary heights as shown, but don't remove leaves. Add the daffodils near irises, then tuck the smaller blooms, thyme, and additional ivy around each floral grouping. Leave a small gap between the two clusters to suggest a woodland path.

Pacific Northwest Checklist

PLANTING

☑ **BARE-ROOT STOCK. Zones 1–3:** As soon as the ground thaws, plant bare-root stock, including ornamental and fruit trees, roses, and perennial vegetables. Keep bare roots moist until you can plant them.

☑ **BEDDING PLANTS. Zones 4–7:** Frost-tolerant plants like dusty miller, lobelia, petunias, and snapdragons can go into beds early in the month. After all danger of frost is past, set out celosia, geraniums, impatiens, and sweet alyssum. In zones 1–3, wait until May to set out bedding plants.

☑ **BERRIES.** Set out blackberries, blueberries, raspberries, and strawberries.

☑ **DAHLIAS. Zones 4–7:** Plant dahlia tubers this month for summer bloom (wait until next month in zones 1–3).

☑ **TREES.** Deciduous and evergreen trees can be planted throughout the Northwest this month.

☑ **VEGETABLES.** Set out cool-season greens and root crops, including cabbage, carrots, lettuce, parsnips, peas, potatoes, radishes, spinach, and Swiss chard.

MAINTENANCE

☑ **AMEND SOIL.** Dig organic matter into the beds once the soil has thawed and is dry. Peat moss, compost, leaf mold, and well-rotted manure are all good amendments. After you dig them in, rake the ground smooth and let it settle for at least a week before planting.

☑ **COMPOST.** To speed the decomposition of new materials, mix them into the old and add high-nitrogen fertilizer. Keep the pile damp but not soggy and turn it regularly.

☑ **GROOM RHODIES.** As rhododendron blooms fade, clip or gently snap off spent flower trusses. Be careful not to break off the new growth buds that emerge just below the flower heads.

☑ **MOVE TENDER PLANTS OUTDOORS. Zones 4–7:** Cymbidiums can go out early in the month, begonias and fuchsias late in the month.

☑ **MOW LAWNS.** You may have to mow grass weekly for the next two to three months.

PEST & WEED CONTROL

☑ **SLUGS. Zones 4–7:** Install beer traps or handpick with a vengeance. The more you send to slug heaven now, the fewer you'll have to deal with in summer and fall.

☑ **WEEDS.** Young weeds are easier to pull than mature plants, and at this time of year, most have not yet set or scattered seed. ◆

Northern California Checklist

PLANTING

☑ **BARE-ROOT STOCK. Zones 1–2:** Deciduous plants such as cane berries, flowering shrubs and vines, fruit and nut trees, grapes, rhubarb, roses, and strawberries can go in the ground now.

☑ **SUMMER FLOWERS. Zones 7–9, 14–17:** All warm-season annuals can be planted now. For your best buy, purchase sixpacks; plants catch up quickly to 4-inch-size plants. If you need instant color, use 4-inch plants. Try ageratum, dwarf dahlias, globe amaranth, impatiens, lobelia, Madagascar periwinkle (vinca), marigold, petunia, phlox, portulaca, salvia, sanvitalia, statice, sunflower, sweet alyssum, verbena, and zinnia.

☑ **TOMATOES. Zones 7–9, 14–17:** 'Brandywine' and 'Black Krim' (both 3–4 inches wide) are winners for flavor. 'Stupice' (2 in. wide) and 'Early Girl' (2–3 in. wide) can't be beat for flavor and production in cooler climates. For a comprehensive list of mail-order heirloom tomato seeds, write Grandview Farms Seeds, 12942 Dupont Rd., Sebastopol, CA 95472. The Natural Gardening Company (707/766-9303) sells organically grown tomato plants (and other edibles) by mail.

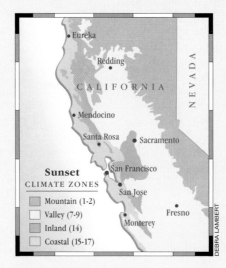

Sunset
CLIMATE ZONES
☐ Mountain (1-2)
☐ Valley (7-9)
☐ Inland (14)
☐ Coastal (15-17)

DEBRA LAMBERT

☑ **TENDER PLANTS. Zones 7–9, 14–17:** Even if they are marginally adapted to Northern California climates, it's hard to resist gorgeous tropicals and subtropicals like bougainvillea, hibiscus, jacaranda, mandevilla, Mexican lime, and plumeria. Set these tender plants out now so they have the growing season to get established. Plant them in protected sites, against a south-facing wall or under an overhang, or grow them in containers that can be moved to a protected spot in winter.

WEED CONTROL

☑ **DESTROY DODDER.** This leafless, parasitic weed has recently appeared in ornamental plantings in Redding. When dodder seeds germinate in spring, thin yellowish stems twine around the first plant they contact, penetrate its tissue, and extract water and nutrients from it. Eventually a mat of stems forms around the host plant and the dodder loses contact with the soil. Remove and destroy infested plants. Treat the area the spring after infestation with a preemergent herbicide to kill the seeds. ◆

Southern California Checklist

PLANTING

☑ **BEDDING PLANTS.** Replace fading cool-season annuals with heat lovers like celosia, dahlias, marigolds, petunias, salvia, verbena, and vinca. Sow some taller annuals for cut flowers, too. Cleomes, cosmos, sunflowers, and zinnias are particularly easy.

☑ **CROPS.** Start beans, corn, cucumbers, eggplant, lima beans, melons, okra, peppers, pumpkins, squash, tomatoes, and other warm-season crops. Delay planting two to four weeks in the high desert (zone 11); frost is still a possibility. Coastal gardeners (zones 21–24) can also continue planting quick-maturing, cool-season crops like leaf lettuces, radishes, spinach, and chard.

☑ **INSECTARY PLANTS.** Beneficial insects like parasitic wasps help keep pests away from your vegetables. Adult beneficial insects eat nectar and pollen, but their voracious young eat aphids, scale, and other undesirables. Flat-topped flowers like scabiosa, Shasta daisies, strawflowers, and yarrow are particularly welcome to beneficials.

MAINTENANCE

☑ **CONTINUE FERTILIZING.** Fertilize trees, shrubs, ground covers, perennials, turf grasses, and other permanent ornamentals not fed last month. Once they stop blooming, feed azaleas and camellias with an acid-based fertilizer. Don't forget house plants. They're growing again and need food too.

☑ **WAIT TO TRIM BULBS.** If you want flowering bulbs to bloom next year, don't be in a hurry to clip yellowing leaves. The bulbs are still gathering nourishment from them for next year's flowers.

☑ **WATCH FOR CHLOROSIS.** In early spring, camellias, citrus, gardenias, hibiscus, and other plants often show signs of iron deficiency. If leaves turn yellow while the veins remain green, treat the plant with chelated iron according to package directions.

PEST CONTROL

☑ **WATCH FOR FIRE ANTS.** Imported red fire ants made an unwelcome appearance in Southern California late last year. To report an infestation of these ants, or to request a brochure on dealing with them, call the California Department of Food and Agriculture hotline at (800) 491-1899. For more information, also check out the Web site at www.cdfa.ca.gov.

☑ **STOP THE ANT PARADE.** If you see ants (other than red fire ants) parading up the trunks of plants such as citrus, chances are they're feeding on the honeydew secreted by aphids or scale insects. Stop the parade with a sticky barrier of Tanglefoot or set out traps containing boric acid. ◆

Mountain Checklist

PLANTING

☑ **BARE-ROOT STOCK.** Early in the month, plant bare-root asparagus, horseradish, and rhubarb. Also plant bare-root berries and fruit and ornamental trees.

☑ **FLOWERS.** Set out annuals (calendulas, English daisies, pansies, primroses, snapdragons, stock, violas) and perennials, including bergenia, bleeding hearts, and wallflowers.

☑ **HARDY VEGETABLES.** As soon as the soil is workable, sow cool-season crops such as beets, carrots, chard, endive, kohlrabi, lettuce, onions, parsley, parsnips, peas, radishes, spinach, and turnips. Set out transplants of broccoli, brussels sprouts, cabbage, cauliflower, and green onions. Also plant seed potatoes. Floating row covers take the edge off cold nights and protect seedlings from wind and sunburn.

☑ **FLOWERING TREES AND SHRUBS.** Buy and plant spring-blooming trees and shrubs such as redbuds, flowering quinces, forsythias, magnolias, and Japanese andromeda (*Pieris* species).

Sunset CLIMATE ZONES
☐ 1-3 ■ 10-11

DEBRA LAMBERT

MAINTENANCE

☑ **FEED LAWNS.** Apply 1 to 2 pounds of high-nitrogen fertilizer per 1,000 square feet of turf (more on heavily used lawns and those growing in poor soil), and water it in well.

☑ **MULCH.** A 3-inch organic mulch suppresses weeds, holds in moisture, and keeps roots cool and growing when the weather heats up. Put it around annuals, perennials, trees, and shrubs, especially if summers are hot and dry where you live. Keep mulch a few inches back from warm-season vegetables—their roots need the warmest soil they can get until hot weather arrives.

☑ **PRUNE.** Early in the month, before new growth emerges, finish pruning deciduous fruit and ornamental trees, grapes, roses, and vines. Wait until after flowering to prune spring-blooming trees and shrubs like forsythia, Japanese apricot, and spiraea, or prune them lightly after buds swell and put the cuttings in vases for an indoor flower show.

PEST AND WEED CONTROL

☑ **HOE OR PULL WEEDS.** When weeds are small and soil is dry, do your hoeing early in the day; sun and dryness will kill tiny roots by day's end. For larger weeds, water thoroughly, then pop weeds out with a hand weeder, roots and all.

☑ **SPRAY FRUIT TREES.** After pruning, but before leaves and flowers appear, spray fruit trees with a mixture of dormant oil and lime sulfur or oil and copper to control overwintering insects and diseases. Dormant oil will smother insects. Copper controls fireblight, peach leaf curl, and shothole fungus. Lime sulfur controls mildew and rust, but don't use it on apricots. If rain washes the treatments off within 48 hours, reapply them. Keep oil and copper spray off walls, fences, and walks to prevent staining. ◆

Southwest Checklist

PLANTING

ANNUALS. Zones 10–13: Early in the month, plant seedlings of ageratum, celosia, cosmos, four o'clock, globe amaranth, gloriosa daisy, kochia, marigold, Mexican sunflower, portulaca, strawflower, vinca rosea, and zinnia.

CITRUS. Zones 12–13: Plant container-grown citrus in full sun. Water two or three times per week at first, tapering to every five to seven days by summer's end. Wrap the young tree's exposed trunk in white cloth or paint it with white latex to prevent sunburn.

LAWNS. Zones 1–2, 10: Sow or reseed bluegrass, fine or tall fescue, perennial rye, or a blend of these. In areas with long, warm summers, consider a blend of buffalo grass and blue grama grass. Zone 11 (Las Vegas): Tall fescue and perennial rye grass are the lawns of choice, but you can also grow common or hybrid Bermuda grass. Zones 12–13: When night temperatures stay above 70°, plant hybrid Bermuda, buffalo, or blue grama.

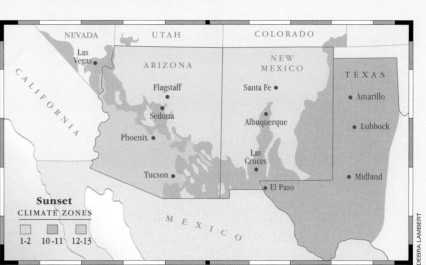

Sunset
CLIMATE ZONES
1-2   10-11   12-13

DEBRA LAMBERT

PERENNIALS. Set out chrysanthemum, columbine, coreopsis, gaillardia, gazania, geranium, gerbera, hollyhock, Michaelmas daisy, salvia, and Shasta daisy.

SUMMER BULBS. After last frost, plant caladium, canna, crinum, dahlia, daylily, gladiolus, iris, and montbretia. You can also buy container-grown agapanthus, society garlic (*Tulbaghia*), and zephyranthes.

VEGETABLES. Zones 10–12: Sow cucumber, melon, okra, pumpkin, soybean, squash, and watermelon; set out seedlings of eggplant, pepper, sweet potato, and tomato; plant Jerusalem artichoke tubers. Zones 12–13: Sow beans and cucumbers by midmonth; set out eggplant, okra, peanut, squash, and sweet potato anytime.

VINES. Zones 10–13: Plant tender vines, including bougainvillea, mandevilla 'Alice du Pont', pink trumpet vine, and queen's wreath, in a warm spot with good winter protection.

MAINTENANCE

FEED LAWNS. About two weeks after Bermuda grass greens up, apply 3 to 4 pounds high-nitrogen fertilizer per 1,000 square feet. Water thoroughly.

MULCH SOIL. Spread a 3-inch layer of organic mulch around annuals, perennials, shrubs, trees, and vegetables to conserve soil moisture, keep roots cool, and suppress weeds. ◆

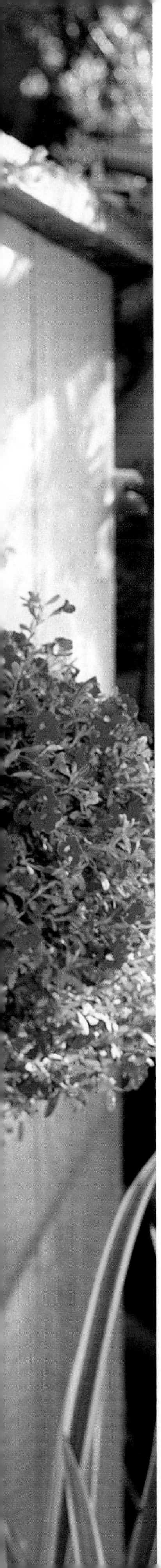

hanging basket magic

No room for a garden? Grow
your flowers and foliage
in baskets, designed to hang

BY LAUREN BONAR SWEZEY • PHOTOGRAPHS BY NORMAN A. PLATE

Bright magenta million bells (*Calibrachoa*) cascade from two terra-cotta pots suspended from the fence by wrought-iron hangers. Arcs above the plants connect to circles of iron that fit neatly under the pot rims to hold the pots in place.

Magic is in the air this spring. Enchanting combinations of flowers and foliage are pairing with offbeat containers to put a fresh spin on the art of hanging baskets. • Imagine an exotic rattan basket, filled with tropical plants, suspended from a beam over your patio. Or a shower of petunia blossoms tumbling from a wire basket outside an arbor. Both are delightful surprises at eye level. And, like the other unique hanging baskets pictured on the following pages, they can transform a patio or entryway from ordinary to magical. • With the right plants and a few simple tips (see page 113), you can create these one-of-a-kind hanging baskets to dress up your garden.

ILLUSTRATIONS: DEBRA LAMBERT (2)

Three-tiered, moss-lined wire basket (left) is filled with **1)** pink polka-dot plant (*Hypoestes*); **2)** silver fern; **3)** white sweet alyssum; **4)** *Pilea depressa* 'Tigers Eyes'; **5)** autumn fern (*Dryopteris erythrosora*); **6)** purple-leaf oxalis; **7)** *Microlepia splendens;* **8)** *Nierembergia hippomanica violacea* 'Purple Robe'; **9)** purple sweet alyssum; **10)** New Guinea impatiens; **11)** baby's tears. Design: Bud Stuckey

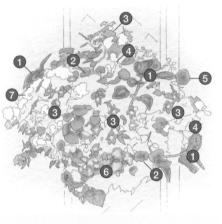

Wall-mounted wire basket (above right) lined with moss holds **1)** coleus; **2)** ageratum; **3)** *Browallia speciosa* 'Blue Bells Improved'; **4)** white fibrous begonia; **5)** magenta impatiens; **6)** *Lamium maculatum;* **7)** white impatiens. Design: Hilda Schwerin, Wegman's Nursery, Redwood City, CA

Six steps to a great hanging basket

■ CHOOSE A CONTAINER

Almost anything that will hold soil can become a hanging planter—wire or rattan baskets, metal pitchers, terra-cotta urns, and wood containers all work well. Hang them with chains, sisal, or wire, and keep in mind that heavier pots need stronger hangers. Use swivel hooks (available at nurseries) atop the hangers; that way, you can rotate the pot occasionally so the plants receive light on all sides.

■ SELECT PLANTS

Choose a style or a theme—all perennials, annuals, succulents, or tropicals, for instance. Next, select your color scheme; use contrasting or complementary colors together, or shades of a single color. Avoid mixing too many colors, which can give a container planting a confetti look. Choose both upright and trailing plants. Make sure the ultimate height of the upright plants will be in scale with the pot. Use sixpack-size plants for tucking into the sides of wire baskets.

■ LINE WIRE BASKETS

Use a preformed, moss-covered sponge liner (MossCraft by

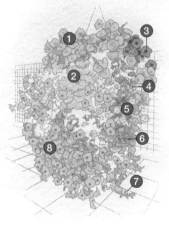

Moss-lined wire basket (above left) contains **1)** petunia Primetime Series 'Rose'; **2)** *Calceolaria* 'Sunshine'; **3)** petunia Celebrity Series 'Red'; **4)** lobelia Color Cascade Mix; **5)** Tapien verbena; **6)** ivy geranium; **7)** parrot's beak; **8)** petunia 'Purple Wave'. Design: Butchart Gardens, Victoria, B.C.

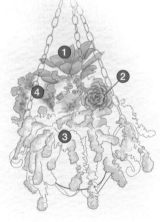

Terra-cotta pot in a wire hanger (above right) contains **1)** *Echeveria gibbiflora* 'Mary Butterfield'; **2)** *E. peacockii;* **3)** donkey tail (*Sedum morganianum*); **4)** pork and beans (*S. rubrotinctum*). Design: Bud Stuckey

---

Mapco, 800/598-9084 or 562/598-9084) or a coco fiber liner (from Kinsman Company, 800/733-4146). You can also use sphagnum moss, but it's much more time-consuming to install.

■ **PREPARE THE POTTING MIX**
Use a high-quality potting mix that contains peat moss, forest products, and perlite. Mix in a controlled-release or well-balanced organic fertilizer. To help retain moisture, you can also mix in soil polymers such as Broadleaf P4. A Rain-Mat (a polymer-containing fabric mat from Kinsman

Company) is particularly good for preventing water from rushing out the bottom of wire baskets. Before filling the container with potting mix, place the Rain-Mat inside the basket on top of the liner.

■ **PLANT THE BASKET**
Depending on the container you use, follow one of these methods.
For top-planted containers: Fill two-thirds to three-fourths of the container with potting mix. Knock plants out of nursery pots and arrange them on top of the soil. Set upright

Indonesian bamboo basket hung with rough hemp holds **1)** agapanthus 'Dark Star'; **2)** *Juncus* 'Oaxaca'; **3)** *Acalypha wilkesiana;* **4)** *Tithonia rotundifolia;* **5)** *Colocasia esculenta;* **6)** *Amaranthus tricolor;* **7)** *Acorus gramineus* 'Ogon'; **8)** *Russelia equisetiformis;* **9)** *Lysimachia procumbens;* **10)** *Scaevola* 'Mauve Clusters'; **11)** *Cordyline australis* 'Albertii'; **12)** *Rhipsalis cereuscula;* **13)** canna 'Technicolor'; **14)** *Crocosmia masoniorum;* **15)** *Plumeria rubra.* Design: Mark Bartos, Hortus Garden Design, Pasadena

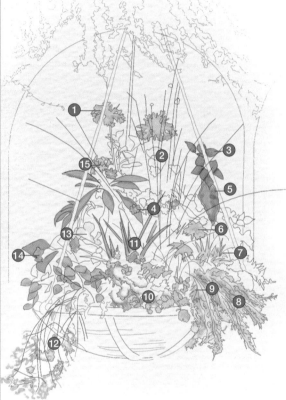

plants in the center of the pot, drapers around the edges. Fill in with soil and water well.

For layered baskets: After lining the basket, fill a third of it with potting mix. Poke holes through the liner (coco fiber can be difficult to cut) or sphagnum moss every 2 to 3 inches around the circumference of the pot, just above the soil (MossCraft liners have premade slits). Push a rootball through each hole so the rootball sits on top of the soil. Add another third of soil, covering the first level of rootballs, and another circle of plants. Finish by filling the rest of the pot with soil and planting the basket top.

■ **WATER REGULARLY**

Keep the soil moist but not soggy. Check containers (particularly baskets) often, since they can dry out quickly in hot weather. In hot inland climates, hang baskets in a spot that gets afternoon shade.

Watering tip: If your hanging basket is drying out too quickly or water seems to run down its sides leaving the rootball unsoaked, dunk the entire basket—soil and all—in a large tub of water for several minutes (or until water stops bubbling). Lift the basket out and let the water drain. ◆

Versatile vines

Whether you train them up a post or let them
sprawl, vines are incredibly obliging.
Here are four easy ways to grow them

BY SHARON COHOON

■ Vines are models of versatility. Once established, they provide privacy and they camouflage, converting unattractive necessities like storage sheds and carports into decorative backdrops. They provide shade, blocking harmful ultraviolet rays from well-used decks all summer. Come winter, when more light is welcome, the deciduous types courteously drop their leaves.

Vines can accentuate an architectural detail by outlining a porch railing, softening a roofline, or curling up a column. They add interest where there is none—greening up the narrow stucco canyons on either side of a tract house, for instance.

Garlanding entryways, vines welcome. Blanketing gazebos in the background, they beckon. Climbing a casual tepee of bamboo poles, vines add drama. Carrying color to the eye and fragrance to the nose, they contribute sensuality.

And those are just the ones that grow upward. Dangling through an overhead lath, vines can envelop a patio in green drapery. Trailing downhill, bold vines like bougainvillea turn slopes into riots of color. Vines can grow horizontally

too. Delicate ones are particularly good this way. Clematis, for example, can weave through campanula as readily as it can reach for a rose.

In addition, vines are notoriously easy to grow. Most are light feeders, and many are drought-tolerant. Best of all, they require little ground space—just enough soil for their roots and stems. Even the smallest garden can squeeze one in. Isn't there room for a vine in yours?

42″

17″

◄——— 25″dia. ———►

1. Garland a trellis.
A different compact clematis grows up each corner of a wire obelisk in the pot at left. A fifth variety is planted in the center. Clockwise from top of obelisk, varieties are 'Lord Nevill', pale blue 'Ramona', crimson 'Gipsy Queen', lavender-blue 'H.F. Young', and pink-and-red 'Dr. Ruppel'. At right, the old bougainvillea is mostly self-supporting; its woody base (behind the gate) is boxed in by brick.

NORMAN A. PLATE (2)   ILLUSTRATION: BARBARA BANTHIEN

2. Cover an arbor. Two grapevines ('Concord' and red 'Flame') and a perennial morning glory vine scramble up posts that flank this entry. All three vines shade the deck in summer, making a fresh-air retreat.

3. Create an outdoor room divider. Potato vine (*Solanum jasminoides*) climbs up 4-by-4 gateposts and over two 2-by-6s across the top to mark the transition from front to backyard in this Southern California garden.

How to choose a vine

• **Find suitable locations** for vines in your garden *before* you shop. Are the potential sites sunny or shady? Are there other factors to consider? Boggy ground suitable only for plants that love wet feet, for instance, or lots of reflected light that heat lovers could tolerate? How's the soil? Is the planting area you have in mind under eaves where the vine won't get rain? How will you irrigate—drip, soaker hose, or by hand?

• **Flowers or foliage or both?** Will the vine be a solid backdrop to set off your flowering plants? If so, evergreens like star jasmine or creeping fig are what you want. For shade in the summer and sun in the winter, on the other hand, shop for something deciduous like grape or wisteria. If it's sky-high flowers you're after, when and in what color do you want them?

• **Clinger or nonclinger?** Vines with their own Velcro-like pads, such as Boston ivy, attach themselves to any rough surface without help. But don't grow them next to wood shingles or surfaces you'll repaint often, because clingers don't detach willingly. The majority of vines, however, climb with clasping tendrils or by twining and need three-dimensional support.

• **What kind of support?** For annual vines, a casual arrangement—like bird netting tacked to a fence—will suffice. But perennial vines require a more permanent toehold: a chain-link fence, trellis, galvanized wire grid, or sturdy pergola. When choosing a support, consider the vine's ultimate bulk and woodiness. A lightweight twiner like Chilean jasmine (*Mandevilla laxa*) will do fine on a nursery-variety trellis, but a woody wisteria will need a sturdy trellis, of 4-by-4s at least, to support its ultimate weight.

NORMAN A. PLATE. TOP: CLAIRE CURRAN

4. Plant an entry pot. 'General Sikorski' (deep blue) clematis climbs a metal frame; it's underplanted with verbena to keep its roots cool. Other clematis varieties for pots include 'Nelly Moser' (pale mauve and lilac) and 'Duchess of Edinburgh' (double white).

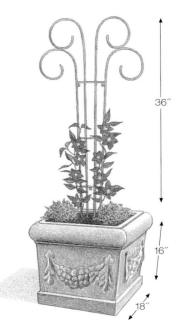

36″

16″

18″

No place for a vine? Try a clematis in a pot

■ Greta Garbo had it. Lauren Bacall still does. Like these two famous actresses, large-flowered clematis have an undeniable mystique. Yet these beautiful vines are no hothouse untouchables; they're versatile, obliging, and easy to grow—even in containers.

If you have no room for a big robust vine, grow a compact clematis in a pot and train it up a small trellis. Now is the perfect time to start; many are in full bloom this month, so you can readily find the flower colors you want.

GETTING STARTED

Buy a big pot, a bag of potting soil, and a trellis. The pyramid obelisk ($57; pictured on page 116) is available by mail from Kinsman Company (800/733-4146). A pot trellis, similar to the one pictured above, is available from Park Seed (800/845-3369). Use compact, large-flowered clematis in 1-gallon pots.

HOW TO PLANT

Thoroughly water the rootballs before planting. Fill the container halfway with potting mix; blend in a balanced, controlled-release fertilizer. Remove each clematis from its pot. Slightly loosen any roots circling the base of the rootball.

Arrange plants in the container near where the trellis supports will go. The crown of the plants (the point where the plant's roots and top structure join) should sit 2 to 3 inches below the soil level and 3 to 4 inches below the pot rim. Cover the rootball with soil and press to firm; water well. Position the trellis in the container, remove existing nursery stakes, and tie stems to the trellis. Keep soil moist during the growing season.

During the first growing season, tie vines to the trellis as they grow. Cut off spent flowers after first bloom to encourage a second flush of blooms. *The following winter* or early spring (depending on climate), cut stems back to about 10 inches to encourage new shoots, cutting just above a single bud or pair of buds. After three pairs of leaves have formed, pinch off the tip of each stem just above a pair of leaves. As the stems grow, tie them to supports. Thereafter, prune annually in late winter or early spring to remove weak and dead stems.

— *Lauren Bonar Swezey* ◆

LUXURIANT GREEN TUFTS between pavers in this Pasadena garden are Korean grass.

What to plant between pavers

Grass makes outdoor "floors" as interesting as indoor carpets

BY STEVEN R. LORTON

Debating whether to use lawn or concrete to fill the large, open space in your garden? A lawn is green and alive but has to be cut, watered, and fertilized. Concrete takes plenty of wear but can look dull and uninviting. Don't choose—pick the best of both: with a little planning, it's easy to mix lawn and paving, as shown in the two gardens pictured above and on the facing page.

Carrie and Marty Davich of Pasadena wanted a cozy patio outside their master bedroom where they could have morning coffee or a moonlit drink. That called for a soft look—not a hard masonry surface. So they hired Mark Bartos of Hortus Garden Design of Pasadena to come up with a solution. Bartos scraped the earth outside the bedroom door flat and smooth. Then he put down 2-inch-thick, off-the-shelf concrete pavers, spacing them 6 inches apart, ran drip irrigation tubes between them, and planted Korean grass (*Zoysia tenuifolia*; *Sunset* climate zones 8–9, 12–24).

The grass forms a fine, bumpy, dark green mat that looks as luxurious as carpet. The owners water it every other day in hottest weather, and occasionally scatter complete granular fertilizer.

Up in Anchorage, Mark Pfeffer and Deb CiCero wanted a handsome surface outside their back door that would stand up to foot traffic and the movement of heavy garden equipment. o Pfeffer placed square pavers in a heckerboard pattern, then cut sections of sod and laid them between the pavers. Now five years old, the surface has held up perfectly. Pfeffer feeds the grass (a hardy local blend) with a high-nitrogen fertilizer in spring and early summer. He waters only when the Alaskan summer is too dry and mows the lawn with a rotary mower, just as he would a regular lawn.

Choice plants to pair with pavers

Grass stands up best to traffic. But if you plan to tread only infrequently on the surface or you're willing to step from paver to paver, avoiding the greenery, you have a greater selection to choose from. Here are some options, each with a different effect.

Ajuga, or carpet bugle (*Ajuga reptans*). Forms a dense mat of dark green to bronzy burgundy leaves. Full sun or part shade. All *Sunset* climate zones.

Baby's tears (*Soleirolia soleirolii*). Forms a dense mat of bright green with a profusion of tiny leaves. Light sun to shade. Zones 4–24.

Chamomile (*Chamaemelum nobile*). Bright green, finely cut, aromatic leaves form a soft-textured mat. Small yellow flowers. Best in full sun, takes some shade. All zones.

Corsican mint (*Mentha requienii*). Tiny leaves form a tight, ground-hugging mat that releases strong licorice fragrance when brushed. Sun or part shade. Zones 5–9, 12–24.

Duchesnea (*Duchesnea indica*). Commonly called Indian mock strawberry; leaves are divided into three leaflets. Small yellow flowers; 1/2-inch red fruits. Sun or shade. All zones.

Erodium, or cranesbill (*Erodium reichardii*). Roundish green leaves with scalloped edges. Profuse flowers, 1/2 inch wide, are white to rose. Full sun or part shade. Zones 7–9, 14–24.

Isotoma, or blue star creeper (*Laurentia fluviatilis*). Oval leaves form a thick mat. Pale

CHECKERBOARD LAWN in Anchorage provides built-in paths between deck and border.

blue, starlike flowers. Full sun or part shade. Zones 4–5, 8–9, 14–24.

Lippia (*Phyla nodiflora*). This tight mat of gray-green leaves takes foot traffic. Flowers are lilac to rose in tight, round heads. Full sun. Zones 8–24.

Lysimachia (*Lysimachia nummularia*). Small roundish leaves on stems that creep and root, forming a dense carpet. Yellow flowers, 1 inch across. Sun or shade. Zones 1–9, 14–24.

Spring cinquefoil (*Potentilla tabernaemontanii*). Dense tufts of tiny leaves with five leaflets. Flowers are yellow, 1/4 inch wide, in clusters. Full sun or light shade. All zones.

Thyme (*Thymus praecox arcticus* and *T. pseudolanuginosus*). Two ground-crawling species of thyme with masses of tiny leaves; the first is green and aromatic, the second known for its woolly gray leaves. Best in full sun. All zones. ◆

'TAHITIAN SUNRISE' flaunts 5-inch-wide flowers.

ALLAN MANDELL

7 DAZZLING DAYLILIES

These hardy daylilies are reliable repeat-blooming varieties. The abbreviations after the variety names refer to the mail-order suppliers listed below.

'Barbara Mitchell' (CFN, SCDG): 6-inch-wide apricot-pink blooms on 2-foot-tall plants.

'Final Touch' (CFN): 5-inch flowers that combine pink and lavender on 32-inch plants.

'Fragrant Light' (CFN): scented, pale yellow flowers 6 inches across on 30-inch plants.

'Lemon Lollypop' (CFN): fragrant, soft yellow flowers 2¾ inches across on 18-inch plants.

'Pink Playmate' (CFN): 4-inch blossoms in deep to rose pink with white ribs on 28-inch plants.

'Stella de Oro' (CFN, SCDG): 2½-inch gold flowers on 12- to 16-inch plants.

'Tahitian Sunrise' (CFN): 5-inch scarlet flowers with a hint of orange on 30-inch plants.

CFN: Caprice Farm Nursery, 15425 S.W. Pleasant Hill Rd., Sherwood, OR 97140; (503) 625-7241; catalog $2.

SCDG: Snow Creek Daylily Gardens, Box 2007, Port Townsend, WA 98368; (360) 385-7572; catalog $3.

Daylilies for colder climates

These hardy beauties reward you with repeat bloom

BY STEVEN R. LORTON

Hybrids of the genus *Hemerocallis* are called daylilies for an obvious reason: each flower lasts only for a single day. Chances are you won't even miss it, for often the very next morning one or more new blossoms pop open. The bloom cycle is likely to continue for weeks or even months, thanks to daylily growers who've bred this repeat-flowering habit into plants. But blooms aren't the whole show: the arching, sword-shaped leaves form handsome clumps.

Order plants now (see sources above). When the tuberous roots arrive, get them into the ground right away. Planted by late May, they'll produce a few flowers their first summer. Daylilies grow in almost any soil. Give them full sun (light shade in the hottest inland areas). Pick off blooms as they fade; when all flowers on the stalk have bloomed, cut it to the ground.

Established plants need only light water during bloom. Apply a balanced granular fertilizer four times each growing season. About every three years, dig up the clumps in late fall or early spring, divide them into sections, and replant the divisions immediately. ◆

'ROCKING CRADLE' bears 3½-inch-wide flowers.

DAZZLING DAYLILIES

'**Bitsy**': 2-inch-wide yellow flowers on 20- to 28-inch stems over 14- to 20-inch-tall leaves.

'**Black Eyed Stella**': 3-inch yellow blooms with reddish eyes on 18-inch stems over 1-foot leaves.

'**Butterscotch Ruffles**': 3-inch ruffled, butterscotch blossoms on 26-inch stems over 16-inch leaves.

'**Little Bobo**': 2-inch soft red flowers with light cream edges on 18-inch stems over 1-foot leaves.

'**Miss Victoria**': Fragrant, 4-inch lemon yellow blossoms on 25-inch stems over 17-inch leaves.

'**Pojo**': 3-inch deep yellow double flowers on 23-inch stems over 16-inch leaves.

'**Pyewacket**': 3-inch peach-and-pink flowers with plum eyes and chartreuse throats on 16-inch stems over 11-inch leaves.

'**Rocking Cradle**': 3½-inch pink-and-ivory blooms on 18-inch-stems over 14-inch leaves.

'**Terra Cotta Baby**': 2½-inch rosy tan flowers on 22-inch stems over 15-inch leaves.

'**Tiny Pumpkin**': 2-inch light pumpkin blooms on 20-inch stems over 15-inch leaves.

These plants are sold by Greenwood Daylily Gardens; (562) 494-8944.

Daylilies for mild-climate areas

10 beauties with evergreen foliage thrive in mild climates

BY LAUREN BONAR SWEZEY

When the compact daylily 'Stella de Oro' was introduced a few years ago, growers raved about its 120-day bloom period and gardeners all over the West planted it. Now, after much trial and error, we've learned that while this plant does fine in colder climates, it doesn't perform as well in mild areas. "'Stella de Oro' goes dormant for three months and needs some winter chill," explains John Schoustra of Greenwood Daylily Gardens in Long Beach, California.

Other compact varieties of daylily (*Hemerocallis*) not only are better suited for mild climates but also bear flowers over a much longer period, Schoustra says. "'Bitsy' and a number of others keep on blooming without a rest period—some for up to 290 days."

Schoustra's favorites are listed above. All make perfect companions with other perennials in borders or beds. When used as a ground cover, "these evergreen types are great for erosion control," says Schoustra. Like other daylilies, they thrive in full sun (afternoon shade in hot, inland or desert areas), in almost any kind of soil, and, once established, with little to regular water. ◆

NORMAN A. PLATE

TAPESTRY IN GOLD: Sunny golds enhance this border. A standard yellow bell pepper from W. Atlee Burpee & Co. is joined by golden pompom marigolds and *Rudbeckia hirta* 'Toto'.

Bright veggies among flowers

Some crops are born beautiful. Why not show them off in floral finery?

BY SHARON COHOON

Floral designers don't segregate vegetables and flowers. Their arrangements mix eggplants, bell peppers, and artichokes with sunflowers, dahlias, and zinnias. Why, they ask, treat vegetables differently from other ornamentals? If eggplants weren't meant to be venerated as art objects before being turned into moussaka, why has nature given them robes of maroon satin? If red peppers aren't supposed to be noticed until they're diced into salsa, why do they glow like lighted lanterns in the garden? If we aren't supposed to admire artichokes before we taste them, why are the globes so graceful that sculptors mimic their form in stone finials?

The answer is obvious: many summer vegetables are gorgeous. That's why last year we grew them in *Sunset's* test garden as if they were star ornamentals. Test garden coordinator Bud Stuckey made a beautiful vegetable the focal point in each of four beds (two are pictured), then gave it a complement of annual flowers and herbs as if he were putting together a bouquet. Since the beds were in close proximity with no borders of greenery between them, he stuck to monochromatic color schemes to keep the plantings from looking too busy. Lavenders and whites complemented violet eggplant, golden tones blended with yellow bell peppers (shown above), and fiery reds paired well with purple bells (shown on the facing page).

For a fourth planting, Stuckey grew scarlet runner beans and hyacinth beans on bamboo poles, then planted marigolds at their feet.

The vegetable-flower combinations thrived; we had wonderful crops as well as beautiful beds. Interplanting caused us only one problem: It was difficult to have to harvest from living bouquets.

Other gardens, other ideas

• Dressing up a bed of low-growing vegetables can be as simple as adding a row of marigolds in front and a row of cosmos in back. Janie Malloy of Home Grown, Edible Landscaping in Pasadena uses this simple technique in many clients' gardens. It looks different in each garden, but unfailingly pretty.

• Tomatillos and bedding dahlias, which grow side by side in Malloy's own garden, are a handsome pair. Dahlias also look great with tomatoes, eggplants, and squash.

• Cannas and corn make great mates. To embellish them further, add a row of zinnias in the foreground.

• The big, silvery leaves of artichokes look wonderful with other gray Mediterranean foliage such as artemisia, lavender, and santolina.

• Don't forget containers. Red chard planted in Italianate terra-cotta urns can be underplanted with a trailing flower such as sweet alyssum or verbena.

The bonus of interplanting

Beauty aside, there are plenty of good reasons to grow flowers with vegetables. At Shoulder to Shoulder Farm in the foothills of the Coast Range in Oregon, growers raise salad greens for gourmet restaurants by interplanting them with flowers that encourage beneficial insects—the farm's main weapons against crop pests.

Parasitic wasps, ladybird beetles, lacewings, syrphid flies, and other beneficials hang around the plants they love—dill, fennel, garlic chives, parsley, ox-eye and Shasta daisies, and yarrow, for instance. The adults feed on flower nectar and pollen and lay eggs on garden crops. When the eggs hatch, the hungry larvae of the beneficials feed on the pests that plague these crops. So the pest/prey ratio remains balanced.

Nectar and pollen-rich flowers also attract honeybees and other pollinators, helping to ensure good fruit set in crops such as eggplants, peppers, squash, and tomatoes.

Finally, interplanting confuses plant pests. When you mass eggplants, for example, sphinx moths can spot these host plants quickly. But when these crops are mixed with other plants in a rich tapestry, the moth is more likely to miss its target and lay its eggs elsewhere.

To learn more about Shoulder to Shoulder Farm and its techniques, send $4 for a catalog to Box 1509, Philomath, OR 97370; (541) 929-4068. ◆

GARNET FRINGE: Purple peppers inspired this planting. Tricolor culinary sage, front left, and 'Firecracker' peppers (center, from Shepherd's Garden Seeds) echo their hue. Revving up the color scheme are the fiercely red, cockscomb-shaped flowers of celosia and the tassel-like seed heads of 'Burgundy Splendor' amaranth. Amaranth seeds come from Ornamental Edibles; celosia is available in nurseries.

DOGWOOD BLOSSOMS unfurl over lacy Japanese maples, mugho pines, and flowering perennials in this Portland garden. For details on this luxuriant living tapestry, see page 134.

May

gardenguide

Botanical treasures

Discover a wealth
of planting ideas
in Albuquerque

■ If you're planning a garden
in New Mexico's high desert
(*Sunset* climate zone 10),
pay a visit to the Rio Grande
Botanic Garden in Albu-
querque. It's full of ideas for
using water-thrifty landscape
plants. Opened in 1996, the
10-acre garden is still young,
but it's already clear that
indigenous Southwest plants
are filling in fastest, just as
they're likely to do in your
garden.

You'll also see non-native
plants used to maximum
effect, like the summer annuals shown at right. The Cere-
monial Rose Garden should

FLOWERS FILL
the home
demonstration
garden (right).
Below,
conservatories
rise over the site.

CHARLES MANN (2)

be in full bloom this month.

Two conservatories house
magnificent collections of
plants. The Mediterranean
Conservatory's herbs and
flowers are most fragrant in
the morning. The adjacent
Desert Conservatory displays
plants of the Chihuahuan
and Sonoran deserts.

Rio Grande Botanic Gar-
den, at 2601 Central Avenue
N.W., is part of Albuquerque's
Biological Park. Admission
($4.50, $2.50 ages 12 and
under or 65 and over) also
includes the Albuquerqu
Aquarium, which is on th
same site. Open 9 to 5 daily,
to 6 Memorial Day and week
ends thereafter; call (505
764-6200.

In May, Friends of th
Rio Grande Botanic Garde
usually holds its annua
Roses & Sage Garden Tou
of 8 or 10 home gardens
plus a weekend garden exp
at the Botanic Garden. Fo
more details, call (505) 292
6910.

— Jim McCauslan

Rhodie paradise in Portland

■ Now in its 52nd year, Portland's Crystal Springs Rhododendron Garden looks better than ever. During peak bloom, from mid-April to mid-May, you'll see clouds of color bursting from a world-class collection of more than 5,000 azaleas and rhododendrons. You can get a panoramic view of the garden from the new public viewing area at the entrance. The 7 acres of landscaped grounds embrace a spring-fed lake and three waterfalls.

The garden is on S.E. 28th Ave., one block north of Woodstock Blvd., across from Reed College. Grounds are open daily during daylight hours; $2 Thu-Mon, free Tue-Wed and for ages 11 and under. For more information, call (503) 256-2483.

— *Steven R. Lorton*

JANET LOUGHREY

Fiesta impatiens

■ Double used to mean trouble, as far as bedding impatiens were concerned. Plants of the Rosebud series, one of the first double-flowered impatiens, bloomed sporadically, dropped buds when unhappy, tended to get leggy, and otherwise misbehaved. But Fiesta, a new line of double-flowered impatiens from Ball Horticultural Company, seems to have addressed all complaints. This new impatiens blooms early and often, sidebranches readily to form full plants, and hangs onto its blooms a long time. It's showy yet solid—just what you want in a bedding plant.

The bushy habit and floriferous nature of Fiesta impatiens make them excellent candidates for hanging baskets, according to Ted Mayeda of M&M Nursery in Orange. 'Sparkler Rose', a pinkish white and bright rose bicolor (shown here), happens to be his favorite, but there are eight other colors on the market. Though Fiesta looks great solo, it mixes well, too. Mayeda especially likes it with lacy ferns or with begonias and trailing ivy.

For a long season of bloom, Mayeda adds 14-14-14 controlled-release fertilizer to the potting soil when planting and feeds his baskets monthly thereafter with a 15-30-15 liquid fertilizer.

— *Sharon Cohoon*

NORMAN A. PLATE

Grow sunflowers for bouquets or for screening

NORMAN A. PLATE (2)

THE BEST VARIETIES FOR CUTTING

■ Sunflowers aren't just sunny yellow anymore. Now they come in a striking range of colors. Midsize varieties are best for cutting. Pollenless types won't shed on tabletops.

Pollenless

All from W. Atlee Burpee & Co. (800/888-1447): 'Del Sol' (early yellow, 5 ft. tall), 'Indian Blanket' (red with yellow tips, 4–5 ft.), 'Lemon Eclair' (lemon yellow, 4–6 ft.), 'Moonshadow' (pale yellow to creamy white, 4 ft.), Parasol Mix (lemon, orange, red, and bicolor in mixed forms, 3–5 ft.).

With pollen

From Park Seed (800/845-3369): Large Flowered Mix (left; yellow, red, and bronze, 6–10 ft.). From Renee's Garden (888/880-7228 or www.garden.com/reneesgarden): 'Bright Bandolier' (yellow and mahogany mix, 5–7 ft.), 'Cinnamon Sun' (cinnamon-bronze, 4–7 ft.), and Renee's favorite, 'Valentine' (chiffon yellow, 4–5 ft.). From Shepherd's Garden Seeds (860/482-3638): 'Prado Red' (red, 3½–4 ft.) and 'Velvet Queen' (bronze, burgundy, chestnut red, and mahogany, 6–8 ft.). — *Lauren Bonar Swezey*

PLANT A SUNFLOWER HEDGE

■ In summer, when sidewalks are busy, Judith Becker McQueen grows an 80-foot-long hedge of sunflowers across the front of her Seattle garden. Dwarf plants (1–2 ft.) such as 'Big Smile' and 'Music Box' grow on the sidewalk side, and tall ones (4–5 ft.) such as 'Floristan' grow on the lawn side. When sidewalk traffic disappears for the winter, so does the hedge.

To make a hedge like McQueen's, you can start the sunflowers from seed, as she did, or from nursery seedlings. Here's how.

From seed. Dig a bed the length you want, and about 24 inches wide. Mix generous amounts of compost into the soil. Plant the seeds about 8 inches apart, in rows for a thick cover. (To extend the bloom season, stagger the planting over a two-week period.) Moisten the soil. After true leaves appear, water the plants deeply once a week using a soaker hose. Fertilize once when plants are actively growing, using a controlled-release complete organic fertilizer. Bait slugs and snails.

▲

From seedlings. Choose sturdy plants in 4-inch pots. Space them 8 inches apart in rows 4 to 6 inches apart. Knock them from their pots, free up any coiled roots, and plant in well-amended soil.
— *S.R.L.*

BEN WOOLSEY

A secret garden

You might say that former astronaut Pete Conrad launched a secret garden for his wife, Nancy. He chose the fountain with the two cherubs shown below. But it was Nancy who realized the fountain demanded new surroundings. "I just knew it called for an English garden," she says, "even though at the time I had no idea what that meant."

Fortunately, garden designer Cory Kelso did. Kelso began by greening up the stucco walls with jasmine, hardenbergia, and trumpet vines. Then she livened up the beds with plants that have interesting foliage, such as silver-laced *Lamium galeobdolon*. In between she squeezed as many flowering shrubs and perennials and bulbs as possible. "To keep things from getting too sweet" and to brighten up a rather shady space, she stuck to bright pastels.

The crowning touch that snaps the garden into focus is the trompe l'oeil gate at one end of the path. Though the "gate" pretends to lead to another English garden, it actually hides a potting shed. Once a woman who never touched dirt, Nancy Conrad has been converted, through her secret garden, into a

Trompe l'oeil gate and burbling fountain make this small garden magical

passionate gardener. And she's become pretty territorial about her space. "Pete and I have a rule," she says. "I stay out of his cockpit, and he stays out of my garden."
PLANTINGS: Cory Kelso, Cory's Cottage Garden, Huntington Beach; (714) 964-2448.
TROMPE L'OEIL GATE: Susan Marosz, Corona del Mar; (949) 644-6240.

— *S.C.*

BRIGHT PASTEL flowers include roses (top) and 'Gartenmeister Bonstedt' fuchsias (flanking fountain, above).

STEVEN GUNTHER (2)

Colorful compromise in Paradise Valley

■ Municipal landscaping codes in Paradise Valley, Arizona, require residential gardens to merge with the surrounding wilderness as seamlessly as possible. Yet homeowners yearn for splashes of color that native plants alone can't always provide. In the garden shown here, Phoenix landscape designer Mary Hoffmann found a way to honor the code and satisfy her client's appetite for color at the same time.

As foundation plants, Hoffmann used sweet acacia trees, 'Green Cloud' sage, thornless Chilean mesquite, and spineless Indian fig. Yellow-flowered brittlebush (*Encelia farinosa*), planted at the outskirts of the garden, echoes the wild plants in the foothills beyond. In May, the brittlebush and the bougainvillea planted near the house compete to see which can put out the most color.

BRITTLEBUSH (foreground) and red 'Barbara Karst' bougainvillea bloom in May.

Native to the Sonoran Desert, brittlebush grows well in zones 11 though 13; it is hardy to about 26°. In the wild, brittlebush plants semidefoliate and look brown in summer. But with supplemental irrigation, they retain their handsome silver foliage and rebloom sporadically throughout the year.

Hoffmann chose the bougainvillea 'Barbara Karst' ("the most reliable variety for the desert," she says). Bougainvillea can be grown outdoors in zones 12 and 13. — *S.C.*

BACK TO BASICS

ALEXIS SEABROOK

Caging large tomato plants yields the most fruit and provides the most protection against sunburn, especially in hot climates. Veteran growers often make their own cages and set them around tomatoes at planting time. To make a cage, buy a 6½-foot length of 5- or 6-foot-wide concrete-reinforcing wire with 6-inch mesh (or use rustproof galvanized fence wire). Roll the wire into a cylinder 24 inches in diameter, as shown in the drawing, bending the ends over to fasten. To anchor the cage so it won't topple in the wind, drive two 2- by 2-inch stakes or lengths of rebar into the ground on opposite sides of the cage and tie them to the wire. — *S.C.*

Paris roses come to Descanso

If you can't make it to Paris this spring to see the famous rambling roses at the Roseraie de l'Haÿ-les-Roses nearby, drop by the Rosarium at Descanso Gardens in La Cañada Flintridge. The rambling roses that twine up posts and weave across steel chains here are the same kind you'd see on the grand trellises at the Roseraie—Wichuraiana hybrids.

Most Wichuraiana hybrids were developed between 1900 and 1920 when the craze of training roses on pillars and pergolas was at its peak. The long, flexible canes and heavy bloom clusters of Wichuraianas make them ideal for swags, according to Mary Brosius, the Rosarium curator. Unlike other climbing roses, which usually get

only light pruning, Wichuraianas should be retrained every year. At the end of the growing season, untwine the canes and cut away all but two or three of the strongest new ones. "It's easier than it sounds," says Brosius. "Just

treat them like blackberries."

Descanso Gardens, 1418 Descanso Dr. 9–4:30 daily. Admission costs $5, $3 ages 62 and over, $1 students.

Where to find Wichuraianas: 'New Dawn' is often available at nurseries.

'Alberic Barbier' (shown above) and the rest of Descanso's Wichuraianas are available by mail from Heirloom Old Garden Roses, 24062 N.E. Riverside Dr., St. Paul, OR 97137; catalog $5; (503) 538-1576. — S.C.

The good and bad news on neem

First the good news: Neem, an organic insecticide/miticide/fungicide derived from the tropical neem tree (*Azadirachta indica*) is now approved for use on edibles such as fruits, nuts, vegetables, and herbs to control insect pests like aphids, mites, various beetles, scales, and whiteflies. Products containing clarified hydrophobic extract of neem oil, which have

a broader application than those with just the active ingredient azadirachtin, can also control plant diseases

such as powdery mildew, anthracnose, and rust.

Now the bad news: Until recently, neem-based insecticides, like other botanical insecticides, were believed to have little impact on beneficial insects such as ladybugs. But researchers at Washington State University have proven otherwise. They found that high concentrations of the pesticide killed large numbers of ladybugs and their larvae.

How does all this stack up? Neem is still a valuable organic pesticide that has much less impact on the environ-

ment than stronger chemicals. But it must be used with caution—only when pest problems are severe and threaten the survival or productivity of your plants. Do not spray it when beneficial insects like ladybugs are active. Chances are, the ladybugs will catch up and eventually control aphids anyway. If not, knock aphids off your plants with a blast of water.

Neem-based products are available in nurseries. Read labels carefully to identify crops on which they can be used and how to apply them properly. — *Lance Walheim*

Great mountain climbers

■ Climbing roses add color and fragrance to arbors and fences. But the harsh climates of the West's mountain regions won't tolerate wimpy plants. Which climbers are tough enough to resist our freezing winters and dry summers? Rosarians and nursery growers helped us compile the list of winners (source information is abbreviated after each item; see key at end). Select and set out any of them this month. Plant deep in a large hole amended with plenty of compost or aged manure, and water deeply during summer. Keep plants mulched year-round.

'Dortmund' (HCR). Large, single, bright red blossoms with white eyes and bright yellow stamens; sharp fragrance; 8 to 10 feet.

'Eden Rose' (HOGR). Fully double blossoms are

'ZÉPHIRINE DROUHIN' has 6- to 10-foot canes.

creamy white tinged with lavender pink; faint scent; 8 to 10 feet.

'Fourth of July' (ER). Red semidouble blossoms striped with white; apple-and-rose perfume; 6 to 8 feet.

'Henry Kelsey' (HCR). Clusters of bright red semidouble blossoms; 6 to 8 feet.

'Mme. Alfred Carrière' (HOGR). Old rose with hybrid-tea-style blooms of softest pink; heady scent of musk and citrus; 15 feet.

Mr. Nash (HCR). A "mystery rose" discovered in Denver in 1940, it bears masses of 4-inch apricot-buff blossoms; spicy fragrance; 10 to 15 feet.

'New Dawn' (HCR). Light pink blossoms; apple-and-rose perfume; 10 to 15 feet.

'Zéphirine Drouhin' (HOGR). Bright cerise pink semidouble blooms; intense spicy scent; 6 to 10 feet.

Source key:

ER Edmunds' Roses (888/481-7673).

HCR High Country Roses (800/552-2082).

HOGR Heirloom Old Garden Roses (503/538-1576; catalog $5).

— *John Starnes*

Lushly layered landscape

A Portland designer weaves a luxuriant living tapestry

■ From the sidewalk to the skyline, layer upon layer of flowers and foliage give the Portland garden pictured on page 126 a richly textured look. Landscape designer Margaret de Haas van Dorsser carefully placed the deciduous and evergreen trees and perennial plants to create multiple levels of interest.

The canopy is formed by the airy branches of Eastern dogwood (*Cornus florida*). In spring, its pink blossoms play off the deep purple leaves of a Japanese maple (*Acer palmatum* 'Bloodgood') growing just below.

The middle layer is formed by the evergreen boughs of two mugho pines, whose branch tips sport "candles" of new spring growth. Beneath the pines is a laceleaf Japanese maple (*A. p.* 'Dissectum Atropurpureum').

Tucked among the trees are low-growing perennials, including white candytuft and blue forget-me-nots. Dotting the foreground are magenta aubrieta and pale blue bellflower.

The owner prunes lightly but regularly to maintain the open, lacy effect. The pines' candles are pinched back halfway to keep the plants compact. She waters weekly during dry summer weather. In late winter or early spring, she gives the garden a thorough weeding and lays down a 4-inch layer of well-rotted manure, which enriches the soil and retards weeds.

— *S.R.L.*

Pacific Northwest Checklist

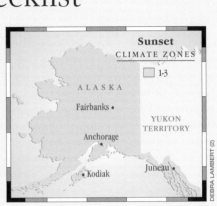

PLANTING

☑ **ANNUAL FLOWERS.** Set out transplants from sixpacks or 4-inch pots as soon as the danger of frost is past.

☑ **DAHLIAS.** Zones 1–3: Set out dahlia tubers. Stake tall varieties at planting time; if you wait until plants are in bloom, you risk puncturing tubers.

☑ **FUCHSIAS AND GERANIUMS.** Zones 4–7: Early in the month, get overwintered plants back into the ground or display them in outdoor containers. In zones 1–3, wait until month's end.

☑ **HERBS AND VEGETABLES.** Once the soil is warm (at least 60°), set out seedlings of herbs (basil, dill, fennel, lovage, rosemary, sage, and thyme) and warm-season vegetables (cucumbers, eggplant, peppers, and tomatoes). Sow seeds of beans, corn, melons, pumpkins, and squash directly in the ground.

MAINTENANCE

☑ **CLIP HEDGES.** If you prune hedges twice annually, shear or clip them between now and early June, then again in mid- to late summer. Prune so the bottom of the hedge is wider than the top, allowing sunlight and rain to reach all the foliage.

☑ **FERTILIZE PLANTS.** Once newly set-out annuals get established, begin feeding them with a liquid fertilizer. For shrubs, scatter a balanced granular fertilizer (15-15-15, for example) around the base of the plant. You can use either liquid or granular fertilizer for perennials. Remember: It is better to underfeed plants than to overfertilize, which results in foliage burn—or worse, death.

☑ **FEED LAWNS.** Midmonth is an excellent time to apply a high-nitrogen fertilizer evenly over lawns to keep grass growing thick and green. Water immediately after fertilizing, unless the rain does it for you.

☑ **PRUNE.** If you prune flowering shrubs like lilacs and rhododendrons while they are in bloom, you can use flowers for indoor bouquets. Remove damaged, crossing, and deformed branches first. Then prune for shape, cutting from the bottom of the plant up and from the inside out.

PEST CONTROL

☑ **APHIDS AND TENT CATERPILLARS.** One of the easiest ways of dealing with these pests is to blast them off plants with a strong jet of water from the hose. Insecticidal soap also works to rid plants of aphids.

☑ **SLUGS.** Handpick, set out beer traps, or turn ducks loose in your garden to control them. To protect young transplants, spread a circle of bait around each plant. ◆

Northern California Checklist

PLANTING

☑ **SUMMER ANNUALS.** Fill bare spots in the garden with summer bedding plants. Choices include celosia, dahlia, gomphrena, Madagascar periwinkle, marigold, petunia, portulaca, salvia, scabiosa, verbena, and zinnia. In shadier areas try begonias, browallia, and coleus.

☑ **FLOWERS FOR CUTTING.** Long-blooming perennials provide a good source of cut flowers. Try alstroemeria, coreopsis, gaillardia, gloriosa daisy, lavender, purple coneflower, scabiosa, Shasta daisy, and yarrow.

☑ **SUBTROPICALS.** Late spring is the ideal time to plant gardenia, hibiscus, mandevilla, plumeria, and other subtropicals that thrive in heat. Locate plants where they'll get as much warmth as possible (against a heat-reflecting wall, for instance). Grow mandevillas and plumerias in large pots; when temperatures begin to cool in fall, move mandevilla under a patio overhang and plumeria indoors for winter.

☑ **VEGETABLES.** May is prime time to plant heat-loving vegetables, such as beans, corn, eggplant, melons, okra, peppers, pumpkins, squash, and tomatoes. Zones 1–2, 17: Grow short-season varieties and plant through black plastic (to protect from late spring frosts). Covering vegetables with row covers can give them an added boost.

Sunset CLIMATE ZONES
- Mountain (1-2)
- Valley (7-9)
- Inland (14)
- Coastal (15-17)

DEBRA LAMBERT

☑ **SET OUT TOMATO SEEDLINGS.** Zones 7–9, 14–17: They're available at nurseries (Upstarts supplies a line of organic tomato seedlings to nurseries throughout the Bay Area). Plant tomatoes deeper than they were growing in the containers. Pull off the lowest one or two sets of leaves and set the plants in the planting holes so the stem is covered to just below the bottom leaf set; roots will form along the stem.

☑ **SHOP FOR MAPLES.** Zones 7–9, 14–17: Wildwood Farm Nursery & Gardens (10300 Sonoma Hwy., Kenwood, CA 95452; 707/833-1161) now carries more than 200 Japanese and other maples. Visit in person or on the Web at www.wildwoodmaples.com. Or order by mail (plants are shipped November-May).

☑ **SHOP FOR ROSES.** Are you having difficulty finding a certain rose? Check out www.findmyroses.com, a Web site that provides sources for thousands of new and antique roses. Amity Heritage Roses in San Jose (408/286-7882 or www.amityheritageroses.com) is one of the sources you'll find there. Amity ships year-round.

MAINTENANCE

☑ **APPLY IRON CHELATE.** If azalea, camellia, citrus, or gardenia foliage is yellowish with green veins, the plants need iron. Apply iron chelate according to label directions.

☑ **REMOVE SUCKERS.** Leafy, fast-growing shoots arising from rootstocks of roses, fruit trees, and some ornamental trees compete for water and nutrients. They also ruin plant form. Cut them back flush with the trunk or ground. On mature trees, snap off any new unwanted growth along the main trunk (retain growth on new trees for a season). ◆

Southern California Checklist

PLANTING

☑ **VEGETABLES.** Set out basil, cucumber, eggplant, melon, pepper, squash, and tomato plants. Sow lima and snap beans, corn, cucumbers, melon, okra, pumpkins, and summer and winter squash. In the low desert (zone 13), plant Jerusalem artichokes, okra, peppers, and sweet peppers.

☑ **SUBTROPICALS.** This is the best time of year to plant avocados, bananas, cherimoyas, citrus, guavas, mangos, and other tropical and subtropical fruits, if appropriate for your area. Late spring is also an excellent time for planting bougainvillea, gardenia, ginger, hibiscus, and other subtropical ornamentals.

☑ **SUMMER ANNUALS.** Choices include celosia, gomphrena, Madagascar periwinkle, marigold, petunia, portulaca, salvia, verbena, and zinnia. In shadier areas try begonia, browallia, coleus, impatiens, and lobelia.

☑ **PERENNIALS.** They're still plentiful at nurseries. For the most show for your money, look for varieties that are just starting their season and will continue blooming well into fall. These include reblooming daylilies, gaillardia, gaura, penstemon, pentas, rudbeckia, salvias, and yarrow.

Sunset
CLIMATE ZONES

1-3 7-9 11 13 14-24

DEBRA LAMBERT

MAINTENANCE

☑ **PINCH BACK MUMS.** For an ample supply of flowers and an attractive bushy plant, continue pinching back the growing tips of chrysanthemum plants through July.

☑ **REPLENISH MULCH.** Three to 6 inches of mulch around trees, shrubs, and established perennials keep roots cool and moist and discourages weeds. Leave a clear area around the base of trunks and stems to prevent disease.

☑ **STEP UP WATERING.** As temperatures warm up, plants need water more often. Carefully monitor seedlings and transplants. Give them frequent shallow watering for a few weeks to establish new roots. Also check container plants frequently. To rejuvenate a dry rootball, set entire pot in large pan of water. When the soil is thoroughly wet, lift out pot and drain.

☑ **TEND TOMATOES.** Late spring/early summer heat waves and overfertilizing can trigger blossom-end rot. To prevent this frustrating disease, be stingy with feeding, mulch deeply, and maintain even soil moisture. In hottest areas, cover plants with shadecloth or screening to prevent sunburn.

PEST CONTROL

☑ **COMBAT POWDERY MILDEW.** Warm days and cool nights are ideal conditions for powdery mildew in susceptible plants like roses. Prevent by hosing off foliage frequently in early mornings to wash off spores. Or spray plants with 1 tablespoon each baking soda and horticultural oil diluted in 1 gallon of water.

☑ **MANAGE INSECT PESTS.** Spray or dust plants that have pest caterpillars (such as cabbage worms) with *Bacillus thuringiensis*. Spray aphids, mites, and whiteflies with insecticidal soap or horticultural oil, or release green lacewings. Trap, handpick, or bait snails and slugs. ◆

Mountain Checklist

PLANTING

☑ **ANNUAL COLOR.** Shop nurseries early to get the best selection of plants. Use row covers to protect seedlings until the danger of frost is past.

☑ **LAWNS.** Sow bluegrass, fescue, perennial ryegrass, or—better—a combination of the three in tilled, raked, and fertilized soil. To overseed bare or worn spots in an existing lawn, rough up the soil surface with a rake, scatter seed, cover lightly with compost or peat moss, and keep the soil moist until the grass is tall enough to mow.

☑ **PERENNIALS.** Plant bleeding heart, bluebell, blue flax, campanula, columbine, coral bells, delphinium, gaillardia, geranium, hellebore, Iceland and Oriental poppy, lady's-mantle, Lamium maculatum, lupine, Maltese cross, penstemon, phlox, primrose, purple coneflower, Russian sage, Shasta daisy, sweet woodruff, veronica, and yarrow.

☑ **LANDSCAPE PLANTS.** Most trees, shrubs, vines, and ground covers can be set out this month.

MONTANA
Helena

Boise
IDAHO   WYOMING

Cheyenne

NEVADA   Salt Lake
City
Reno   Denver

UTAH   COLORADO

Las
Vegas

Sunset
CLIMATE ZONES
☐ 1-3   ☐ 10-11

DEBRA LAMBERT

☑ **VEGETABLES.** Set out seedlings of cool-season crops. Sow seeds of corn, cucumbers, eggplant, melons, peppers, squash, and tomatoes right away for transplanting after danger of frost is past; if frost is no longer a threat in your area, you can sow all of these, plus beans, directly in the ground now. One good source for seeds of warm-season crops is D.V. Burrell Seed Growers Co., Box 150, Rocky Ford, CO 81067; (719) 254-3318. This nearly century-old firm specializes in melons, peppers, squash, and tomatoes, including many open-pollinated varieties. Try 'Aztec Hybrid' zucchini (butter yellow fruit) or 'Navajo Sweet' watermelon. Burrell also sells herbs and flowers.

MAINTENANCE

☑ **CARE FOR TOMATOES.** Stake or cage indeterminate kinds, which keep growing all season, to stop them from flopping over. Keep soil moisture even to minimize blossom-end rot.

☑ **FERTILIZE.** Dig 1 to 2 pounds of complete fertilizer per 100 square feet into the soil before planting flowers or vegetables. Feed spring-flowering shrubs after they bloom. Start a monthly fertilization program for long-blooming annuals and perennials and container plants.

☑ **MOVE HOUSE PLANTS OUTDOORS.** After the last frost, most house plants (but not orchids) can move outside to a shady, windless place for the summer.

☑ **MAKE COMPOST.** Alternate 4-inch-thick layers of green matter (grass clippings and fresh weeds) and brown matter (dead leaves and straw), watering the pile between layers. Turn the pile weekly and you'll have compost within two months.

☑ **MULCH PLANTS.** Spread ground bark, compost, grass clippings, or rotted leaves around plants to hold in soil moisture and retard weeds.

☑ **PRUNE FLOWERING ORNAMENTALS.** After bloom ends, prune spring-flowering plants such as azalea, lilac, mock orange, rhododendron, and spiraea. ◆

Southwest Checklist

PLANTING

☑ **FLOWERS. Zones 10–13:** Set out ageratum, celosia, coreopsis, cosmos, firebush (*Hamelia patens*), four o'clock, gaillardia, globe amaranth, gloriosa daisy, kochia, lantana, lisianthus, nicotiana, portulaca, salvia, strawflower, tithonia, vinca rosea (*Catharanthus roseus*), and zinnia. Zones 1–2: Set out all of the above after danger of frost is past.

☑ **LANDSCAPE PLANTS. Zones 1–2, 10–11:** Set out trees, shrubs, vines, and ground covers from containers.

☑ **LAWNS. Zones 12–13:** Plant Bermuda grass, blue grama, or buffalo grass when night temperatures average 70° or warmer. Zones 1–2, 10 (Albuquerque): Plant or overseed with bluegrass, fescue, ryegrass, or a blend of these early in the month.

☑ **SUMMER BULBS.** Plant canna, crocosmia, dahlia, daylily, gladiolus, and Mexican shell flower (*Tigridia*). In zones 12–13, also plant agapanthus, caladium, and crinum. In zone 13 (Phoenix), plant society garlic (*Tulbaghia violacea*).

☑ **VEGETABLES. Zones 12–13:** Set out eggplant, Jerusalem artichokes, okra, peanuts, peppers, soybeans, summer squash, and sweet potatoes. Zones 10–11: Plant all of the above plus cucumbers, melons, pumpkins, and Southern peas; in zone 10 also plant

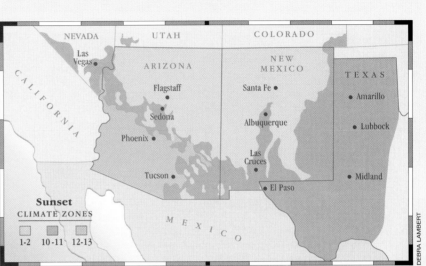

beans, corn, radishes, and tomatoes. Zones 1–2: Set out cool-season crops, and sow warm-season crops such as corn, cucumbers, eggplant, melons, peppers, squash, and tomatoes right away for transplanting into the garden after danger of frost has passed.

MAINTENANCE

☑ **CARE FOR CITRUS.** After watering, spread 1 cup ammonium sulfate per inch of trunk diameter, then water again. To treat chlorosis, apply chelated iron, zinc, and magnesium. Irrigate mature trees by soaking the ground two to three hours every two to three weeks (more in sandy soil, less in clay); soak young trees one to two hours each week.

☑ **CARE FOR ROSES. Zones 11–13:** Water, mulch, deadhead, and fertilize.

☑ **FERTILIZE.** Feed long-blooming annuals, perennials, and container plants monthly. Feed flowering shrubs after bloom.

☑ **INCREASE WATERING.** When the first 100° days come, check plants (especially new growth) at least twice a day for wilting. ◆

SUNSET MAGAZINE'S

Idea Gardens

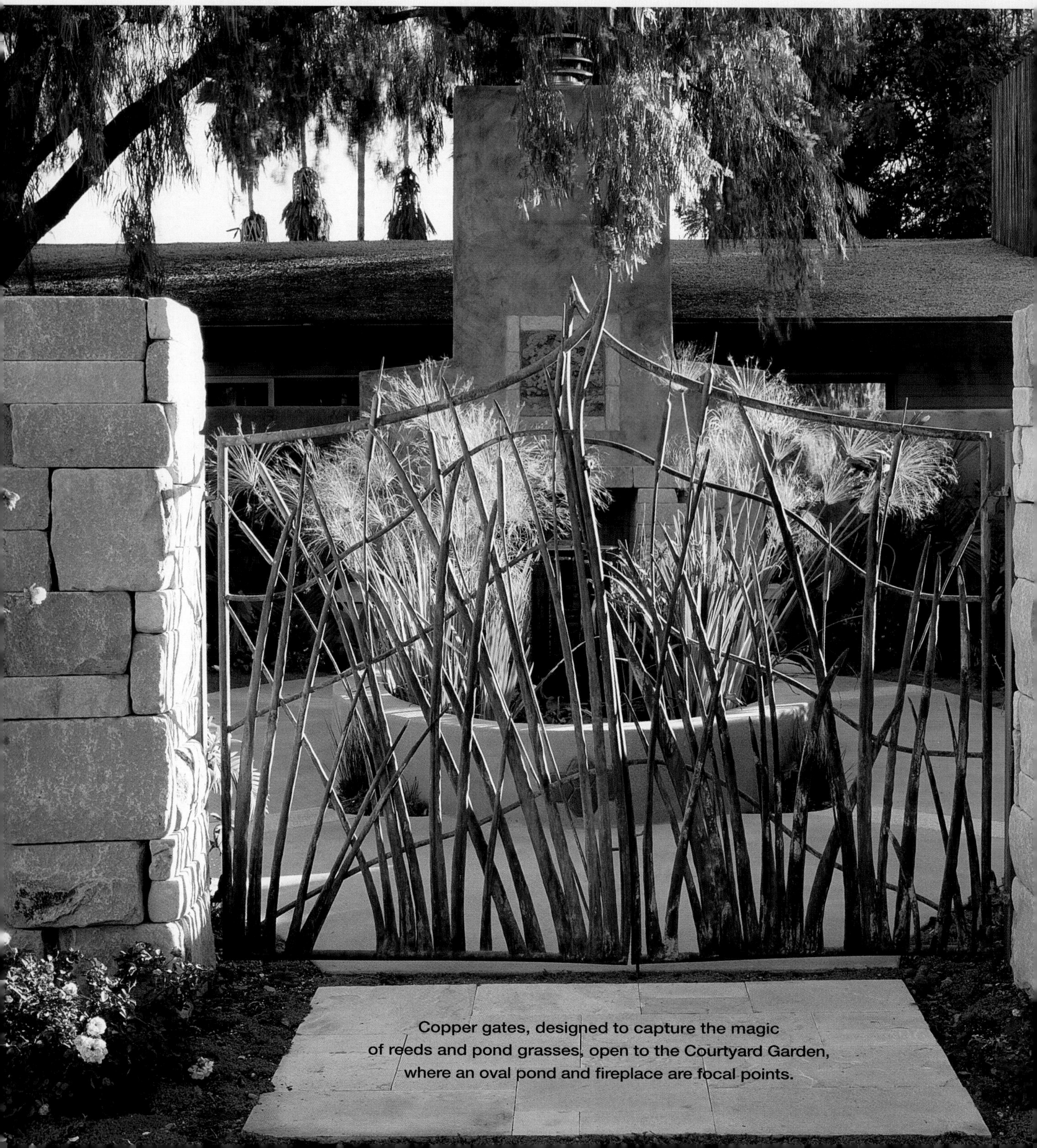

Copper gates, designed to capture the magic of reeds and pond grasses, open to the Courtyard Garden, where an oval pond and fireplace are focal points.

Sunset and the Arboretum of Los Angeles County team up again
to showcase the latest designs for outdoor living in the West

BY KATHLEEN N. BRENZEL AND PETER O. WHITELEY

Photographs of beautiful gardens may inspire, but there's nothing like a walk down a real garden path to bring design ideas to life. That's the intent of *Sunset's* new demonstration garden at the Arboretum of Los Angeles County.

For more than 40 years, our garden—just inside the entrance to the arboretum's parklike grounds—has provided visitors with ideas for everything from paving and fencing to water features, furnishings, and plantings. Scores of visitors (including classes of landscape design students) have collected ideas here.

But times change. So do garden styles, materials, and the way we use our outdoor spaces. In 1996, *Sunset* and the arboretum staff, under the direction of arboretum superintendent John Provine, began planning the new gardens. *Sunset* editors identified the types of outdoor living spaces that today's homeowners want most. Then, to bring widespread community thinking to the project, we invited Southern California landscape architects to submit plans. In 1998, we leveled the old garden to make way for the new ones.

The master plan divides the 1½-acre space into eight small gardens plus an education/demonstration area, all linked by a serpentine walkway. Each garden presents a theme that translates well to a broad range of residential situations. In each garden you'll see the latest products for landscaping and outdoor living, from synthetic wood decking to state-of-the-art barbecues.

On the following pages are ideas from the gardens that you can use no matter where in the West you live. And if travels take you to the Arcadia area, drop by the garden for a visit.

Arboretum of Los Angeles County, 301 N. Baldwin Ave., Arcadia, CA; 9–4:30 daily. $5, $3 students and ages 62 and over, $1 ages 5–12. (626) 821-3222.

Sunset Magazine Demonstration Garden
Visit and take away ideas

Gardening under the Oaks

STEVEN GUNTHER (2)

Inspired by California's native oak woodland, this garden shows plants growing as they might in their native habitat. Ornamental grasses planted among stones change their appearance with the seasons; they're as beautiful when dry and brown in fall as they are when green. Other plantings are minimal, drought-resistant, and appropriate for this timeless California environment.

A straw bale wall in the background has an undulating surface of hand-laid plaster. Subtle "petroglyph" paintings of animals that once might have lived among the oaks embellish its adobe-colored surface.

Sculptural rock pyramids indicate the presence of man. In the spaces between the stones are native succulents.

Design: Jana Ruzicka, Hortulus, Laguna Beach, CA

Deck Garden

Decks have long been popular in Southern California. This one—embraced by water features and lush plantings and edged on one side by a bronze-red wall—is as beautiful as it is environmentally friendly.

Made of recycled plastic and wood pulp, the decking rests on a foundation that uses an existing concrete stem wall. The metal frames of the benches were salvaged from the waste stream, and the tops are of certified redwood. Low-voltage lighting, sculptural elements, handmade pavers, and an arbor of redwood (from an environmentally certified source) also enrich the space.

Design: Jane MacDonald Adrian, Environmental Interests, La Crescenta, CA

▼ **Dining and Entertainment Patio.** This timeless patio has all the comforts of home: a state-of-the-art barbecue with tile counter and sink, a firepit for toasting marshmallows, a water feature for a touch of serenity, and an outdoor fireplace to gather around on chilly evenings. Anchoring each of these elements are large, man-made boulders, manufactured on the site.

In the background is a screen, made of recycled timbers colored with copper verdigris paint, and underfoot is a stained, embossed concrete floor as interesting as a Persian carpet. The fireplace, counter base, and wall are formed with Rastra blocks (made of recycled plastic foam and cement).

Small beds and planting pockets around the garden contain a richly textured mix of succulents and drought-tolerant plants.

The garden is both fun and functional.

Design: Nick Williams, Nick Williams & Associates, Tarzana, CA

Dining and Entertainment Patio

Courtyard Garden

The classic elements of life—water, fire, earth, and air—come together in this luxuriant small garden.

As you enter through copper gates, designed to mimic reeds and pussy willows that grow near creeks, the comforting sound of spilling water greets you. The water cascades from a shallow copper bowl atop a tall sculpture in a densely planted pond. With the flip of a switch, a blue-orange flame bursts from the center of the bowl, infusing the garden with a magical, rosy glow. Fragrant citrus trees grow in urns on either side of the courtyard; behind them, lush plantings include azaleas, espaliered Sasanqua camellias, and dwarf mondo grass. Against the back wall, the notched hearth of a tall fireplace provides intimate tête-à-tête seating. Low night lighting and metal sculptures contribute to the courtyard's magic.

Design: Nick Williams, Nick Williams & Associates, Tarzana, CA

▼ **Nostalgia Garden.** The romance of our grandmothers' gardens is captured in the perennial borders and broken concrete paths of this outdoor space. A gently sloping site helped shape the garden's simple, straightforward design.

Around the circular lawn—just big enough for romping toddlers and perhaps a picnic blanket or two—shrubs, perennials, and herbs provide fragrance, color, and texture. Recycled broken concrete, stacked without mortar, makes the low retaining wall and also the path, where it is set on sand. Pale yellow Adirondack chairs invite relaxation, and a collection of colorful birdhouses atop posts, in beds opposite the patio, reinforces the garden's tribute to the natural world.

Design: Jerry Williams, Outer Spaces, Toluca Lake, CA

Nostalgia Garden

Woodland Garden. Step into this garden with its stately conifers and mounding shrubs and suddenly you're in the cool, soothing mountain woods on a Sunday outing (for inspiration, the designers turned to coastal redwood forests and riparian habitats of Southern California's canyons). Off to one side of the path, a dry streambed filled with rounded boulders, cobblestones, pebbles, and sand typical of mountain washes meanders through low perennials and a meadowy collection of ornamental grasses. The designers chose plants that thrive in a warm Southern California climate but are in scale with an average suburban property.

On the other side of the path is a dry pond/vernal pool, designed to collect rainwater and irrigation runoff. A flagstone sitting area with a stone bench faces the garden and mountain vista; a stepping-stone path extends through areas not accessible from the main walkway.

Design: Anna Armstrong and Richard Walker, Armstrong & Walker Landscape Architecture, Monrovia, CA

Water Retreat. A curvaceous pond edged with layers of plants is the soothing focal point for this wooded retreat. Visitors step off the main walkway onto a serpentine gravel path inside a wall of trees, which will in time create a leafy screen.

Set back from the path is a secluded bench that invites contemplation or conversation amid low, plant-covered berms.

Design: David Squires, SAA Planning and Design, Santa Monica

▼ **Native Plant Garden.** A sculptural representation of a peaceful spring is at the heart of this garden, designed to capture the spirit of nature. Flowing paths that mimic a dry streambed lead to a seating area where boulders nudge the edges of the black granite slab. The highly polished slab is sandblasted with curves, stone shapes, and concentric circles to look as if stones had been thrown into water and the resulting ripples frozen in time.

Behind the "pool," easy-to-grow mahonia forms an informal hedge.

Design: Ronnie Siegel, Swire Siegel, Landscape Architects, La Cañada Flintridge, CA

Woodland
Garden

Native Plant
Garden

STEVEN GUNTHER (2)

NORMAN A. PLATE (5)

5 DETAILS

Adapt them to your own garden

All eight of our gardens are filled with ideas you can adapt to your own garden. Whether handmade pavers or faux-painted fireplaces, such details help enrich an outdoor room. Watch for other examples in upcoming issues of *Sunset*.

HANDMADE PAVERS, ABOVE, are colored-concrete squares that step up to the Deck Garden. Designer Jane Adrian textured them by lining wood frames with burlap and other materials, and setting in bits of tile, shells, and half slices of bamboo. (Watch for how-to details in an upcoming issue.)

WALL, BELOW, which edges the Dining and Entertainment Patio, uses recycled pieces of broken concrete that have been colored with chemical stains to impart warm tones. Planting pocket in front contains a tapestry mix of succulents and cactus.

FOUNTAIN, ABOVE, is etched-granite slab that slopes down to a shallow pool. The water rises through the deck and stone via a tube—from a recirculating pump hidden in a plastic pot below the grasses at right—then burbles down the trough to the rock below. The pool, beside the entry to the Deck Garden, is a shallow depression in the soil, covered with a plastic liner and river rock.

POLISHED STONE POND, ABOVE, has "water circles" formed by sandblasting and water jet (supplier on page 149). The red granite inset mimics a real mahonia leaf from nearby plants in the Native Plant Garden. Lightweight, manmade boulders that look like granite edge the "pond."

FAUX PAINT, BELOW, colors a stucco fireplace in the Courtyard Garden. Several layers of paint, in different muted colors, were applied with rags and brushes. Inset tile, an oak tree by Laguna Studio for Mission Tile, embellishes the chimney. Tiles around it are also faux-painted.

The plan and the architect

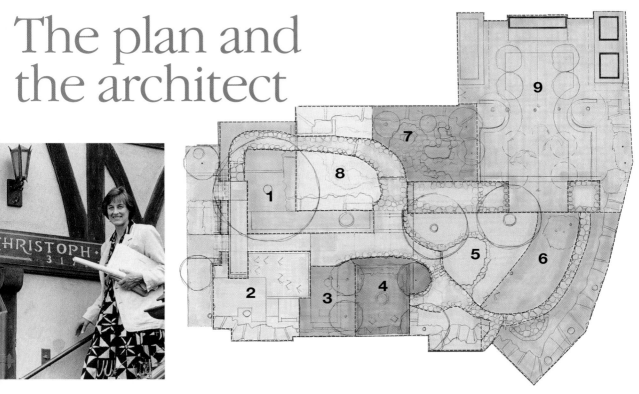

The master plan, designed by landscape architect Ann Christoph of Laguna Beach, California, divides the garden into eight theme gardens, detailed on the preceding pages: (1) Gardening under the Oaks; (2) Deck Garden; (3) Dining and Entertainment Patio; (4) Courtyard Garden; (5) Nostalgia Garden; (6) Woodland Garden; (7) Water Retreat; (8) Native Plant Garden; (9) education/demonstration area (under construction), designed by Bob Cardoza of Nuvis, Costa Mesa, California. "We wanted to unify the various spaces," Christoph says of the plan.

A sturdy arbor, designed by Ann Christoph, marks the entrance to the Sunset Magazine Demonstration Garden. Redwood for the arbor was donated by the California Redwood Association.

The contributors

Gardening under the Oaks

DESIGN
Jana Ruzicka, Hortulus,
530 Cress St., Laguna Beach, CA 92651;
(949) 494-8871

INSTALLATION: Jose Benitez Garcia, Hortulus
ARTIST: Leah Vasquez, 606 Bluebird Canyon Dr., Laguna Beach, CA 92651; (949) 494-5787
PLANT MATERIAL: Tree of Life Nursery, Box 635, San Juan Capistrano, CA 92693; (949) 728-0685
LIGHTING: Nightscaping, 1705 E. Colton Ave., Redlands, CA 92374; (909) 794-2121

Deck Garden

DESIGN AND INSTALLATION
Jane MacDonald Adrian, Environmental Interests, 3704 Foothill Blvd., La Crescenta, CA 91214; (818) 248-5221

SPONSOR
DECKING: Trex Company, 20 S. Cameron St., Winchester, VA 22601; (800) 289-8739

CONTRIBUTORS

TREATED FIR SUBSTRUCTURE: Western Wood Preservers Institute, 7017 N.E. Hwy. 99, Suite 108, Vancouver, WA 98665; (360) 693-9958

IRRIGATION: J. Harold Mitchell Co., 305 Agostino Rd., San Gabriel, CA 91776; (800) 675-7305

PLANT MATERIAL:

El Nativo Growers (wholesale), 200 S. Peckham Rd., Azusa, CA 91702; (626) 969-8449

Magic Growers (wholesale), 2800 Eaton Canyon Dr., Pasadena, CA 91107; (626) 797-6511

Native Sons Wholesale Nursery, 379 W. El Campo Rd., Arroyo Grande, CA 93420; (805) 481-5996

Persson's Nursery, 3115 E. Sierra Madre Blvd., Pasadena, CA 91107; (626) 792-6073

Hi-Mark Nursery (wholesale), 1635 Cravens Lane, Carpinteria, CA 93013; (805) 684-4462

REDWOOD:

Eco Timber International, 1020 Heinz Ave., Berkeley, CA 94710; (510) 549-3000

Certified Forest Products Council, 14780 S.W. Osprey Dr., Suite 285, Beaverton, OR, 97007; (503) 590-6600

GRANITE FOUNTAIN: Yoshikawa, 6190 Temple Hill Dr., Los Angeles, CA 90068; (323) 462-7139

FOUNTAIN AND POND, CERAMIC WALL PANELS: Antje Hamer, 22546 Sunlight Creek, Lake Forest, CA 92630; (949) 581-9759

WALL PAINTING, STEPPINGSTONES: Lynda Fenneman, 13007 Debby St., Van Nuys, CA 91401; (818) 785-3239

POTS: Asian Ceramics, 2600 E. Foothill Blvd., Pasadena, CA 91107; (626) 449-6800

LIGHT FIXTURES: Santa Barbara Illumination, Box 30176, Santa Barbara, CA 93130; (805) 962-2929

CONSTRUCTION: New Method Termite Control, 787 E. Washington Blvd., Suite 3, Pasadena, CA 91104; (626) 797-6012

Dining & Entertainment Patio

DESIGN

Nick Williams & Associates, 18751 Ventura Blvd., Suite 200, Tarzana, CA 91356; (818) 996-4010
Construction Coordinator: Tom Torre
Project Coordinator: Suzanne Manaugh
Landscape Coordinator: Kenny Vlasak

SPONSOR

Weber-Stephen Products Co.; Summit Grill

SUBCONTRACTORS

FIREPLACE: Sunwest Construction, 6586 Bernal St., Simi Valley, CA 93063; (805) 522-1546

CONCRETE: Lee's Lasting Impressions, 3859 Old Conejo Rd., Newbury Park, CA 91320; (805) 498-6303

WOOD SCREEN: Marvin "Spike" Dinovitz

MANUFACTURED BOULDERS: Preston Waterscapes

BARBECUE: Ortega Masonry

STONEWORK: SierraScapes

ARCHITECTURAL DRAWING: Erich Stein

SUPPLIERS

STONE AND BUILDING MATERIALS: Malibu Stone & Masonry Supply, 3730 Cross Creek Rd., Malibu, CA 90265; (310) 456-9444

SUCCULENTS: California Nursery Specialties, 8925 Densmore Ave., North Hills, CA 91343; (818) 894-5694

BARBECUE TILE: Busby Gilbert Custom Tile, 16021 Arminta St., Van Nuys, CA 91406; (818) 780-9460

WALLS AND BARBECUE MATERIAL: Environmental Building Technologies, 537 Newport Center Dr., Suite 365, Newport Beach, CA 92660; (949) 720-8712

PLANTS:

Pacific Arbor Nursery, 305 W. Hueneme Rd., Camarillo, CA 93012; (800) 426-2150
San Marcos Growers

IRRIGATION SUPPLIES: Yosef Amzalag Supply, 13650 Vaughn St., San Fernando, CA 91340; (818) 896-6633

LIGHTS: Rockscapes, 7924 Deering Ave., Unit B, Canoga Park, CA 91304; (818) 704-5195

REBAR: Bellis Steel, 8740 Vanalden Ave., Northridge, CA 91324; (818) 886-5601

CONCRETE: Spragues Ready Mix, 230 E. Longden Ave., Irwindale, CA 91706; (626) 445-2125

GARDEN ART: Zach Swanson

SPECIAL THANKS TO:

Del Anderson, Cal Mat, Miguel, Bernardino, Sergio, Luis, Homero, Hector, Carlos, Zach & Shana Swanson, Gail Goldstein, Tod Williams, Larry Heller, California Landscape Lighting, John Boething, Abel Hagoepian, Karen, Tree, Dawn, Nelson, Adrienne, Paul, John Taylor

Courtyard Garden

DESIGN

Nick Williams & Associates, 18751 Ventura Blvd., Suite 200, Tarzana, CA 91356; (818) 996-4010
Construction Coordinator: Tom Torre
Project Coordinator: Suzanne Manaugh
Landscape Coordinator: Kenny Vlasak

SUBCONTRACTORS

GATES: Copper Gardens, Box 341, Rough and Ready, CA 95975; (530) 432-9598

FIREPLACE PAINTING: Michael Pennington Fantasy Finishes; (805) 689-8690

WALLS: Ortega Masonry

FIREPLACE: Kinzel Construction

CONCRETE PANELS: Lasting Impressions

CONCRETE: SierraScapes

POND: Nicholas Waterscapes

SUPPLIERS

PLANTS: Green Thumb Nursery, 7659 Topanga Canyon Blvd., Canoga Park, CA 91304; (818) 348-9266

TILE: Mission Tile West, 853 Mission St., South Pasadena, CA 91030; (626) 799-4595

POTS: Pottery Etc., 7441 Canoga Ave., Canoga Park, CA 91303; (818) 704-0741

FIREPLACE: FCM Fireplaces, 4505 Manhattan Beach Blvd., Suite C, Lawndale, CA 90260; (310) 973-3537

MATERIAL FOR WALLS: Environmental Building Technologies, 537 Newport Center Dr., Suite 365, Newport Beach, CA 92660; (949) 720-8712

REBAR: Bellis Steel, 8740 Vanalden Ave., Northridge, CA 91324; (818) 886-5601

CONCRETE: Spragues Ready Mix, 230 E. Longden Ave., Irwindale, CA 91706; (626) 445-2125

IRRIGATION SUPPLIES: Yosef Amzalag Supply, 13650 Vaughn St., San Fernando, CA 91340; (818) 896-6633

STONE AND BUILDING MATERIALS: Malibu Stone & Masonry Supply

OAK TILE: Manufactured by Laguna Studio for Mission Tile

LIGHTS: Mica Lamp Company

FOUNTAIN: Tory Williams

BUILDING MATERIALS: Cal Mat

GARDEN ART: Zach Swanson

SPECIAL THANKS TO:

Del Anderson, Cal Mat, Miguel, Bernardino, Sergio, Luis, Homero, Hector, Carlos, Tory Williams, Zach & Shana Swanson, Matt Plaskoff, Tyler Bennett (deck builders), Joe Nolan, Peter Whiteley, Dan MacDonell, Jim

Gibbons, John Boething of Treeland, California Landscape Lighting, Joe Sperling, Abel Hagoepian

Nostalgia Garden

DESIGN

Jerry Williams, Outer Spaces, 10612 Bloomfield St., Toluca Lake, CA 91602; (818) 762-3163

CONTRIBUTORS

LANDSCAPE CONTRACTOR: Pierre Sprinkler & Landscape, 16015 Sherman Way, Van Nuys, CA 91406; (818) 373-0023

PLANT MATERIAL: Monrovia, Box 1385, Azusa, CA 91702; (888) 752-6848

LAWN: Southland Sod Farms, Box 579, Port Hueneme, CA 93044; (805) 488-3585

IRRIGATION: Toro Company, 5825 Jasmine St., Riverside, CA 92504; (909) 688-9221

LIGHTING: Lumiere Design & Manufacturing, 2382 Townsgate Rd.; Westlake Village, CA 91361; (805) 496-2003

SOIL AMENDMENTS: Kellogg Supply, 350 W. Sepulveda Blvd.; Carson, CA 90745; (310) 830-2200

MULCH: Whittier Fertilizer, Box 596, Pico Rivera, CA 90660; (562) 699-3461

BIRDHOUSES: Jim Hall, Burbank, CA

Woodland Garden

DESIGN

Armstrong & Walker Landscape Architecture, 434 N. Grand Ave., Suite 3, Monrovia, CA 91016; (626) 357-4599

CONTRIBUTORS

BOULDER PLACEMENT: Larry's Bobcat Service, 11450 San Felipe Ave., Chino, CA 91710; (626) 337-5587

COBBLE ROCK: Hanson Aggregates, Irwindale Plant, 16080 Arrow Hwy., Irwindale, CA 91706; (626) 856-6700

SOIL AMENDMENT: Cal-Blend Soils and Amendments, 13530 Live Oak Ave., Irwindale, CA 91706; (800) 425-3631

SOIL CONDITIONERS:

Plant Health Care, Mitchell Pest Control, 305 Agostino Rd., San Gabriel, CA 91776; (626) 287-1106

Broadleaf Industries P-4, 1041 W. 18th St., Suite A103, Costa Mesa, CA 92627; (800) 628-7374

IRRIGATION MATERIALS: Hunter Industries, 1940 Diamond St., San Marcos, CA 92069; (760) 744-5240

SPRINKLER HEADS: J. Harold Mitchell Company, 305 Agostino Rd., San Gabriel, CA 91776; (626) 287-1101

IRRIGATION PIPE AND INSTALLATION: Land Re:Vision, 1000 Fair Oaks Ave., Suite 110, South Pasadena, CA 91030; (626) 441-0455

STONE BENCH CONSTRUCTION: Dale Naber Masonry, 10352 Mountair Ave., Tujunga, CA 91042; (818) 353-1078

FERTILIZER: Gro-Power, 15065 Telephone Ave., Chino, CA 91710; (800) 473-1307

TREES: Arbor Nursery, Box 1138, Duarte, CA 91009; (626) 357-4823

MONETARY DONATION: Leroy Quisby Foundation

SHRUBS AND PERENNIALS:

Norman's Nursery, 8635 E. Duarte Rd., San Gabriel, CA 91775; (626) 285-9795

Magic Growers (wholesale), 2800 Eaton Canyon Dr., Pasadena, CA 91107; (626) 797-6511

Desert to Jungle Nursery, 3211 W. Beverly Blvd., Montebello, CA 90640; (323) 722-3976

NATIVE PLANTS: Rancho Santa Ana Botanic Garden, 1500 N. College Ave., Claremont, CA 91711; (909) 625-8767

TREE STAKES AND TIES: Home Depot, 1625 S. Mountain Ave., Monrovia, CA 91016; (626) 256-0580

RECYCLED BARK MULCH: Whittier Fertilizer, Box 596, Pico Rivera, CA 90660; (562) 699-3461

INSTALLATION ASSISTANCE: Ute Baum, Richard Fellows, Howard Miller, Teresa Proscewicz, David Walker, Theresa Roberti, Greg Wood

Water Retreat

DESIGN

David Squires, SAA Planning and Design, 940 14th St., Suite E, Santa Monica, CA 90403; (310) 393-6772

CONTRIBUTORS

POND: Under the Sea, 904 N. Ave. 67, Los Angeles, CA 90042; (213) 478-9835

Custom Stone, 3681 Kampton Dr., Los Alamitos, CA 90720; (562) 430-1881

LANDSCAPE LIGHTING: Lumen-8, 20452 Carrey Rd., Walnut, CA 91789; (909) 595-6884

LIGHTING, IRRIGATION, HARDSCAPE: Nakae & Associates, 705 Lakefield Rd., Suite G, Westlake Village, CA 91361; (805) 373-5342

IRRIGATION: Rainbird Sprinkler Manufacturing, 145 N. Grand Ave., Glendora, CA 91741; (800) 247-3782

HARDSCAPE: Bourget Bros., 1636 11th St., Santa Monica, CA 90404; (310) 450-6556

GARDENING:

Guerrero Landscape, 3819 W. 109th St., Inglewood, CA 90303

Living Designs, Box 9923, Marina del Rey, CA 90295; (310) 305-7337

PLANT MATERIAL: San Gabriel Nursery & Florist, 632 S. San Gabriel Blvd., San Gabriel, CA 91776; (626) 286-3782

Squires & Associates, 940 14th St., Suite E, Santa Monica, CA 90403; (310) 393-6772

Marina del Rey Garden Center, 13198 Mindanao Way, Marina del Rey, CA 90295; (310) 823-5956

FURNITURE: Design Resource, 140 Pine Ave., Third Floor, Long Beach, CA 90802; (562) 624-4144

Native Plant Garden

DESIGN

Ronnie Siegel, Swire Siegel, Landscape Architects, 5166 Oakwood Ave., La Cañada Flintridge, CA 91011; (818) 952-8626

CONTRIBUTORS

GRADING, IRRIGATION, LIGHTING, PLANTING, AND SOFT PATH: Picture Perfect Landscaping, Monrovia, CA; (626) 303-5902

GRANITE BOULDER PLACEMENT: Manmade Boulder Construction, Site Development Studios, 711 W. 17th St., Suite E-1, Costa Mesa, CA 92627; (949) 515-4270

GRANITE SANDBLASTING AND WATER JET CUTTING: Charisma Design Studio, 13227 San Fernando Rd., Sylmar, CA 91342; (818) 364-8383

GRANITE SLAB INSTALLATION: G.C. Masonry, Granite Flame Finishing, GL Ventura, 12595 Foothill Blvd., Sylmar, CA 91342; (818) 890-1886

WALL ART: Hillary Hunter, Box 530, La Cañada Flintridge, CA 91012

BLACK GRANITE: Intertile Distributors, 126 Pioneer Place, Pomona, CA 91768; (909) 595-7900

PLANT MATERIAL:

El Nativo Growers (wholesale), 200 S. Peckham Rd., Azusa, CA 91702; (626) 969-8449

Tree of Life Nursery, Box 635, San Juan Capistrano, CA 92693; (949) 728-0685

IRRIGATION AND LIGHTING SUPPLIES: Ewing Irrigation, 1405 Grand Central Ave., Glendale, CA 91201; (818) 551-9550

STONE DUST: Azusa Rock, 3901 Fish Canyon Rd., Duarte, CA 91010; (626) 856-6160 ◆

Stars of the shade: Hydrangeas

Here are six, familiar to rare

BY LAUREN BONAR SWEZEY

'TELLER RED' lace cap hydrangea mixes beautifully with 'Royal Purple' smoke bush at Gossler Farms Nursery in Springfield, Oregon.

Few shrubs can compete with hydrangeas' dramatic show of summer flowers—especially when you're dealing with shade. In addition to the familiar blue, red, pink, and white globular flower clusters of garden hydrangea (*H. macrophylla*), there are unusual species with strikingly different flowers and foliage.

Some develop huge flower heads, while others are more delicate. Leaves may be narrow or lobed, hairy or glossy.

The six we've chosen represent the range of choices. All grow well from the Pacific Northwest to coastal Southern California. Several are hardy in the coldest climates. Those listed here grow 4 to 6 feet tall except as noted. For planting and care tips, see page 87.

H. arborescens 'Annabelle' (also sold as *H. arboreum* 'Annabelle'). Huge white globes cover the plant all summer. Withstands some drought; grows in shade or sun. Hardy to −30°.

H. aspera, H. robusta, H. sargentiana. These have lavender-blue or white lace cap flowers and hairy, pointed leaves. The form sold as *H.a. villosa* has a spreading habit. *H. robusta* and *H. sargentiana* grow 9 to 12 feet tall. Prune hard if plants get leggy. Hardy to 0° (−10° if protected).

H. macrophylla. This large category of familiar plants includes mopheads (large, round heads) and lace cap hydrangeas (flat heads with small, star-petaled flowers surrounded by large showy flowers). *H.m.* 'Ayesha' has small, waxy pink flowers several times thicker than those on other *H. macrophylla* varieties. Hardy to 0° (-10° if protected).

H. quercifolia (oakleaf hydrangea). Long-lasting flowers in conical clusters turn from white to pale pink. 'Snow Flake' has double flowers. 'Snow Queen' has 12-inch-long flowers. Deeply-lobed foliage turns bronze or crimson in fall. Hardy to −30°.

WHERE TO BUY PLANTS

The following mail-order sources carry many unusual kinds.

Forestfarm, 990 Tetherow Rd., Williams, OR 97544; (541) 846-7269. Catalog $4. Sells 46 kinds.

Gossler Farms Nursery, 1200 Weaver Rd., Springfield, OR 97478; (541) 746-3922. Catalog $2. Sells 30 kinds (accepts orders September through April 15).

Greer Gardens, 1280 Goodpasture Island Rd., Eugene, OR 97401; (800) 548-0111. Catalog $3. Sells 45 kinds.

Heronswood Nursery, 7530 N.E. 288th St., Kingston, WA 98346; (360) 297-4172. Catalog $5. Sells 75 kinds.

Hydrangea Plus, Box 389, Aurora, OR 97002; (503) 651-2887. Catalog $4.50. Sells 74 kinds.

DOUBLE FLOWERS of 'Snow Flake' oakleaf hydrangea (left) cascade gracefully over a stone wall. Above, 'Enziandom' produces many gorgeous dark blue flowers. Below, lilaclike flowers of 'Ayesha' form dense, 8-inch-wide clusters.

Hydrangea basics

Growing. Hydrangeas tolerate full sun near the coast; inland, give them partial shade. Plant them in rich, porous soil (lighten heavy clay soils by mixing in plenty of compost or peat moss). Hydrangeas prefer moist soil, but established plants can get by on less water in coastal areas. Plants are especially beautiful when massed in large beds, or planted singly in pots.

Pruning. To control size and shape, prune plants after flowering. Cut out stems that have flowered, leaving those that have not. For big flower clusters, reduce the number of stems. For numerous medium-size clusters, keep more stems.

Changing the flower color. In acid soils, pink and red garden hydrangeas often turn blue or purple. To make (or keep) flower color blue, apply aluminum sulfate (¼ ounce to 1 gallon of water) to the soil several times in spring and fall, at weekly intervals. To keep flowers red or make them redder, add lime to the soil (apply ½ pound to every 5 feet of surface area under branches once or twice a year). ◆

Lily ponds fringe the perfect party deck

A city gardener turns his backyard into a country escape

BY SHARON COHOON

WILLOW CHAIRS, cool drinks, and sunbathing Irish setters—Marc LaFont's deck is a laid-back summer place.

Marc LaFont is one entertaining guy. His idea of a good time is coming up with a party theme, executing it with theatrical style, and watching guests become enchanted by the spell he's created. So it's no coincidence that LaFont's backyard in Santa Ana, California, has evolved into the perfect setting for great parties. Arriving guests walk into a scene that could have been painted by Monet. A wood deck "floats" above ponds filled with water lilies, and a verdant tangle of shrubs and vines frames the picture.

LaFont knew what kind of mood he wanted to create in his backyard from the day he bought the property. "I wanted it to feel like a country escape, in England or France perhaps, and I wanted it to be suitable for all kinds of outdoor entertaining." LaFont's vision took form in stages.

The first was the rear deck, which was built to take advantage of the shade of a large avocado tree. Next, LaFont extended the deck to encircle a liquidam-

bar tree and installed a large lily pond (see drawing on facing page). When the avocado tree became diseased and was removed, the landscape was reshaped into its current configuration. But without the avocado, the back deck lacked a focal point, so LaFont installed a new centerpiece—a handsome English gazebo—and narrowed the middle of the deck to form a "bridge" over the water. He also added a second, smaller lily pond on the other side of the bridge. Though the two ponds are separate, they create the illusion of being one body of water.

The ultimate compliment comes when partygoers tell LaFont, "I can't believe I'm still in the city." He says, "Sometimes I forget, too."

FRINGED BY PONDS and furnished with a gazebo rigged with overhead lights, the rear deck is a comfortable outdoor room by day or night.

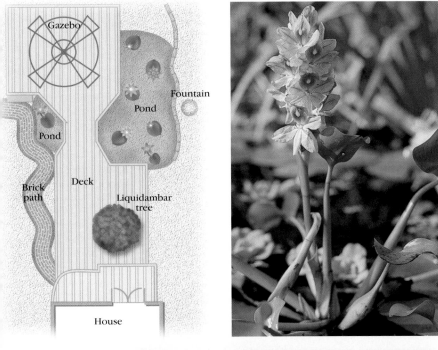

WATER HYACINTHS (middle photo) add splashes of lilac blue to the ponds. Water lilies (right), including tall-stemmed tropical types and shorter hardy kinds, are planted in submerged pots.

The details

Deck. Though LaFont chose unfinished fir instead of redwood primarily to keep costs down, he likes the wood's rough, weathered look.

Ponds. Excavated holes were padded with old carpeting, followed by a standard PVC pond liner, then a layer of chicken wire, which was capped with concrete. LaFont mixed his own concrete, using soil rather than sand in the mix to create a stickier material that's easier to work with and forms more natural-looking pond edges.

Water plants. The ponds are planted with a mixture of hardy and tropical water lilies, other flowering plants, and oxygenating grasses. To find the right balance of plants, LaFont gleaned information from books on water gardening; visits to specialty nurseries like Van Ness Water Gardens (see below); and Internet chats with experienced water gardeners. Water hyacinth, a natural purifier, plays a crucial role in maintaining the balance of LaFont's aquatic ecosystem. (Water hyacinths must be confined to home gardens and should never be released into natural waters, where they can be serious pests.)

Good sources for aquatic plants:
• Daydreamer Aquatic and Perennial Gardens, Route 1, Box 438, Belpre, OH 45714; (800) 741-3867. Write for a free list or visit www.daydreamergardens.com.
• Moorehaven Water Gardens, 3006 York Rd., Everett, WA 98204; (425) 743-6888. Free list.
• Van Ness Water Gardens, 2460 N. Euclid Ave., Upland, CA 91784; (800) 205-2425. Free catalog.

Accessories. The Ogee gazebo of nylon-coated steel, made by Agriframes (about $1,250, plus shipping), was purchased from New England Garden Ornaments (508/867-4474). The rustic bent-willow furniture has cushions covered in Sunbrella, an acrylic fabric made for outdoor use, and filled with fast-drying foam used in boat cushions. ◆

RAISED BEDS are filled to bursting with summer crops in Monsen's 26- by 56-foot vegetable garden (above), installed over a season in a corner of this previously bare backyard (right).

Bare earth to beauty

Mel Monsen turned an empty lot into a productive garden. His secret? Raised beds

BY STEVEN R. LORTON

PHOTOGRAPHS BY NORMAN PLATE

■ Mel Monsen's garden is to vegetables what the perfect closet is to clothes: everything has its place. Vegetables grow in neat raised beds by kind—tomatoes in one bed, green beans in another, pumpkins in yet another. There's a place for growing raspberries (along the fence), a place for compost (in the corner), a place to hang the hose and to mount a rain gauge (by the retaining wall), and a place for fruit trees (beside the entry trellis). Decorative trellises dotting the garden are home to climbing roses, clematis, and sweet peas.

But the best part about Monsen's garden is that he did the work himself, transforming part of the empty lot behind his new house in Anchorage into a productive vegetable garden in just four months. The four-step plan on page 70 shows how he did it and, in the process, gave new meaning to the expression *starting from scratch*.

Working in his garage, Monsen built 22 raised beds of varying widths and lengths. He also built the trellises. Then he planted. A few tricks (on page 156) helped his garden grow.

Four easy steps to bountiful raised beds

1 **Build raised beds.** Monsen used cedar 2-by-8s set on edge and capped with flat 2-by-4s. Most of the beds measure 4 feet wide by 8 feet long and are 10 inches deep. Also build trellises.

2 **Prepare the soil.** Use a rented rotary tiller if necessary to turn soil. Move the raised beds and trellises into place. In gopher country, line the beds with chicken wire or hardware cloth to keep the critters from nibbling plant roots.

3 **Build retaining walls and paths.** Monsen used 4-by-6s set on sides to edge two sides of the garden. For paths, he covered the ground with black plastic sheeting and topped it with a 3-inch layer of gravel.

4 **Fill beds with soil, then plant.** Monsen used a rich mix of commercial soil, compost, and well-rotted horse manure, then blended in some granular fertilizer (8-32-16). He planted nursery seedlings, giving the largest beds to the crops that need room to ramble.

Raised bed

8'

4'

Garden plot plan

Compost bins

Asparagus

Raspberry

Strawberry

Broccoli

Dill

Onion

Green pepper

Strawberry

Cabbage

Greens
Romaine
lettuce

Green
pepper

Strawberry

Sweet pea

Annuals

Carrot

Raspberry

Green
bean

Tomato

Muskmelon

56'

Pumpkin

Kiwi

Cucumber

Parsley

Thyme

26'

Monsen's secrets

Mulch. To warm the soil for heat-loving crops (necessary in cool climates), Monsen covers it with infrared-transmitting plastic sheeting. He cuts slits in the plastic and plants seedlings through the slits. For added heat, he fills clear 1-liter plastic beverage bottles with tea and lays them atop the plastic over the plants' root zones. The dark liquid absorbs solar heat during the day and releases it at night.

Row covers. If spring and summer weather is chilly, Monsen covers beds with row cover, a lightweight spun fabric that transmits light and holds in heat. It's available by the roll at nurseries.

Crop rotation. To keep diseases at bay, Monsen never grows the same crop in the same bed more than once in a three-year period. Each year he makes a map of what was planted in each bed.

Calling all gardeners: We'd love to hear from you if your gardening plans this spring and summer include planting a flower or veggie garden from scratch or doing a garden makeover—spiffing up a front yard, backyard, patio, perennial border, kitchen garden—or if you've recently completed such a project. • Drop us a note describing the garden before (bare dirt or overgrown?), what you transformed it into, how you completed the work, and how long the project took. Snapshots or plans are welcome. Mail your letters to Grow with Us editor, *Sunset Magazine,* 80 Willow Rd., Menlo Park, CA 94025. ◆

Foolproof perennials

Plant them now to spruce up summer beds and borders

BY LAUREN BONAR SWEZEY

F all may be the best time to set out perennials so they can settle in during the cooler winter months, but May is when most nurseries tempt you with great selections of blooming plants in gallon containers.

Don't resist: it's okay to indulge in a little instant gratification. In all but the hottest desert areas, gardeners can still plant perennials this month.

LEFT: Clockwise from top center are purple penstemon, yellow coreopsis, pink *Diascia vigilis,* 'Pink Mist' pincushion flower (at center), lavender-blue catmint, pink 'Heidi' yarrow, and blue delphinium. **RIGHT:** Vivid red 'Firebird' penstemon mingles with Temari Violet verbena. Design: Maile Arnold, Sebastopol, California

14 EASY PERENNIALS TO BUY IN BLOOM

Aster frikartii **'Mönch'.** Daisylike lavender-blue flowers; plants 3 ft. tall. Sun. All *Sunset* climate zones.

Blanket flower (*Gaillardia grandiflora*). Daisylike flowers in shades of red and yellow with orange or maroon bands. Sun. All zones.

Cape fuchsia (*Phygelius*). Shrubby perennial with drooping, fuchsia-like flowers in pink, red, or pale yellow; to 4 ft. tall. Sun or light shade. Zones 4–9, 14–24.

Catmint (*Nepeta faassenii*). Spikes of lavender-blue flowers on mounding plants with gray-green foliage. Sun. All zones.

Coreopsis. Daisylike flowers in yellow, orange, maroon, or red. Full sun. Zones vary.

Diascia. Low-growing plants with coral, pink, or lavender flowers on ends of stems. Full sun to partial shade. Zones 7–9, 14–24.

Gaura lindheimeri. Branching flower spikes of white or pink blossoms. Full sun. All zones.

Nemesia fruticans. Vanilla-scented lavender and pink or white flowers on a bushy evergreen plant; to 1 ft. tall. Zones 16–24.

Penstemon hybrids. 'Apple Blossom' (pink), 'Firebird' (red), and 'Midnight' (purple) are particularly long-blooming varieties. Sun. Zones vary.

Pincushion flower (*Scabiosa* 'Butterfly Blue' and 'Pink Mist'). Lacylooking, 1-inch-wide blue or pink flowers. Blooms much of year in mild climates. Full sun. All zones.

Salvia. *Salvia coccinea* (red; zones 14–24) blooms from spring to fall if deadheaded. Mexican bush sage (*S. leucantha;* purple; zones 10–24) blooms from late spring to late fall. Sun.

Santa Barbara daisy (*Erigeron karvinskianus*). Bears masses of ³⁄₄-inch white and pinkish daisies. Sun or light shade. Zones 8–9, 12–24.

Scaevola aemula. Sprawling plants produce masses of 1½-inch-wide lavender-blue flowers. Full sun. Zones 8–9, 14–24.

Verbena. Mostly ground cover plants that thrive in heat. 'Homestead Purple' grows up to 18 in. tall and has large (2 in.) purple flower heads. Varieties of *V. peruviana* come in pink, purple, red, and white, and stay 3 in. tall. Sun. Zones vary.

PLANTING TIPS

• Before planting, soak the rootballs by immersing nursery cans up to the rims in a water-filled sink or tub as long as overnight.

• Amend the soil in the planting hole with organic matter such as compost to improve water retention.

• If roots are tightly coiled, gently pry them apart with your hands or use a sharp knife to score the root mass.

• After planting, spread a 2- to 3-inch layer of mulch around plants to keep roots cool and soil moist. Keep mulch off crown of plant.

• Be prepared to water plants as often as twice a day until their roots get established.

• About two weeks after planting, begin regular feeding with a gentle liquid fertilizer such as fish emulsion.

• Clip faded blooms regularly. Shear off spent blossoms of ground-hugging plants, such as catmint, diascia, Santa Barbara daisy, and verbena, when 80 percent of the flowers have faded. Pinch or snip off blossoms of blanket flower and pincushion flower one at a time. On penstemon, cut the entire stalk down to the base of the plant. ◆

KOKOPELLI FIGURINE presides over a Colorado garden composed entirely of container plants. For details on these colorful pots, see page 166.

June

gardenguide

Simply pretty summer combos

A few good plants carry the show in these high-desert gardens

■ The Old Town section of Albuquerque is full of historic adobe structures, gift shops, restaurants—and pocket gardens. Photographer Charles Mann of Santa Fe spotted the two plantings pictured here. In both cases, only two or three different plants were used to form eye-catching combinations.

Mann found the foreground planting (above left) in Patio Escondido in early summer. Created for owner Richard Sanchez by landscape designer Susan Wachter, the composition is as pretty as a still life painted with desert hues. Purple wands of Rocky Mountain penstemon (*P. strictus*) play off the fragrant, bright yellow flowers of Spanish broom (*Spartium junceum*). A mulch of brown Santa Fe gravel around the plants complements the rustic feel of the garden. Rocky Mountain penstemon is hardy in *Sunset* climate zones 1–3 and 10–13; Spanish broom grows in zones 10–13.

Later in summer, Mann saw a pocket garden with a distinctly tropical flavor. In the circular island bed (above right), the hot orange and red flowers of cannas contrast with a blue-trimmed window behind. The surrounding beds are edged with orange and yellow marigolds and zinnias in shades of red, salmon, and pale yellow. Cannas are tuberous-rooted perennials that can stay in the ground year-round in all but the coldest areas (in zones 1–3, lift roots in fall and store for winter).

ABOVE: Zinnias (foreground), tall cannas, and marigolds (left rear) add sizzle to an Albuquerque patio. ABOVE LEFT: Spanish broom forms a backdrop for purple penstemon in Patio Escondido.

Light up a living lantern

■ The sun is setting, the air is balmy, and the outdoor dining table is set for two. A romantic summer supper such as this calls for soft lighting. What better way to provide it than by hanging an ivy topiary lantern like the one pictured at right? Shaped like a coachman's lamp, it contains a three-wick candle (about 8 inches tall) that burns brightly inside a hurricane glass.

Landscape designer Chris Jacobson purchased the 24-inch-tall, four-sided topiary basket in the photo 20 years ago. He's kept it going all these years with a simple maintenance schedule: overhead watering as needed to wash the foliage (which helps stave off mite infestations) and irrigate the soil, liquid fertilizer three times a year, and trimming and training new growth twice a year.

You can buy an unplanted lantern frame by mail from Nature's Alley (Allied Arts Guild, 75 Arbor Rd., Menlo Park, CA 94025) and train your own topiary. The frames come in two sizes: small (22 inches tall by 19 inches wide; $29) and large (24 inches by 22 inches; $36). Line the basket with sphagnum moss and fill it with potting mix, then plant rooted ivy stems (use rooted stems from two 4-inch pots of English ivy) 1½ inches apart around the edges; leave space in the center for a candleholder. Topiary pins ($1.75 for 100 to 125 pins) hold the ivy in place. As the stems grow, twine some of them up the corner wires, others down around the lantern's base. The topiary should begin to fill out in a season.

— *Lauren Bonar Swezey*

NORMAN A. PLATE

A hardy maple with Oriental grace

■ When it comes to graceful form and beautiful foliage, it's hard to beat the Japanese maple (*Acer palmatum*). Unfortunately, this species won't survive in areas where temperatures fall below −15°. However, it has a lovely cousin native to Korea and Manchuria with a hardier constitution. The Korean maple (*A. pseudo-sieboldianum*) has all the grace and beauty of the green-leafed Japanese maples, but is unfazed by temperatures as low as −35°.

Korean maples grow 12 to 18 inches a year, to an eventual height of 18 to 30 feet and a width of almost 30 feet. The leaves are kelly green in summer, turning spectacular hues of red and orange in fall. Each leaf has 9 to 11 lobes. The overall form and effect are identical to those of the larger Japanese maples, and the trees' cultural requirements are the same. Korean maples prefer moist, well-drained, slightly acidic soil. In hot-summer areas, the tree needs protection from afternoon sun to keep foliage from scorching.

This maple may be planted bareroot in spring or from containers anytime. If you can't find it at a nursery, call Forest Farm (541/846-7269; 1- to 2-foot plants in 1-gallon containers, $12) or Mountain Maples (707/984-6522; up to 5-foot trees, $55).

— *Richard D. Rifkind*

Two ways to dress up a garden party table

NORMAN A. PLATE (2)

■ You love your garden. That's why you want to share it—literally—by sending guests home from a summer party with charming souvenirs. Here are two ways to do that.

1. Blooms by the bunch

Two or three stems each of flowers that dry well—purple sea lavender (*Limonium perezii*) and *L. latifolium*—with a spray of deep green camellia leaves behind make up the little bouquet pictured above. Snip the stems to 3 inches long, gather the flowers as shown, and tie them with natural-colored raffia.

Other flowers to try: globe amaranth in mixed colors, sprays of lavender with coral bells (*Heuchera*), or yarrow. Other foliage: citrus, sprenger asparagus fern, or sword fern.

2. Button-size bouquets

Some plants bear diminutive but bouquet-perfect blooms with enough stem to help them last up to two weeks when cut. The ones pictured above right come in sunny fiesta colors; all, except where noted, are summer annuals that grow well throughout the West and should be in nurseries this month. For a softer look, try asters, feverfew, or miniature roses.

THE PLANTS

•*Asteriscus maritimus* (also sold as Gold Coin). Showy yellow daisylike flowers, about 1½ inches across on foot-tall plants. Evergreen perennial in

Sunset climate zones 9 and 15–24. (In colder climates, substitute coreopsis.)
•Creeping zinnia (*Sanvitalia procumbens*). Not really a zinnia, but it looks like one; this plant grows only 4 to 6 inches tall and trails to a foot or more. Yellow or orange daisylike flowers, up to an inch across, have dark purple-brown centers.
•*Zinnia angustifolia* Starbright Mix. Inch-wide flowers are orange, bronze, gold, and cream on compact plants to 8 inches tall.
•*Zinnia haageana* Old Mexico. Mahogany flowers overlaid with shades of golden yellow are less than 1½ inches across on compact plants (to 16 inches tall).

THE VASES: Tiny glass vases (3½ to 4 inches tall) like the one above are available at some florists and florists' supply stores, or you can use straight-sided spice bottles. Embellish them with natural raffia ties.

THE STRATEGY: Set a bouquet at each place to send home with your guests. A center arrangement can display larger summer flowers in the same colors and shapes: gaillardia, gloriosa daisies, and *Zinnia elegans* with yellow or red blooms.

— *Kathleen N. Brenzel*

Butterflies on the Net

■ All around me, fluttering spots of color—sherbety oranges, glowing yellows, bright reds and purples, shimmery sky blues—zip and dip. Here a sleepy orange sips from a fairy duster, there a two-tailed swallowtail floats onto a New Mexico thistle, and nearly everywhere little marine blues twinkle in the morning light.

I'm watching the butterflies in the demonstration garden of the Sonoran Arthropod Studies Institute (SASI) in the foothills of the Tucson Mountains. The desert Southwest is home to over 250 species of butterflies; to attract many of them, SASI's garden is filled with 67 species of plants that provide nectar and/or food. Some of the butterflies' favorites are listed here.

• Goodding verbena (*V. gooddingii*): Perennial with sky blue, nectar-bearing flowers.

• New Mexico thistle (*Cirsium neomexicana*): Biennial with pink, nectar-bear-

A PAINTED LADY draws nectar from a flower of groundsel.

STEVEN J. PRCHAL

ing flowers; larval food for painted ladies.

• Pipevine (*Aristolochia watsoni*): Perennial vine with cream and maroon flowers provides larval food for pipevine swallowtail.

• Skeleton milkweed (*Asclepias curassavica*): Annual with pinkish white, nectar-bearing flowers; larval food for monarchs and queens.

• Sweet bush (*Bebbia*

juncea): Perennial with yellow, nectar-bearing flowers.

You can take an on-line tour of SASI's garden by visiting www.sasionline.org. SASI and the Arizona Native Plant Society have published *Desert Butterfly Gardening*, a 36-page booklet. Order a copy on-line or send $3 to SASI, Box 5624, Tucson, AZ 85703; (520) 883-3945.

— *Roseann Hanson*

NORMAN A. PLATE

Sharpen those edges

■ Just as knives grow dull with use, so do the edges of your hoes, shovels, and other garden tools. The Quicksharp Single Edge Tool Sharpener works on any tool that has one sharp beveled edge, such as lawn mower blades and pruning shears (the latter must open wide enough for the tool's sharpening edge to fit over the shear blade). The tool sharpener is available at many home improvement stores (call 800/621-7433 for a source near you). Cost is about $7.

— *L.B.S.*

Rainbows swim through the garden

■ Owners Molly and Jay Precourt of Vail wanted to make their long, narrow side yard an engaging summer place. So they turned to landscape architect Glen Ellison. He, in turn, drew inspiration from a wild stream that flows nearby—Vail's Mill Creek. The water feature Ellison designed looks natural and even sustains a few stocked rainbow trout during the summer.

Fed by a recirculating pump, the watercourse starts at the pond pictured above, which flows into a 60-foot-long creek with another pond in the middle and a third pool at the other end.

The banks are planted with perennials, all hardy enough to endure the bitter cold winters here at 8,200 feet. Bergenia, columbine, and ferns share space with peach-leafed campanula, red-hot poker, and Siberian iris. Along one side of the watercourse, a flagstone path is seamed with purple-flowered thyme and other creeping perennials.

In fall, the water feature is drained before freezing weather arrives.

— Jim McCausland

Catch the 'Misty Lilac Wave'

■ Don't let the color fool you. Hue is the only delicate thing about 'Misty Lilac Wave' petunia. Its many flowers, which open lavender and gradually fade to white, are 3 inches across. Its 4-foot-wide spread is equally impressive; the 28-inch-diameter bowl pictured above contains just three plants. In borders, 'Misty Lilac Wave' makes a handsome edging, especially with blue flowers behind it.

'Misty Lilac Wave' is widely available in nurseries. To find a source near you, consult www.wave-rave.com.
— *Sharon Cohoon*

A pink cloud in Seattle

■ When breeder Richard Jaynes called mountain laurel (*Kalmia latifolia*) "one of the most beautiful evergreen flowering shrubs that grows in temperate climates," he could have been describing the 60-year-old specimen shown at right in Lyn White's Seattle garden. Probably started from a cutting taken at nearby Washington Park Arboretum, this plant is now 6 feet tall, 10 feet wide, and absolutely covered with pink flowers from mid-May through early June.

Mountain laurel grows wild in eastern American forests and takes well to cultivation throughout the Pacific Northwest (*Sunset* climate zones 1–7). You'll find named varieties with flowers in pinks, burgundy, and white, and some are banded. The star-shaped buds are nearly as beautiful as the flowers that follow.

A relative of the rhododendron, mountain laurel

MAGGIE MACLAREN

has similar needs: partial shade to full sun in mild climates, a light fertilizing in early spring and again just after bloom, and a thick leaf mulch to keep roots moist. Never let the root zone dry out completely.

Look for mountain laurels at nurseries throughout the Northwest, or order plants by mail from Greer Gardens (800/548-0111), Gossler Farms Nursery (541/746-3922), or Whitney Gardens (800/952-2404). —*J.M.*

Pretty in white

■ "Bright, buoyant, joyous ... a celebration of the season." That's how designer Bob Clark describes his exuberant summer- and fall-blooming flower border in this Northern California garden. The sunny bed is so packed that it appears much wider than 3 feet. The trick, says Clark, is creating a tiered effect using plants of different heights.

Clark chose crisp and refreshing colors. Apricot orange miniature 'Holy Toledo' roses, apricot and white *Salvia coccinea*, guara, 'Morning Light' miscanthus, *Salvia guaranitica* (cobalt blue), and 'Sundowner' flax (spiky bronze-coral leaves) form the bed's backbone. Silvery lamb's ears are permanent fillers at the front. Between these staples are summer annuals, mostly with white flowers: baby's breath and cosmos in the rear; nicotiana and *Salvia farinacea* 'Silver White' and 'Victoria' in the middle; and feverfew, lobelia, and petunias—with a splash of blue ageratum—toward the front. — *L.B.S.*

NORMAN A. PLATE (2)

Iris seedlings are surprising beauties

■ Japanese irises produce big, sumptuous blossoms in the wettest spots without missing a beat. Normally, these beardless irises are grown from named varieties of rhizomes planted in fall or spring. But Northwest grower George Yamamoto noticed that Japanese iris seedlings (unnamed varieties grown from seed) also have great beauty.

Most of Yamamoto's seedlings come in single-flowered forms, 4 to 5 inches across, in shades of purple, violet, pink, rose, yellow, and white. Because these seedlings are random crosses, you won't know exactly what color you're getting until they bloom. If you set out plants from 4-inch containers this month or next, some will start blooming late next spring, and all will flower by the following year.

Japanese irises need rich, moist soil and regular water. They flourish along the damp edges of ponds and streams.

You can choose your plants from the field at Yamamoto Nursery in Port Orchard, Washington. Call ahead to time your visit during this month's peak bloom. (From State 16, take the Sedgwick Rd. exit and drive east ½ mile to the traffic signal, then go left ¼ mile to 5765 Sidney Rd., on your left.) Or mail-order seedlings by color (from $4.50 each, plus $3.50 for shipping); (360) 876-1889. —*J.M.*

Prize container garden in Colorado

■ On a cycling vacation through the Italian countryside near Assisi, Don and Nada Graves were captivated by the profusion of container plantings they saw in every village. The couple wanted to re-create this Old World charm in the adobe-walled courtyard of their new home near Denver. So they enlisted landscape designer Annie Huston of Columbine Design in Englewood, Colorado. Huston helped the Graveses achieve their vision by creating a garden composed entirely of container plants. The resulting design (featured on page 158) earned Huston's firm the grand award for use of color from the Associated Landscape Contractors of Colorado.

In the plantings Huston mingled alyssum, marguerites, marigolds, petunias, yellow archangel (*Lamium galeobdolon*), and trailing *Vinca minor* with showy vertical plumes of purple fountain grass. Burgundy-leafed 'Red Emperor' canna erupts from the container at top center, while 'Purple Wave' petunias and silvery licorice plant (*Helichrysum petiolare*) tumble over the rim.

Originally, the Graveses used clay pots, but they switched to terra-cotta-colored plastic containers 28 to 30 inches in diameter. The plastic containers hold moisture better and weigh much less than clay, making them easy to stack and store over the winter. To further reduce weight, the bottom third of each container is filled with plastic foam "peanuts," which are covered with weed barrier fabric. The plants are in a soilless potting mix amended with controlled-release fertilizer, supplemented by biweekly doses of liquid fertilizer to keep them growing strong all season. The Graveses do their watering by hand.

— *Marcia Tatroe*

BACK TO BASICS

How to choose seedlings. Ideal seedlings are sturdy and stocky, not leggy. Choose well-established plants, each with at least four true leaves that have a healthy green color. Don't buy seedlings with roots that protrude from the bottom of the container (they're rootbound) or those with premature fruits. If the rootball is like the one shown—firm with roots but not quite rootbound—loosen the roots with your fingers before planting. This will help the roots grow out into the surrounding soil instead of circling the rootball.

STEVEN GUNTHER

Summertime blues at Rancho Los Alamitos

■ The lavender blue canopy of jacaranda trees has been a staple of the Southern California summer landscape for more than a century. But *Jacaranda mimosifolia* has lost favor in recent years; homeowners no longer seem willing to deal with its sticky flower drop.

Fallout is never a problem, however, near the barns at Rancho Los Alamitos Historic Ranch and Garden. "Our horses gobble up the flowers like gumdrops," says Doug McGavin, chief horticulturist at the Rancho. If you want the familiar tunnel-of-blue experience, he says, check out the Jacaranda Walk behind the tennis courts. "It's off-limits to the horses."

Florence Bixby, the last private owner of the Rancho, planted the Jacaranda Walk in 1926. She chose the flowering trees for their summer show, of course, but also for their tolerance of heavy clay soil and drought.

The Rancho is at 6400 Bixby Hill Rd., Long Beach, and is open 1–5 Wed-Sun. Admission is free. (562) 431-3541. — *S.C.*

FALLEN JACARANDA petals are like candy from heaven for the Rancho's horses.

FRAGRANT, old-fashioned sweet peas include 'Blanche Ferry', 'Janet Scott' (center photo), and 'America' (right).

Sweet peas on trial in Oregon

■ After growing scores of different sweet peas in the past few years, Pat Sherman has developed some well-founded opinions about them. "People say they want sweet peas for the fragrance, so I grow lots of the old-fashioned kinds. Though their flowers are small, they really do smell best. But when I'm at the farmers' market, the modern sweet peas always sell out first. They may not smell best, but they have *great* flowers, always large and often with ruffles."

To satisfy all sweet pea lovers, Sherman grows both the old and the new at her Fragrant Garden Nursery near Canby, Oregon. This year, she's trying nearly 100 varieties. "The secret to growing good plants is to start right. I sow mine in February in 2-inch plastic pots, then transplant them into the garden in March and April."

In 1999, Sherman offered a catalog (50 cents) listing 76 varieties of sweet peas. The nursery was open for tours during the last few weekends in June (by appointment only; space limited). To get more information, write to Fragrant Garden Nursery, Box 627, Canby, OR 97013.

—*Jim McCausland*

Pacific Northwest Checklist

PLANTING

☑ ANNUALS. Sow seeds of cosmos, marigold, portulaca, sunflower, sweet alyssum, and zinnia. For faster bloom, set out nursery seedlings of those plants, plus geranium, impatiens, Madagascar periwinkle, and petunia.

☑ BULBS. For late summer color, plant canna, crocosmia, dahlia, gladiolus, tigridia, and tuberous begonia.

☑ HERBS. Plant all kinds from pots this month.

☑ PERENNIALS. Plant aster, blanket flower, campanula, columbine, coreopsis, delphinium, erigeron, feverfew, foxglove, gilia, heuchera, Oriental poppy, penstemon, potentilla, purple coneflower, salvia, Shirley poppy, and Siberian wallflower. For foliage fillers, try artemisia, dusty miller, or golden or purple sage.

☑ LANDSCAPE PLANTS. Plant balled-and-burlapped or container-grown trees, shrubs, vines, and ground covers.

☑ VEGETABLES. Sow seeds of cucumbers and squash, plus successive crops of beets, bush beans, carrots, chard, kohlrabi, lettuce, onions, parsnips, peas, radishes, spinach, and turnips. Set out seedlings of eggplant, peppers, and tomatoes.

MAINTENANCE

☑ TIP-PRUNE PINES. After the needles have opened on new shoots, called candles, you can break the candles in half to limit growth. This is an old bonsai trick that also works with pines in the landscape.

☑ DEADHEAD. Keep faded blossoms picked to prevent seed from setting; this slows or stops the bloom cycle.

☑ DIVIDE PERENNIALS. Immediately after flowering, dig perennials and divide them. Some plants, like Oriental poppies, can be separated root by root; others, such as irises, have to be cut apart with a knife or spade. Discard dead or woody parts of the root.

☑ FERTILIZE. Feed spring-flowering plants right after bloom.

☑ PRUNE SPRING-FLOWERING SHRUBS. Thin and shape them now, before they set next spring's buds.

☑ THIN APPLES. To keep apple trees from producing too much small fruit, wait until after June drop (when trees spontaneously abort unpollinated fruit), then remove excess fruit. Thin triple clusters to doubles, and double clusters to singles. (Exception: Don't thin at all if you have an alternate-bearing tree and this is the light year.) Other kinds of fruit—especially Asian and European pears—also need heavy thinning to guarantee large fruit. ◆

Northern California Checklist

PLANTING

✔ **PLANTS FOR DAD.** Nurseries carry a wide and wonderful assortment of interesting plants this month, just in time for Father's Day. Consider a blooming bonsai, bougainvillea, daylily, gardenia, or new kind of citrus, such as a 'Clementine' tangerine or 'Improved Meyer' lemon.

✔ **BULBS, CORMS, AND TUBERS.** Zones 1–2: For late summer color, plant begonias, dahlias, gladiolus, montbretia, and tigridia.

✔ **LOW-MAINTENANCE SHRUBS.** Zones 7–9, 14–17: For attractive color and form with minimal water needs, plant blue hibiscus, cape mallow, cape plumbago, ceanothus, euphorbia, feathery cassia, flax hybrids, Jerusalem sage, lavender, plumbago, rockrose, Russian sage, and tree mallow.

✔ **VEGETABLES.** June is prime planting time for warm-season vegetables. Sow seeds of beans (plant both bush and pole types) and corn (our favorite is still 'Breeder's Choice', a sugary enhanced type from W. Atlee Burpee & Co.; 800/888-1447). Buy transplants for cucumbers, eggplant, melons, okra, peppers, pumpkins, squash, and tomatoes.

Sunset
CLIMATE ZONES
▢ Mountain (1-2)
▢ Valley (7-9)
▢ Inland (14)
▢ Coastal (15-17)

DEBRA LAMBERT

✔ **UNUSUAL PLANTS.** Gardeners seeking rare and unique plants should check out the Great Plant Company's new catalog. To order, call (800) 441-9788 or visit www.greatplants.com. Two other favorites for finding unusual plants are Heronswood Nursery in Kingston, WA (360/297-4172 or www.heronswood.com), and Forestfarm in Williams, OR (541/846-7269 or www.forestfarm.com).

MAINTENANCE

✔ **MULCH ROSES.** Spread a 3- to 4-inch layer of mulch under rose bushes to help conserve water and keep roots cool. Keep mulch away from the trunks.

✔ **PICK HERBS.** For the best flavor, harvest individual leaves or sprigs before flower buds open. If plants are blooming, use the flowers as garnish for foods such as cheeses or pâté.

✔ **PROTECT JAPANESE MAPLES.** Zones 7–9, 14–15: When temperatures rise, these sensitive trees often suffer from tip burn. Leaves turn brown along the edges, which detracts from the tree's beauty. An easy way to minimize damage is to spray the foliage with an antitranspirant, such as Cloud Cover (available at many nurseries and home improvement stores). Also mulch the soil under the branches (keep mulch away from trunks) and water trees regularly.

✔ **REMOVE FIRE HAZARDS.** In fire-prone areas (any natural scrub or forested areas, such as the coastal range, Oakland/Berkeley hills, and Mt. Tamalpais area), clean up brush and debris to reduce the fuel volume. When grasses turn brown, mow them to about 4 inches. Prune out dead and diseased wood from trees and shrubs. Prune tree limbs to at least 20 feet off the ground. Cut branches back at least 15 feet from the house. Clean off any plant debris that have accumulated on the roof. ◆

Southern California Checklist

PLANTING

☑ **ANNUALS.** It's not too late to set out summer bedding plants. Sun-loving choices include celosia, dahlia, gomphrena, marigold, petunia, portulaca, salvia, scabiosa, verbena, vinca, and zinnia. In shadier areas, try begonia, browallia, caladium, coleus, impatiens, and lobelia.

☑ **SUBTROPICALS.** They are widely available in nurseries now. Choices include flowering trees (bauhinia, crape myrtle, tabebuia); fruit trees (avocado, banana, citrus); shrubs (gardenia, hibiscus, princess flower); and a lot of vines (bougainvillea, mandevilla, stephanotis, and trumpet vine).

☑ **VEGETABLES.** Set out transplants of cucumbers, eggplant, melons, peppers, and tomatoes. Sow seeds of beans, corn, cucumbers, okra, pumpkins, and summer and winter squash. In the high desert (zone 11), plant short-season varieties.

☑ **SHADE LOVERS.** Foliage choices include ferns, heavenly bamboo, holly, ivy, lamium, ligularia, palms, and pittosporum. For flowers, consider abutilon, begonias, coral bells, fuchsia, heliotrope, impatiens, and shrimp plant (*Justicia brandegeane*).

Bishop
NEVADA
CALIFORNIA
San Luis Obispo
Bakersfield
Tehachapi
Santa Barbara
Lancaster
Los Angeles
Palm Springs
Sunset
CLIMATE ZONES
1-3 7-9 11 13 14-24
San Diego
MEXICO

DEBRA LAMBERT

MAINTENANCE

☑ **FEED GROWING PLANTS.** Roses, warm-season lawns, annual flowers and vegetables, and just about anything actively growing in the garden will benefit from fertilizing now. But don't feed natives or drought-tolerant Mediterraneans—summer is the dormant period for them.

☑ **SHAPE FUCHSIAS.** If fuchsias are growing leggy, pinch off branch tips just above a set of leaves to force growth into side branches. Groom plants by picking flowers as they fade.

☑ **STAKE TOMATOES.** For easy picking and to prevent fruit rot, keep tomatoes off the ground by supporting them with cages, stakes, or a trellis. As plants grow, tie them to supports with plastic ties or strips from an old pair of panty hose.

☑ **TREAT IRON DEFICIENCIES.** Gardenias, citrus, and other susceptible plants often exhibit green veins on upper leaves at this time of year—a signal that they require iron. To treat, apply chelated iron as a soil drench or foliar spray, following package directions.

PEST CONTROL

☑ **COMBAT ROSE PESTS.** Along the coast, "June gloom" creates ideal conditions for powdery mildew. Combat by hosing down foliage frequently, early in the morning, to wash off spores. Or spray with 1 tablespoon *each* baking soda and fine-grade horticultural oil diluted in a gallon of water; avoid spraying when temperatures exceed 85°. Inland, watch for spider mites. To hold down mite populations, keep foliage clean by spraying often with water, particularly the undersides of leaves.

☑ **CONTROL CATERPILLARS.** Spray or dust plants that have pest caterpillars (such as cabbage worm, tomato hornworm, or geranium budworm) with *Bacillus thuringiensis*. Apply sparingly, starting when caterpillars are small. ◆

Mountain Checklist

PLANTING

✔ **ANNUALS.** Sow seeds of cosmos, marigold, portulaca, sunflower, and zinnia. Or set out seedlings of those plants, plus African daisy, baby snapdragon, bachelor's button, calendula, clarkia, forget-me-not, globe amaranth, lobelia, pansy, snapdragon, spider flower, sweet alyssum, sweet William, and viola. After last frost, set out coleus, geranium, impatiens, Madagascar periwinkle, nasturtium, and petunia.

✔ **BULBS.** For late-summer color, plant canna, crocosmia, dahlia, gladiolus, and tuberous begonia.

✔ **LANDSCAPE PLANTS.** Now is the time to set out ground covers, shrubs, trees, and vines.

✔ **PERENNIALS.** Sow seeds of aster, basket-of-gold, campanula, columbine, delphinium, erigeron, gilia, heuchera, penstemon, perennial sweet pea, potentilla, and purple coneflower. Or set out seedlings of those plants, plus blanket flower, coreopsis, penstemon, and salvia.

✔ **NATIVE GRASSES.** Sow seeds or set out plugs or sod of blue grama, buffalo grass, and crested wheatgrass.

Sunset
CLIMATE ZONES

◻ 1-3 ▨ 10-11

DEBRA LAMBERT

✔ **VEGETABLES.** Sow seeds of cucumber and squash, plus successive crops of beets, bush beans, carrots, chard, lettuce, onions, parsnips, peas, radishes, spinach, and turnips. If the season is long and warm enough in your area, sow seeds of corn, pumpkin, and watermelon, and set out seedlings of eggplant, peppers, and tomatoes.

MAINTENANCE

✔ **FERTILIZE.** Feed lawns, flower beds, and vegetable gardens.

✔ **MOW LAWNS.** Cut bluegrass, fescue, and ryegrass to about 2 inches, bent grass to 1 inch or less.

✔ **MAINTAIN ROSES.** Deadhead faded flowers, fertilize, then build a moat around each plant to direct water to the root zone.

✔ **MULCH.** Spread a 3-inch layer of organic mulch around permanent plants.

✔ **PROTECT FRUITS.** Use bird netting or row covers to protect strawberries and ripening cherries until fruit is ready to harvest.

✔ **PRUNE SPRING-FLOWERING SHRUBS.** As soon as forsythia, lilacs, spiraea, and other spring-flowering shrubs finish blooming, prune them before they set next spring's buds.

✔ **THIN FRUITS.** To get larger fruit, thin apples and pears so they are 6 to 8 inches apart; apricots and most plums should be 4 to 5 inches apart.

✔ **TREAT CHLOROSIS.** When plants lack iron, their leaves turn yellow while their veins remain green. Correct chlorosis by applying chelated iron over the plant's root zone.

✔ **WATER.** Irrigate permanent plants deeply. Water new plantings and container plants frequently. ◆

Southwest Checklist

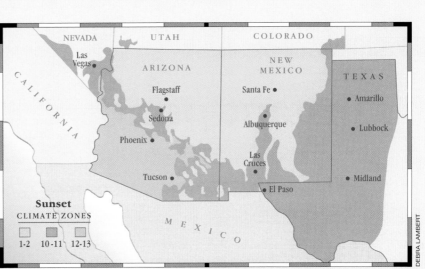

PLANTING

✔ PALMS. Plant them in a hole that's the same depth as the rootball and twice as wide. Tie the fronds up over the bud to protect it. After new growth begins, cut the twine.

✔ SUMMER COLOR. Zones 10–12: Set out cockscomb, firebush, globe amaranth, Madagascar periwinkle, portulaca, purslane, salvia, starflower, and zinnia right away. It helps to put them in a place that gets filtered sun in the hottest part of the day.

✔ SUMMER CROPS. Zones 10–11: Plant cucumbers, melons, and summer squash by midmonth, or corn early in the month. Zones 12–13: You can still plant black-eyed peas, corn, melons, okra, peanuts, sweet potatoes, and yard-long beans.

✔ FALL VEGETABLES. Zones 1–2, 10 (Albuquerque): Sow seeds of brussels sprouts, cabbage, and carrots anytime, but wait until midmonth to sow broccoli and cauliflower. Zones 12–13: Sow tomato seeds indoors for transplanting into the garden in late July. Some good varieties include 'Champion', 'Early Girl', 'Heatwave', 'Solar Set', and 'Sunmaster'.

MAINTENANCE

✔ CARE FOR ROSES. Cut off faded flowers just above a set of five leaflets (not three), then build a moat around each plant to concentrate water around the root zone. Mulch each plant well. Wet the soil, fertilize, and water again immediately.

✔ MOW LAWNS. Cut Bermuda, St. Augustine, and zoysia grass 1 to 1½ inches high. Keep hybrid Bermuda at about 1 inch.

✔ MULCH TREES, SHRUBS. Zones 10–13: Spread a 2- to 4-inch mulch over the root zones of trees, shrubs, flowers, and vegetables. Use organic mulch for cool soil over shallow roots, gravel mulch where wind or water would carry a light organic mulch away.

✔ WATER. Water deeply by flooding or drip irrigation; if you use drip, flood-irrigate monthly to wash salts out of the root zone.

PEST CONTROL

✔ BEET LEAFHOPPERS. These greenish yellow, inch-long insects spread curly top virus to cucumber, melon, and tomato plants. Protect crops by covering them with shadecloth. Remove infested plants.

Instant pond

Install this water feature in five easy steps

BY PETER O. WHITELEY

PHOTOGRAPHS BY NORMAN A. PLATE

■ The heart of any tranquil garden is surely a pond. Mirror-smooth water reflects surrounding plants and clouds overhead; in its depths, goldfish swim lazily, glinting softly in sunlight. And a small fountain emits the soothing sound of burbling water.

You can add a pond to your garden in a day or less by starting with a preformed plastic shell from a garden supply store or home improvement store. Installing one is easy, but it does require gloves, a good shovel, and a strong back. You just dig a hole, drop in the shell, and fill it with water and plants. Edged with stones and low-growing plants, the pond becomes graceful and inviting.

Preformed pond shells come in a variety of shapes, sizes, and depths. Some have smooth, vertical sides (which discourage raccoons); others have textured walls. Some have shelves around the sides to hold containers of water plants. Despite their bulk, most shells are lightweight—made of a heavy-duty, UV-stabilized polyethylene. Shapes range from tidy ovals to free-form; volume ranges from about 30 gallons to several hundred. Costs increase with size. The pond shown here, sold by Beckett Corporation, is available in a 42-gallon size ($52) and an 85-gallon size ($120). Call Beckett for a local merchant; (888) 232-5388.

To help keep the pond clean, you'll need a pump. Submersible models are fine for a small pond like ours. We used a solar pump, powered by a small photovoltaic collector ($129 from Smith & Hawken; to order, call 800/776-3336). Obviously, it runs only when sunlight hits the collector.

Water plants also help keep ponds clean: as a rule, they should cover about two-thirds of the water's surface.

FLAT STONES cover the pond's edges, giving it a natural finish. Floating duckweed (A) helps keep algae in check. Low plants in foreground include mosslike *Scleranthus biflorus* (B), blue fescue (C), pink-flowered thrift (*Armeria juniperifolia*) (D), and *Sedum* 'Baby Tears' (E). *Boronia megastigma* (F) grows at right, and Mexican feather grass (G), blue oat grass (H), and reddish *Stipa arundinacea* (I) grow behind.

MATERIALS

- Pond shell and pump
- Yardstick
- Several bags of sand
- Shovel
- Contractor's level
- Wheelbarrow (for moving sand)
- Edging stones (Thin, broad ones, such as flagstone, are best. To determine the number of rocks you'll need, make a paper outline of your pond as a guide and take it with you to the stone yard. Allow space between some of the stones for growing plants.)

DIRECTIONS

1. Select the site; trace the shell. Open areas are better than areas beneath trees with leaves or needles that will build up debris on the pond's bottom over time. To install a pond in a lawn, remove the sod and keep it moist and protected in a shady area so you can reuse it later. Set the pond shell on the cleared, level site, adjusting it to face the direction you want. Holding a yardstick vertically against the outside edge, trace around the pond shell to outline it in the soil.

2. Remove the pond shell and trace the soil outline with sand (as shown, or use a hose or length of rope).

3. Dig the hole following the outline. The hole should be 2 inches deeper and wider than the shell to accommodate a layer of sand. Using a carpenter's level, make sure the bottom of the hole is flat. Remove protruding stones or roots, then cover the bottom with 2 inches of packed damp sand. Recheck flatness with level.

4. Place the pond shell in the hole. It should sit slightly higher than the surrounding ground, and the top lip should be level. (To check it, you may have to place the level on a straight 2-by-4 to span the pond.) Adjust the shell as necessary. Start filling the pond with water, setting a garden hose to run slowly. Working in 4-inch increments, add moist backfill sand around the shell as shown, tamping as you go. Periodically recheck that the top is level. Continue until pond and hole are filled, adding backfill to create a gentle slope of soil away from the pond's edges.

5. Position edging stones around the pond so they hide the lip from view. Cantilever them beyond the lip of the shell, but keep most of their weight on surrounding soil, not on the lip.

Solar-powered fountain

A small photovoltaic panel powers the submersible pump for this pond. It comes with 16½ feet of wire; to operate properly, it must be in a sunny, south-facing spot near the pond. The small pump comes with a variety of spray heads that put out gentle streams of water. For a larger pond, use a standard, electric-powered pump that will circulate the pond's volume every two hours. Such pumps require 110 volts and should plug into an outdoor receptacle with a GFCI (ground fault circuit interrupter). ◆

A garden designed for parties

This small backyard has everything for entertaining:
seating, lighting, a barbecue, and more

BY PETER O. WHITELEY • PHOTOGRAPHS BY JAMIE HADLEY

I t's almost like being in a room," says Cia Foreman of the outdoor dining area she designed on one side of her 30- by 50-foot rear garden in Palo Alto. A patio floor paved with Connecticut blue stone defines the area, and finishing touches—sculptural, freestanding lighting columns, a built-in barbecue, and an antique metal baker's rack against one wall that substitutes for a buffet table—serve her well for entertaining.

To accentuate the roomlike feeling, Foreman covered two of the sections of fence that hug the dining area with the same siding as the house, then painted the back one soft lavender and the side one gray to match the house. Copper-and-glass light fixtures mounted near the tops of 6-by-6 redwood posts function like wall sconces to bathe the patio in soft light. (Channels routed in the posts accommodate the electrical lines.)

But this small remodeled garden offers more than its dining patio for summer entertaining. At the heart of the garden is an elevated planter, with a fountain and a vine-covered trellis; it's edged on two sides by a wide seat wall. At night, light fixtures hidden in the planter splash the fountain, background foliage, and fence with light.

At the other end of the garden, an outdoor sitting area containing two

7 must-haves for outdoor entertaining

- Comfortable seating for everyone. Built-in seating or seat walls can supplement garden furniture for large groups and keep the garden from looking cluttered.
- Serving or buffet surfaces. These can be portable (carts or side tables) or built-in countertops.
- Barbecue, cooktop, pizza oven, or built-in wok.
- Easy access to the kitchen (even just a pass-through window). Also, good traffic flow from house to garden and within and around outdoor living spaces.
- Bug control. Burn citrus candles to help keep a variety of bugs at bay, and keep ponds stocked with mosquito fish. For yellow jackets (daytime nuisances, mostly), try traps from your nursery or garden center; hang them at least 5 yards downwind of a barbecue or picnic table, waist-high or lower. Cover food, especially meat and sweet drinks, on a buffet table.
- Umbrellas or other shademakers for afternoon parties in hot climates. (They add visual interest too.)
- Outdoor lighting for evening parties.

AN ELEVATED FOUNTAIN (above) fills the garden with the sound of falling water. Behind it, vines climb a freestanding trellis. The fountain rises from a large planter that divides the dining area from a sitting area (right) at the garden's opposite end.

comfortable chairs is backed by a generous lattice-covered screen.

THE PLANTS

Golden coreopsis, blue delphinium, daylilies, species geraniums, penstemons, and lamb's ears (*Stachys*) mix with blue *Salvia farinacea* and violas in the stucco-clad planter. Morning glory (*Ipomoea*) and polyanthus jasmine cling to the trellis behind the fountain, and scented herbs—lavenders and thyme—grow close to the sitting area with spiky New Zealand flax as accent.

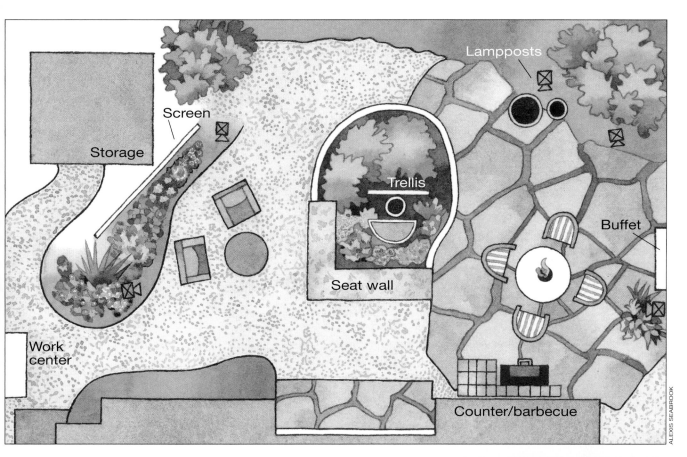

Screen

Storage

Lampposts

Trellis

Buffet

Seat wall

Work
center

Counter/barbecue

ALEXIS SEABROOK

PLAN SHOWS HOW the slender, rectangular garden—which once contained only a struggling lawn and a small brick patio—is now divided into a dining area on the right and a sitting area on the left. A seat wall wraps the central planter to provide extra seating for parties. There's also storage (hidden behind the sitting area's angled lattice screen) and easy access to the house.

RIGHT: Copper-topped lantern from Arroyo Craftsman (888/227-7696) hangs from a cantilevered hook mounted to the post. Garden installation by Harris Landscaping, Redwood City, CA (650/261-1858).

7 magic-makers

■ Portable lighting. Candles, luminarias, miniature white lights strung between trees or posts, or white paper lanterns dangling from trees can supplement built-in lighting and take a patio from ordinary to spectacular.

■ Water. A trickling fountain or a glazed pot containing a single water lily adds magic. Or float summer blossoms in a birdbath.

■ Fragrance. Perfumed flowers are en-chanting on warm summer nights. Plant some of these in pots: *Bouvardia longiflora,* citrus, gardenia, *Jasminum nitidum,* plumeria. Put the pots on the edge of the deck or patio where their fragrance can be enjoyed.

■ Colorful pillows. It's best if they're covered with outdoor fabrics. Scatter them on garden benches or seat walls.

■ Outdoor speakers. Play your favorite tunes—soft classical guitar, bossa nova, or Hawaiian slack key, anyone? All of these are especially soothing outdoors on balmy evenings.

■ Fireplace. Or it could be a portable firepit (gas, or wood-burning, fitted with a spark-arresting top).

■ Outdoor bouquets. Fill terra-cotta wine coolers or colorful painted buckets with bunches of cut flowers to dress up a patio or buffet table.

— *Kathleen N. Brenzel* ◆

Party pots

Containers can set the stage for backyard summer parties

BY LAUREN BONAR SWEZEY

Colorful, flower-filled pots make your garden sparkle for a summer celebration. And by continuing your party theme—for a fiesta or wedding, for instance—container plantings add to your garden's festiveness.

Theme pots are Keeyla Meadows's specialty. "They're conversation starters," says this Albany, California, garden designer and artist. "They can really make a garden shine." One of her party pot collections—for a backyard fiesta party—is pictured at right. The fiesta pots are so colorful they need nothing else, except perhaps a mariachi band, to set the scene.

Any occasion is an excuse to revel with container gardens. Imagine pots filled with red, white, and blue flowers for a Fourth of July bash. Or pots painted with stripes or polka dots filled with candy-colored zinnias for a birthday party. Even the smallest gatherings lend themselves to themed pots.

Last-minute party planners can take advantage of the wide array of blooming plants available in nurseries this month for instant displays. Those with more time before the event can go for a cost-effective option: start with young plants and fill in with additional bloomers right before the party. Whichever route you choose, your party pots will help you celebrate the season.

PARTY POT PLANNER

Design your plantings ahead on paper, or wait until you're at the nursery, where you can see what's in bloom.

1. Decide on a theme. "Let your imagination run wild," advises Meadows. Even old shoes filled with plants would enhance a Walk on the Wild Side dinner.

2. Select a color scheme. Choose colors to suit the holiday or event. Then bend the rules. Instead of red, white, and blue flowers for a Fourth of July pot, you could vary the blue tones by mixing in purple, and add orange flowers beside red ones.

3. Set a timetable. *The two-month plan:* Use small plants and pot them two months before the date of the event. The week of the event, fill holes between them with blooming 4-inch or 1-gallon plants as needed. *The two- to seven-day plan:* Use 4-inch and 1-gallon flowering plants and pot them right before the event. Allow at least a couple of days for the plants to settle in.

4. Determine your party location. Will it be on the patio, deck, or back lawn? Then figure out how many pots will fit the site. Combine large and small pots in clusters around patios, on steps, and by doorways. Use odd numbers—clusters of three and five pots—for striking vignettes. Make sure that the scale of the containers is in keeping with the location.

5. Shop for plants, containers, and accessories. Go all out for a big event like a wedding. Buy more plants than you think you'll need. If you want the pots to last for a season, pack them with plants for the occasion, then remove some afterward to allow room for the remaining ones to grow. Use all kinds of plants—vines, bulbs, annuals, and perennials. Even colorful house plants work outdoors during the summer season.

If you plan to keep the pots long after the event, buy quality planters such as glazed containers or Italian terra-cotta. Pots for one-time use and giveaways (as party favors) can be made of anything that will hold soil. Try secondhand and antiques stores for unusual containers.

6. Plant the pots. Fill the pot partway with a good potting mix. Mix in a controlled-release fertilizer. Then plant, following tips in the box below.

ABOUT THOSE PAINTED POTS

Using a slightly moist rag, Meadows wiped Mexican terra-cotta pots with one to three layers of diluted acrylic paint (allowing it to dry between layers).

Planting and care guide

- Think of the pot as having a grid dividing it into three sections—back, center, and front.

- Plant the tallest plant in back, two medium-size plants in the center on either side of the tallest plant, and a cascading plant in front.

- Tuck intensely colored annuals and bulbs on either side of the cascaders. Fill in around plants with potting mix.

- Water after planting, and again often enough to keep the soil moist. Once plants fill in, small pots might need watering daily. If you start with young plants, feed them with 0-10-10 (follow label directions) beginning two weeks before the event. ◆

Fiesta time. A playful theme pairs hot colors in terra-cotta pots. Tall plants: Spiky-leafed 'Solfatare' crocosmia and lime green nicotiana. Midsize plants: Yellow-green coleus, red gerbera daisies, pink and coral New Guinea impatiens, yellow ornamental peppers, orange ursinia, and yellow to deep red zinnias. Yellow Dahlberg daisies, 'Harlequin' marigolds, and petunias round out the festive palette. Design: Keeyla Meadows, Albany, CA; (510) 524-7106.

A wreath in a wink

How to make an aromatic herb wreath in minutes, using your own wreath jig

BY SHARON COHOON

LEFT: Scott Williams tucks eucalyptus and rosemary branches into a wreath jig.
ABOVE: Minutes later, three completed wreaths. Red dahlias and rosebuds embellish wreath at top. Violet blue statice, ivory roses, and lavender complement the blue-gray herbal foliage, at left. Succulents and eucalyptus pods add texture to the wreath at right.

Fragrant wreaths of lavender, eucalpytus, summer savory, and thyme disappear from Scott Williams's stand at the Saturday Farmers Market in Santa Barbara almost as quickly as he can make them. And when he's surrounded by crowds and his adrenaline is up, that's darn fast—less than five minutes per wreath. What many of his customers really covet, however, is the neat little gizmo he uses to make them. "Boy, could I use one of those," said one gardener, with undisguised envy. "At the end of the season, I have all these herbs that need to be pruned, and it just kills me to toss them. With this, I could make wreaths for all my friends."

Williams, an organic herb and flower grower, understands her point of view. A desire not to let any of his harvest go to waste is what led him to design this tool, which is a simplified version of a commercial jig. So he's generously sharing instructions for making one, as well as providing suggestions for how to use the jig to create simple wreaths from end-of-the-season garden clippings.

Williams's jig, which is nothing more than a ring of evenly spaced dowels secured in a plywood base, frees his hands. The dowels hold the herb cuttings in place as he assembles them, then guide the twine when he's ready to bundle the lot together into a wreath. The directions on page 183 are for a jig to make a wreath that is 10 inches in diameter, Williams's most popular size, but you can make a larger or smaller jig.

Enjoy your wreath while the herbs retain their savor and color. Then toss it into the compost and make another.

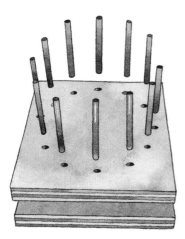

How to make a wreath jig

You can make your own jig following the directions below. But if you'd rather buy a jig than build one, Williams can oblige. Write or call Santa Barbara Gardens & Company, Box 6701, Santa Barbara, CA 93160 (805/964-0679; fax 805/964-4233) for a Wreath Wizard brochure. The jigs come in five sizes; a 10-inch wreath jig costs $49.99.

TIME: 1½ hours to make, plus several hours to dry

COST: $10 to $15

MATERIALS

• Two squares of ¾-inch-thick plywood a few inches larger than the desired diameter of your wreath. For example, cut two 13-inch squares for a 10-inch wreath.

• Compass, pencil, drill with ½-inch bit, wood glue, clamps, mallet

• A dozen ½-inch-thick hardwood dowels, cut to 4¾-inch lengths

DIRECTIONS

1. Using the compass, draw a 10-inch circle in the center of one plywood square.

2. To place dowels, mark 12 equally spaced spots around the circle.

3. At each mark, drill a ½-inch-wide hole completely through the plywood.

4. Coat one side of the second plywood square with a generous amount of glue. Affix the first square on top. Use clamps to hold the two squares together while the glue dries (or weight them with heavy books).

5. Drip glue inside each dowel hole and pound dowels into place with a mallet.

Wipe off any excess glue. Allow glue to dry thoroughly—for at least several hours—before using the jig.

How to make a wreath

1. Use plants with sturdy but still pliable stems for your bottom layer. Williams favors baby blue eucalyptus (shown at right), rosemary, curly willow, cedar, and pine. One stem at a time, place the cuttings inside the dowel circle. Start with stem ends, tucking them under foliage. Alternate starting points on opposite sides of the jig. "That way the wreath stays balanced," he says.

2. Pile on herbs with a light texture—lavender, savory, thyme, and scented geraniums ("whatever needs pruning," says Williams). Save the most fragrant clippings (such as rosemary, right) and those with blossoms for the top layer.

3. Cut a 5-foot piece of twine (about two arm's lengths). Starting at any point, tie the twine around all layers of the wreath. Hide the knot on the inside of the wreath; don't trim the ends yet. Working from the inside out, loop the twine around the wreath, using the dowels to help guide the twine. Pull the twine taut with each wrap.

4. Tie the end of the twine to your original knot. Clip twine ends.

Variations on a theme

• Add flowers. Statice, strawflowers, and other blooms make attractive finishing touches.

• Fill the centers. A row of 6-inch wreaths filled with votive candles makes a great tabletop display. Small potted plants can be added to larger wreaths.

• Turn a wreath into a decorative basket (not meant to be picked up). Strip a eucalyptus branch, notch the ends, and bend into a handle; poke ends into the base. Add more clippings to the bottom side of the wreath. Set a pot of grass and/or fresh farm eggs in the center. ◆

ASIATIC LILIES BLOOM over a carpet of feverfew in this Montrose, Colorado, garden. For details on this pretty pairing, see page 192.

July

gardenguide

STEVEN GUNTHER

Monet in Mandeville Canyon

Plantings give this pool a natural elegance

PAINTERLY HUES— provided by pink society garlic, gray lamb's ears, and blue agapanthus— surround the pool and reflect in its mirror-smooth water.

■ It would be easy to pretend you were floating in a pond in the middle of a meadow while in this backyard swimming pool in Mandeville Canyon. Flowers and foliage come right up to the water's edge and lean over to admire their reflected images, just the way they do in nature. But Teresa Yang doesn't see things from that vantage point very often. She can't tear herself away from her garden.

It wasn't always that way. With a dental practice and two young children to manage, Yang assumed she wouldn't have time to garden. So she planned a landscape that would require minimal maintenance for the pool area. But she soon found it boringly tame and tucked in a few cosmos dahlias, geraniums, and other annuals for color. Then she added some perennials—columbine, coneflower, daylilies, gaillardia, lamb's ears, and yarrow—for a bit more. Soon she was squeezing in flowering shrubs like shrimp plant and rockrose and colorful vines such as bougainvillea.

Good-bye, low maintenance. Hello, well-worn garden gloves. "Now I'm out there at dusk with a flashlight sometimes, trying to get one more job done before dark," Yang admits. "But gardening is so relaxing and therapeutic, it never feels like work."

Her family loves the results. Her husband, John Coo, finds pruning from *inside* the pool an amusing diversion. Their daughter, Danielle, and son, Spencer, enjoy the butterflies and bees the flowers attract. And the mirror images on the pool's surface delight everyone, especially Yang. "It's like having Monet's pond in my backyard," she says.

— *Sharon Cohoon*

Harvest of history at Fort Vancouver

■ In 1825 the Hudson's Bay Company established Fort Vancouver, a key supply post on the Washington shore of the Columbia River. Early residents there enriched their diet by growing fresh vegetables and medicinal herbs. They also planted flowers to add a touch of beauty to a lonely frontier fortress.

Last year, the Fort Vancouver National Historic Site celebrated its 50th anniversary as a unit of the National Park Service. Under the direction of park ranger Rick Edwards and landscape specialist Patti Norberg, a corps of 25 volunteers maintains a 1-acre garden that represents the historic plantings.

The harvest begins this month. Visit the site to see the fruitfulness of a garden maintained with sustainable techniques, including crop rotation, composting (in big double bins), and planting "green manure"—cover crops such as buckwheat and crimson clover—to enrich the soil. You'll see hops growing atop an arbor, scarlet runner beans climbing split-log fences, and cardoon, whose succulent stalks taste like celery. Among the heirloom flowers are dahlias, lemon lilies, and monarda (bee balm), whose leaves were steeped to make Oswego tea. When you visit, pick up packets of seed harvested on-site to grow in your own garden; just leave a donation in the watering can.

The garden is open 9 to 5 daily. A $2 entry fee includes access to the entire fort. From Interstate 5 in Vancouver, Washington, take exit 1C and follow signs. For information, call (360) 696-7655, ext. 17, or visit www.nps.gov/fova.

— *Steven R. Lorton*

Lavender time in Oregon

■ Though lavender starts blooming in late May in the Pacific Northwest, it doesn't peak until July. That's when most plants are covered with fragrant flower spikes—and when you should pay a visit to Sawmill Ballroom Lavender Farm in Lorane, Oregon, about 30 minutes south of Eugene.

The farm grows about 30 varieties of lavender, including a favorite called 'Tuscan' that owners Nancy and Joey Blum brought back from Italy 11 years ago. You can buy a 4-inch potted lavender (from $3) or one in a 1-gallon can ($8) as well as fresh and dried flowers and sachets. The farm also stocks a dozen kinds of rosemary and a few varieties of butterfly bush, penstemon, and sage. The pace is relaxed; kids can watch the donkeys while parents ponder plants.

Sawmill Ballroom Lavender Farm is at 29251 Hamm Rd., about 11 miles from Interstate 5. (From I-5, take exit 182 at Creswell and drive west through town on Oregon St., which becomes Camas Swale Rd., which turns into Hamm Rd.) For more information, call (541) 686-9999. — *Jim McCausland*

FLANKING A PATH are billowy blue oat grass (on right) and scarlet pineleaf penstemon (on left).

A gallery of great plants in Santa Fe

■ Filled with art galleries and museums, Santa Fe makes it easy for visitors to see its cultural riches. The city's horticultural treasures are harder to find because so many beautiful gardens are tucked behind adobe walls. Many of those gardens are stocked with rugged, cold-hardy plants raised by a local grower—Santa Fe Greenhouses. Happily, the firm's own gardens have blossomed into an expansive display of annuals, perennials, grasses, and shrubs that perform well in the high-desert and mountain areas of the West.

Visitors are welcome to stroll paths through gently bermed beds. Some star performers are shown above. At left is scarlet pineleaf penstemon (*Penstemon pinifolius*); in front a rosy carpet of 'Reiter's' thyme creeps around 'Sea Urchin' blue fescue. At right, golden seed heads of blue oat grass (*Helictotrichon sempervirens*) wave beside a soft mound of silver-leafed 'Powis Castle' artemisia.

The gardens are open year-round for self-guided tours (9–5:30 Mon-Sat, 10–5 Sun). During peak bloom, from late May to late August, visitors can join a one-hour tour led by knowledgeable employees (10 A.M. Wed, 10 and 11 A.M. Sat). In mid-August, the nursery hosts a Hummingbird & Butterfly Festival featuring guest speakers and a plant sale.

Santa Fe Greenhouses is at 2904 Rufina St.; (505) 473-2700. If you can't visit in person, order a free copy of the catalog from High Country Gardens (800/925-9387), the firm's mail-order arm. — *Judith Phillips*

Sleek and sporty hose-end sprinkler

■ It's durable, yet lightweight, it delivers water gently and quickly, and the squeeze handle is much easier to operate than comparable devices. That's what we like about the new Waterquick watering wand.

Its Miracle Nozzle resembles a bubbler in softness of flow, but it delivers aerated water at maximum volume to a specific point (standard bubblers emit water in a wide circle), so there's no splashing or waste. The water stream is so gentle that you can hold the nozzle a couple of inches above the soil, delivering water right to the root zone without displacing soil or showering plant foliage. The unit, made of brightly colored, high-impact plastic and powder-coated aluminum, includes an optional spray device.

Waterquick is available at some nurseries and home improvement stores, or directly from KSM ($20 including shipping); (800) 396-8585. — *Lauren Bonar Swezey*

Foliage carries the show

NORMAN A. PLATE (2)

■ Designed for a sunny patio, this container combines three plants with contrasting leaf colors and textures: purple fountain grass, heavenly bamboo (*Nandina domestica*), and dusty miller (*Senecio cineraria*). For a shady area, try cast-iron plant (*Aspidistra elatior*), Myers asparagus, and sword fern. Any of these plants, if snipped judiciously, can also provide cuttings to use in floral bouquets.

PLANT A FOLIAGE POT

- Choose a 16- to 20-inch container to hold from three to five plants in 1-gallon cans.
- Plant on-site. Filled with soil and plants, the container will be heavy and difficult to move.
- Fill the container about halfway with potting mix. Stir in a controlled-release fertilizer to provide a steady supply of nutrients.
- Remove plants from 1-gallon cans and position them in the container, placing the tallest plant toward the rear and shorter ones in the middle or front. Fill in around plants with more potting mix.
- Water regularly. — *Kay Motley*

Pretty as a petunia—without problems

■ *Calibrachoa* is destined to make its mark in gardens over the next few years, due to its easy-care habit and long-lasting bloom.

Native to Brazil, it was hybridized in Japan; hybrids began appearing in Western nurseries about four years ago. Now a new color range—from white to pink to purplish blue—is available from Paul Ecke Ranch (known for its poinsettias) and Proven Winners.

Plants of Ecke's first series, called Liricashower, are very low-growing trailers. The latest series, called Colorburst, has mounding and trailing habits; the plants are not as flat as the Liricashower series. Liricashower comes in blush white, pink, rose, and blue. Colorburst comes in cherry, rose, red, and violet. Proven Winners offers three trailing types and one compact variety sold under the common name million bells.

COLORBURST SERIES includes rose, red (bottom left), and violet (bottom right).

"We're excited about *Calibrachoa*," says Laurie Scullin of Ecke Ranch. "Unlike petunias, these have wiry stems that don't break easily, the flowers are self-cleaning [they drop off naturally when spent], budworms don't eat them, and the plants continue to produce flowers up and down the stems all season long."

The plants are marvelous in hanging baskets and containers. In milder parts of the West, they can be grown as perennials. Elsewhere, grow them as annuals. Plants thrive in full sun and moist soil.

Look for *Calibrachoa* at nurseries that carry a wide selection of plants. Or visit www.provenwinners.com to find a source near you.

— *L.B.S.*

STEVEN GUNTHER (3)

DEEP GREEN SANTOLINA and ornamental grasses form showy mounds.

Lush and rugged in Boulder

Maintaining a beautiful garden in the middle of deer country might seem like an impossible dream, especially where the water supply is limited. Despite these challenges, landscape designer Robert Howard and his associate Mike Ransom created a dreamy landscape in the Boulder, Colorado, garden shown above. They used unthirsty plants—ornamental grasses, perennials, and shrubs—to compose a naturalistic garden that tolerates grazing deer, yet fits handsomely into the foothills.

The grasses—blue fescue, blue oat grass, feather reed grass, maiden grass, and *Panicum virgatum*—provide interesting color and form much of the year. "Deer regularly move through the garden and munch on the ornamental grasses, but you don't notice any damage because of the plants' informal shapes," says Howard. Around the grasses grow Apache plume (*Fallugia paradoxa*), *Rosa rugosa*, santolina, and three-leaf sumac (*Rhus trilobata*). Boulders of local sandstone "moss rock" anchor the landscape and blend with the hilly terrain.

— *L.B.S.*

BACK TO BASICS

Container plants can be difficult to keep watered during the heat of summer, especially if the potting mix dries out at any time, or if the plant is rootbound. Water runs off the surface of dry soils. To rewet dry soil, try these two tricks. **1.** Using a pointed stick, poke four to six holes in the rootball so water can penetrate it. **2.** Add a drop of mild liquid dish soap to a gallon of water and soak the soil. This helps break the surface tension of peat moss–based potting mix so water can soak in. — *L.B.S.*

ALLAN MANDELL

Perfect pair: Lilies, feverfew

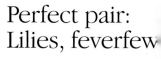

■ The sunny bed in Fred Maxted's Montrose, Colorado, garden (pictured on page 184) is a shining example of serendipity. Several years ago when Maxted was driving through Minnesota on vacation, he happened to pass a field of Asiatic hybrid lilies in full bloom at Hartle-Gilman Gardens, a specialty nursery. He stopped the car, picked out two varieties that he liked, and ordered bulbs then and there. When the bulbs arrived that fall, Maxted planted them in a spot where he "had a hard time growing anything,"

In their first summer, the lilies produced only a few blooms, so Maxted planted feverfew (*Chrysanthemum parthenium*) among them to brighten the bed. The next summer, Maxted's patience was rewarded: The lilies bloomed profusely over a carpet of feverfew that had reseeded from the previous year.

The lilies Maxted chose are golden yellow 'Candle-flame' and pale yellow 'Indian Princess'. Both are still available, though 'Indian Princess' is in limited supply. Order now for fall planting. Bury bulbs about 8 inches deep in well-drained soil. Next spring, sow feverfew or set out nursery seedlings. The shade cast by feverfew creates a cool root run that lilies appreciate. *Hartle-Gilman Gardens, 4708 E. Rose St., Owatonna, MN 55060; free price list, (507) 451-3191. — D.B.*

Five pots full of summer glory

■ A deck forms the stage for D'Nece and Andy Soulé's container garden in Redmond, Washington. Designed by Karen Kienholz Steeb, the whole garden grows in five pots filled with evergreens and ornamental grasses for year-round interest and cascades of summer flowers and foliage.

The containers, ranging from 12 to 20 inches in diameter and depth, are made from double-walled plastic and filled with lightweight potting mix. Steeb plants everything "very close, with rootballs almost touching, so growth is forced up and out. That's how I get that bouquet look," she says. She starts with permanent plants like blue oat grass, sedge grass, heavenly bamboo, *Hypericum moseranum* 'Tricolor', leucothoe, *Mahonia repens,* and *Viburnum da-* *vidii.* Then she plugs in midheight flowers like 'Tango Red' geranium. Finally, she fills in with plants that spill and trail like variegated *Vinca major,* 'Merlin Blue' petunia, and deep blue and red verbenas.

At planting time, Steeb sprinkles controlled-release fertilizer over the soil and waters it in. She applies 20-20-20 fertilizer every two weeks until July. After the summer annuals fade, they'll be replaced with pansies for fall/winter color, and tulips in spring. — *J.M.*

NORMAN A. PLATE

Pouch for phone and pruners

■ These days when people putter around the garden, they're as likely to carry a cordless phone as pruning shears. But balancing phone and tools is tricky. With that in mind, Fiskars has devised a way to tote both items securely, yet still keep your hands free. Just strap the Phone & Garden Pocket around your waist. It has one mesh pouch to hold a portable phone of any size and another pocket for small garden tools. There's also a sturdy metal clip for attaching a pocket knife or a spare set of house keys. *$13; for local retailers, call (800) 500-4849 or visit www.fiskars.com.*

— *Dick Bushnell*

Pacific Northwest Checklist

PLANTING

☑ **ANNUALS.** Act right away and you can still plant annuals that will bloom until frost, often putting on a better late-summer show than ones that were planted in May.

☑ **CROPS.** Seed for beets, broccoli, bush beans, carrots, chard, Chinese cabbage, kohlrabi, lettuce, peas, radishes, scallions, spinach, and turnips can be sown directly into the ground now. You can also plant a second crop of early potatoes for fall harvest if you do it by July 4.

MAINTENANCE

☑ **CARE FOR FUCHSIAS.** Snip or pick off blooms as they fade to keep flowers coming—but expect bloom to slack off during hot weather. Feed plants monthly with a complete liquid plant fertilizer (every two weeks if plants are in containers).

☑ **COMPOST.** Keep adding organic matter and turning the pile at least weekly. Keep the pile moist.

☑ **FEED CHRYSANTHEMUMS.** For best bloom this autumn, feed plants with a low-nitrogen liquid fertilizer (often called a bloom formula) every three weeks until buds start to show color. When the first blooms open, feed weekly.

☑ **IRRIGATE.** Water annuals and perennials early in the morning to reduce evaporation and give plants time to dry off before mildew gets going.

☑ **MAINTAIN GROUND COVERS.** After they've bloomed, shear ground covers back to keep them neat and compact. After shearing, scatter a complete dry fertilizer over the bed and water it in well. This is a good time to bait for slugs, which frequently use ground covers as hideouts.

☑ **MONITOR HOUSE PLANTS.** Watch for infestations of insects; they can explode this time of year. Check plants daily to make sure they have enough water. Hose off dusty leaves or rinse them in a lukewarm shower. If normally green leaves take on a bronze cast, give plants more shade.

☑ **MULCH SHRUBS.** Put a 3- to 4-inch layer of organic mulch under shrubs—especially azaleas and rhododendrons—to conserve moisture.

☑ **TEND STRAWBERRIES.** On everbearing kinds, keep fruit picked so plants will keep producing. After harvest on June-bearing strawberries, feed plants with 2 pounds of 10-10-10 fertilizer per 100 square feet.

WEED. Hoe young weeds on a warm, dry morning and the sun will kill them by evening. Water before you pull mature weeds, whose taproots come out of damp soil more easily than dry. ◆

Northern California Checklist

PLANTING

☑ **A PATRIOTIC POT.** Nurseries sell many plants in full bloom right now. For a patriotic display in a flowerpot on the Fourth of July, mix red, white, and blue flowers. For red, try annual phlox, celosia, geranium, nicotiana, petunia, *Salvia* coccinea, and scarlet sage. For white, try alyssum, annual phlox, dahlia, dwarf cosmos, geranium, heliotrope, nicotiana, petunia, and a white variety of scarlet sage. For blue, try gentian sage, lobelia, mealycup sage, petunia, and verbena.

☑ **FALL VEGETABLES.** Zones 1–2: For fall harvest (except in highest altitudes), plant beets, broccoli, bush beans, cabbage, carrots, cauliflower, green onions, peas, spinach, and turnips. Below 5,000 feet, plant winter squash among spinach; the spinach will be ready to harvest before the squash takes over.

☑ **IRISES.** Plant new rhizomes or dig up overcrowded clumps six weeks after flowers fade. Discard dried-out or mushy rhizomes; cut apart healthy ones, and trim leaves back to 6 inches. Plant new or just-divided irises in full sun in fast-draining soil that's been well amended with compost.

☑ **MUMS.** To add rich, bright colors to the fall garden, plant garden chrysanthemums now. If plants haven't formed flower buds yet, pinch growing tips to keep plants compact.

Sunset
CLIMATE ZONES

Eureka

Redding

CALIFORNIA

NEVADA

Mendocino

Santa Rosa · Sacramento

San Francisco

San Jose

Monterey · Fresno

☐ Mountain (1-2)
☐ Valley (7-9)
☐ Inland (14)
☐ Coastal (15-17)

DEBRA LAMBERT

MAINTENANCE

☑ **CARE FOR LAWNS.** Keep the mowing height high during the heat of summer; mow when the grass is about a third taller than the recommended height. For bluegrass and fescue, mow when the grass is 3 to 4 inches tall, with your mower set at 2 to 3 inches. Cut Bermuda grass when it's not quite 2 inches tall with the mower set at 1 inch. If your lawn is full of crabgrass (broad-spreading weed with blue-green foliage) and it has set seed, collect the clippings after mowing to keep the weed from spreading.

☑ **COAX BOUGAINVILLEA BLOOM.** Bougainvillea flowers best if it's kept on the dry side. Allow the top several inches of soil around it to dry out between waterings.

☑ **POLLINATE MELONS, SQUASH.** When the weather is hot, high temperatures may inhibit fruit set. To aid pollination, use an artist's brush to gather yellow pollen from freshly opened male flowers and dust it onto the stigmata of female flowers, which have slightly enlarged bases. You can also pull off male flowers, gently remove petals, and shake directly over the female flowers.

PEST CONTROL

☑ **CONTROL BUDWORMS.** If your geraniums, nicotiana, penstemons, and petunias appear healthy but have no flowers, budworms are probably eating the flowers before they open. Look for holes in buds and black droppings. Spray the plants every 7 to 10 days with *Bacillus thuringiensis* (BT), available at most local nurseries or by mail from Harmony Farm Supply and Nursery (707/823-9125). ◆

Southern California Checklist

PLANTING

☑ **BIENNIALS.** For blooms next spring, sow seeds of Canterbury bells, foxglove, hollyhocks, sweet William, and verbascum now. Transplant seedlings to the garden in fall when they are about 4 inches high.

☑ **PATRIOTIC POTS.** Decorate for the Fourth with some tricolored container plantings. For red, consider begonias, pentas, petunias, verbena—even miniature roses. White: candytuft, petunias, sweet alyssum, verbena, vinca. Blue: annual salvia, Chinese delphiniums, foamflower, petunias.

☑ **SUBTROPICALS.** Add palms, philodendron, tree ferns, and other evergreens; flowering shrubs like cestrum, datura, hibiscus, and princess flower; avocado, citrus, guava, sapote, and other exotic fruits; and bougainvillea, passion vine, *Stephanotis floribunda,* thunbergia, and trumpet vine.

☑ **SUMMER VEGETABLES.** For a late-summer harvest, continue to plant vegetables in coastal and inland gardens (zones 22–24 and 18–21, respectively). Set out cucumber, eggplant, pepper, squash, and tomato plants. Sow snap beans and corn. Plant basil, chervil, chives, parsley, rosemary, sage, savory, and thyme. In the low desert (zone 13), start pumpkins and winter squash.

CALIFORNIA
NEVADA
Bishop
San Luis Obispo
Bakersfield
Tehachapi
Santa Barbara
Lancaster
Los Angeles
Palm Springs
Sunset
CLIMATE ZONES
San Diego
1-3 7-9 11 13 14-24
MEXICO

DEBRA LAMBERT

MAINTENANCE

☑ **CARE FOR CYMBIDIUMS.** Next year's flower spikes are developing now. To encourage proper development, water plants weekly and feed them with a high-nitrogen fertilizer.

☑ **MOW LAWNS.** To keep their roots shaded, allow tall fescues to grow to 2 to 3 inches tall. Keep warm-season grasses like Bermuda and St. Augustine below 1 inch tall to lessen thatch buildup.

☑ **HARVEST CROPS.** Pick beans, cucumbers, peppers, and tomatoes frequently to encourage further production. Check fast growers like squash almost daily. Cut off seed heads of cosmos, dahlias, rudbeckias, and zinnias to encourage more flowers for cutting.

☑ **WATER CAREFULLY.** Last winter was a dry one, which stressed plants. Give shade trees a slow, deep soak once a month to ensure good health. Water established shrubs and perennials deeply, too. Shallow-rooted citrus and avocados need more frequent irrigation. Water once a week inland, every other week along the coast.

PEST AND WEED CONTROL

☑ **CONTROL CATERPILLARS.** Spray or dust plants that have pest caterpillars (such as cabbage worm, tomato hornworm, and geranium budworm) with *Bacillus thuringiensis*. Apply sparingly, starting when caterpillars are small. Handpick large hornworms from tomato plants.

☑ **MANAGE GIANT WHITEFLY.** Examine the underside of leaves of target plants like hibiscus and banana for white waxy spirals where eggs are deposited. Remove leaves—bag in plastic and dispose of them—or wash away the spirals with a strong stream of water. ◆

Mountain Checklist

PLANTING & HARVEST

☑ **HARVEST VEGETABLES, FLOW-ERS.** All plants, be they vegetables or flowers, exist to set seed. If you remove the fruit before the seed ripens, the plant will usually try to produce more flowers and fruit. Use this to your advantage by keeping vegetables and flowers picked so the harvest will continue.

☑ **PLANT FALL VEGETABLES.** Zone 1: Plant warm-season vegetables in large pots. If nighttime temperatures are predicted to drop below 60°, move them under cover for the night. Zone 2 (Denver, Salt Lake City): Plant beets, broccoli, bush beans, cabbage, carrots, cauliflower, green onions, peas, spinach, and turnips. Below 5,000 feet, plant winter squash among spinach; it will fill the space after you harvest the spinach.

☑ **PLANT IRISES.** Set out new rhizomes in rich, well-drained soil in full sun. Sprinkle on some complete fertilizer at planting time and water in well.

Sunset
CLIMATE ZONES
☐ 1-3 ☐ 10-11

DEBRA LAMBERT

MAINTENANCE

☑ **CARE FOR CONTAINER PLANTS.** To encourage bloom and fruit production, apply a liquid fertilizer every two weeks.

☑ **COMPOST.** Add leafy garden debris and grass clippings to the compost pile. To keep it working, turn it weekly and water it so it stays as moist as a damp sponge.

☑ **CONTROL SPIDER MITES.** Mottled leaves and fine webs indicate the presence of spider mites; spray foliage with a strong jet of water, then treat with insecticidal soap or a stronger miticide.

☑ **DIVIDE IRISES.** Dig and divide overcrowded clumps three weeks after flowers fade. Discard dry or mushy rhizomes as you cut apart healthy ones, trimming leaves back to 6 inches, and replant in well-drained soil in full sun.

☑ **FERTILIZE.** Feed annuals and vegetables with high-nitrogen fertilizer and water it in well.

☑ **MAINTAIN SPRING-BLOOMING BULBS.** In coldest climates, pluck faded flowers and seed heads from daffodils, tulips, and other spring-flowering bulbs. After bloom, feed with high-phosphorus fertilizer, then water periodically until leaves turn brown. Let plants dry until fall rains.

☑ **STAKE TALL PLANTS.** Stake beans, delphiniums, peas, peonies, and tomatoes against high winds. Drive stakes at least 1 foot into the ground and tie plants loosely but securely.

☑ **TEND FRUIT TREES.** On trees with lots of fruit, thin plums to 2 inches apart and apples, nectarines, and peaches to 4-inch intervals.

☑ **TEND ROSES.** After each bloom cycle, remove faded flowers, cutting them off just above a leaf node with five leaflets. Then fertilize and water deeply in preparation for the next round of bloom.

☑ **WATER.** Continue a regular deep-watering program for ground covers, lawns, shrubs, and trees. ◆

Southwest Checklist

PLANTING & HARVEST

☑ **HARVEST VEGETABLES, FLOW-ERS.** Pick ripe vegetables every day or two to keep new ones coming and to prevent crops from becoming overmature (cucumbers, zucchini) or downright rotten (tomatoes). Pick flowers before they go to seed to encourage continued bloom.

☑ **PLANT VEGETABLES.** Zones 1–2, 10–11: Plant beets, broccoli, cabbage, carrots, cauliflower, green onions, leaf lettuce, peas, spinach, and turnips for fall harvest. Zone 10 (Albuquerque): Plant cantaloupes, eggplant, okra, peppers, pumpkins, tomatoes, watermelons, and winter squash. Potatoes go in at month's end.

MAINTENANCE

☑ **FERTILIZE.** Zones 1–2, 10–11: Feed annuals and vegetables with high-nitrogen fertilizer and water it in well.

☑ **IRRIGATE.** Water annual vegetables and flowers only after the top inch of soil has dried out. Deep-rooted permanent plants can be watered less often, but give them a thorough soaking when you irrigate.

☑ **MULCH.** Apply a 3-inch layer of organic mulch around permanent plants to reduce evaporation, inhibit weeds, and keep roots cool.

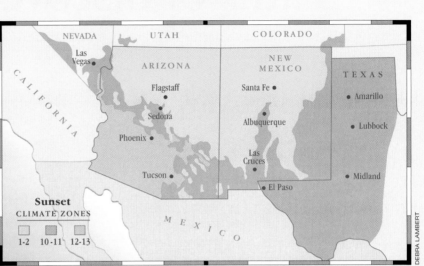

☑ **POLLINATE MELONS, SQUASH.** In hot-summer areas, high temperatures inhibit fruit set on squash. You can improve matters by dabbing pollen-bearing male flowers with a small artist's brush, then "painting" the pollen onto female flower parts (pistils); identify pistils by their swollen bases.

☑ **TEND ROSES.** After each bloom cycle, remove faded flowers, cutting them off just above a leaf node with five leaflets (nodes closest to the flower have three leaflets). Then fertilize and water deeply to stimulate the next round of bloom.

☑ **THIN TREES.** Thin top-heavy trees like acacia, Brazilian pepper, mesquite, and olives to open them up and protect them from strong winds.

PEST CONTROL

☑ **SPIDER MITES.** Mottled leaves and fine webs indicate the presence of spider mites; spray foliage with a strong jet of water, then treat with insecticidal soap or a stronger miticide.

☑ **TOBACCO BUDWORMS.** They eat through the buds of geraniums, nicotiana, penstemons, and petunias, thus preventing bloom. Spray plants every 7 to 10 days with the biological control *Bacillus thuringiensis.* ◆

Paths of discovery

How to blaze a garden trail with style—and the right materials

BY JIM McCAUSLAND

ABOVE: A gravel path leads through an arbor in Eugene, Oregon. Perennials crowding the path's edges give the garden a well-established look.

JANET LOUGHREY

■ Paths beckon. They invite you into a garden or through it, perhaps for a look at some fresh mallows that have unfurled near the birdbath or a sniff of the honeysuckle whose scent wafts from a sunny spot by the pond. They also give structure to the garden—and direction to its visitors. And when tufts of moss or creeping thyme grow between their pavers, paths urge you to slow down for a look underfoot. Paths will even eventually make themselves:

You cut across the lawn to the mailbox, the compost pile, or the gate enough times, and soon a path of flattened grass marks your trail.

Before that happens, map out circulation patterns in your garden and draw a plan—one that allows just enough twists and turns to reveal the garden slowly, area by area. A garden can do with a little mystery, which serpentine paths provide. The design ideas on these pages can spark inspiration.

Rules of the path

1. Choose the right materials. The most durable paths are designed for use in all weather conditions. That implies good drainage when it's wet, good traction when it's icy. Gravel and crushed rock are nearly perfect for this, as are loose-laid brick, pavers, and slightly crowned (higher in the center) paths made from textured concrete, brick, or stone.

Use solid paths (brick, concrete, pavers, or stone) for routes that you're likely to travel barefoot (the path from hot tub to house, for example), so you won't pick up dirt on wet feet. Use bark or gravel in places that call for a more natural look.

2. Make it wide enough. Main garden paths should be wide enough for two people to walk side by side; 5 feet is about right. Small subsidiary paths should be wide enough for a wheelbarrow (handles have a 24- to 30-inch spread). Two feet is a generous minimum, as long as plants don't crowd the edges.

Organize a network of paths like a river system, with smaller paths feeding into larger ones.

3. Add plants wherever possible. Allow at least 2 inches of soil between pavers, stones, or bricks in which to plant thyme or other low creepers. Amend the soil well so plants can establish roots; it should be light (on the sandy side) so it won't become packed down with foot traffic and kill the plants' roots.

Which path's for you?

Here's a quick guide to common path materials that can be loose-laid. Prices are approximate and do not include edging or base materials such as sand or gravel.

The easiest paths are laid over packed sand, or a combination of sand and gravel. More difficult to build are those set in concrete or mortar; such paths usually call for expert installation or guidance from a book like the *Sunset Complete Patio Book* (Sunset Publishing Corporation, Menlo Park, CA, 1998; $19.95).

Aggregate and concrete steppingstones. Textured concrete or aggregate steppingstones are attractive and have good traction in icy conditions. Cost is $4 to $7 per 16-inch-square paver, or $20 to $35 per square yard if you butt them together.

Bark. Good choice for woodland gardens, since it has the look and feel of forest duff, but it must be renewed frequently. You can cover a square yard of path 3 inches deep for about $1.15 to $4.

Brick. High-fired all-weather bricks are a great choice for formal paths. Most are 4 by 8 inches, give or take ¼ inch in either dimension. Enough brick to pave a square yard (about 40 bricks) costs $13 to $26.

TERRENCE MOORE

ABOVE: Bordered with boulders, crushed rock path is as informal as the Phoenix garden around it.
RIGHT: Grass path is soft underfoot and blends beautifully with surrounding greenery.
BELOW: Colored pavers give structure to this formal garden in Oregon.

JANET LOUGHREY (2)

irregular stone

cut stone

crushed rock

aggregate

grass

brick

bark

gravel

pavers

Crushed rock. The irregular shapes of the crushed particles allow them to pack well, giving a firm surface that can easily support a wheelbarrow. Let crushed rock pack down by itself or rent a compactor (similar to a jackhammer, but with a flat foot) to do the job for you. Cost is about $1.40 to $2.25 to cover a square yard of path 3 inches deep.

Grass. Works best in combination with stone. Alone, use it in wide swaths that spread out traffic to prevent worn trails. The heavier the use, the more you'll need to fertilize and overseed to compensate. Costs less than a nickel for enough seed to sow a square yard of ground.

Gravel. Makes a fine natural surface. But because gravel particles are round, it isn't great for heavily used paths; the particles shift as you walk on them. Most is sold in the $3/8$- to $3/4$-inch size; smaller grades are usually easier to walk on. Cost is $1.40 to $2.25 for enough gravel to cover a square yard of path 3 inches deep.

Pavers. Available in lots of beautiful patterns and textures. You can mix and match pavers of different colors and sizes. They cost $20 to $30 per square yard.

Stone (cut or irregular). Flagstones make wonderfully formal walks, while flat fieldstones work best in informal steppingstone paths. Cost is $30 to $100 per square yard.

SOURCES
Gravel, bark, rock, aggregate (this page), and materials for path (page 201) from Lyngso Garden Materials, Redwood City, CA; (650) 364-1730. Stone, brick, pavers, and aggregate (this page) from Peninsula Building Materials, Redwood City; (650) 365-8500.

JAMIE HADLEY (8)

Install this path in a day

Before building a path, you need to prepare the site. Concrete, aggregate, bark, gravel, and stones can be set directly on stable soil; paths of other materials need a base. Sand is a good choice, but be careful: It can wash out from under pavers and bricks, making them settle unevenly, especially in rainy areas. To prevent washout, layer sand over a 2-inch gravel base. Many people also put landscaping fabric under any loose-laid material (like gravel) to keep it from mixing with the sand or soil below. That can be effective, but often the fabric's edges work up to the surface. Keep the fabric down by stuffing its edges under the benderboards. You can make grade changes either with steps or simply by sloping the path.

1. Install benderboard edging first, then put down landscape fabric (available at nurseries) to prevent weeds. Secure fabric edges under the benderboard edging.

2. Pour a 2-inch-thick layer of sand over the landscape fabric, raking it smooth. (In rainy areas, put down a 2-inch gravel layer first.)

3. As you rake, moisten the sand with a fine spray from the hose.

4. Firm the sand. Using a drum roller or a hand tamper, pass over the moist sand several times to pack it down.

5. Add steppingstones, then wiggle them in so they're firmly embedded.

6. To finish, fill cracks between stones with gravel as shown, or—to hold flagstones more firmly—use something smaller like decomposed granite. ◆

FINISHED PATH features flagstones set in Salmon Bay gravel. As edging plants (blue fescue and petunias) grow, they'll create a graceful, soft edge.

NORMAN A. PLATE (7)

CLASSIC BENCH, left untreated to weather naturally, stands out against a climbing hydrangea hedge on a Seattle patio, at left. Above, a 'Chinatown' shrub rose climbs over an arbor bench.

Romancing the bench

Outdoor benches give a garden enduring graciousness and invite you to sit and enjoy your surroundings

BY STEVEN R. LORTON

Magical things happen on a garden bench. Grandmothers amaze us with tales of jitterbugging. Dads break their silence on the war. Lovers spin dreams for the future. And children speculate about what the dog might do if it had wings.

There's a reason for this magic. Put two people on a garden bench surrounded by trees and flowers, let them look out at something (a view of distant hills, or even clouds overhead), and suddenly their souls soar. Thoughts open up. Language relaxes. Pauses are soothing. Life expands to its proper perspective.

No garden should be without a bench—better two or three. A bench can capitalize on good views; it's a place where you can linger to enjoy a sweep of grass, the plop of a fountain, or the activity of a bird darting in and out of a nesting box to feed its young. And a good bench provides a logical place to stop and rest between wanderings along a garden path.

Most gardeners like their benches against something, whether a rock retaining wall or fence, a stand of dark conifers, or a big rambunctious shrub. A freestanding trellis supporting a

scramble of vines makes a fine backdrop for a bench. Simple as it sounds, the trick is this: *Place the bench where you'd like to spend time sitting.* The photos on these pages can give you some ideas.

Benches come in a wide variety of materials, colors, and styles, from natural or painted wood to stone or twiggy prunings. There are traditional English teak benches and wrought-iron reproductions of Victorian classics. Many of them could stand alone as garden ornaments. Well-placed boulders, long stone slabs, or wood planks can also

be used to provide seating.

No matter which bench you choose, pay special attention to where you put it, then sit back and let the magic happen.

TOP: Rustic bench has a frame of alder branches and a seat of milled lumber, painted deep green to echo its surroundings in a Willow, Alaska, garden. Design: Jerry Conrad. CENTER: Washed with a soft turquoise paint, weathered wood bench beckons in a Santa Fe garden. BOTTOM: Loveland buff sandstone bench was built into a hillside retaining wall in this Boulder, Colorado, garden. It is surrounded by catmint, woolly thyme, and gold flame honeysuckle. Design: Robert Howard.

BENCH BASICS

• Like all outdoor furniture, benches must be able to stand up to sun, rain, insects, fungus, and smog year-round. The most durable materials include metal (wrought iron, steel, cast aluminum, or enameled aluminum) and wood (especially teak or redwood).

• When shopping for a bench, pay special attention to the joinery. A good joint, where the bench leg or armrest meets the seat, looks nearly seamless. And it is strong.

• Give the bench good footing— poured concrete, pavers, decking, or lawn—so that it stays level and won't sink into the soil when you sit on it. You can make wood runners that will support each pair of legs: where bench legs will sit, sink two pressure-treated 4-by-4s into the ground so their tops are level with the surrounding soil.

• A small table on one or both ends can hold a tray of beverages, a book, or binoculars. A couple of pillows or a throw can make your bench more comfortable. ◆

NOTHING BEATS SUNFLOWERS for stunning summer bouquets. For tips on choosing the right varieties for cutting and on harvesting to prolong vase life, see page 210.

August

gardenguide

'REGAL MIST' deer grass and pink penstemon edge the patio fountain.

TERRENCE MOORE

A cooling interlude in Phoenix

Compact water feature is a mini-oasis that attracts birds and refreshes viewers

■ Just outside Jeffrey Weaver's living room in central Phoenix, finches splash in a gurgling fountain. Weaver's cooling patio scene was created by Phoenix landscape designer Susan Raymond of Dig It. Inspiration for the design came from the irrigation standpipes that dot this older neighborhood, which still receives flood irrigation to water lawns and gardens. Made of cast-in-place concrete, the recirculating fountain is 3 feet in diameter and 20 inches deep; its catch basin, covered by a metal grate, is hidden under red rocks. Water spirals up from the bottom, then gently flows over the edges and onto the rocks below.

Around the fountain, Raymond placed pavers made from recycled chunks of an old concrete driveway, which had been removed during remodeling. Randomly shaped and ranging in size from about 1 foot to 3 feet in diameter, the concrete slabs were set 3 inches apart in sand.

Between the pavers are seams of *Dichondra micrantha,* kept green by regular irrigation from pop-up, low-flow spray heads.

(Other drought-tolerant ground covers such as creeping or woolly thyme could be used in place of dichondra.) The fountain is backdropped by a drift of deer grass (*Muhlenbergia rigens* 'Regal Mist') and Gregg ash (*Fraxinus greggii),* supplemented by penstemon and other perennials to provide seasonal color and attract birds.

— *Nora Burba Trulsson*

Trading lawn for flowers in Denver

A few summers ago, our previously pampered front lawn disappeared in a single afternoon when my husband, Randy, and I buried it under 2 tons of stone. We placed random-size slabs of 2-inch-thick red flagstone directly on top of the living sod, effectively smothering the lawn. Spacing the stones 4 to 6 inches apart, we used glyphosate to kill the grass between them.

Originally, we planned to fill the spaces between the stones with woolly thyme, and we vowed to wait until the following spring to plant the thyme. But temptation got the better of me during the fall nursery clearance sales. A shameless plant addict, I came home with dozens of plants. The empty terrace beckoned, and free-for-all planting ensued.

Countless nursery visits

NARROW GAPS between flagstones are toehold enough for masses of blossoms.

ROB PROCTOR

and plant sales later, thyme now shares the terrace with an ever-changing riot of ground covers, rock garden plants, and wildflowers. From early spring through late fall, flowers fill every nook and cranny, and tending our crazy quilt of a garden requires leapfrog and

hopscotch skills.

The photo above shows the terrace in early summer, when the flagstones are nearly obscured by billowing mounds of golden flax (*Linum flavum*), native tufted primrose (*Oenothera caespitosa*) with white blooms that

fade to pink, pink 'Fairy Wings' Shirley poppy, lavender blue *Scabiosa lucida,* and various species of dianthus. Penstemons, salvias, red-hot poker, and lupine send up their spiky flower heads here and there.

— *Marcia Tatroe*

Window on the garden

Any structural opening that permits a partial glimpse of the garden is automatically perceived as a framed picture, explains Santa Barbara landscape architect Sydney Baumgartner. So what's seen through the framework ought to look like an ordered composition, she says. That's true whether the opening is an entry portal, an arched gateway, or a "window" between two garden rooms.

When Baumgartner decided she wanted a view corridor in the hedge separating her

outdoor dining alcove from the main garden, she created an opening that lined up precisely with the stone birdbath at the far edge of the lawn so the view would have a clear focal point. Then she installed an old wood picture frame bolted to two sturdy upright posts to clearly outline exactly what she wanted observers to see. The result, pictured at left, is a composition so satisfying it looks as if it were painted rather than planted.

— *Sharon Cohoon*

NORMAN A. PLATE (2)

TRELLIS IN A POT holds hydrangeas and lavender—tied with raffia—to dry.

Air-dry flowers. . . with style

■ Summer flowers such as hydrangea and lavender are beautiful, even when tied in bunches and hung upside down to dry. So rather than dangle them from the rafters in a garage or garden shed, why not let them dry where you can see them better? The drying rack pictured at left is pretty enough to set on a patio or in a corner of the garden. It's also convenient: You can clip and hang bunches of blooms without leaving the garden. (Where summer rains are common, keep your trellis indoors.)

TIME: Less than 1 hour, plus drying paint

COST: Less than $25

TOOLS AND MATERIALS

- Spray or exterior latex paint (optional)
- Terra-cotta pot, 13 inches in diameter
- Trellis, about 24 inches square, with two "feet," each about 10 inches long
- Gravel or crushed rock
- Colored rock (sold in pet stores for aquariums; optional)

DIRECTIONS

1. Paint the pot and trellis; allow them to dry.

2. Holding the trellis in the center of the pot with its bottom horizontal piece resting on the pot rim and its feet deep in the pot, pour gravel or crushed rock into the pot to within 3 inches of the pot rim. When the pot is full, the gravel will hold the trellis upright. If desired, finish with a 1-inch layer of colored rock.

— *Kathleen Norris Brenzel*

5 unusual flowers for drying

Baby's breath, cockscomb, hydrangea, larkspur, roses, statice, and strawflowers have long been favored flowers for drying. But the five unusual ones listed below also dry well. Harvest the flowers in the morning.

- Cupid's dart (*Catananche caerulea*). Lavender blue perennial to 2 feet tall. Harvest when fully open.
- Immortelle (*Xeranthemum annuum*). Annual in mixed colors to 2½ feet tall. Har-

vest when fully open and at peak color.
- Safflower (*Carthamus tinctorius*). Yellow-orange annual, 1 to 3 feet tall. Harvest when in bud or just at peak color.
- Sea holly (*Eryngium amethustinum*). Light to dark metallic blue perennial, 2 to 3 feet tall. Harvest when flowers turn blue.
- Pincushion flower (*Scabiosa stellata*). Greenish to bronze annual to 1½ feet tall. Harvest as soon as petals drop.

FOUNTAIN GRASS edges the pool, while flaming cannas stand as tall as Jeff Goldblum.

Jurassic Park revisited

■ When Robert Cornell was asked to replant actor Jeff Goldblum's slope and pool area after El Niño damage, the Pasadena landscape designer immediately knew his theme. "After starring in two *Jurassic Park* movies, it seemed only fitting that Jeff have a *Jurassic Park* garden," says Cornell. Besides, he says, the warm peach tones of his saltillo-tiled patio and the bright flecks of tile in his handsome, vintage pool all seemed to lead to the same conclusion: This setting called for exotic, tropical plants.

Since the pool was the obvious focal point of the yard, Cornell situated the garden's showiest plants, 'Durban' and 'Tropicanna' cannas, along its far edge to reinforce its star status. Ornamental grasses—*Pennisetum setaceum,* variegated pampas grass, and *Carex glauca*—soften the remaining edges.

The wide (40 ft. by 150 ft.), steep slope behind the pool is a natural backdrop, and Cornell painted it in bold swaths for dramatic effect. Thirstier plants, such as orange trees and yellow-flowered *Cuphea micropetala* (immediately behind Goldblum in the photo above), grow on the shadier side of the slope. The sunnier half is planted with drought-tolerant species—Mexican sage, *Tagetes lemmonii,* and coral fountain (*Russelia equisetiformis*).

Though still young, Goldblum's garden is already a pretty convincing jungle. But give it a few years, says Cornell. "When the flowering tropical trees [*Chorisia* and *Markhamia*] are big enough to form a canopy, we'll take out the remaining silk oaks," he says. "Then it will really look like a set for *Jurassic Park*."

— S.C.

Armored sleeves for prickly tasks

■ Terrie Murphy was fed up with the scratches she sustained while pruning rose bushes. "My arms would always be torn up from the thorns," says Murphy, who operates a garden maintenance business in Albuquerque. So she created her own protective sleeves by sewing together pieces of scrap canvas. Seeing her wearing the sleeves, gardeners asked Murphy where they could get a pair. "Since they weren't on the market, I decided to make them," she says. Called Armadillos, the sleeves are made of heavy-duty canvas over duck canvas, well suited to working around prickly plants such as agave and cactus. They come in one generous size that fits almost anyone. Cost is $34.95 plus $6 postage and handling. Order from Murphy's Earthworks, Box 7508, Albuquerque, NM 87194; (505) 899-3825.

— Dick Bushnell

ARMADILLOS shield her arms from spiny agave.

NORMAN A. PLATE

Lawn bowling, anyone?

Sunflowers for bouquets

■ Liz Floyd has mastered the art of growing sunflowers. Late each summer, her cutting garden in Des Moines, Washington, comes alive with vibrant blooms. Some plants are volunteers from years past, others are sown every year. Floyd makes good use of all of them, cutting bunches for bouquets (see example on page 204).

If you planted some last spring, use these harvest tips to prolong your blooms' vase life: Cut blooms in the cool of the morning and plunge the cut stems into buckets of cool water. Before arranging, recut stem ends diagonally while holding them in a bowl of hot water. Then arrange the flowers loosely in a vase. Floyd's bouquets last as long as 10 days outdoors, slightly less indoors.

■ Alien creatures paying homage to their lustrous leader? Incubating offspring of a giant metallic bird? Bocce balls for Brobdingnagians? San Diego landscape architect William Burton likes to imagine cocktail party guests circling this assembly of silver balls, coming up with their own interpretations. The truth is he was just having fun. His company, Burton Associates, wanted to do something whimsical and memorable at this model home (at Rosegate in Irvine), and he came up with this novel way of using gazing globes.

The globes in this garden fit into sleeves made out of PVC pipe, buried flush with the ground. Gazing globes have short stems on the bottom to make it easier to affix them to pedestals; the stems slip into the buried pipes, holding the globes in place in the lawn. (I guess that rules out the bocce theory.) When it's time to mow, the globes can be removed.

To duplicate the idea, use a dibble or other narrow digging tool to make holes in your turf for 6- to 8-inch lengths of PVC pipe. Use pipe that is a ½ inch or so wider than the stems of your globes, so the "necks" can slide in and out easily. Position globes. Cocktails and imaginative guests are optional.

— *S.C.*

Now, when gardens and farmers' markets are filled with sunflowers, is a good time to choose varieties to try. Floyd's favorites include 'Lemon Queen' (creamy pale yellow, 6-inch flowers with chocolate centers on 6-foot plants), 'Music Box' (4- to 5-inch blooms in mixed colors on 28-inch plants), and 'Valentine' (bright lemony yellow, 6-inch flowers on 5-foot plants); all are available from Park Seed (800/845-3369 or www.parkseed.com). 'Sunrich Lemon' (lemon yellow petals with black centers on 3-foot plants) is sold by Territorial Seed Company (541/942-9547 or www.territorial-seed.com). — *K.B.*

BACK TO BASICS

NORMAN A. PLATE

How to get rid of tree suckers: Many trees and shrubs, especially grafted ones like roses and some fruit trees, send up suckers from the base of the trunk or roots. These are weak shoots that should be pruned off before they get too large. Otherwise, they'll compete with or possibly overtake and dominate the plant. Using sharp pruning shears, cut them off as close as possible to the trunk or root.

— *Lauren Bonar Swezey*

CORAL-COLORED *Aloe saponaria* mingles with fall-planted California poppies, treelike *Euphorbia lambii, Scabiosa* 'Butterfly Blue', and white Santa Barbara daisies.

Under the Berkeley sun

■ French impressionist painter Paul Gauguin would have felt right at home in Susan Springer's garden. Rich colors and sculptural forms fill planting beds like paints on canvas. Succulents, wildflowers, cactus, and perennials play off one another in the meadowlike garden.

Springer, an artist and former fashion designer, has a strong sense of color and texture. It came in handy when—with the help of landscape designer David Feix—she renovated her garden. "Since I left the garment business, my garden has become my palette," she explains.

The sun-loving plants here are not widely grown in Berkeley, California, which is often foggy. But Springer took advantage of her mostly sunny exposure. "I take great pleasure in the succulents and cactus, which have evolved through millions of years," says Springer. "Like me, they're real survivors." This garden would be an inspiration to any artist.

This month or next, gardeners in Northern California's mildest climates can plant Santa Barbara daisies, scabiosa, and succulents, then sow seeds of California poppies around them.

— *L.B.S.*

EXOTIC PLANTS fill these Indonesian pots made of metal and aged terra-cotta. Colored glass balls float in water-filled bowl.

Tropical pleasures

■ No time this summer for a vacation in Bali? Why not create a tropical paradise at home instead, with an exotic collection of potted foliage and flowering plants?

San Francisco landscape designer Chris Jacobson's exuberant lemon grass forms the backdrop for the richly hued arrangement pictured above. Yellow bird-like heliconia flowers appear to flutter beside it.

No tropical garden would be complete without a leathery-leafed yellow and red croton. This one, growing in an Indonesian pot, is underplanted with spiky-leafed bromeliads. At right is a white-leafed caladium in an aged terra-cotta container. A red and green bromeliad in a metal pot grows in front.

Water is the key to keeping these lush beauties healthy. All prefer moist soil (except the bromeliads, which need water poured into their center cups). In winter, protect bromeliads, caladiums, and crotons from frost. Lemon grass is hardy in *Sunset* climate zones 16–17, 23–24, and, in warmest years, 15 and 21–22. Plants (except the lemon grass) were supplied by Green Thumb Nursery in Los Gatos, California; (408) 395-6050.

— *L.B.S.*

A clearly different pond near Santa Cruz

■ The backyard pond pictured below, in Soquel, California, looks as though nature planted it over many years. The water is so clear that you can see koi and bluegill swimming among the lily pads. Mallards occasionally drop in, and bobcats and herons have been spotted at the water's edge.

As natural as it looks, it's the culmination of an intricate system that carries gray water from the house (except for effluent from the kitchen, toilets, and the garage sink) through two filtration tanks topped with iron-removing parrot's feathers and water hyacinths. Finally, a gurgling waterfall aerates and purifies the water.

"Water is gold here in California," says retired field biology instructor John Shower, who designed this system with his wife, Marty. "By diverting reusable wastewater from our house, we were able to enhance the landscape without diminishing groundwater supply."

Shower dug his 2,500-gallon pond into a 300-square-foot area with the help of contractors and skilled friends. It's lined with mortarlike sprayed cement, which was smoothed into place over a steel rebar grid (total cost: $4,000).

While properly designed gray-water systems are permitted in Santa Cruz County, regulations vary by municipality. To build an inexpensive natural-looking pond with fresh water, use a plastic liner or preformed shell, a submersible pump, and water plants. (See "Instant Pond," June, page 174.)

— *Kirsten Whatley*

Everlasting blooms at Sundance Farms

PLUMES OF AMARANTH (right) and orange calendula (below) are dried for bouquets and potpourri.

■ Standing in the gardens of Sundance Farms in Utah, you're surrounded by drifts of burgundy and gold amaranth, pastel poppies, yellow and red sunflowers, and blue statice. The fragrances of lavender and mint infuse the air. And lush plantings of basil, sage, and oregano are enough to whet your appetite.

Robert Redford started Sundance Farms in 1988 to produce organically grown vegetables, flowers, and herbs for his Sundance Resort, about 20 miles to the east. Situated in the fertile Heber Valley at an elevation of about 5,800 feet, the gardens also produce flowers and herbs for potpourris, wreaths, and other products sold through the Sundance catalog and retailers.

Sundance favorites

Liz Sprackland, general manager of Sundance Farms, favors these dried flowers and leaves for use in wreaths or potpourris.

Flowers: Bee balm or bergamot (*Monarda didyma*), English lavender, fernleaf yarrow (*Achillea filipendulina*), feverfew (*Chrysanthemum parthenium*), 'Hot Biscuits' and 'Pygmy Torch' amaranth.

Foliage: 'Dark Opal' basil, lamb's ears (*Stachys byzantina*), silver king artemisia.

Visitors are welcome to stroll through the gardens and the drying barn where blossoms and herbs are arrayed for drying; wildflower seed mixes, wreaths, and other Sundance products are sold in the small garden shop.

Sundance Farms is just off State 113, about 4 miles south of Midway. Summer hours are 9 to 4 Mondays through Fridays, 11 to 4 Saturdays. For more information, call (435) 654-2721.

— *Kurt Repanshek*

MELBA LEVICK

Japanese style in West Coast gardens

■ At the turn of the century, Japanese immigrants began to influence American horticultural style in gardens along the Pacific Coast. A new book documents this stylistic evolution and the gardens that best exemplify it: *Japanese-Style Gardens of the Pacific West Coast* (Rizzoli International Publications, New York, 1999, 176 pages; $50; 800/522-6657). In his introduction, author Kendall H. Brown explains how "Japanism" (the American fascination with Japanese culture) has affected our

RED-LEAFED Japanese maple and spires of conifers show their sculptural form at Bloedel Reserve.

gardens from the late 19th century to the present.

Handsome color photos by Melba Levick show 20 gardens, from Bloedel Reserve on Washington's Bainbridge Island to the Japanese Friendship Garden in San Diego's Balboa Park. Four other Northwest gardens are included: Kubota Garden and Washington Park Arboretum Japanese Garden in Seattle, Portland's Japanese Garden, and Nitobe Memorial Garden at the University of British Columbia in Vancouver. If you aspire to Japanese garden design, the photos offer a wealth of ideas from exquisite water features to raked gravel beds. Information on visiting the gardens is included in a directory.

— *Steven R. Lorton*

Vegetable secrets from Alaska

■ Gaze at the 59-pound zucchini John Evans grew last summer. Later this month, Evans will take such behemoth vegetables to Palmer, Alaska, to compete in the state fair. In recent years, Evans has won 165 first-place awards and the fair's grand-champion prize 16 times.

How does he do it? For one thing, Evans's garden, in the fertile Matanuska Valley northeast of Anchorage, is blessed with nearly 20 hours of sunlight a day during summer. But Evans is also a master technician, and his methods can be used by any gardener to grow better, if not giant, crops.

Evans begins preparing his soil in the fall by adding cow manure. About three months before planting time, he starts seedlings in his solarium. In early May, he warms up the soil with 70° water applied by soaker hoses. Then he amends the soil with fish and kelp fertilizer, controlled-release fertilizer (14-14-14), and a compost of newspapers, sawdust, and birch ashes. In mid-May, he sets plants outdoors, mulches them with hay, and uses drip irrigation to keep the soil surface constantly moist.

To coax top performances from warm-season vegetables like zucchini, Evans grows them inside a self-designed "poly-tunnel" covered with polyethylene sheeting. As the weather warms up, he regulates the heat inside the tunnel by raising and lowering flaps on both sides.

— *Maria Lorraine Binchet*

CHARLES MANN

EVANS PAMPERS a prize zucchini.

Pacific Northwest Checklist

PLANTING & HARVEST

☑ **HARVEST HERBS FOR DRYING.** Pick in the morning just after the dew has dried. To air-dry herbs, set them on a clean window screen in a cool, dry place out of direct sunlight and wind. Spread the herbs out on the screen. Once leaves are completely dry, you can store them in jars.

☑ **PLANT FALL CROPS. Zones 4–7:** Early in the month, plant seedlings of cole crops (cabbage family members) and sow seeds of beets, kale, mustard, onions, radishes, and spinach.

☑ **SET OUT SUMMER COLOR. Zones 4–7:** There's still time to spruce up summer beds and containers with fuchsias, impatiens, marigolds, and pelargoniums. Given proper care, they should continue to bloom well into October.

MAINTENANCE

☑ **CONTROL SLUGS, SNAILS.** If you've noticed an increase in snails lately, you're not alone. It's likely these hard-shelled invaders sneaked into the Northwest by riding along on nursery plants imported from California. They are just as damaging to plants as slugs are, and they can be controlled using the same means: handpicking, beer traps, or bait.

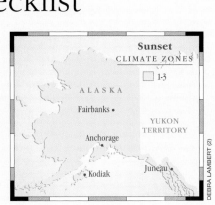

☑ **DIVIDE PERENNIALS.** Dig up clumps of perennials such as bearded irises and Oriental poppies. Use a spade to cut small clumps in half, large clumps into quarters. Replant the divisions immediately in amended soil.

☑ **PROPAGATE SHRUBS.** Growing plants from cuttings is a great way to get more plants just like their parents. Evergreen candidates include azaleas, camellias, daphne, euonymus, holly, and rhododendrons. Deciduous plants like hydrangeas develop well from cuttings, too. Cut a 4- to 6-inch section of branch tip in the morning and strip off all but the top three or four leaves. Dip the cut ends into rooting hormone, then insert the cuttings into 4-inch pots filled with sterile potting soil; water well. Place the cuttings in a spot out of direct sunlight and keep them thoroughly moist. Before frost hits, move them into a greenhouse or sunroom. By next spring, you'll have rooted plants to transplant into 1-gallon cans or set out in the garden.

☑ **PRUNE CANE BERRIES.** Remove all canes that bore fruit this season on June-bearing plants. On everbearing varieties, cut back by half any canes that have already borne.

☑ **WATER.** When weather is dry and water-use ordinances permit, irrigate plants such as rhododendrons deeply twice a week. Spray the foliage to wash accumulated dust off leaves and help stressed plants absorb water quickly. ◆

Northern California Checklist

PLANTING

☑ **LATE-SUMMER, FALL ANNUALS.** Zones 7–9, 14–17: If you're planning a summer garden party and need instant color to spruce up the garden, nurseries should still have a good supply of warm-season annuals in 4-inch pots. Look for alyssum, lobelia, marigolds, petunias, vinca, and zinnias. For fall- and winter-blooming annuals, start seeds of calendulas, Iceland poppies, pansies, primroses, stock, and violas.

☑ **SELECT PLANTS CAREFULLY.** Most nurseries care for their plants meticulously, but in summer a missed watering can stress them severely. When shopping, check plants carefully. Unless a particular variety is going through summer dormancy, foliage should look perky and lush, without burned leaf edges. Avoid leggy plants or ones that are overgrown and rootbound.

☑ **SHRUBS FOR SUMMER-TO-FALL BLOOM.** Zones 7–9, 14–17: Annuals and perennials aren't the only plants that bring color to the garden over a long season. For a show of flowers that lasts well into fall, try one of the following long-blooming shrubs or shrubby perennials: blue hibiscus, Brazilian plume flower, butterfly bush, cape fuchsia, lavatera, oleander, plumbago, princess flower, and a variety of salvias (check hardiness before purchasing; not all plants are hardy in every zone listed here).

Sunset
CLIMATE ZONES

- ☐ Mountain (1-2)
- ☐ Valley (7-9)
- ☐ Inland (14)
- ☐ Coastal (15-17)

DEBRA LAMBERT

☑ **SWEET PEAS.** Zones 7–9, 14–17: To get a crop of early flowers, sow an early-flowering variety now, such as knee-high 'Explorer Mix' (crimson, light pink, navy blue, purple, rose, scarlet, and white) or 'Winter Elegance Mix' (cream, lavender, pink, salmon, and white). These types will bloom when days are short. Protect new growth from slugs and snails, and provide support for the tall vines. Seeds are available at nurseries. To find a local retailer, call Renee's Garden; (888) 880-7228. For more information, visit www.reneesgarden.com.

MAINTENANCE

☑ **DEEP-WATER LARGE TREES AND SHRUBS.** Trees and shrubs may need a deep soaking now, even if they're watered by a sprinkler system (some systems don't run long enough for water to penetrate the soil deeply). Use a soaker hose, deep-root irrigator, or hose (turned on slowly in a basin) and run it until the soil is soaked to a depth of 12 to 18 inches (use the deeper amount for larger shrubs and trees) under the drip line of the plant. Check moisture penetration with a trowel.

☑ **LIGHTLY SHAPE SHRUBS AND VINES.** After a summer of growth, some plants may need minor trimming for shape. Snip out long, wayward shoots and thin interior growth, if necessary, but avoid major pruning.

☑ **PICK UP FALLEN FRUIT.** Collect decaying fruit such as peaches and nectarines that could be harboring diseases. Toss them in the garbage if they look suspect; don't compost them.

☑ **PREPARE BEDS FOR FALL PLANTING.** Cultivate the soil at least 12 inches deep (if possible), then turn in a 2- to 3-inch layer of organic matter or compost. ◆

Southern California Checklist

PLANTING

✔ **COOL-SEASON ANNUALS.** Start seeds of calendula, Iceland poppies, nemesia, pansies, phlox, snapdragons, stock, and sweet peas in flats. (This is often the only way to obtain tall-stemmed varieties or a large quantity of a single color.) By October—prime planting month—the seedlings will be ready to transplant into the garden.

✔ **FINAL SUMMER CROPS.** Coastal (zones 22–24), inland (zones 18–21), and low-desert (zone 13) gardeners can sow a final crop of beans and corn. Coastal gardeners can also set out transplants of eggplant, peppers, squash, and tomatoes for a fall harvest.

✔ **SOUTH AFRICAN BULBS.** Freesias, ixia, sparaxis, and other South African bulbs—the best bulbs for naturalizing in Southern California's low elevations—begin appearing in nurseries this month. Shop early for best selection, and plant immediately.

✔ **WINTER CROPS.** Coastal, inland, and high-desert (zone 11) gardeners can start germinating cool-season vegetable seeds in flats. The seedlings will be ready to transplant to the garden in 6 to 8 weeks. Candidates include broccoli, brussels sprouts, cabbage, cauliflower, chard, collards, kale, lettuce, Oriental greens, peas, and spinach. Direct seed beets, carrots, and turnips, or start seeds in peat pots and transfer plants to the garden, pots and all.

Bishop

NEVADA

CALIFORNIA

San Luis Obispo

Bakersfield

Santa Barbara

Tehachapi

Lancaster

Los Angeles

Palm Springs

Sunset
CLIMATE ZONES

1-3 7-9 11 13 14-24

San Diego

MEXICO

DEBRA LAMBERT

MAINTENANCE

✔ **PROTECT AGAINST BRUSHFIRES.** Santa Ana winds and dead vegetation are an inflammatory combination. In fire-prone areas, begin removing all dead limbs and leaves from trees and shrubs, particularly those that grow near the house. Keep tall grasses and weeds cut down to stubble. Clear leaves from gutters, and remove woody vegetation growing against structures. For more information, contact your local fire department for literature on firescaping.

✔ **GROOM PLANTS.** Lightly trim plants that have grown rangy or leggy so they'll have time to put out new growth before winter. On perennials, watch for new basal growth; cut back spent flower stalks to just above this growth to shape plants.

✔ **RENEW MULCH.** It insulates roots, helps retain soil moisture, discourages weeds, and enriches the soil when it decomposes. Apply ground bark or other material around plants throughout the garden, forming a layer 3 to 4 inches deep. Keep it away from tree trunks and the crowns of plants.

✔ **DIVIDE BEARDED IRISES.** Dig up old, overgrown clumps of bearded irises, and divide the rhizomes with a sharp knife. Discard the woody centers. Trim the leaves of remaining rhizomes to 6 inches. Replant the divisions 1 to 2 feet apart.

PEST CONTROL

✔ **COMBAT LAWN GRUBS.** Irregular brown patches in lawns may be caused by beetle larvae, which feed on grass roots. Pull up sections of dead turf and examine them. If you find grubs, treat lawn with parasitic nematodes, following label instructions. ◆

Mountain Checklist

PLANTING & HARVEST

☑ **HARVEST CROPS.** Pick early apples, beets, broccoli, bush beans, cauliflower, new potatoes, peaches, raspberries, strawberries, summer squash, sweet corn, tomatoes, and zucchini.

☑ **HARVEST HERBS.** Pick in the morning, just after dew has dried. Use them fresh or dried; to dry, lay them on a screen in dry shade, put them in a dehydrator, or hang them from the rafters in a garage.

☑ **PICK FLOWERS FOR DRYING.** Cut blooms with long stems, strip off the leaves, bundle them together, and hang upside down to air-dry in a garage or basement. Good candidates for drying are baby's breath, goldenrod, lavender, love-in-a-mist, rose, statice, strawflower, and yarrow.

☑ **PLANT CROPS FOR FALL HARVEST.** Where frosts aren't expected until late October, sow beets, carrots, radishes, and spinach for fall harvest. In mildest climates, set out transplants of broccoli, cabbage, and cauliflower.

☑ **SOW WILDFLOWERS.** Sow bachelor's buttons, blue flax, coreopsis, Mexican hat, poppies, prairie aster, Rocky Mountain penstemon, and yellow coneflower. (In coldest areas, do this in September.) Cultivate soil lightly, spread seeds, then mulch with ¼ to ½ inch of ground bark or other organic matter.

Sunset
CLIMATE ZONES
☐ 1-3 ☐ 10-11

DEBRA LAMBERT

MAINTENANCE

☑ **CHECK FOR CHLOROSIS.** When leaves turn yellow but their veins remain green, suspect chlorosis, an iron deficiency; correct it by applying chelated iron. If leaves are yellowish overall and you can spot no insect or cultural problems, apply a complete fertilizer.

☑ **DEADHEAD ANNUALS.** Remove faded flowers of long-blooming annuals, then water and fertilize to encourage bloom through summer's end.

☑ **DIVIDE PERENNIALS.** After they bloom, divide large clumps of delphiniums, irises, Oriental poppies, and Shasta daisies. Dig up and cut the root mass into several sections. Weed and amend soil, then replant divisions. (In shortest-season areas, wait until next spring to dig and replant.)

☑ **MAKE COMPOST.** As you pull out annuals and early vegetables, put them on the compost pile. Keep the pile as moist as a wrung-out sponge and turn it often. By frost, the compost should be ready.

PEST CONTROL

☑ **POWDERY MILDEW.** The foliage of cucumbers, dahlias, peas, squash, and zinnias are particularly susceptible to this white, powdery fungus. Rake up and destroy fallen leaves, and remove diseased leaves and stems. To control, spray the tops and bottoms of leaves weekly with a solution of 2 teaspoons baking soda and 2 teaspoons summer oil in 1 gallon of water.

☑ **SLUGS.** Handpick or set out beer traps for these nighttime nibblers. If you spread poison bait, be careful to keep it away from children and pets. ◆

Southwest Checklist

PLANTING

☑ **VEGETABLES.** Zone 10 (Albuquerque): Sow seeds of beans, corn, cucumbers, and squash; plant potatoes; and sow or set out seedlings of cabbage family members, spinach, and Swiss chard. Seeds go in early in the month, seedlings later. Zone 11 (Las Vegas): Sow beets, carrots, radishes, spinach, and transplants of broccoli, cabbage, and cauliflower for fall harvest. Zones 12–13 (Tucson and Phoenix): Plant beans, cabbage family members, carrots, corn, cucumbers, green onions, leeks, lettuce, and squash for a late harvest.

MAINTENANCE

☑ **CARE FOR ROSES.** To prepare roses for strong fall bloom, acidify the soil with soluble sulfur (Disper-Sul), fortify it with complete fertilizer, and apply chelated iron. Water everything in thoroughly.

☑ **FERTILIZE SHRUBS.** In the evening, give them a half-strength application of complete fertilizer, watering it in deeply to help them recover from heat stress.

☑ **MAKE COMPOST.** Haul garden waste to the compost pile, mixing weeds, lawn clippings, and nonmeat kitchen waste. Water the pile enough to make it feel like a damp sponge, and turn the pile regularly; it should be ready to use within two months.

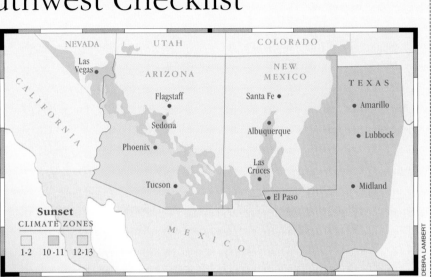

☑ **WATER.** This year's plantings need regular irrigation the most, since they don't yet have the deep roots it takes to survive drought. Also pay special attention to container plants and anything growing under house eaves or otherwise sheltered from monsoons. Drench the roots of landscape plants with a soaker hose, deep-root irrigator, or hose running slowly into a basin around the plant.

PEST CONTROL

☑ **LAWN INSECTS.** Chinch bugs can cause St. Augustine to dry out and die back; microscopic Bermuda grass mites can do the same to Bermuda grass lawns, giving them a shaving-brush look. You can treat both pests with an application of chlorpyrifos (Dursban) or Diazinon.

☑ **SOUTHWESTERN CORN BORERS.** Skeletonized, translucent patches on corn leaves are usually caused by corn borer larvae. Spray plants, especially where leaves join the stalk, with *Bacillus thuringiensis,* a biological control.

☑ **SPIDER MITES.** Mottled leaves and fine webs give away the mites' presence. Control them by keeping leaves well washed (that gives predators a clear shot at the mites) and spraying with a miticide. ◆

Perfect picks

How to tell when your summer garden's ready to harvest

BY JIM McCAUSLAND
PHOTOGRAPHS BY NORMAN A. PLATE

■ OPPOSITE PAGE: Red tomato is ready, but blushing yellow fruits can also be picked to ripen indoors.
■ LEFT: When leafy onion tops wither, bend them to the ground and let the bulbs cure.
■ BELOW: Three weeks later, lift the bulbs and remove the tops.

■ YOU'VE WEEDED, WATERED, FERTILIZED, AND FOUGHT OFF A legion of pests. At last, the fruit of your labor is ready to harvest—or is it? Pick that corn too early and its kernels will be watery; pick it too late and it will be starchy and tough.

How do you know exactly when to harvest your summer crops? Keep an eye on them and compare your observations with the hints listed in the guide that follows. Our harvest and storage tips reflect the experience of *Sunset's* garden and food staff, as well as the advice of farmers and university horticulturists.

While some crops slip easily off the plant when they're ready, others need a helping hand. Use a sharp knife or pruning shears to harvest vegetables such as green or snap beans and eggplant, which should be picked when they are slightly immature.

With many vegetables, the act of harvesting fruits that contain developing seeds stimulates the plants to keep producing (corn, melons, and onions are exceptions). Prompt harvest also prevents crops like summer squash from getting too big and pithy to use, and fruits like tomatoes from rotting on the vine. If you do spot overripe or rotten vegetables, pick and toss them on the compost pile.

LEFT: When shelling bean pods are plump but not split, harvest the pods and strip the beans to eat fresh.
ABOVE: Nicked with a thumbnail, a kernel of ripe corn exudes milky liquid.

HARVEST TIPS

BEANS. *Green or snap types* (such as 'Blue Lake'). Nip beans off as sides of pods start to swell, but before they get stringy and lose their ability to snap. **Storage:** Refrigerate unwashed beans in plastic bags for up to four days. Freeze or can for longer storage. *Shelling and dry beans* (such as scarlet runner or 'Vermont Cranberry'). **Shelling stage:** Shell beans after pods become too stringy to eat and beans inside are full size, but not crisp and hard. Eat immediately. **Dry stage:** Strip the beans out with your thumb after pods have dried and shattered (started to split). **Storage:** You can refrigerate shelling beans for a couple of days, but it makes more sense to eat them fresh. Store dry beans in sealed jars.

CORN. When silk tassels start to dry, peel husk from an ear and pop a kernel with your thumbnail. If water comes out, it's immature. If it's toothpasty, the corn is past its prime. If milky fluid comes out, it's perfect. The "milk" of white corn is clearer, while liquid from yellow corn is yellowish. **Storage:** Never refrigerate; the whole point of growing sweet corn is to eat it immediately, before sugars convert to starch. Freeze whole ears or kernels.

CUCUMBERS. *For fresh eating.* Pick standard cukes at about 8 inches long, Armenian and Japanese types up to 20 inches, lemon cukes under 3 inches. **Storage:** Store bagged, fresh cukes in the refrigerator for up to two weeks.
For canning. Pick sweet pickles at 2 to 3 inches long, dill pickles at 5 to 6 inches.

EGGPLANT. Shiny-skinned, immature eggplant is tender and good. Dull-skinned, mature eggplant has hard seeds and flesh that separates into channels—not what you want. **Storage:** You can refrigerate eggplant for a few days. Freeze or dry sliced eggplant and store in containers.

MUSKMELONS (CANTALOUPES). After the skin has become netted, give the fruit a gentle tug, bending the vine slightly as you do; when it's ready, it will "slip" (separate) from the vine. **Storage:** Store in a cool, humid spot (like a cellar) for two to four weeks.

ONIONS. Before bulbs mature, harvest green onions (scallions) for chopping into salads. When bulbs are large enough to pick, use your foot to bend the leafy tops down to the ground and let the bulbs harden and cure for three weeks before you pull them. **Storage:** Refrigerate green nions or store in a cool, humid place for up o three months. Store bulbs in a cool, dry pot for three weeks to seven months, depending on variety. Or freeze, can, or dry.

PEPPERS. You can pick any pepper when the pod is firm and fully developed, egardless of color. But for maximum flavor, ook for these signs.

Hot peppers. They develop the most flavor

and heat after pods show color. Jalapeños turn red at maturity; serranos can go red, orange, brown, or yellow. Harvest both red and green pods for salsa.

Sweet peppers. These are sweetest and most flavorful when fully mature. That's usually (but not always) signaled by a color change. Bell peppers can mature green, yellow, red, orange, maroon, or brown; pimiento ripens red; wax types go from yellow to orange or red.

Storage: Keep fresh peppers cool and humid for up to six weeks. Dry, freeze, or can for winter storage.

SQUASH. *Summer squash.* Harvest fruits before they mature. Pick zucchini at 5 to 8 inches long, yellow crookneck at 4 to 7 inches, scalloped squash (pattypan) before it turns ivory white.

Winter squash (acorn, Hubbard, spaghetti, pumpkin). Harvest when the shell hardens, after the vine dries.

Storage: Eat summer squash immediately.

Cut winter squash with 2- to 3-inch stems; store in a dry place between 45° and 55°.

TOMATOES. In summer, harvest after fruit colors fully. In fall, when night temperatures drop below 55°, pick any tomato with color to ripen indoors on a windowsill (dark green fruit will never ripen). Or pull the whole plant up and hang it upside down in a warm garage or porch; most of its fruit will ripen. **Storage:** Store between 55° and 70°, or put fruits on a windowsill for faster ripening. Don't refrigerate (temperatures below 55° stop flavor development). You can dry paste tomatoes; purée and freeze standard varieties.

WATERMELONS. Look—and listen—for these four signs of ripeness: 1. A withered tendril where vine meets melon. 2. Creamy white belly (or yellowish on seedless kinds). 3. Dull skin. 4. A hollow sound when thumped. **Storage:** Watermelons don't ripen further after harvest. Refrigerate or can chunked fruit. ◆

■ ABOVE: Most bell peppers (front) reach peak sweetness when they develop full color—orange, yellow, red, or purple, depending on variety. Hot peppers (rear) can be harvested at any color stage.
■ TOP RIGHT: Watermelon is ready to leave the vine when the tendril next to the stem withers.
■ RIGHT: Eggplant with glossy skin is slightly immature but perfectly ready to eat.

the ultimate small garden

It packs lots of big
ideas into a
16- by 24-foot space

BY KATHLEEN N.
BRENZEL AND
PETER O. WHITELEY

PHOTOGRAPHS BY
NORMAN A. PLATE

How much good living can you get into a very small garden? That's what we wanted to find out when we planned the one pictured on these pages. After asking ourselves what we considered "must haves" for outdoor living, we designed and built this space-efficient garden at *Sunset's* headquarters in Menlo Park, California. Fresh and innovative, it combines new building materials with a rich tapestry of plants to create a garden that's as attractive as it is intimate. All the amenities of a larger garden are here: freestanding benches with storage beneath, a water feature, a barbecue, a deck big enough for a table and four chairs, and planting beds for herbs, vegetables, fruit trees, and flowers. There's even a birdhouse on a post and a doghouse (see page 228) to match the garden's decor.

In spite of its limited size

FLANKED by potted bougainvilleas and lighted by a single candle in an overhead lantern, the entry arbor is colorful and inviting. Granite-textured pavers on the entry floor are set in sand.

LEFT: Planting bed to the right of the entry is packed with assorted culinary herbs. Golden sage and lime thyme spill from a pot set on its side.
BELOW: Wood boxes from a nursery, dressed up with paint and plastic lattice, are centered in low beds fringed with blue fescue. They contain 'Eureka' lemons and lemon thyme.

the garden feels airy and inviting—thanks to a few visual tricks. The peaked-roof arbor at its entrance is generous (4 feet wide and more than 8 feet tall in the center). The lattice-trimmed fence around it looks lacy and open, and the window frames—which hang from the beams of a triangular arbor in one corner—provide the deck with a sense of enclosure without closing it off.

You can copy the whole plan for your own small garden, fit it into a corner of a large garden as an outdoor living room, or adapt its individual components to suit your specific needs. The photograph on page 226 details the plan.

All garden structures were designed for easy construction using a few hand-held electric tools and materials readily available at home improvement stores and garden centers.

The structures

To maintain a unified look, the same materials and colors are used throughout the garden. The framing (use redwood, cedar, or pressure-treated wood) is painted with gray-green exterior latex. (The color is Eucalyptus Wreath from *Sunset's* paint palette; see "Colors for the Western Home," March 1998, page 88). The white plastic lattice and matching trim pieces forming the fence, entry arbor, and bench sides—and embellishing the citrus containers and doghouse—are from Tuff-Bilt (800/394-6679); they're sold in 4-by-8 panels.

■ FENCE. Its lattice panels, cut to 2 feet tall and up to 8 feet long, are edged with ready-made plastic trim and framed top and bottom with wood 2-by-4s; vertical posts are 4-by-4s. Decorative post

the **ultimate** small garden

corner trellis

entry arbor

planters

benches

herb bed

flower bed

deck

fence

vegetable bed

caps (optional) top the 4-by-4s.

■ ENTRY ARBOR. Each side of the arbor has 86-inch-tall 4-by-4 posts framing 4-by 6-foot lattice panels; there are 2-by-4s at the top and bottom of the panels. The gable-shaped "roof" is also lattice. Two containers, both filled with 'James Walker' bougainvillea, flank the entrance.

■ DECK. Just 13 square feet, it's built of Trex, a synthetic lumber. Nine modules each measure 52 inches square (size can be scaled up or down). For each module, we spaced the decking boards evenly and screwed them from the underside to four pressure-treated 2-by-2 sleepers. Since the modules are portable, they can be used to cover an existing concrete patio. You can arrange them any way you want; we alternated the direction of the boards, square by square, to create a checkerboard pattern (see photo above).

■ CORNER TRELLIS. Three vertical posts, each 8 feet tall (aboveground), are topped with 2-by-8 beams. Seven

evenly spaced 2-by-4 joists cap the beams. Lattice fencing covers the lower part of the arbor.

■ BENCHES. Two benches that sit on the decking and butt against the sides of the trellis also have lattice on the exposed fronts and ends. The bench frames are 2-by-4s; to support the removable top, they have crosspieces at 16-inch intervals. Bench tops are also of Trex to match the deck; the front edges were rounded over with a router.

■ PLANTERS. We purchased four redwood containers (each 16 inches square) at a garden supply center. After painting, these were covered with lattice, cut to fit.

The plantings

Three planting beds provide just the right amount of space for weekend gardeners. Flanking the entry arbor are an herb bed and a vegetable bed, each 5 by 6 feet. Along the fence, the third (3 feet wide by 14½ feet long) shows off a colorful mix of

annuals, perennials, and shrubs.

■ HERB BED. Golden sage spills from a green-stained terra-cotta urn set on its side in the center of the bed (see photo on page 225). Around it grow culinary herbs, including basil, chives, dill, oregano, parsley, and thyme. Taller

■ ABOVE: Bench seats are removable for access to storage below. "Windows" hang from heavy-duty picture wire and eye screws set in overhead beams and window frames.

■ RIGHT: Lettuce and tomatoes are stars of the vegetable bed; marigolds and a fringe of purple sweet alyssum add color.

■ **FLOWER BED.** To keep the planting (behind foreground fence in top photo on the facing page) from looking too busy in this small space, we chose a controlled palette of cool colors: blues, lavender, and purple with splashes of pink, yellow, and white. Tall plants (blue delphiniums, *Echium vulgare* 'Blue Bedder', and catmint) grow against the fence, and tall 'Tara's Pink' cape mallow grows in one corner. Medium-size plants (asters, pink snapdragons, and golden yarrow) grow in the center, and low plants (purple and lavender verbena, white Santa Barbara daisy, and white sweet alyssum) grow in front.

■ **CONTAINER PLANTINGS.** Four 'Eureka' lemon trees, underplanted with lemon thyme and blue fescue, grow in the 16-inch-square containers; together they act as room dividers between the working garden and the deck.

■ **WATER FEATURE.** A 16-inch glazed stoneware bowl nestles among the flowers. In it float blossoms such as roses and bougainvillea.

plants—lavender and rosemary—are placed in back; low ones such as lemon thyme are in front. A path of granite-textured pavers edges the beds.

■ **VEGETABLE BED.** It's just big enough for a few favorite homegrown crops (bush and dwarf vegetable varieties are best in such mini-gardens): patio tomatoes ('Sweet 100'), two zucchini (Lebanese white zucchini), one squash ('Eight Ball'), four bell peppers, mixed lettuces, and—for color—a scattering of flowers (marigolds, Johnny-jump-ups, and nasturtiums).

Distinctive dog digs

An eye-catching layer of lacy lattice paneling makes this midsize doghouse a charming addition to any garden. Durable and easy to work with, the white plastic lattice adds pattern and depth to the painted plywood shell. The doghouse roof can be covered with any type of shingle—wood, composition, cement, stone, or metal. Simple enough for a beginning-to-intermediate woodworker to build in a weekend, the doghouse is constructed of materials available at home improvement stores.

■ **IT'S A CANINE COTTAGE** worth barking about, made from one sheet of plywood.

Cost: About $50

Materials

- Tape measure
- Yardstick
- Combination square (for drawing pattern)
- 4- by 8-foot ½-inch exterior plywood
- Circular saw
- 4- by 8-foot plastic lattice panel
- Saber saw
- Two 8-foot lengths 2-by-2
- 50 1¼-inch self-tapping deck screws
- Screwdriver
- Electric drill (for screws)
- Scraps of carpet or tile for floor (optional)
- 1 quart exterior latex paint
- Paintbrush
- Miter box and saw
- Four 8-foot lengths plastic-lattice trim
- Shingles
- Nails for shingles
- Hammer

Directions

1. Draw pattern on plywood as shown in diagram at right. With circular saw, cut out pieces, except opening for door.

2. Determine height of door opening by laying the lattice panel over the plywood front piece so that the diagonal grid of the lattice aligns with the peaked roofline and the top of the opening. (The bottom of the 12-inch-wide opening is 2 inches above the bottom of the plywood piece.) Mark and cut out door opening, using saber saw.

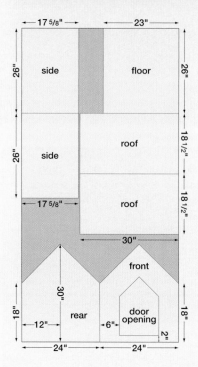

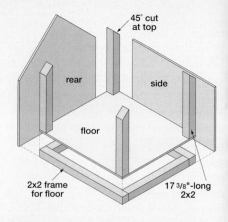

3. Measure and cut four pieces from one 2-by-2 to be flush with the edges of the underside of the floor; screw in place. Then screw plywood side pieces to the 2-by-2s, bottom edges flush.

4. Place the rear piece so it overlaps floor and sides. To make bevel-topped corner posts, place remaining 8-foot 2-by-2 against corner of rear piece and mark height and pitch of first post (it should be 17⅜ inches on high side). Cut. Use it as a guide to make three more. Screw flush with edges of the side pieces (see diagram).

5. Carpet or paint floor, or cut adhesive tiles to fit.

6. Attach the front and back with screws, then center and attach the roof pieces with screws.

7. Paint the shell.

8. Cut the lattice end pieces so that, with trim pieces, they'll be the same size as their plywood counterparts. Cut the lattice side pieces slightly shorter than the plywood sides to allow for the roof pitch. Using miter box for angles, cut lattice trim pieces to fit. Attach lattice and trim pieces with screws or nails.

9. Add shingles (or other roofing material). Cut off or bend nail tips that protrude inside.

10. Add dog. ◆

The merits of organic mulch

Spread some now to help plants, foil weeds, and save water

BY LANCE WALHEIM

In late summer, as air and soil temperatures rise, plants can be heat-stressed right down to their roots. One of the best things you can do for them is to spread a blanket of organic mulch over their root zones. A layer of mulch not only cools plant roots but conserves soil moisture, reducing plants' heat stress and your water bill at the same time. Mulch also helps to control weeds and gives the garden a tidy look.

Nurseries and garden supply centers usually sell a selection of different organic mulches by the bag or in bulk amounts. Here are some of the merits and drawbacks of the most commonly available mulches.

BARK. Many kinds of trees yield bark that makes attractive, long-lasting mulch. You can buy bark graded into small, medium, or large pieces or shredded into a stringy fiber called "gorilla hair." Since bark breaks down slowly, it's not suitable for use in flower or vegetable beds where you'd normally till mulch into the ground at the end of the season.

COMPOST. One of the best mulches, compost improves soil fertility and texture as it breaks down. Homemade compost from your own pile works great if it is weed-free. County waste-disposal sites often sell or give away compost; some is made only from plant debris, but others may include ground-up lumber (with nails removed) and possibly paint chips. Commercially made compost often includes manure, wood by-products, and even sewage sludge—which could contain toxic heavy metals.

When buying compost, read the label on the bag or ask the nursery staff what it contains. Good compost should appear clean and thoroughly decomposed and have that nice earthy smell. Since it breaks down fairly quickly, compost mulch has to be replenished often.

LEAF MOLD. Ground-up and partially decomposed leaves make a very attractive mulch. Leaf mold tends to acidify the soil, making it ideal for mulching around azaleas, rhododendrons, and other acid-loving plants. Usually sold by the bag, leaf mold needs to be replenished often.

PEAT MOSS. Sold in compressed bales, peat moss is a relatively expensive mulch. The acidic property of peat moss makes it ideal around acid-loving plants. However, once it dries out, it repels water and is hard to rewet. Also, conservationists are concerned that the mining of peat moss is seriously depleting the fragile bogs where peat is formed. An alternative to peat moss is coconut fiber; made from coconut husks, the fiber isn't acidic like peat moss. It is becoming more widely available.

OTHER MATERIALS. Chipper debris may be available free from tree maintenance firms. Aged or nitrogen-fortified sawdust is preferred over the raw stuff, which can rob nitrogen from plants as it breaks down. Locally available agricultural by-products like cotton gin waste and rice hulls are useful mulches. Especially around vegetables and strawberries, straw and hay work well, although they often contain weed seeds.

HOW MUCH MULCH?

For denser materials like peat moss or sawdust, a 1- to 2-inch layer is usually sufficient. Mulches made of larger or looser pieces like bark should be spread 3 to 4 inches deep. Very loose materials such as leaf mold can be spread as much as 6 inches deep. Generally, you should spread a deeper layer of mulch around larger trees and shrubs than you would around young transplants, flowers, or vegetables. Keep all mulches a few inches away from the trunks, crowns, and stems of plants. ◆

Rent a chipper and turn prunings into mulch

Disposing of garden prunings can be a daunting task, especially when you're cutting hedges, trees, and shrubs. Try renting a machine to turn that woody waste into a pile of chips you can use as mulch.

You'll find gasoline-powered machines in various sizes at rental yards. They're rated according to the branch size they'll take without jamming. Small units, often referred to as "shredders", rent for around $9 per day; medium and large units (recommended for pieces thicker than 2 inches) are called "chippers" and rent for $105 to $210 per day. Most units are rented in half-day or one-day increments.

Plan a chipping party with a couple of neighbors. Prune your gardens a day ahead and gather all the waste in a central location, such as a vacant driveway. When the chipper arrives, work as a team, feeding waste into the machine and sharing the mulch.

Whatever their size, these machines all tend to choke on green or fibrous material such as cedar boughs, cornstalks, and blackberry canes, which can wrap around the chipping mechanism and make it stall. The trick is to feed the green stuff into the chute with woody material; then all goes through more easily.

Only small units can be carried home in the back of a truck or van. Medium and large chippers must be towed. Rental yards will sometimes deliver and pick up a unit for an additional charge.

It's essential to follow the safety guidelines posted on the unit and to wear eye and ear protection. Keep children well away from the work area.

—Jim McCausland

Hidden pleasures

A private new courtyard replaces a very open front lawn

BY SHARON COHOON

Not long ago, David and Nan Holt's front yard in Manhattan Beach, California, was stuck in a 1950s–'60s time warp: flat carpet of grass out front, red brick planter boxes tucked up against the foundation, dominant driveway. You'd pass it by without a second glance.

Now their garden is another story, thanks to a new wall, courtyard, and planting beds that replaced much of the lawn. A path of rosy flagstone leads to a

handsome gate that opens to the inviting interior courtyard. The scene is welcoming, yet private. The simple changes add up to a big difference because each was carefully thought out.

Take the wall. After consulting with an architect and designer, the Holts were convinced that creating an interior courtyard would solve two vexing problems. It would eliminate an ugly view of parked cars and enable them to dispense with drawn drapes, which pro-

vided privacy but darkened the house.

Deciding where to put the wall—as far from the house and as close to the street as city ordinances permitted—was not an issue. But determining the best height was. Chris Scuitto, a landscape designer at Artscape, drew several perspectives to help the Holts visualize how the courtyard space would look. The Holts also erected poles and strung wire across the tops to simulate a wall and get a feeling for different heights. "But I still couldn't

PROJECT BUDGET BREAKDOWN (Includes materials and construction)	
Courtyard wall	$9,500
Flagstone hardscape	$5,800
Irrigation system	$2,400
Outdoor lighting	$1,500
Plant material	$5,000
TOTAL	$24,200

BEFORE: House had square lawn, no privacy. AFTER: Sandstone path winds to furniture-quality gate. RIGHT: Inside, paved surfaces are fringed by fine-textured foliage. Climbing roses soften the wall.

"I've seen walkways this size done with just eight or nine pieces," he says. "Yes, it's quicker and cheaper, but the scale is way off, so the path looks skimpy."

Plants were also selected with care. Around the existing black pine, Japanese anemone, campanula, and other shade lovers were chosen to create a woodland look. In the courtyard, the emphasis was on small stature and fine texture—delicate ferns, diosma, nandina, euonymus. "Again," says Scuitto, "scale was key. We wanted variety without overwhelming the space." In the beds that screen the driveway from view are tall, narrow plants such as the mayten tree.

Nan is particularly pleased with the majestic kangaroo paws flanking the garden's side entrance. "When they're at their peak, they canopy over the path, and walking through them feels like a ceremony," she says.

David concurs. "Even though it would be quicker to go through the garage, I always come back out and come into the house through the path and the gate for the sheer pleasure of the experience. It never fails to delight me."

picture it," says Nan. So she and her husband checked out neighbors' gardens for a firsthand experience of how walled-in spaces of various dimensions feel.

The homework paid off. The 5-foot, 9-inch height they finally chose is perfect, says Nan. From inside, it provides privacy without blocking views of the outside world. "So you never feel claustrophobic," she says.

Like the wall, the walkway was thoughtfully planned. The flagstone was laid to create a free-form edge that gives the path a weathered look. "The walkway doesn't scream 'freshly installed,' so it's not such an obvious addition," says Scuitto. Other notable details: dyed-to-match grouting and smaller-than-usual flagstone pieces.

TWO BITS OF ADVICE BEFORE TACKLING A RENOVATION

• Know your taste *before* you engage a designer. Stroll through public gardens, visit model homes, and look through magazines to find out what moves you. Take photographs and cut out pictures of designs you like. "The more information you give us, the better we can tailor a garden to your style, and the more value you get for your dollar," says Scuitto.

• Shop for skill as well as price. If you want careful craftsmanship, you'll have to invest in time as well as materials, says David Holt. "We were more worried about finding someone concerned with careful workmanship than we were with obtaining the lowest estimate," he says. ◆

WHO SAYS FLOWERS can't stand up to salt spray and ocean breezes? A rainbow of blooms—including cosmos (scarlet), coreopsis (yellow), and sea lavender (blue)—flourish in this terraced seaside garden in South Laguna. For details, see page 238.

September

gardenguide

'SHINKO' bears big fruit with richly flavored flesh.

MICHAEL S. THOMPSON

Choice Asian pears for homegrown flavor

Small-scale trees produce delicious fruit at an early age

■ If you enjoy crisp, crunchy Asian pears, why not grow your own? Although standard market varieties such as 'Chojuro' and 'Twentieth Century' are tasty, other delicious kinds can be grown by home gardeners. Here are four varieties that do well in the coastal Northwest, often bearing fruit their first year after planting.

'Kikusui' bears medium to large yellow-green fruit with a crisp texture and mildly tart flavor. It ripens from early to mid-September.

'Korean Giant' lives up to its name by bearing pears that weigh as much as 1 pound each. Bronze russet-skinned fruit has crisp, juicy flesh with a high sugar content. It ripens late, beginning in October.

'Shinko' is a very productive tree that bears large, golden brown fruit with distinctively rich, tangy flavor. Harvest begins in late September.

'Shin Li' has sweet and spicy cinnamon-flavor fruit with yellow-green skin. Pears are ready for harvest in mid-September.

'Kikusui' and 'Korean Giant' are hardy in *Sunset* climate zones 3–7, 'Shinko' and 'Shin Li' in zones 4–7.

Shop nurseries for container-grown trees to set out this fall, or order bare-root stock for planting this winter or next spring. 'Kikusui' and 'Korean Giant' are sold on dwarf rootstock

(10 to 12 feet tall) by Raintree Nursery in Morton, Washington (360/496-6400). 'Shinko' and 'Shin Li' are sold on standard rootstock (12 to 15 feet tall) by One Green World in Molalla, Oregon (503/651-3005).

Plant in full sun and well-drained soil. Young trees should receive a deep weekly watering during dry months. Asian pears must ripen on the tree to develop full sweetness and flavor. Harvest when color has fully developed and fruit is still firm. — *Kris Wetherbee*

Pop-and-grow perennials

■ The way Carl Loeb figures it, the first year in the life of a perennial is the most important. If you can get a plant through that—and into the garden without transplant shock—success follows easily. It took Loeb, a nursery owner, and his lead propagator several years to come up with a formula for reliable starts. The result is now being sold under the Etera label at retail nurseries. Etera, based in Mt. Vernon, Washington, offers about 80 kinds of perennials for fall planting, more than 370 varieties for spring.

Unlike perennials sold in plastic containers, Etera's plants come in 4-inch-diameter plantable pots that can go directly into the ground. You set the coconut-fiber pots just below the soil surface, firm the earth around them, and water well. The roots quickly grow through the coconut fiber, which eventually decomposes.

In *Sunset* garden trials, Etera's one-year-old plants became established quickly and flowered reliably. By season's end, their performance nearly equaled that of the same perennials sold in 1-gallon cans.

For a free catalog or the names of local retailers that sell Etera plants, or to order plants directly, call (888) 840-4024 or visit www.etera. com. —*Jim McCausland*

COCONUT-FIBER POTS of 'Firewitch' dianthus go directly into prepared soil.

NORMAN A. PLATE

BEN WOOLSEY

A late clematis with a sweet surprise

■ Not to be outdone by its spring- and summer-flowering brethren, one member of the clematis family waits patiently in the wings. And sweet autumn clematis is worth the wait, as billowy masses of fragrant blossoms cascade from the vine in late summer or fall. The inch-wide blooms open creamy white over glossy dark green leaves. When the flowers fade, they form showy plumed seeds—fuzzy silver pinwheels that hang on well into the winter.

Native to Japan, sweet autumn clematis is hardy in zones 2–9. The vine climbs vigorously to 20 to 30 feet. Like other clematis, it flourishes in a site where its roots are shaded but its flowers and leaves grow in sun.

Currently, sweet autumn clematis is known as *Clematis dioscoreifolia,* but you may also find the plant sold as *C. terniflora, C. paniculata,* or *C. maximowiczina.* Shop for blooming plants in nursery containers or order (as *C. terniflora*) from Joy Creek Nursery, 20300 N.W. Watson Rd., Scappoose, OR 97056; (503) 543-7474. Catalog $2.

If you buy one now, get it in the ground soon. Before freezing weather hits, spread a 6-inch layer of organic mulch over its roots to protect them during the first winter. Once the vine is established, prune it in early spring or after it flowers. — *Steven R. Lorton*

FLAMBOYANT spikes of penstemon and mounds of desert marigolds skirt the courtyard wall.

Cheery face-lift for an old Phoenix yard

■ When Vic Vasquez and Scott Aycock let their lawn die, neighbors fretted. Then a red stucco wall sprouted in their front yard, and more brows furrowed. After all, their 1929 adobe house was the pride of the Willow Historic District in Phoenix. Wasn't the wall going to overpower it?

Trust us, said Peter and Carrie Nimmer, the architect/landscape designer team responsible for the project, who also happen to live across the street. Once acacia and palo verde trees were planted, and desert marigolds and penstemons began to flower, the 32-inch-high wall seemed perfectly proportioned.

The remodeled front yard is a much more sociable space. The wall includes a built-in seating area that wraps around a patio paved with red-tinted concrete. Now neighbors drop by to chat, and Aycock and Vasquez use the patio for outdoor entertaining. And since there's no lawn to tend, notes Vasquez, "we spend our time enjoying the garden instead of working in it."

— *Sharon Coboon*

Floating island of conifers

■ Landscape designer Peggy Quaid collects unusual plants. While working at the nursery she started, "I was always trading plants with friends at other nurseries," she says. Her contacts with West Coast specialty growers inspired her to plant dwarf conifers, as well as offbeat bulbs and perennials, in her Fort Bragg garden.

Quaid has dozens of species and varieties, arranged in orderly beds. The alpine conifers form an "island," while the gravel path mimics a dry streambed. Foliage is more important than flowers; it ranges from gold to lime green, apple green to deep plum. Many of the conifers change color in cold weather.

To build the island, Quaid scraped off an old lawn and mounded the turf

pieces in the center of the garden. She added compost, turning the pile regularly for six months until it became rich soil. Then she started planting.

QUAID'S FAVORITE DWARF CONIFERS

•*Chamaecyparis obtusa* 'Chabo Yaderi'. Dome-shaped shrub with fan-shaped foliage that turn to plum in winter. FF

•*C.o.* 'Nana Lutea'. Upright shrub with vivid lemon-gold foliage. FF
•*Chamaecyparis pisifera* 'Boulevard'. Dense, conical habit with steel blue foliage. FF
•*Chamaecyparis thyoides* 'Heather Bun'. A round-topped cedar; olive green foliage has soft plum overtones, turns intense plum in winter. M
•*Cryptomeria japonica*

'Jindai-Sugi'. A compact, conical cedar with green foliage. FF
•*Picea abies* 'Little Gem'. Dense, flat-topped globe with rich green needles. M

SOURCES: FF=available by mail from Forestfarm nursery, Williams, OR; (541) 846-7269. M=ask your nursery to order from Monrovia (wholesale only).

— *Lauren Bonar Swezey*

A river runs through it

■ The Brazilian *Aechmea* bromeliad running through Andy Butler's garden near Honolulu is as flame red as a river of lava. This pineapple relative likes it here; it has naturalized with abandon in the arid climate in this part of Oahu. Since Butler loves the plant's dramatic, 5-foot-tall flower stalks and incendiary red-orange leaves—especially in late summer when their color is most intense—he doesn't fight the flow. He gave

up on a lawn, and now lets the plant produce pups (side shoots) to root freely. Succulents and other bromeliads are happy in the same conditions and cool down the color scheme slightly.

If he could wean himself from the rest of his "tropicalia," gardening would be a breeze, admits Butler. "My red bromeliads practically take care of themselves," he says. "They're the easiest plants in my yard." — *S.C.*

FLAME-COLORED bromeliads thrive in heat.

SAN DIEGO

JEFF LANCASTER

Grapevines for your garden

■ John and Carol Rayes installed a vineyard in their front yard not because it was glamorous but because it was inexpensive. Lots are very large in the Elfin Forest area of northern San Diego County; the slope from the couple's front yard to the street covers nearly an acre.

Carpeting their garden with sod would have cost a fortune, and irrigating it would have cost at least several hundred dollars a month. Installing 500 grapevines in the front (and 300 in another location), on the other hand, cost the Rayeses only about $6,000— they did much of the labor themselves. And their irrigation expenditure is just $80 a month.

But, more important, managing a vineyard has become an adventure. The Rayeses have become experts on subjects they couldn't have defined a few years ago, such as spur pruning. And they have brought in their first harvest a year ahead of schedule. The crush resulted in 50 gallons of wine. It's too early to judge the red, but the Rayeses liked the white so well they entered it in the Del Mar Fair. Elfin Forest Vineyards Viognier '98 was a very good year.

If you're interested in viticulture, call (619) 694-2845 to order cooperative extension's packet on grape growing. And read *From Vines to Wines: The Complete Guide to Growing Grapes and Making Your Own Wine,* by Jeff Cox (Storey Books, Williamstown, MA, 1999; $18.95; 802/823-5810 or www.storeybooks.com).

— *S.C*

A seaside fantasy

■ For Evonne Kane, the urge to create something beautiful on property she rented close to the beach in South Laguna was irresistible, especially after she found rock benches, walls, and other remnants of an old garden buried underneath the overgrown vegetation. She began pulling up ice plant and putting in roses.

As she worked, she learned: Geraniums bloom nearly year-round at the beach. Roses do fine, provided you wash the salt off their foliage regularly (and early in the day). Cottage garden plants can contribute their magic, too: Agapanthus, bachelor's buttons, coreopsis, dahlias, foxgloves, gaura, nasturtiums, and yarrow do fine in coastal breezes.

Containers bring in additional color. Kane set pots of princess flower (*Tibouchina urvilleana*), mandevilla, and lavender on stone benches adjacent to her "meadow" border.

The results are featured on page 232. Kane even created something beautiful out of the stones she found buried under vegetation (see photo below).— *S.C.*

BACK TO BASICS

NORMAN A. PLATE

Before you plant vegetable or flower beds this fall, your soil could probably use some additional compost or organic mulch.

If the soil is already a good clay loam, dig in a 2- to 3-inch layer. For heavy clay soil, you'll need to add twice that amount. One cubic yard (27 cubic feet) of mulch covers 108 square feet with a layer about 3 inches deep. A 2-cubic-foot bag covers 8 square feet 3 inches deep. — *L.B.S.*

VIOLET SPIKES of *Salvia superba* sweep around grasses and blue-and-white Rocky Mountain columbine.

TERRENCE MOORE

Summer success under the Montana sky

■ Gardening in the hills near Flathead Lake in Bigfork, Montana, landscape architect Chris Moritz has to contend with sandy soil, a short growing season, and winter cold. Yet Moritz has managed to find perennials that shine under these conditions. All can be planted this month in most areas (if your garden soil usually freezes deep before

it snows, wait until spring to plant).

Backed by a stand of native pines and firs, the bed shown above is split by a violet-blue stream of *Salvia superba*. It blooms for almost a month in June, and by mid-July it's ready to be cut back and fertilized to spark a second round of bloom in late summer or early autumn.

Two ornamental grasses back up the sage: tufted hair grass (*Deschampsia caespitosa* 'Goldgehaenge') with 2- to 3-foot-tall blond seed heads, and feather reed grass (*Calamagrostis arundinacea* 'Karl Foerster'), an extremely hardy clumping grass that reaches 5 to 6 feet tall. Blue-and-white Rocky Mountain columbine

(*Aquilegia caerulea*), tall blue delphiniums, and white peonies complete the picture. Moritz also likes to tuck pockets of bulbs, including daffodils, tulips, and lilies, among the perennials.

Moritz feeds the bed with a complete fertilizer twice a year, once in spring and again in midsummer.

— *J.M.*

Grow your own fertilizer

■ Healthy plants start with healthy soil. And one way to improve your soil is to plant a cover crop (sometimes called green manure)—a kind of miracle worker for the soil made of fast-growing nitrogen-fixing legumes or grains.

Cover crops not only add nitrogen to the soil and increase organic matter content but also help choke out weeds; improve air, root, and water penetration; and encourage earthworms and beneficial microorganisms.

In addition, while they grow, they also provide habitat, nectar, and pollen for beneficial insects.

Many of the best cover crops are cool-season plants you start in fall (before heavy rains start in cool, wet climates; two months before the first hard frost in cold climates). They can be used in a bed of any size. If you don't want to give up your entire vegetable garden to cover crops, plant one section each season. It may take several years of

cover cropping to get significant results in poor soil.

Two types of cover crops we like are fava beans and mixes. If you're a first-time cover cropper, you might want to start with a mix of different crops for maximum soil building.

FAVA BEANS are probably the best-known cover crop. They make nodules on their roots that "fix" nitrogen in the soil. Use 2 to 3 pounds per 1,000 square feet.

MIXES for mild climates include Austrian winter peas, bell beans, vetch, and sometimes oats. Use these kinds of mixes if your winter temperatures don't drop

below 20°; they're available from Harmony Farm Supply & Nursery (707/823-9125) and Peaceful Valley Farm Supply (888/784-1722). If temperatures drop below 20°, use Cold Zone Soil Builder (which contains hairy vetch and cereal rye) from Peaceful Valley Farm Supply. Plant the mixes according to label directions. Adding a legume inoculant to the seeds before planting will increase nitrogen fixation (available from both sources; follow package directions). Cut the cover crop down when 50 percent of the mix starts to bloom.

— L.B.S.

Teatime for flowers

■ English-born gardener Joyce Smith of Willow, Alaska, has one of the most prolific raised-bed flower gardens we have ever seen. To keep the blooms coming, she regularly treats her plants to tea—*manure* tea, that is. Here is her recipe: Empty a 1-cubic-foot bag of well-rotted steer manure into an old pillowcase and put it in a garbage can filled with water. Stir until the manure is completely diluted; let stand until water turns the color of rich coffee—about a week. Pull out the pillowcase, pour the nutrient-rich tea around the root zones of plants, and dump the depleted manure into the garden when finished. — *S.R.L.*

Pacific Northwest Checklist

PLANTING

☑ **COOL-SEASON VEGGIES.** If you act very soon—ideally no later than Labor Day weekend—you can still sow seeds for fall and winter cole crops (cabbage and kale) and salad crops (arugula, leaf lettuce, mustard greens, radishes, and spinach). You can also plant nursery-grown seedlings of most of these, plus cabbage and purple-sprouting broccoli, which you harvest in spring.

☑ **LANDSCAPE PLANTS.** Autumn is the best time to set out trees, shrubs, vines, ground covers, and many perennial plants.

☑ **LAWNS.** If your lawn has thin spots, overseed them with the same kind of grass that grew there originally (if you sow something different, the color will be off, like a bad paint job). This month is also a good time to sow new lawns.

☑ **SPRING-BLOOMING BULBS.** These arrive at nurseries shortly after Labor Day. Plant tulips and hyacinths or, for long-term performance, try daffodils and crocus.

MAINTENANCE

☑ **CARE FOR ROSES.** After the fall flush of bloom, don't deadhead. By letting the spent blossoms produce hips, you get the plant ready to wind down for winter.

☑ **CLEAN GREENHOUSES.** While you can still keep tender plants outside, empty the greenhouse, wash it down (a combination of bleach and water makes short work of moss and algae), replace weather-stripping, check out heating and venting systems, and clean out flats, pots, and seedbeds. When frosty weather comes, you'll be ready to press the greenhouse into service.

☑ **DIG AND DIVIDE PERENNIALS.** Divide and replant spring- and summer-flowering perennials now, including astilbe, daylilies, Oriental poppies, peonies, Shasta daisies, Siberian irises, and yarrow. Divide fall bloomers such as asters after they flower or in spring.

☑ **MAKE COMPOST.** Use grass clippings, fallen leaves, weeds, and vegetable waste to build an autumn compost pile. Keep it damp and turned, and you'll have compost to turn in to the soil before winter.

☑ **MULCH.** Zones 1–3: Apply a 3-inch layer of organic mulch to minimize winter freeze damage and erosion.

☑ **TEND FLOWERS.** Keep fuchsias, annuals, and long-flowering perennials deadheaded, fed, and watered to keep bloom coming until near frost.

☑ **WEED.** Don't let weeds get started now or they'll be tough to remove next spring. Keep the garden hoed and mulched to prevent weeds from sending down roots over winter. ◆

Northern California Checklist

PLANTS

☑ **COLORFUL CABBAGES AND KALE.** Zones 7–9, 14–17: Although not actually flowers, ornamental cabbages and kale provide striking midwinter color in the garden. Peacock series kale has feathery leaves. Nagoya series kale has frilly leaf edges. Color Up cabbage has smooth cabbagelike leaves. Most nurseries carry several different types. Or you can grow them from seed (all are available from Park Seed Company; 800/845-3369).

☑ **FALL-BLOOMING PERENNIALS.** Zones 7–9, 14–17: Some good choices include asters, chrysanthemums, gaillardias, gloriosa daisies, Japanese anemones, lion's tails, purple coneflowers, and salvias.

☑ **LESS COMMON BULBS.** Zones 7–9, 14–17: Try these charmers in your garden; all will give a colorful display in spring: African corn lily (*Ixia*), baboon flower (*Babiana*), *Freesia*, grape hyacinth (*Muscari*), harlequin flower (*Sparaxis*), *Homeria*, poppy-flowered anemone (*A. coronaria*), ranunculus, species and other dwarf *Narcissus*, species tulips such as *Tulipa clusiana* and *T. saxatilis*, and *Tritonia*.

Sunset
CLIMATE ZONES
- Mountain (1-2)
- Valley (7-9)
- Inland (14)
- Coastal (15-17)

DEBRA LAMBERT

☑ **NEW LAWNS.** Zones 1–9, 14–17: Toward the end of the month, sow seed or lay sod over soil that's been rotary tilled and amended with plenty of organic matter. Zones 1–2: Plant new lawns early in September (at highest elevations, wait to plant seed until October; it will germinate in spring when the snow melts).

☑ **EDIBLE-POD PEAS.** Zones 1–9, 14–17: The best snap peas? Try 2- to 3-foot-tall 'Super Sugar Mel' (from Renee's Garden; (888) 880-7228 or www.garden.com.reneesgarden) or 2-foot-tall 'Sugar Ann' or 6-foot-tall 'Sugar Snap' (from Nichols Garden Nursery; 541/928-9280).

MAINTENANCE

☑ **DISBUD CAMELLIAS.** Zones 7–9, 14–17: To get huge, show-quality blooms in spring, remove all but one bud per stem.

☑ **DIVIDE PERENNIALS.** Dig and divide perennials, such as agapanthus, candytuft, coreopsis, daylily, and penstemon, that are overgrown or not flowering well (zones 1–2: do this early in the month). Use a spading fork or spade to lift clumps; then cut clumps into sections with a spade, a sharp knife, or pruning shears. Replant sections in well-amended soil; keep moist.

☑ **FEED ROSES.** Zones 7–9, 14–17: If you haven't fertilized recently, give roses a shot now to encourage autumn blooms. Make sure the soil is moist before fertilizing; water well afterward.

PEST CONTROL

☑ **CONTROL POWDERY MILDEW.** Zones 7–9, 14–17: This white powdery disease infects a number of plants including dahlias, roses, zinnias, and many vegetables. Spray foliage with a mix of 2 teaspoons baking soda, 2 teaspoons lightweight summer oil, and 1 gallon of water (reapply to new growth), or dust with sulfur at the first sign of damage (sulfur can damage some melons and squash; test on a leaf and wait a few days first). Do not apply sulfur to roses in very hot weather. ◆

Southern California Checklist

PLANTING

☑ **BULBS.** Spring-flowering bulbs begin arriving in nurseries this month. Shop early while stock is fresh. Bulbs that naturalize easily in Southern California's climate include acidanthera, babiana, Dutch iris, freesia, narcissus, *Sparaxis tricolor,* and watsonia. Anemone and ranunculus don't need to be prechilled but do need to be replanted every year. Also buy tulips, spring-flowering crocus, and hyacinths now but wait until after Thanksgiving to plant them. Store bulbs in paper bags in the crisper section of the refrigerator in the interim. In the medium to high desert (zone 11) where no prechilling is necessary, plant bulbs immediately.

☑ **COOL-SEASON CROPS.** From midmonth on, coastal (zones 22–24) and inland (zones 18–21) gardeners can set out seedlings of broccoli, brussels sprouts, cabbage, cauliflower, celery, and parsley. Sow seeds for beets, bok choy, carrots, chard, collards, kale, lettuce, parsnips, peas, radishes, spinach, and turnips. Plant sets of garlic, onions, and shallots. In the high desert, plant lettuce, radishes, and spinach.

Sunset CLIMATE ZONES

1-3 7-9 11 13 14-24

DEBRA LAMBERT

☑ **SWEET PEAS.** Plant seeds soon to have sweet peas for the winter holidays. Look for varieties designated "early-flowering" such as 'Winter Elegance Mix'. To speed germination, soak seeds overnight before planting. Provide a fence, trellis, or several tall poles for the vines to climb.

MAINTENANCE

☑ **FEED ROSES.** For gorgeous fall roses, cut back spent flowers to just above a five-leaflet leaf. Then fertilize, water well, and replenish mulch. Jan Weverka, editor of *The Rose Gardener,* a monthly newsletter out of Monrovia, suggests applying the following formula per rose bush: 3 cups alfalfa meal, 1 cup cottonseed meal, 1/2 cup Ironite, 1/4 cup kelp, and 2 tablespoons sulfur. Scratch it into the soil surface before watering. For details about Weverka's newsletter, call (626) 301-0013.

☑ **FEED PERMANENT PLANTS.** Fertilize trees, shrubs, ground covers, perennials, tropicals, subtropicals, and warm-season grasses for the final time this year. Don't feed California natives or drought-tolerant Mediterranean plants.

☑ **DIVIDE PERENNIALS.** Dig and divide agapanthus, daylilies, ornamental grasses, and other plants that are overcrowded or are not flowering well. Use a spading fork to lift and a sharp knife to divide.

☑ **OVERSEED BERMUDA GRASS.** If you don't like the tawny look of dormant grass, overseed your lawn with annual rye. Mow the lawn short, then scatter rye seed (1 lb. per 100 square feet), cover it with top dressing, and water it regularly until the seed germinates.

PEST CONTROL

☑ **PROTECT CABBAGE CROPS.** The minute you plant a brassica, squadrons of cabbage white butterflies seem to descend on it to lay their eggs. The easiest way to thwart them is to cover your cabbage crops with row covers right from the start. The next best option is spraying with *Bacillus thuringiensis* to kill the young caterpillar larvae. ◆

Mountain Checklist

PLANTING

☑ **FORCE INDOOR BULBS.** For holiday bloom, pot amaryllis and paper white narcissus by month's end. Water the bulbs and put them in a warm, bright spot to encourage strong flower stems.

☑ **SET OUT BULBS.** Plant crocus, daffodil, hyacinth, *Iris reticulata,* scilla, and tulip bulbs. Bury daffodils and tulips 10 to 12 inches deep, smaller bulbs 5 inches deep.

☑ **PANSIES.** These hardy workhorses provide fall color when they become established, bloom during winter mild spells, then come on strong again in spring. Put them in a place where they won't be buried in snow for more than a few days at a time.

☑ **PERENNIALS.** Set out campanula, candytuft, catmint, coreopsis, delphinium, dianthus, foxglove, gaillardia, geum, penstemon, phlox, salvia, and yarrow. Put them in well-prepared garden soil and water well. In areas where the soil freezes deeply every winter, spread a thick layer of mulch around plants to keep them from being heaved out of the ground.

☑ **SEED OR SOD LAWNS.** Early fall is ideal for seeding a lawn or laying sod. Keep the grass well watered until cold weather stops its growth.

Sunset
CLIMATE ZONES

☐ 1-3   ☐ 10-11

DEBRA LAMBERT

MAINTENANCE

☑ **CLEAN UP THE GREENHOUSE.** Scrub out seedbeds and flats with a weak mixture of bleach and water. Then check and replace weather-stripping, broken glass, and torn plastic. Finally, check vents, filters, and heaters, replacing or repairing broken components before winter comes.

☑ **DIG AND STORE SUMMER BULBS.** When foliage dies down, lift cannas, dahlias, and gladiolus. Let them dry for a few days, then store at 35° to 50° in a well-ventilated space. Store cannas and dahlias in sand, peat moss, or vermiculite. Leave begonia tubers in the containers they grew in, but bring them indoors.

☑ **DIVIDE PERENNIALS.** In all but the very highest elevations, lift and divide crowded clumps of bleeding hearts, daylilies, hostas, peonies, and Shasta daisies. Then mulch to protect plants against freezing and heaving.

☑ **FERTILIZE LAWNS.** Apply about 10 pounds of 10-10-10 fertilizer per 1,000 square feet of turf.

☑ **MAKE COMPOST.** Compost all the vegetable waste that comes out of your garden this month. Make a pile 4 feet in diameter, putting down alternating layers of green matter (like grass clippings) and brown (dried leaves). Water enough to keep the pile as moist as a squeezed-out sponge, and turn the pile weekly with a pitchfork.

☑ **PREVENT SNOW MOLD.** Rake the thatch that harbors snow mold out of the lawn, then spray turf with a fungicide, such as benomyl.

☑ **WATER.** Pay special attention to plants growing under eaves and in containers.

☑ **WEED.** Hoe, pull, or spray weeds with herbicide before they go to seed. ◆

Southwest Checklist

PLANTING

☑ **ANNUALS.** Zone 12 (Tucson): Plant delphinium, larkspur, lobelia, pansy, stock, and viola. All should be well established by Halloween and bloom through April or May.

☑ **BULBS.** Zone 11 (Las Vegas): Plant bearded iris rhizomes. Zones 1–2, 10–11: Plant spring-flowering bulbs like crocus, daffodil, grape hyacinth, hyacinth, and tulip. Zones 12–13: Buy spring bulbs now, put them in paper bags, and refrigerate them until the soil cools down enough to plant, around Thanksgiving.

☑ **COOL-SEASON CROPS.** Zones 10–13: As soon as temperatures drop below 100°, sow beets, carrots, celery, chard, endive, green onions, kale, kohlrabi, leeks, parsley, parsnips, peas, potatoes, radishes, spinach, and turnips. Sow lettuce and cabbage-family members (broccoli and cauliflower) in flats for transplanting in October.

☑ **LANDSCAPE PLANTS.** Zones 10–11: Set out hardy trees, shrubs, and ground covers.

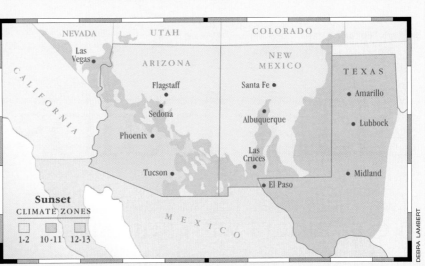

☑ **LAWNS.** Zones 1–2, 10–11: Early fall is ideal for seeding a lawn or laying sod. Just keep it well watered until cold weather stops its growth.

☑ **PERENNIALS.** Zones 1–2, 10–11: Plant perennials like campanula, candytuft, catmint, coreopsis, delphinium, dianthus, diascia, foxglove, gaillardia, geum, penstemon, phlox, salvia, and yarrow. Zones 10–13: Start seed of carnation, columbine, coreopsis, feverfew, gaillardia, hardy aster, hollyhock, lupine, penstemon, phlox, Shasta daisy, statice, and yarrow; transplant in about eight weeks.

☑ **WARM-SEASON CROPS.** Zones 12–13: Plant beans and corn around Labor Day and you'll be harvesting by Thanksgiving.

MAINTENANCE

☑ **CARE FOR LAWNS.** If you plan to overseed your Bermuda grass lawn, stop feeding it. If you don't plan to overseed, apply high-nitrogen fertilizer now at 1 pound actual nitrogen per 1,000 square feet and water it in well to keep the grass actively growing for as long as possible.

☑ **FEED ROSES.** Water deeply, then apply a complete fertilizer (preferably one that contains chelated iron), water again, and apply a 3-inch layer of organic mulch.

☑ **WATER.** Pay special attention to anything you planted this year, plants under eaves, and those in containers. Water citrus deeply every 10 to 14 days; regular irrigation helps to prevent split fruit. ◆

Three great ways to plant bulbs

In containers with annuals, by themselves, or in beds for months of bloom

BY SHARON COHOON AND JIM McCAUSLAND
PHOTOGRAPHS BY NORMAN A. PLATE

■ A daffodil is an alchemist's dream come true. Think about it: You drop a brown lump into the soil in fall and add some water. In the dead of winter, succulent spears push up through the damp mulch. Swelling with promise, buds form in January and, by February or March, golden flowers emerge—heralding spring. The transformation from tulip bulb to bloom is just as impressive. Ditto hyacinth, Dutch iris, anemone, and freesia. Science explains it: Bulbs, corms, rhizomes, and tubers are all storage organs that contain more than enough nutrients for a brief and brilliant season of color. But explanation doesn't dilute the mystery. The metamorphosis from fall bulb to spring flower never fails to feel like magic. • To make the most of that magic, on the following pages we present three great ways to show off fall-planted bulbs. In large pots, you can mix them with annuals or mass them by kind; both methods make a big splash without demanding that you spend a small fortune for bulbs. (You don't have to worry about overcrowding them. Since they're only for the season and you don't expect them to multiply, you can plant bulbs cheek-to-jowl for maximum flash. And, when the flowers have faded, you can move the withering foliage out of sight.) • In garden beds, you can prolong a daffodil show by mingling early-, middle-, and late-flowering kinds to get two full months of bloom.

■ Buy plump, top-quality bulbs as soon as they appear in nurseries. Generally, the bigger the bulbs' circumference, the more flowers you will get.

■ In mild climates, chill tulips and hyacinths at 40° to 45° in the refrigerator for six weeks before planting.

■ Soil for bulbs must drain quickly. In pots, use light, fibrous potting mix. In garden beds, add organic matter such as compost or redwood soil conditioner before planting.

■ In garden beds, plant bulbs so they're covered with soil three times as deep as the bulb's diameter. In pots, follow the directions for solo bulbs on page 250.

■ All bulbs thrive in full sun (dappled shade in hot inland climates).

■ Apply complete fertilizer between leaf emergence and bloom. If you're growing daffodils in containers, use half-strength liquid fertilizer applied at leaf emergence, at bloom, and again when bloom is finished.

■ After bulb leaves start to die, stop watering to let bulbs go dormant for the summer. (Exceptions are tulips, which don't perform reliably the second year, and bulbs planted with annuals.) For daffodils, pull off faded blooms, but allow leaves to remain and rebuild the bulbs. If you planted annuals with the bulbs, you can keep watering to prolong bloom; cut down or tuck fading bulb foliage under them.

■ ORANGE GROVE TULIPS rise above blue forget-me-nots and orange violas; ivy softens pot edges. Pot design: Sharon Cohoon with Jean Manocchio. House and garden design: Lynn Hollyn Associates.

METHOD ONE

Bouquets in pots:
Bulbs with annuals

Classic bulb/annual combinations like pansies with daffodils or tulips with linaria are as elegant in pots as they are in borders. The photos on these pages suggest some great pairings. Forget-me-nots (*Myosotis sylvatica*) are foolproof; their clear blue flowers seem to complement bulb flowers of any color—from orange tulips to red ranunculus or yellow daffodils. Sweet alyssum is another "goes-with-anything" choice. A ruff of burgundy lettuce is unexpected when paired with blue hyacinth, and after the blooms quit, you've got a crop to harvest. Nemesia, dwarf stock, snapdragons, and primroses—especially *Primula polyantha* and lacy-flowered *P. malacoides*—are other good companions for bulbs.

There are two ways to plant your bulb companions.

From seed: Some annuals (forget-me-nots, sweet alyssum) and grasses are easy to start from seed; you just plant the bulbs, cover them with soil almost to the pot rim, then scatter seeds over the surface, press them in place, and water well. The seeds will sprout, grow, and bloom right along with the bulbs.

From cell-packs: For small bulbs like anemones, freesias, or ranunculus, it's easier to plant the bedding plants first, then tuck in the bulbs. Fill the container with pansies, for instance, then poke the bulbs into the empty spots, using your finger or a pencil as a dibble. For larger bulbs such as tulips and daffodils, plant the bulbs first, mark their locations where you put in the bulbs with stakes or twigs, then add bedding plants. Or you can wait until the bulbs send up shoots before adding plants.

■ LEFT: Pink 'New Design' tulips and blue pansies mingle around silver spear (*Astelia nervosa chathamica*). Design: Jackie Gray for Stanford Shopping Center.
■ ABOVE: 'Blushing Beauty' tulips are fringed with pink English primroses and cyclamen. Design: Bud Stuckey.
■ RIGHT: 'Bismarck' hyacinth is fringed with 'Lollo Rosso' red-leaf lettuce.

great ways with bulbs

■ PAPER WHITE NARCISSUS grow through a meadow of winter rye. Bulbs were planted first, then grass seeds sown on top.

METHOD TWO
Solo show in pots

The simplest way to plant bulbs in containers is to mass a single variety in a pot. Bulbs with starchy foliage, like tulips and daffodils, look especially good this way. A half-dozen tulips and a handsome pot is all it takes to make a pretty vignette. (For a meadow look, overseed with grass as shown above.)

For a planting like the daffodil pot pictured at right, fill a large (16- to 18-inch) pot to within 4 inches of the pot rim with light, fibrous potting mix. Set the bulbs on the soil base so they're almost touching (a 16-inch pot will hold nearly 50 tulip bulbs or about 40 daffodil bulbs). Cover the bulbs with soil, leaving 1½ inches at the top for watering space. Tamp the soil firmly to press it against the bulbs. Move the pots to a cool, shaded spot and water well. When green shoots appear (in three to four months), move pots into full sun.

■ LEFT: 'Passionale' daffodils fill this pot; California poppy foliage grows among the bulbs.
■ ABOVE: 'King Alfred' daffodils fill bucket at Van Lierop Bulb Farm in Puyallup, Washington.

ABOVE: CONNIE COLEMAN

A word about the late 'King Alfred'

■ Introduced exactly a century ago, the yellow trumpet daffodil 'King Alfred' achieved such fame that gardeners continued to choose it over improved daffodil varieties that were developed later. Not to be denied, retailers started selling the improved varieties as "King Alfred types," 'King Alfred Improved', or worse, just 'King Alfred'. Almost no true 'King Alfred' daffodils are grown these days; when you buy them, you're usually getting 'Golden Harvest', 'Dutch Master', or some other worthy yellow trumpet daffodil.

In garden beds: The longest daffodil parade in town

Daffodil blossoms normally last about three weeks. But by planting early, mid-, and late-season varieties, you can have spring's most trouble-free signature flowers for two months or more. Just group one to two dozen bulbs of each kind in kidney-shaped drifts, putting taller plants at the back, shorter ones in front.

Use our chart to choose daffodils that will flower in sequence over the longest possible season. Most of the varieties listed are widely available, though you may have to order some by mail to complete your planting scheme.

Though most of us call them daffodils, the plants in this chart are technically narcissus. Serious horticulturists consider plants from only one division—the trumpet narcissus—to be true daffodils. In the other divisions, plants are grouped generally by the proportions of the flower's cup (the center corona, also called the crown or trumpet) and the segments (petals) that flare out to the sides.

We mention daffodils from most divisions here. Some division names, like large-cupped, small-cupped, and double, are self-explanatory. The triandrus, jonquilla, and tender tazetta types bear flowers in (usually fragrant) clusters; cyclamineus have swept-back segments; papillons are split-corona types, which have a sunburst of color in their centers; and poeticus are fragrant, with disk-shaped centers. The miscellaneous group serves as a catch-all for a variety of new flower forms.

Most kinds of narcissus will flower the spring after they're planted in any *Sunset* climate zone, but not all will come back in perpetuity. Some are limited by cold, others by winter warmth. In areas with poor soil, plant in containers. For help in choosing the best types for your area, see note on chart top.

early

'Ice Follies' (foreground) and 'Dutch Master' (rear).

mid

'Geranium' (left) and white-cupped 'Thalia' (rear).

late

'Yellow Cheerfulness' and 'Cheerfulness'.

QUICK TIP

How to use daffodils in bouquets

After you cut daffodil flowers, place stems in a bucket of water. Fill a vase with a solution of commercial flower preservative and warm water according to package directions, or use a mixture of 1 part lemon-lime soda (not a diet kind) to 2 parts warm water.

Before arranging, snip off the bottom ½ inch of each stem while holding it under water (a wide bowl of water works well for this). Immediately transfer the blooms to the vase. Here, daffodils combine with goldenrod and forget-me-nots.

Bulbs for all seasons:
Two months' worth of daffodils

For plants limited by cold, we list the coldest zones in which they're likely to survive. If you garden in a mild-winter place (like Southern California or mild parts of Arizona), choose varieties listed for warmer climates.

Variety or species	Cool areas	Warm areas	Height	Comments
Early				
'Dutch Master'	●		16″	Yellow trumpet.
'February Gold'	●	●	12″	Yellow cyclamineus. Naturalizes.
'Jenny'	●	●	10″	White cyclamineus.
'Ziva'		●	18″	White tazetta with strong fragrance. Won't take frost.
Early midseason				
'Amor'	●		18″	White small-cupped with yellow-red cup.
'Carlton'	●	●	14″	Yellow, vanilla-scented large-cupped. Naturalizes to zone 3.
'Gigantic Star'	●	●	18″	Yellow, fragrant large-cupped. Naturalizes. Hardy to zone 3.
'Ice Follies'	●	●	14″	White large-cupped with yellow cup. Naturalizes.
'Mount Hood'	●		16″	White trumpet.
'Peeping Tom'		●	12″	Yellow cyclamineus. Naturalizes.
'Tête à Tête'	●		6″	Yellow and fragrant. Miscellaneous division.
Midseason				
'Cassata'	●		16″	White split-corona type with fading yellow cup.
'Geranium'	●	●	15″	White, fragrant tazetta with red-orange cup. Hardy to zone 4.
'Golden Harvest'	●		16″	Yellow trumpet. Naturalizes.
'Jack Snipe'		●	12″	White cyclamineus with yellow cup. Naturalizes.
'Las Vegas'	●		16″	White trumpet with yellow cup.
'Minnow'	●	●	6″	Yellow to white tazetta with yellow cup.
Narcissus bulbocodium	●	●	6″	Yellow species that's mostly trumpet. 'Golden Bells' variety naturalizes. Called "hoop petticoat daffodil."
'Quail'	●	●	14″	Yellow, fragrant jonquilla.
'Suzy'	●	●	16″	Yellow, fragrant jonquilla with orange cup. Naturalizes.
Late midseason				
'Actaea'	●	●	16″	White, fragrant poeticus with yellow-red cup, green eye.
'Baby Moon'	●	●	4″	Yellow jonquilla with intense fragrance.
'Coquille'	●	●	14″	Pink large-cupped with salmon-pink cup. Takes sun well.
'Dickcissel'	●	●	12″	Yellow jonquilla whose cups fade to white.
'Pink Charm'	●	●	16″	White large-cupped with red-orange-pink cup.
'Salome'	●		14″	White large-cupped with apricot-pink cup.
'Sir Winston Churchill'	●	●	14″	White, fragrant double with orange cup.
'Sorbet'	●	●	15″	White papillon with yellow-orange pinwheel cup.
'Thalia'	●	●	16″	White, fragrant triandrus. Vigorous, even in dry, warm areas.
Late				
'Cheerfulness'	●	●	14″	White, fragrant double with a yellow center.
'Hawera'	●	●	8″	Lemon yellow miniature triandrus.
Narcissus canaliculatus	●	●	6″	White, fragrant species with a yellow cup.
Narcissus poeticus recurvus	●		16″	Yellow, fragrant poeticus with red-edged cup and golden green eye. Naturalizes. Called "Poet's daffodil."
'Sun Disc'	●	●	5″	Yellow miniature jonquilla.
'Yellow Cheerfulness'	●		14″	Yellow, fragrant double with a hint of orange. ◆

MEXICAN FEATHER GRASS, blue-green festuca, and carefully placed stones add textural interest to a hill covered with lush blue star creeper. Lacy bamboos and 'Soquel' redwoods create a leafy screen behind.

Lessons in green

This serene garden in Sonoma, California, offers inspiration for combining foliage plants

BY JOAN STAPLETON ROCKWELL
PHOTOGRAPHS BY NORMAN A. PLATE

■ THERE IS SILENCE IN THIS MOIST, woodsy garden. And there is peace; soft shades of green—emerald, jade, and yellow-green—prevail.

"It's a California-Japanese-with-art Zen garden," says Victor Levine of the garden he created for Deborah Hill. The plantings are soothing and simple. Except for a scattering of tiny, pale blooms on the blue star creeper, there's not a flower in sight. Yet the garden is richly textured, thanks to a masterful combination of foliage in shades of green.

"Gardening with compassion is important to me," says Levine, who turned for inspiration to the gentle rolling hills along Sonoma Valley's western skyline and to the region's natural plant communities. To re-create the look of hills, Levine hauled in a ton of soil and shaped low mounds behind the house. He embedded boulders in the "hill," then planted blue star creeper, Mexican feather grass, festuca, and variegated bamboos around them.

Beyond these grassy hills, he created a raked-gravel courtyard encircled by native California shrubs, vines, and trees. Here, a pond is ringed with low grasses and ground covers. And a cluster of silvery artemisia billows over raked gravel. To Levine, these puffs of foliage represent "wispy clouds floating over a lake of gravel."

"Remember how restful it was lying in green grass making pictures of fluffy clouds?" he asks. "In this garden, you don't have to imagine it."

DESIGN: Victor Levine, Sonoma, CA; (707) 939-1712.

Hill's garden owes its tapestrylike quality to a pared-down palette of greens.

Cool green to gray

• *Artemisia* 'Powis Castle'. Silvery mound to 3 feet tall. Grows in all *Sunset* climate zones. • *Festuca amethystina, F. glauca.* Tight clumps of narrow bluish or grayish leaves 6 to 18 inches tall. Sun to part shade; all zones. • Coast redwood (*Sequoia sempervirens*). 'Soquel' (used in this garden) has bluish green foliage. 'Aptos Blue' and 'Majestic Beauty' have deeper blue-green foliage. 'Filoli' and 'Woodside' are distinctly blue. Grows fast to 70 to 90 feet. Sun (part shade when young). Zones 4–9, 14–24.

Warm green

• Bamboos. Levine used golden bamboo and black bamboo; both are running types, hardy to 0°. Clumpers with graceful foliage include golden goddess bamboo and Mexican weeping bamboo. • Blue star creeper (*Laurentia fluviatilis,* also sold as *Isotoma fluviatilis*). Apple green leaves on creeping plant to 3 inches tall. Sun to part shade. Zones 4–5, 8–9, 14–24.

Lessons in foliage

Play leaf colors off one another. Place apple green fern fronds beneath a red Japanese maple, for instance, or clumps of yellow-green feather grass next to gray-green woolly thyme. Plant ribbons of blue fescue through low blue star creeper and baby's tears. Fringe the edges with silvery lamb's ears.

Pair plants for shape, texture, and height. Plant billowing clumps of feathery grasses next to low, neat mats of creeping thyme, or variegated liriope (stiff, upright leaves) next to a groundhugger such as dymondia.

Repeat the plantings. Use the same plants—bamboo, for instance—in several parts of the garden. "Balance is vital," says Levine. "It unifies a garden."

Add art. Tuck water basins, stones, or garden statuary amid the foliage for interest and a bit of whimsy. ◆

TOP: Rock wall of Sonoma fieldstone edges the gently curving deck; it's fringed with blue festuca. Bamboo screen at garden's far end frames the view of distant hills. ABOVE: *Artemisia* 'Powis Castle' billows around center stone.

ABOVE LEFT: White-ash basket (foreground) holds a bushel of apples. Natural white color warms to honey gold after exposure to sunlight for several weeks. Hardware is brass to avoid corrosion. Small bamboo nesting basket (middle), handmade in Vietnam to carry everything from rice to coal, comes in 21-, 16-, 11½-, and 7-inch diameters. Flower-filled English trug (rear) is made from natural split willow and unpeeled sweet chestnut; copper nails hold rims together. Sold in eight sizes; this one is 13 by 7 by 8 inches. ABOVE RIGHT: Galvanized-wire vegetable harvest basket from Germany has a wood handle; you can rinse and drain vegetables right in the basket. This one is 18½ by 10½ by 6¼ inches.

Harvest baskets

Luggage for your vegetables

BY JIM McCAUSLAND

Meticulously arranged on a broad woven trug, fresh-cut flowers can make the trip from garden to vase without crimping a petal. It's no accident: Harvest baskets like the ones shown above took centuries to perfect, a task that fell mostly to gardeners who wanted the best for the crops they had worked so hard to grow.

Such baskets are designed to carry everything from apples to root vegetables. Use them once and you'll wonder how you ever did without them. Most are multipurpose: Flatish trugs, for example, work equally well for asparagus and flowers, and bushel baskets can haul anything from potatoes to apples.

The more tender the crop, the more important it is to use the right kind of basket. Here are some guidelines to help you select the perfect harvest aid.

■ **Bushel baskets.** The advantage here is in the volume they provide: You can use them to easily carry apples, avocados, cherries, citrus, corn, melons, nuts, pears, potatoes, slicing cucumbers, or squash. (This assumes that you pick avocados and pears firm.)

■ **Shallow round baskets.** Best for crops that are on the small or tender side, like beans, herbs, hot peppers, leafy vegetables, or pickling and lemon cucumbers.

■ **Trugs.** With perhaps the most interesting name of the lot (and its etymological origins are unknown), the trug is best for carrying crops that shouldn't be crushed or bent: apricots, asparagus, berries, figs, fresh-cut flowers, peaches, peppers, persimmons, plums, and tomatoes. Arrange soft fruits and vegetables one layer deep.

■ **Wire baskets.** These are designed for toting root crops like beets, carrots, radishes, rutabagas, and turnips; you can rinse the vegetables directly in the basket. ◆

Cool-season crops need a head start

Now's the time to sow seeds of cabbage, lettuce, and their kin

BY SHARON COHOON

Chard Silverado
Chard Charlotte

SEEDLINGS thrive in peat pots (at left), 4-inch plastic pots (center), and nursery flats.

Cabbage and cauliflower are not the crops most on our minds in late summer. We're too preoccupied trying to find recipes to use up our surplus zucchini. But put down that cookbook for a moment and pick up some potting mix: This is the ideal time to start seeds of cool-season vegetables and salad greens.

It's too hot now in much of the West to sow directly into the ground. But seeds started in flats or pots will be ready to transplant in six to eight weeks, when growing conditions are perfect. The air will be cooler and the soil just warm enough to encourage young plants to put down roots quickly. Depending on the crop, you can reap a harvest this fall, or overwinter plants in the ground for harvest early next spring.

COOL OPPORTUNITIES

Start seeds of any of the following crops as described in "Easy Steps" (at right).

Cole crops: Broccoli, brussels sprouts, cabbage, cauliflower, and kohlrabi. Gardeners in all but the coldest Western climates (*Sunset* zones 1–3) can start sowing these crops now. In areas with shorter growing seasons, such as the high desert (zone 10) and the coastal Pacific Northwest (zones 4–7), sow right away.

Leaf and salad crops: Chard, collards, kale, lettuce, mustard, and spinach. Most of the West can start leaf crops now. In the low and intermediate deserts (zones 11–13) and in the hot interior valleys of Southern California (zones 18–19), wait until cooler weather comes in late September or October.

Peas: Start edible-pod snap and snow peas now in all mild-winter areas except the low and intermediate deserts and zones 18–19, where you should wait until October or November.

Root crops: Beets, carrots, onions, parsnips, rutabagas, and turnips. Start seeds now through September in all but desert zones 11–13. In zones 1–3, protect plants against freezing winter weather with straw mulch.

EASY STEPS

In *Sunset's* test garden, we start seeds of cabbage and other cole crops, as well as peas, in 3- or 4-inch plastic pots, leaf crops in nursery flats, and root crops like beets and turnips in peat pots, which can be planted directly in the ground without disturbing the roots. We follow these steps.

1. Fill containers with potting mix. Moisten the mix well.

2. Distribute seeds evenly on top of soil. Sow seeds for lettuce and other greens about ½ to 1 inch apart. If using pots, two or three seeds per pot is plenty. Cover seeds with mix to the depth recommended on the seed packet. Water again, taking care not to displace the seeds; use a hose with a misting nozzle or a watering can with a sprinkler head.

3. Lay plastic wrap loosely over containers to hold in moisture. Set the containers in a sheltered area such as the bottom shelf of a potting bench or the top of a refrigerator. Because peat pots dry out quickly, it helps to nest them in a nursery flat filled with moistened potting mix. Check containers regularly to ensure that soil remains constantly moist.

4. As soon as seeds sprout, move containers into an area with good light—but no direct sun—such as under shadecloth or fluorescent lights, or in bright, dappled shade. Feed seedlings with a dilute solution of fish emulsion. Cull scrawny seedlings by using scissors to cut off their stems at the base.

5. Once seedlings develop their first set of true leaves, they're ready to transplant. Before they go into the garden, harden them off by gradually exposing them to ever-brighter sunlight. Give them an hour or so of direct morning sun the first day, two hours the next day, and so on until they're able to take full sun all day long. ◆

JAMIE HADLEY

SWEET PEAS don't have to be wallflowers. They can take center stage if you grow them in pots and train them up trellises of tree prunings or, as shown here, last year's Christmas tree. For more on these beautiful sprawlers, see page 266.

October

gardenguide

Azaleas with rich autumn color

Unlike their evergreen cousins, these azaleas turn blazing shades

RHODODENDRON LUTEUM is one of the showiest deciduous azaleas.

JANET LOUGHREY

■ If you've never associated azaleas with spectacular fall foliage, one look at *Rhododendron luteum* will change your thinking. This deciduous azalea is a showstopper not only during spring bloom, but also in autumn, when its leaves turn brilliant crimson, orange, or deep yellow. Hardy to –15°, it grows 4 to 8 feet tall with an equal spread and an open, upright form. Tubular yellow blossoms, which appear on leafless branches in April and May, are very fragrant.

Other deciduous azaleas with fiery autumn foliage include *R.* 'Mollala Red', *R. quinquefolium,* and *R. schlippenbachii;* their leaves turn color slowly but hang on several weeks before dropping.

Whether they're wearing their autumn colors or spring flowers, these azaleas look especially good against a background of deep green conifers.

Handsome as these azaleas are, they aren't widely sold at nurseries. If you can't find the plant you want, ask the nursery staff to order from a specialty grower. One good mail-order source is Greer Gardens, 1280 Good Pasture Island Rd., Eugene, OR 97401; (541) 686-8266.

If you buy a deciduous azalea this fall, plant it before really cold weather sets in. Azaleas like gentle morning sun and filtered afternoon light; avoid locations in full sun or near south- or west-facing walls. Plant in quick-draining soil enriched with plenty of organic matter. Spread a layer of mulch around the base of the plant to keep the roots moist but not wet. — *Steven R. Lorton*

LETTUCE and other greens grow in coldframes with plastic covers that prop open to ventilate the crops.

Salad crops thrive under the covers

■ Even during frosty weather, the chefs at Sooke Harbour House on Vancouver Island fill their salads with fresh greens harvested from an extensive kitchen garden. To protect the crops, chief gardener Byron Cook grows them in covered coldframes like those at left.

Each 42- by 96-inch frame is made with 2-by-10s. The arched cover is formed by three half-circles of plywood topped by horizontal lath strips with 6-mil plastic sheeting stapled over them (the ultraviolet-resistant plastic lasts about three years.) At 2 feet tall, the cover allows enough headroom for taller crops like miner's lettuce. The covers are put on the frames in October before the first frost hits. During the cold months, the hinged covers are opened on mornings when the temperature is above freezing and closed in the evening. The frames remain closed only when the weather is very cold and cloudy; even then, gardeners open them for at least a half-hour every couple of days to let in fresh air. The covers are removed in spring after frost danger is past.

For salad greens, Cook grows arugula, chickweed, lettuces ('Black-seeded Simpson', 'Four Seasons', 'Oak Leaf', 'Red Sails', and 'Rouge Grenobloise'), mesclun, miner's lettuce, and two kinds of sorrel. He also grows assorted leaf vegetables for cooking (chard, collards, kale, and spinach), root crops (beets, carrots, Jerusalem artichokes, potatoes, and radishes), and edible flowers (calendulas, English daisies, pansies, and violas). — *Jim McCausland*

Weave a wreath of rose hips

■ Left uncut, rose blossoms develop into seed pods called hips. Species such as *Rosa rugosa* and many old garden roses are especially prolific producers of hips in shades of red or orange. To enjoy their beauty all winter long, garden writer Georgeanne Brennan weaves hip-laden canes into wreaths. Follow her method, described here.

1. Choose a relatively thornless rose with hips that grow every 4 to 6 inches along the cane. Cut off three or four canes, each about 3 feet long.

2. Twist one cane into a circle and fasten the ends with a piece of uncoated florist's wire.

3. Position the second cane on the wired circle 3 to 4 inches from where the first circle started. Wire the second cane to the first, fastening it at the beginning, middle, and end to overlay another circle. Repeat this step with the remaining canes.

4. Place the wreath on a rack in a warm, dark place with good air circulation until the hips are dry.

5. Hang the wreath on a door or gate, or display it on a mirror or table.

Brennan's wreath is one of dozens of projects she describes in her new book *Flowerkeeping: The Time-Honored Art of Preserving Flowers* (Ten Speed Press, Berkeley, 1999; $17.95; 800/841-2665). — *Dick Bushnell*

Showers of spring flowers in Tucson

Perennials and cool-season annuals join forces for a dazzling display

TERRENCE MOORE (2)

LEFT: Delicate pastel blossoms play off the bold forms of agave and cactus.
ABOVE: Pots of petunias encircle a mesquite tree.

■ From late winter through spring, Kevin Casey and Ken Bowling invite family and friends to their Tucson home for a series of backyard brunches and pool parties amid a dazzling display of color. Cool-season annuals and classic spring flowers team up with perennials to put on a coordinated show in terraced beds that wrap around the back of the house.

Preparations start in October, when Casey and Bowling strip the beds down to permanent plants, which include cactus, succulents, and perennial ground covers such as lantana and Mexican evening primrose.

First they sow seeds of free-blooming spring annuals, scattering them in swaths so they'll form drifts of color. Casey and Bowling have good luck with California poppy (*Eschscholzia californica*), Oriental poppy (*Papaver orientale*), Shirley poppy (*P. rhoeas*), golden columbine (*Aquilegia chrysantha*), scarlet flax (*Linum grandiflorum* 'Rubrum'), flowering sweet peas, and African daisies (*Dimorphotheca auranti-aca*) in shades of orange, yellow, pink, and salmon.

Next they set out seedlings of cool-season annuals, including calendulas, lobelia, nasturtiums, pansies, petunias, snapdragons, and violas. These plants go into beds as well as poolside pots and hanging baskets suspended from mesquite trees. Casey and Bowling also like to pepper the pots with spring bulbs, including Dutch irises and tulips.

To get plants off to a good start, Casey and Bowling scatter a complete fertilizer (6-8-6) over the beds in October.

— *Nora Burba Trulsson*

How to store dahlias for winter

■ When dahlia foliage is fully withered and the plants are dormant, it's time to dig up the tender tubers and store them for winter. (In frost-free areas, you can leave tubers in the ground through winter. But to ensure superior flowers, most gardeners dig and lift their dahlias each year.) Follow these steps.

1. Cut back flower stalks to within 4 inches of the ground.

2. Carefully dig a 2-foot-diameter circle around each plant (photo A).

3. Using a spading fork, gently pry up the clump of attached tubers (photo B).

4. Shake off loose soil (photo C). Let the clumps dry in the sun for several hours.

5. Before storing the tubers, label them so you won't mix up the different varieties. Attach a tag to record details such as variety name, color, and comments ("'Tequila Sunrise', caramel-orange, cactus-type, 7-inch bloom, superior foliage," for example). Or write the variety name directly on the tuber with an indelible pen.

6. To prevent mildew or rot, dust the tubers with sulfur.

7. Fill nursery flats, wood boxes, or paper bags with dry peat moss, clean sand, sawdust, vermiculite, or perlite, then bury the tubers in single layers inside, leaving labels exposed (photo D). Store the containers in a cool (40°–45°), dry place.

8. In the spring, two to four weeks before planting time, divide the tuber clumps. Cut the clumps apart with a sharp knife, making sure that each tuber is attached to a portion of stalk and shows a visible growth bud.

— *Lauren Bonar Swezey*

BLOOMS UNFURL in summer on plants that grow from spring-planted tubers.

TINGED WITH FALL COLOR, Japanese maple trees are among the many new plants in Descanso's recently renovated Japanese Garden.

Festival time at Descanso Gardens

■ The Japanese Garden at Descanso Gardens, installed in 1966, has a new look. Under the supervision of Sierra Madre landscape designer Lew Watanabe, it has been spruced up with new paths, redwood gates, a carefully pruned tree canopy, and new plants—including 10 varieties of Japanese maples that will be in fall color soon.

If it's been a while since you've visited this garden, the Japanese Garden Festival in late October would be a good time to check it out. The 1999 festival entertainment included traditional Japanese dancing, taiko drumming with audience participation, koto and flute playing, ikebana demonstrations, a chrysanthemum show, and children's crafts.

Descanso Gardens, 1418 Descanso Dr., La Cañada Flintridge; 9–4:30 daily (except Christmas). $5, $3 ages 62 and over and students with I.D., $1 ages 5–12, under 5 free. (818) 952-4401.

— Sharon Cohoon

Ideas from a redhead's garden

Orange is still a hard sell at most nurseries—except when Sarah Steidel walks in. The Sierra Madre gardener naturally gravitates toward coral, copper, persimmon, and tangerine—the same shades you'd find in her closet. Real redhead colors. Steidel's roses are shades of apricot ('Livin' Easy' and 'Polka') rather than pink. Her abutilons are named 'Pumpkin' instead of 'Roseus'. And her fuchsia is, of course, the coral-trumpeted 'Gartenmeister Bonstedt'.

Steidel also likes the acid green color that the fashion industry loves but only redheads seem to look good in. So there is a lot of chartreuse foliage in her garden, such as that of golden zonal geraniums and golden lamium. Instead of using blue flowers to temper this warm-hued scheme, she opts for burgundy foliage—dark-leafed coleus, 'Palace Purple' heuchera, and Lobelia cardinalis, for instance.

Steidel's palette would work in many California gardens, as the photo above shows. "These colors don't blanch out in the sun like soft pastels do," she says, "and they look rich and luscious in the shade." — S.C.

RED LANTANA "TREE" presides over coleus, red-flowered begonias, geraniums, and scarlet chenille plant.

STEVEN GUNTHER (2)

BACK TO BASICS

JAMIE HADLEY

Growing garlic isn't tricky

It just takes well-drained soil with a moderate amount of organic matter mixed in. (If your soil is heavy, grow garlic in raised beds.)

To plant, gently break a garlic bulb into cloves (avoid bruising them). Space the cloves 4 to 6 inches apart; set the scab end down, then cover the cloves with 1 inch of soil (3 to 4 inches in cold climates). Apply several inches of mulch over the soil. — *L.B.S.*

CLIPPINGS

•Sonoma nursery-hopping. If you plan to nursery shop in Sonoma County, pick up a copy of *The Guide to Sonoma County Nurseries,* by Rita and Michel Ter Sarkissoff (Spring Hill Press, Sebastopol, CA, 1998; $24.50, tax and shipping included; 707/829-2355). The 203-page book lists and describes 67 nurseries in the Sonoma area.

Select plants for the new millennium

■ Each year since its inception in 1997, the Plant Select program cosponsored by Colorado State University and Denver Botanic Gardens has been responsible for introducing worthy new plants to intermountain gardens. Five more winners made the Plant Select honor roll for the year 2000. They take full sun or partial shade. Look for plants bearing the Plant Select tag at participating nurseries next spring. 'Coral Canyon' twinspur (*Diascia integerrima*), a 15-inch-tall perennial, is topped with coral-pink flowers from June through frost. Give it moderate water below about 7,000 feet. 'Pawnee Buttes' sand cherry (*Prunus besseyi*), a ground-cover form of the Rocky Mountain native, stays under 18 inches tall but can spread to 6 feet. Fragrant

'CORAL CANYON' twinspur works well in borders and rock gardens.

white flowers rise above its shiny green leaves in April, black cherries follow in summer (birds love the fruit), and the leaves turn red and purple in fall. It can grow at elevations up to 9,000 feet. 'Prairie Jewel' penstemon (*P. grandiflorus*) is the showiest of the northern Great Plains penstemons.

Its blooms come in lavender, rose pink, violet purple, and white. Plant this 2-foot perennial in full sun in a well-drained spot. 'Princess Kay' plum (*Prunus nigra*) is bedecked with double white flowers in spring, a neat green crown in summer, and spectacular red foliage in autumn. This

tree grows fairly quickly to 20 feet tall and 15 feet wide. 'Spanish Gold' broom (*Cytisus purgans*) develops into a 6-foot-wide, 4-foot-tall mound of green stems covered with a mass of yellow flowers every spring. This shrub does well in the southern Rockies at elevations up to 8,000 feet. — *J.M.*

Sweet peas climb the old Christmas tree

■ Sweet peas are usually confined to the perimeters of a garden, where they have fences or walls to lean against. But this year, for a change, why not move them to center stage where you can appreciate their baby powder–clean scent?

You don't need an expensive trellis to support these beautiful sprawlers; use garden prunings instead.

Look for dead branches in

trees and shrubs that you can prune off and put to use. Or save your discarded Christmas tree, as Brita Lemmon of Brita's Old Town Gardens in Seal Beach, California, likes to do (see photo on page 258). "Watching a dead tree [or branches] turn into a tower of flowers is a kick," she says.

Lemmon puts the spent Christmas tree in a 16- or 18-

inch container, adds packaged potting soil, then sows seeds around the tree. As the seedlings grow, she helps them twine around the tree's branches.

Sweet peas aren't fussy about support, but they do appreciate good soil. Before planting them in the ground, dig a 1½-foot trench.

Add a layer of manure to the bottom. Mix 1 part com-

post or other soil conditioner to 2 parts garden soil. Add some low-nitrogen fertilizer according to package directions. Backfill the trench with soil mixture, then plant the seeds.

Loosely cover the trench with netting to protect emergent seedlings from birds. Be sure to remove the netting when seedlings are 4 to 6 inches tall). — *S.C.*

Pacific Northwest Checklist

PLANTING

☑ **AUTUMN COLOR.** The fall foliage spectacle is on. Shop nurseries for container-grown trees and shrubs in full color. Set out plants this month and water them well until fall rains take over.

☑ **BULBS.** Nurseries and garden centers are bulging with spring-blooming bulbs. Shop early for the best selection, choosing bulbs that are plump and firm. Get them into the ground as soon as possible.

☑ **COVER CROPS.** As annuals come out, sow seed of cover crops such as Austrian winter peas, crimson clover, and tyfon greens. They'll minimize erosion during harsh winter weather and enrich the soil with organic matter after you till them under the next spring.

☑ **GARLIC.** Zones 4–7: Set out cloves for harvest next summer (see "Back to Basics" on page 265). One good Northwestern source is Filaree Farm in Okanogan, Washington (509/422-6940 or www.filareefarm.com; catalog $2).

☑ **PERENNIALS.** Planted now, perennials will have the entire winter to put out roots, then grow and flower next spring. In contrast, some spring-planted perennials won't flower the first year; they'll be too busy trying to become established.

MAINTENANCE

☑ **ANNUALS.** Zones 1–3: When frost hits, pull plants, shake soil off the roots, and toss them on the compost pile. Zones 4–7: Continue to deadhead spent blooms and fertilize one last time early in the month.

☑ **CARE FOR LAWNS.** If you want to rejuvenate an old lawn, mow it first, then rough up bare spots with a rake, scatter a generous amount of seed, cover with a thin layer of soil, water well, and keep the seedbed moist until autumn rains begin.

☑ **CARE FOR ROSES.** Continue to remove faded blooms. As you cut flowers to take indoors, shape plants. Allow a few flowers to form hips.

☑ **FEED FUCHSIAS.** Continue to feed until two weeks before the first frost is expected.

☑ **INSTANT MULCH.** As you cut back perennials for the season, chop up the prunings and spread them around plants as winter mulch.

☑ **MAKE COMPOST.** As you harvest, mow, rake, and prune, put everything but diseased material on the compost pile. Turn the pile and keep it moist. By next spring compost should be ready to dig into beds.

☑ **WATER.** Until rains begin, deep-water established plants. Drought-stressed plants are far more likely to be damaged in a hard freeze. ◆

Northern California Checklist

PLANTING

☑ **LARGE GROUND COVERS.** Zones 7–9, 14–17: To cover large areas, consider these spreading ground covers: *Arctostaphylos* 'Emerald Carpet', *Ceanothus* 'Centennial', ivy, varieties of *Juniperus chinensis procumbens* and *J. horizontalis,* kinnikinnick, myoporum, and trailing rosemary ('Corsican Prostrate' or 'Huntington Blue'). For the fastest coverage, put plants in offset rows in groups of four to form diamonds. To check spacing for individual plants, see listings in the *Sunset Western Garden Book*.

☑ **A SALAD POT.** Zones 7–9, 14–17: Start with a large, low bowl (at least 18 inches in diameter) filled with potting mix. Plant seedlings of green- or red-leaf, butter, or romaine lettuces (two or three heads) with arugula, curly endive, mâche, and mustard. Tuck chives and Johnny-jump-ups or other small-flowered violas (which are edible) between them. If you prefer to start with seeds, buy a mesclun mix (available from Ornamental Edibles, 408/946-7333, or Renee's Garden, on seed racks or at www.garden.com/ reneesgarden) and sow seeds very thinly over the top of the soil. When seedlings need thinning, harvest and use the thinnings in a salad. Whether you plant seeds or seedlings, start harvesting the greens when they're 3 to 5 inches long. Replant when the pot has been completely harvested.

Sunset
CLIMATE ZONES

☐ Mountain (1-2)
☐ Valley (7-9)
☐ Inland (14)
☐ Coastal (15-17)

DEBRA LAMBERT

☑ **SPECIALTY FRUIT TREES.** If you'd like to purchase trees of special varieties of apples, grapes, peaches, or other fruit, order them soon so you're sure to get the varieties you want. Some nurseries (Orchard Nursery & Florist of Lafayette, for instance; 925/284-4474) take special orders in fall for delivery in winter. You can also order fruit by mail (try Sonoma Antique Apple Nursery in Healdsburg, 707/433-6420, or Bay Laurel Nursery in Atascadero, 805/466-3406).

☑ **SOW WILDFLOWERS.** For a colorful show in spring, sow wildflowers now. Choose an area that's free of weeds and their seeds, or—several weeks before sowing wildflower seeds—kill the weed seeds by pregerminating them (water the soil so seeds germinate, then hoe down). You still have time to do this in zones 7–9 and 14–17, but in cold climates, you'll have to weed in spring. (To fig-

ure out which are wildflowers and which are weeds, sow a flat of wildflower seeds in late winter so you can compare this foliage with what's popping up from the ground.)

MAINTENANCE

☑ **DIVIDE PERENNIALS.** If blooms on your perennials—asters, bellflowers, callas, daisies, daylilies, helianthus, heliopsis, rudbeckias, and yarrow—were smaller than normal this year, and if the plants are weak and crowded, it's time to divide them. Dig out the clump so the rootball comes up intact. Wash or gently shake off excess soil so you can cut divisions using a sharp knife or pruning shears. Each division should have leaves and plenty of roots. Plant immediately.

☑ **FEED ANNUALS.** Zones 7–9, 14–17: To get annuals off to a strong start, feed them with a nitrogen fertilizer (moisten soil first). If you use a dry fertilizer, water thoroughly after applying it. ◆

Southern California Checklist

PLANTING

✔ **BULBS.** Plant anemones, daffodils, ranunculus, and all the South African bulbs that thrive in our climate—like *Babiana,* freesia, *Ixia, Sparaxis,* and watsonia. Buy hyacinth and tulip bulbs but chill them in the refrigerator for four to six weeks before planting.

✔ **COOL-SEASON ANNUALS.** Coastal, inland, and low-desert gardeners (zones 13 and 18–24) can set out transplants of calendulas, cyclamen, dianthus, Iceland poppies, ornamental kale, pansies, primroses, *Schizanthus pinnatus,* snapdragons, stock, violas, and other early-blooming bedding plants. For more variety and for cutting flowers, try seeding *Agrostemma githago* (corn cockle), forget-me-nots, godetia, larkspurs, Shirley poppies, and sweet peas directly into garden beds. (Sow seeds in raked, weed-free soil.)

✔ **WINTER CROPS.** Gardeners in frost-free areas can continue to sow beets, carrots, chard, fava beans, onions, parsley, peas, radishes, and turnips, and set out transplants of broccoli, cabbage, and other cole crops. Coastal area gardeners can also start lettuces and other leafy crops from seed or transplants.

Bishop

NEVADA

CALIFORNIA

San Luis Obispo

Bakersfield

Tehachapi

Santa Barbara

Lancaster

Los Angeles

Palm Springs

Sunset
CLIMATE ZONES

1-3   7-9   11   13   14-24

San Diego

MEXICO

DEBRA LAMBERT

✔ **NATIVES.** Deep, dense roots make ceanothus, toyon, and other native shrubs great choices for erosion control on slopes. Plant selection at many nurseries is excellent this month. Also, most native plant societies host plant sales, as do many public gardens. Check the garden calendar of your local newspaper for listings.

MAINTENANCE

✔ **DIVIDE PERENNIALS.** Dig up agapanthus, daylilies, Shasta daisies, and other perennials that are overcrowded. Divide and replant.

✔ **FEED ROSES.** Give roses one last feeding early this month. Many rosarians also sprinkle a handful of Epsom salts—about ¼ cup per mature plant—around their plants now. The salts help roses absorb nutrients from alkaline soils.

✔ **REJUVENATE LAWNS.** If you have a cool-season lawn such as tall fescue, this is the time to rake out thatch and uproot crabgrass. If fungus has been a problem, treat the lawn with a commercial product before rains start. To boost growth, give the grass a complete lawn fertilizer. If you have a warm-season lawn such as Bermuda that goes brown in winter, overseed it with annual ryegrass now. Before overseeding, cut grass short. Afterward, mulch the grass and seeds with manure or a fine-grained soil amendment. Keep the ground damp until seeds sprout.

PEST CONTROL

✔ **PROTECT COLE CROPS.** Cabbage loopers—small, green worms—can do quick damage to young, tender seedlings. Cover cole crops with floating row covers to prevent white butterflies from laying their eggs on the leaves. Or dust the leaves with *Bacillus thuringiensis*, a biological control that kills the larvae.

✔ **MANAGE INSECT PESTS.** Aphids and whiteflies multiply when temperatures cool off a bit. Dislodge them from plants with blasts of water from a hose. Or use an insecticidal soap. ◆

Mountain Checklist

PLANTING

☑ BULBS. Before the ground freezes, set out crocus, daffodils, hyacinth, *Iris reticulata,* scilla, and tulips. To protect them from soil temperature fluctuations, plant daffodils and tulips 6 to 8 inches deep and small bulbs 5 inches deep. Set out garlic immediately (see "Back to Basics" on page 265).

☑ PERMANENT PLANTS. Set out hardy ground covers, trees, shrubs, and perennials; water in well.

☑ WILDFLOWERS. Early in the month, broadcast seed over rock gardens, fields, and hillsides. If possible, lightly rake seeds into the soil and cover them with a ¼-inch layer of organic matter.

MAINTENANCE

☑ CUT BACK PERENNIALS. After the first hard freeze, cut back flowering perennials such as aster, campanula, daylily, phlox, and veronica, leaving 2-inch stubs above the ground.

☑ DIVIDE RHUBARB. For improved production next season, divide and transplant overcrowded roots after the first killing frost.

Sunset
CLIMATE ZONES

☐ 1-3 ☐ 10-11

DEBRA LAMBERT

☑ FLUSH DRIP IRRIGATION SYSTEMS. To prevent mineral buildup and cracked tubing, flush drip systems before the soil freezes. Remove end caps from the main lines, turn the water on for a few minutes, then shut it off. Drain all the water, then replace the end caps. If you have an ooze-type system, store it in a dark, protected place for the winter.

☑ HARVEST AND STORE CROPS. Pick broccoli and brussels sprouts before a killing frost hits. Cut pumpkins and winter squash with 2-inch stems; store at 50° to 60°. Beets, carrots, potatoes, and turnips keep best at 35° to 45° in barely damp sand. Onions and shallots need cool, dry storage in mesh bags or slotted crates. Store apples and pears indoors in separate containers at around 40°.

☑ MULCH FOR WINTER. After a hard freeze, spread 2 to 3 inches of compost, weed-free straw, or other organic matter to protect bulbs, perennial flowers and vegetables, permanent plants, and strawberry beds. Mulch conserves soil moisture and helps minimize freezing and thawing of soil, which can heave plants out of the ground.

☑ PREPARE PLANTING BEDS. For earlier planting next spring, spade beds now, digging in generous amounts of organic matter such as compost or manure. Leave soil rough so it absorbs winter moisture; recurrent freezes and thaws will break apart clods.

☑ PROTECT YOUNG TREE TRUNKS. Bright winter sunlight can make young tree trunks split and crack down their south sides. Protect them with a coat of white latex paint or a length of corrugated drainpipe split lengthwise. After trees are three or four years old, their thickening bark prevents sunburn.

☑ WATER. Before leaves drop, water everything regularly until fall rains take over. After leaves fall, irrigate deciduous trees deeply—but only when the temperature is above freezing. ◆

Southwest Checklist

PLANTING

☑ **BULBS.** Zones 1–2, 10–11: Plant spring-blooming bulbs as soon as they become available in nurseries. Zones 12–13: Plant amaryllis, anemone, calla, daffodil, grape hyacinth, harlequin flower, iris, oxalis, ranunculus, and watsonia; prechill crocus, hyacinth, and tulip bulbs in the refrigerator for at least six weeks before planting.

☑ **COOL-SEASON ANNUALS.** Zones 10–11: Plant aubrieta, candytuft, English daisy, forget-me-not, primrose, snapdragon, and stock. Zones 12–13: Plant calendula, dianthus, English daisy, Iceland poppy, lobelia, nemesia, ornamental cabbage and kale, pansy, petunia, primrose, snapdragon, and stock.

☑ **COOL-SEASON VEGETABLES.** Zones 12–13: Plant beets, broccoli, brussels sprouts, cabbage, carrots, cauliflower, chard, endive, garlic (see "Back to Basics" on page 265), kale, kohlrabi, lettuce, onions, parsley, peas, radishes, and turnips.

☑ **GROUND COVERS.** Zones 10–11: Plant low-growing junipers and *Acacia redolens.* Zones 12–13: Plant Baja and Mexican evening primroses, *Dalea greggii,* dwarf rosemary, gazania, lippia, low-growing junipers, snow-in-summer, and verbena.

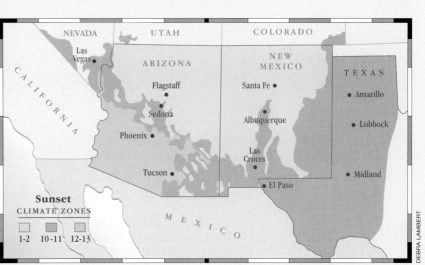

☑ **PERMANENT PLANTS.** Set out trees, shrubs, and hardy native perennials now so they'll have the winter to become established.

☑ **STRAWBERRIES.** Plant anytime after midmonth for a crop next spring. In zones 10–11, two varieties that do well are 'Fort Laramie' and 'Ogallala'. In zones 12–13, try 'Sequoia' and 'Tioga'.

MAINTENANCE

☑ **DIVIDE PERENNIALS.** Zones 10 (Albuquerque), 12–13: Dig and divide crowded clumps of bee balm, catmint, daylilies, hostas, and Shasta daisies. Replant the divisions immediately and water well.

☑ **FEED AND SEED LAWNS.** Zones 12–13: If you want to overplant your Bermuda grass lawn with cool-season grass, first mow it to about ½ inch, then overseed with perennial ryegrass and water deeply. Let the newly planted grass grow for six weeks, then feed with 1 pound actual nitrogen per 1,000 square feet of turf. If you don't overseed, apply the same amount of fertilizer now.

☑ **STORE SUMMER BULBS.** Zones 1–2, 10–12: Lift cannas, dahlias, and gladiolus. Let them dry for a few days, then store at 40° to 50° in a well-ventilated space. Store cannas and dahlias in sand, peat moss, or vermiculite. ◆

A WESTERNER'S GUIDE T

tulips

Even mild-climate gardeners can grow
tulips successfully. We show you how,
and share our favorite color combinations

BY LAUREN BONAR SWEZEY

PHOTOGRAPHS BY NORMAN A. PLATE

■ As anyone who has been to Holland knows, tulips thrive best in cold-winter climates. Nature blesses the land of windmills with months of winter chill that urges the bulbs to robust growth. In spring, swaths of silky-cupped beauties splash the landscape like strokes of paint on canvas.

In mild-winter climates, though, growing tulips might seem more of a struggle; without winter chill, many kinds bloom poorly, if at all. But with a little extra care and the right varieties, even gardeners in mild-winter climates such as San Diego and Phoenix can grow them successfully every year. After all, in public gardens from British Columbia to Southern California, gorgeous displays of tulips flaunt their irresistible jewel-tone colors each spring.

how to combine tulips
for a spectacular color show

One reason for growing tulips is the glorious color they present. The trick is to create harmonious combinations that bloom all at once. But how to achieve a coordinated display?

To learn the answer, we asked growers which bulbs bloom at the same time and pair well for color. Then we planted groupings of bulbs in *Sunset's* test gardens last fall. The photos on these pages show tulip combinations that work. If you wish to reproduce these color schemes in your own garden, select the types

'Queen of the Night'

'Maureen'

'Shirley'

guide to **tulips**

'Dreaming Maid'

'Yellow Present'

'Maureen'

'Beauty Queen'

listed in "The Magnificent 7," at right.

Keep in mind that the colors of real flowers may differ slightly from the pictures of tulips on these pages, on box labels, or in catalogs. Colors may fade in warm weather. Unison blooming can also be thrown off by weather.

tulip planting and care

In the West, tulip planting time begins in September in the coldest climates, and in December in Southern California and the desert (to allow for the soil to cool). To get the best selection, shop at nurseries or by mail as soon as possible. Buy only top-quality bulbs.

In mild climates, chill tulips before planting. Store the bulbs in paper or netted bags—not plastic—for six to eight weeks in the vegetable drawer of the refrigerator. Do not mix them with fruit.

IN THE GROUND

• Plant in full sun and well-drained soil. If the soil is heavy, add plenty of organic matter or plant in raised beds. In coldest climates (*Sunset* zones 1–6), where

bulbs will live on for more than one season, mix a bulb fertilizer into the soil.

• Plant at the right depth. Follow instructions for your climate in our chart on page 276 (measure from the top of the bulb).

• Space them correctly. Set tulip bulbs 2 to 4 inches apart. Exception: When planting forget-me-nots, pansies, violas, or other flowers above the bulbs, plant the tulips 8 inches apart on center and the flowers 10 inches on center.

• Water well after planting, and often enough to keep the soil from drying out if rain doesn't come. When stems emerge from the soil, water to keep the soil moist.

• After bloom, in mild climates, pull out and discard the bulbs. In cold climates, for bloom next year, snip off spent flowers. Then fertilize with nitrogen and allow the leaves to manufacture nutrients. Cut the leaves off when they turn yellow.

IN A CONTAINER

• Plant bulbs so they're touching.

• Arrange the outermost bulbs so their

flat sides are against the rim of the container (the first big leaf appears from the flat side of a bulb and will gracefully drape over the edge of the pot).

• Cover with 2 to 4 inches of soil. Water well and monitor the soil to make sure it doesn't dry out. Set the container in shade until stems first emerge, then move the container to full sun. Water regularly after bulbs emerge.

bulbs by mail

Marde Ross & Company, Box 1517, Palo Alto, CA 94302; (650) 328-5109.

McClure & Zimmerman, 108 W. Winnebago St., Box 368, Friesland, WI 53935; (920) 326-4220.

Van Lierop Bulb Farm, 13407 80th St. E., Puyallup, WA 98372; (253) 848-7272.

Wooden Shoe Bulb Company, 33814 S. Meridian Rd., Woodburn, OR; (800) 711-2006.

'Mrs. John T. Scheepers'

'Daydream'

the magnificent 7

We tested hundreds of bulb pairings. These were our favorites

1. 'West Point' (yellow), 'White Triumphator' **2.** 'Beauty Queen' (salmon and pink), 'Dreaming Maid' (lavender), 'Hibernia' (white), 'Ivory Floradale' (creamy white) **3.** 'New Design' (pink and yellow), 'Rainbow Warrior' (creamy yellow) **4.** 'Queen of the Night' (dark maroon), 'Douglas Baader' (rose) **5.** 'Estella Rijnveld' (red and white), 'White Parrot' **6.** 'Burgundy Lace' (wine red), 'Emmy' (red and apricot), 'Fringed Elegance' (yellow) **7.** 'Angelique' (pink), 'Mount Tacoma' (white).

guide to **tulips**

Zone	Chilling required?	Planting time	Bloom time	Rebloom	Depth	Best varieties	Tips
Northwest	No	Mid-September to October	Early March to late April	3–5 years	6″-8″	All are adapted	Plant from every classification for continuous color
Northern California	Taller with chilling	October to early December	Late February to April	Sometimes	4″-6″	All but Single Early types (except 'Apricot Beauty' and 'Beauty Queen')	Darwin hybrids and others sometimes return a second year
Southern California	Yes	Late November to mid-January	Late February to April	No	4″-6″	All but Single Early types (except 'Apricot Beauty' and 'Beauty Queen')	Plant after Thanksgiving to avoid drying effects of Santa Ana winds
Desert	Yes	December to mid-January	Mid-March	No	4″-6″	Plant Darwin hybrids	Plant some in pots, which can be moved into partial shade if it gets hot
Mountain	No	Mid-September to early November	Mid-April to May	3–5 years	6″-8″	All are adapted	Use cloches or boxes to protect young tulips from late snows

tulips: which class is best for your region?

•**SINGLE EARLY:** NW, MTN (with exceptions as noted). Large, single blooms on sturdy 12- to 18-inch-tall stems. Favorites: 'Apricot Beauty', 'Beauty Queen' (salmon and pink). Both also perform well in Northern and Southern California. Early.

•**FOSTERIANA** (Emperor): NW, NC, SC, MTN. The largest flowers of all varieties grow on 12- to 16-inch-tall stems. Come back reliably in colder climates. Favorites: 'Orange Emperor', 'Red Emperor'. Early.

•**TRIUMPH:** NW, NC, SC, MTN. Hybrids of Single Early and late-flowering tulips with large flowers on 12- to 20-inch-tall stems. Favorites: 'Douglas Baader' (light pink), 'Dreaming Maid' (lavender), and 'New Design' (pink and yellow). Midseason.

•**DARWIN HYBRIDS:** NW, NC, SC, D, MTN. Known for their tall (20- to 24-inch), strong stems and bright flowers. Widely adapted; the best tulips for the desert. Come back reliably in colder climates. Favorites: 'Apeldoorn' (red), 'Daydream' (apricot-orange), 'Pink Impression'. Midseason.

•**FRINGED:** NW, NC, SC, MTN. Petal edges are fringed. Stems grow 20 to 24 inches tall. Favorites: 'Emmy' (red and apricot), 'Fringed Elegance' (yellow), 'Swan Wings' (white). Mid- to late-season.

•**DOUBLE LATE (PEONY):** NW, NC, SC, MTN. Full, double flowers that look like peonies. Stems grow 14 to 20 inches tall. Favorites: 'Angelique' (pink), 'Mount Tacoma' (white). Late.

•**SINGLE LATE (Mayflowering):** NW, NC, SC, MTN. Large blooms in a wide color range, and strong 24- to 28-inch-tall stems. Favorites: 'Maureen' (yellowish white), 'Menton' (pink, rose, and apricot), 'Renown' (carmine-rose). Late.

•**LILY-FLOWERED:** NW, NC, SC, MTN. Graceful blooms with pointed, flaring petals. Stems grow 18 to 24 inches tall. Favorites: 'Mariette' (deep rose pink), 'West Point' (yellow), 'White Triumphator'. Late.

•**PARROT:** NW, NC, SC, MTN. Exotic-looking tulips with frilled, ruffled, and flared petals. Stems grow 16 to 26 inches tall. Favorites: 'Apricot Parrot', 'Estella Rijnveld' (red and white). Late.

NW=Northwest (*Sunset* climate zones 4–6). NC=Northern California (zones 7–9, 14–17). SC=Southern California (zones 18–24). D=desert (zones 10–13). MTN=mountain (zones 1–3).

tulip types

Single

Lily-flowered

Double Late

Parrot

tips for using **color**

If you'd rather design your own color combinations, here's advice.

•**Combine bulbs** from the same class (all Single Early tulips, for example). The photo at left shows the main tulip types. Or plant single colors in containers, then combine pots of bulbs as they come into bloom.

•**Combine varieties** whose flower colors are opposites on the color spectrum, such as orange and purple, or two or three colors that are in a close range—such as red with pink and orange, as shown at right.

•**Consider height** when choosing varieties (a 10-inch-tall tulip may be dwarfed next to a 24-inch-tall tulip).

FIESTA FLAIR: 'Pink Impression', orange-scarlet 'Holland's Glory', and 'Orange Emperor' bloom above purple violas and anemones in this Palo Alto garden.

Beautiful borders

The secret? Choose a theme, then buy the plants to fit

BY LAUREN BONAR SWEZEY • ILLUSTRATIONS BY ALEXIS SEABROOK

■ A BEAUTIFUL BORDER IS LIKE AN ORCHESTRA: THE PLANTS IT CONTAINS ARE THE NOTES—OF COLOR, texture, and height—that play off one another to form a harmonious composition.

To create such a border, you could stroll through a nursery, buying plants that appeal to you, then try to orchestrate them when you get home. But it's difficult to keep such a casually designed border from looking like anything but a hodge-podge—rather like having too many horns and not enough violins to make pleasing sounds. A better solution is to choose a theme, then buy plants to suit it.

Designers use this trick regularly when planning a border. They may focus on specific types of plants (herbs, for instance) or mix two groups of plants together (such as grasses and perennials).

On the following pages, we present four borders, created by designers around the West. You can use one of these plans to re-create a border in your own garden. (If necessary, adjust the size and the number of plants to fit your space.) Or design your own theme to fit your garden's style.

Except for the desert border, all designs work well throughout the West. In mild climates, October is the time to start planting.

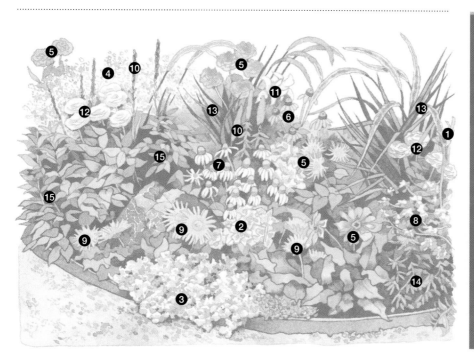

1. Agapanthus
2. Alstroemeria
3. Alyssum
4. Baby's breath
5. Dahlia
6. *Echinacea purpurea* 'Magnus'
7. *E.p.* 'White Swan'
8. *Gaura* 'Siskiyou Pink'
9. Gerbera daisy
10. Liatris
11. Lily
12. Lisianthus 'Mariachi Mixed'
13. Purple fountain grass
14. Snapdragon
15. *Viburnum tinus* 'Spring Bouquet'

NORMAN A. PLATE

A border for bouquet-making: Perennials, bulbs, and more

■ *Sunset* test garden coordinator Bud Stuckey, who regularly harvests flowers from our test garden for making big bouquets, designed the border pictured above. A skillful blend of shrubs, bulbs, grasses, and long-stemmed perennials, this border yields enough plant material for making several bouquets per week. And it's as beautiful as it is bountiful. Shrubs such as nandina and viburnum form the backdrop. Fountain grass catches the late-afternoon sun and shivers in the slightest breeze. Purple sweet alyssum edges the path with lacy flowers.

To keep the border looking neat and colorful as he cuts from it, Stuckey included several plants of each variety, and he cuts only a few stems at a time from each plant. He allows the shrubs to grow for at least a year before cutting from them. Thanks to regular waterings through ooze tubing, and weekly doses of fish emulsion, plants stay healthy and bloom heavily.

To create a similar border, plant the shrubs, perennials (alstroemeria, *Echinacea*, fountain grass, gaura, liatris) and annuals (baby's breath and sweet alyssum) this fall. Then in early spring, set out the warm-season flowers (dahlias, gerberas, and lisianthus).

Fanciful foliage: Grasses, ground covers, and shrubs

1. Blue oat grass
2. Catmint
3. Feather reed grass
4. *Helenium autumnale*
5. Japanese barberry
6. Japanese blood grass
7. *Lysimachia nummularia* 'Aurea'
8. Purple *Viola corsica*
9. *Salvia officinalis* 'Icterina'
10. 'Vera Jameson' *sedum*
11. White fir
12. White viola
13. Woolly thyme

■ "Full, informal, with the feel of a cottage garden." That's how landscape designer Robert Howard describes the border he created along a driveway outside Connie Hill's Boulder, Colorado, house.

Howard started with a color theme—blue, purple, and yellow—and with ornamental grasses for year-round texture. The bed is designed to be viewed from all sides, with tall plants in the middle and low growers planted around them.

Although the grasses turn brown in winter, their shapes remain attractive most of the year (Howard cuts them back in late April).

Design: Robert Howard Associates, Boulder, CO; (303) 449-1624.

All-seasonings border: Culinary herbs and flowers

■ This handsome herb bed, at Elizabeth F. Gamble Garden Center in Palo Alto, combines edible herbs with a few colorful ornamentals. Just 3½ feet wide, the L-shaped border wraps around a sunny corner of the garden. It contains culinary favorites that are perennials in mild climates—chives, oregano, rosemary, sage, and thyme—with such agreeable companions as yellow yarrow and pink society garlic. To these basics you can add your favorites, such as cilantro or tarragon. Every good cook also needs basil, and many kinds grow in a square bed across the path from this border.

Design: Don Ellis, Palo Alto; (650) 329-1356.

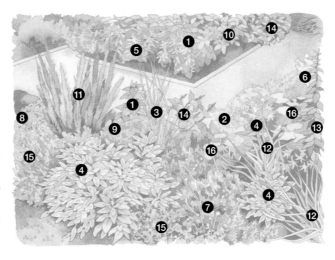

1. 'Broadleaf Sweet' basil
2. Chamomile
3. Chives
4. Common sage ('Icterina', 'Purpur-ascens', 'Tricolor')
5. 'Fino Verde' basil
6. Golden oregano
7. Marjoram
8. *Origanum vulgare* 'Humile'
9. Parsley
10. 'Red Rubin' basil
11. Rosemary
12. Society garlic
13. Spearmint
14. 'Thai' basil
15. Thyme
16. Yarrow

Waves of color, with bold accents

RICHARD MAACK

■ In desert gardens, building a border takes a different strategy than elsewhere in the West. "Our intense light makes everything look flat and washed out," explains landscape architect Steve Martino, "so bold textures are important." For Martino, plants with sculptural shapes make the best border subjects—especially when they're placed where light can play through them, casting shadows on nearby walls and on the ground.

In this border, designed for a display garden at Arid Zone Trees nursery outside Phoenix, Martino used a wavy, terra-cotta-colored wall as a backdrop; in front, colorful perennials and bold succulents create their own shadows.

Watering is critical in a desert border. Drip irrigation is the most efficient method of delivering the water, so little is lost to evaporation.

Design: Steve Martino & Associates, Phoenix; (602) 957-6150.

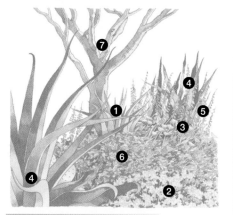

1. *Agave desmettiana*
2. *Chrysactinia mexicana*
3. Desert marigold
4. Octopus agave
5. *Penstemon eatonii*
6. *Salvia greggii*
7. Sonoran palo verde

Design tips for creating your own border

■ Select a location. Determine its exposure (sun, partial sun, or shade).

■ Measure the site's dimensions; make a sketch to use as a handy reference.

■ Choose a theme. Take your cues from the color or style of your house, or from the types of plants (such as ferns or succulents) that thrive naturally in your area. Or choose a theme to suit a particular use (to attract birds or butterflies, for instance).

■ Buy plants to fit the exposure and the theme.

■ Prepare the soil; mix in generous amounts of compost or other soil amendment, then rake it smooth.

■ Arrange the plants. Place plants—still in their pots—on the soil, and adjust as needed before planting. *For one-sided viewing:* Put tall plants in the back, ground huggers in the front, and short to medium growers in the middle. *To view from all angles:* Put the tall plants in the middle and low-growers around them.

■ Plant in groups. Cluster several plants of a kind together; odd numbers, such as threes or fives, are best. For large borders, repeat the groupings every few feet.

■ Incorporate accents. Use dramatic plants (agaves or tall grasses, for instance) as exclamation points throughout the border. ◆

Capture the spirit of the desert

A naturalistic approach to landscaping

BY LAUREN BONAR SWEZEY

Inside the gates of this urban Tucson garden, birds sing in the trees, lizards scamper through bushes, and visitors feel miles away from civilization. That's exactly the effect landscape designer Jeffrey Trent sought to achieve. "The homeowners and I wanted a southern Arizona garden that blends with the existing trees," explains Trent.

The lot was shaded by mature native mesquites, but shrubs blocked views out of the living room window, and the existing plantings lacked cohesiveness.

Trent opened up the garden and surrounded a new flagstone patio with a series of beds. He filled the beds with a mix of native and desert-adapted plants selected for their handsome colors, textures, and forms. "I chose a loose, natural planting scheme, not one that's manicured," says Trent. "The style may not speak to everyone, but it's particularly suited to this site."

In the low and intermediate deserts, the fall planting season is the best time to install a naturalistic landscape. Trent offers these guidelines.

• Study the natural landscape for ideas on how to arrange plants in your garden.

• Combine desert natives and non-native plants that have similar water requirements.

• Use bold foliage plants such as aloes and opuntia to provide accents and year-round structure. Avoid large-leafed tropical plants.

• Soften the spiky forms of agave and cactus by playing them off against small-leafed plants such as Baja fairy duster and trailing indigo bush.

• Plant spring-blooming wildflowers after the soil cools in fall. Once the seeds have germinated, don't overwater plants: Let them adapt to the natural wet-dry cycles of the desert.

• For winter-spring color on patios, set out pots of cool-season annuals such as pansies and petunias between October and mid-November.

• For summer color, plant seedlings of annuals such as portulaca, Madagascar periwinkle, and zinnias in spring.

ABOVE: The sculptural branches of an old mesquite tree arch over pink-flowered globemallow, desert spoon, penstemon, and assorted wildflowers.

LEFT: Barrel cactus punctuate a planting of *Salvia greggii,* poppies, and phacelia, backed by a fence of ocotillo stems.

Five plantings—fresh as a desert morning

■ Aloe, deer grass, globemallow.
■ *Aloysia wrightii,* Baja fairy duster, desert spoon, jojoba.
■ Blackfoot daisy, desert spoon, globemallow, *Opuntia macrocentra,* penstemon.
■ Deer grass, octopus agave, primrose jasmine, trailing indigo bush.
■ 'Green Cloud' Texas ranger, Mt. Lemmon marigold (*Tagetes lemmonii*), *Opuntia ficus-indica.* ◆

STEVEN GUNTHER (2)

Late performers for a grand finale

BY STEVEN R. LORTON

BLOOMING IN FALL, mauve and rose flowers of Scotch heather (*Calluna vulgaris*) contrast with the green hues of broad-leafed and coniferous shrubs.

FLOWER HEADS of 'Autumn Joy' sedum measure 6 inches across.

M ost gardeners plant for peak color in spring. Not Steve Walker. His garden in Olympia, Washington, features a cast of characters that put on a spectacular show in October, just before winter brings the curtain down. Why the late show? Walker's philosophy is simple: "As beautiful as the garden looks in April, May, even June, we don't spend much time in it. In summer, we're out on the water or in the mountains. But in autumn, the weather is great, the kids are back in school, and we're home. That's when I really want to be out there.

"The garden's last act is often the most sensational," he adds. With that in mind, Walker has landscaped with plants that reach peak bloom or foliage color in fall. In his garden this month,

late-blooming perennials provide drifts of color, ornamental grasses wave their seed heads like magic wands, and berries and foliage paint the landscape with autumnal hues—reds, oranges, and yellows.

As aesthetically pleasing as autumn is, it can also satisfy a gardener's urge to get down and dirty. October is one of the best planting months in much of the West. When Walker goes nursery shopping and sees a plant he wants, he buys it and plants it. Most plants get off to a better start in fall than at other times of the year: The cooler air and soil temperatures reduce the stress on plants, and winter rains will promote deep root growth.

Walker's garden is home to hundreds of species of plants. His favorite autumn performers are named at right.

Favorite fall flowers

"I'm always amazed that people don't pay more attention to autumn bloom," says Walker. Here are his top picks, listed in the order that he favors them.

***Sedum telephium* 'Autumn Joy'.** Grows to a height of 2½ feet with large domed-shaped flower clusters that are deep rose, turning coppery as the season advances. Succulent leaves are light sage green. Flower heads turn brown after a freeze, but plants stand through winter, erect after all but the heaviest snows.

Sedum spectabile. A close cousin to 'Autumn Joy' but smaller (to a height of 1½ feet), this plant comes in a number of named varieties with flowers ranging from deep rose to white.

Japanese anemone (*A. hybrida*). Semidouble flowers (reminiscent of apple blossoms or small dahlias) in white and shades of pink on graceful, branching stems 2 to 4 feet tall.

Scotch heather (*Calluna vulgaris*). There are dozens of named varieties, but the late-bloomers like 'David Eason' (mauve flowers) and 'Finale' (rosy purple) make carpets of color in the autumn garden. Many have foliage that turns color after the first frost.

Aster frikartii. Masses of 2½-inch-wide single flowers—clear lavender to violet blue with yellow centers—top 3-foot stems.

ALLAN MANDELL (2)

AS PAPERBARK MAPLE sheds its shaggy old bark, a smooth new layer is revealed.

Striking seeds, berries, and bark

"Gardening is more than cultivating flowers," says Steve Walker. "Plants are interesting from the time they pop out of the ground until they die back."

Crocosmia **'Lucifer'.** This variety produces tall flower spikes filled with bright red blooms that form plump seed pods in October. Its erect 4-foot leaves resemble gladiolus foliage.

Himalayan honeysuckle (*Leycesteria formosa*). Deep-purple berries dangle in glistening clusters among bright green, spade-shaped leaves on fleshy stalks that reach 6 feet tall.

Liatris spicata. After this perennial's mauve pink blooms fade, the 2-foot-tall flower spikes are left in place to form striking rows of seeds that turn from green to brown.

Paperbark maple (*Acer griseum*). This maple is grown for its cinnamon-colored bark (shown above). The tree eventually reaches a height of 25 feet, and Walker prunes it high, so that trunk and lower limbs are open to the light. "It glows with warm autumn colors, even before the leaves turn color," he says.

Foliage accents and backgrounds

Walker combines plants that contrast handsomely in foliage color and form. Low-growing conifers like mugho pines anchor the garden floor. Tall ones, like cedars and Douglas firs on the perimeter of the garden, form dark backgrounds for his tapestry of plants.

Colorado spruce (*Picea pungens*). Varieties such as 'Koster' and 'Fat Albert' make rich blue accents around the garden.

Eulalia grass (*Miscanthus sinensis*). This ornamental grass grows in graceful clumps reaching 5 to 6 feet tall. It brings sound and motion to the garden as it rustles its leaves and waves its fluffy tan seed heads in the wind.

Japanese forest grass (*Hakonechloa macra* 'Aureola'; shown below). Thick clumps of arching, bamboolike leaves of pale green variegated with gold stripes stand 12 to 18 inches tall.

Plume poppy (*Macleaya cordata*). Growing to a height of 7 feet, celadon stems sporting big fig-leaf foliage of the same color are topped by plumes of tiny pinkish tan flowers. (Note: Don't confuse this plant with *M. microcarpa*, its nearly identical but highly invasive cousin.) ◆

JAPANESE FOREST GRASS thrives in partial shade. In autumn, its feathery leaves develop a pink tinge.

Meadow in a pot

Yellow Point Reyes meadowfoam and baby blue eyes, which sprinkle coastal meadows, fill a 24-inch-diameter bowl; Idaho fescue grass rises in the center. Lowry also plants pots with 'Mahogany Red' California poppy and *Ceanothus thyrsiflorus*, or *Clarkia bottae* and globe gilia. To create your own little meadow, fill a large bowl with potting mix, then sprinkle seeds evenly over the surface. Cover the seeds with a ¼-inch layer of potting mix; water with a fine spray. Continue to irrigate regularly if winter rains are light. Depending on variety, seeds germinate in two to four weeks. As seedlings grow, thin the weakest ones to give vigorous plants room to grow.

Wild beauties

Judith Lowry's garden is filled with ideas for using wildflowers and grasses

BY LAUREN BONAR SWEZEY

You won't find roses or lavender in Judith Lowry's garden. Just native wildflowers, grasses, and perennials that thrive on her mesa near the Northern California coast.

During the 1976–77 drought, Lowry—who owns Larner Seeds, a native plant seed mail-order business—became interested in the plants growing on nearby hills and meadows. Since then, her love of these wild beauties has been the driving force behind her passion for "backyard restoration gardening," or "gardening to root yourself in a place," Lowry explains.

Her garden is both a showcase of local wildflowers and a repository for plants that, in the wild, are being overrun by introduced non-native species.

Coyote brush forms the "bones" of the garden; coffeeberry and toyon are background shrubs for "islands" of plants from coastal dunes and scrub communities. Pictured above are two of the many ways Lowry uses wildflowers; you can copy these ideas with plants native to your own area.

"I'm trying to re-create the qualities I've seen in surrounding plant communities and work them into my garden," Lowry says.

Coastal scrub corralled

In this "island" bed, native perennials such as bleeding heart (*Dicentra formosa*) and monkey flower (*Mimulus guttatus*) mingle with leopard lily (*Lilium pardalinum*), 'Blue Bedder' penstemon (placed where it gets more sun), and sword fern. Behind them is a vine maple. Plant in native soil and mulch with organic matter. Near the coast these plants need no additional water once established. ◆

Sensational small trees

BY STEVEN R. LORTON

A single tree growing in a large, handsome container adds a significant grace note to any garden. Carefully placed, it can become a sculptural focal point. It can define an entry or an outdoor living area—or screen one. Place it on a sunny deck or patio and it will obligingly cast shade for you or a cluster of smaller potted plants.

The keys to success are selecting a tree that grows slowly to a manageable size (see "Eight Trees Made for Containers," below), potting it in an ample container, and providing proper long-term care.

A tree in a container is like a bird in a cage: To keep it happy and healthy, you have to provide the right environment. Choose a generous pot that will allow the roots to develop; a 4-foot-tall tree will need a pot at least 20 to 24 inches in diameter and 16 to 24 inches in depth. Plastic and glazed ceramic containers won't crack in freezing weather, and they retain soil moisture much better than unglazed terra-cotta and wood containers.

Fill the container with a high-quality potting mix. Most trees (except pines) benefit from controlled-release fertilizer mixed into the soil at planting time. Use about ¼ cup of fertilizer for every 5 gallons of potting mix.

A big container filled with soil and a tree is heavy; it will be much easier to move around a deck or patio if you set the pot on a mobile platform with wheels or casters attached to the undercarriage.

Remember that trees in containers need water more frequently than those in the ground. Every three years or so, take the tree out of its container and prune off the large old roots that have coiled around the outside of the rootball. Repot the tree immediately in fresh mix, moving it to a larger container if necessary.

LACELEAF JAPANESE MAPLE thrives in a terra-cotta pot set on river rocks.

Eight trees made for containers

■ **Bristlecone pine** (*Pinus aristata*); *Sunset* climate zones 1–6. Dense, rich green needles on a tree that grows slowly, rarely to more than 20 feet. Nursery-grown stock has a pleasing conical form. Cold-hardy and drought-tolerant. One mail-order source is Forestfarm Nursery, 990 Tetherow Rd., Williams, OR 97544; (541) 846-7269 or www.forestfarm.com. Catalog $4; pines from $12.

■ **Dwarf Alberta spruce** (*Picea glauca* 'Conica'); zones 1–6 and 14–17. This conifer with a pyramidal form and bright green, thickly set needles will reach 7 feet in 35 years. Protect it from hot, drying winds and intense reflected light.

■ **Holly** (*Ilex*); zones vary by species. Glossy evergreen leaves, often with ruffled edges and prickly tips, sparkle in sunlight or rain. A number of small-scale varieties such as *I.* 'September Gem', *I. fargesii*, and *I. altaclarensis* 'Wilsonii' will live for years in containers. One good source for hollies is Heronswood Nursery, 7530 N.E. 288th St., Kingston, WA 98346; (360) 297-4172 or www.heronswood.com. Catalog $5; hollies from $6.

■ **Japanese maple** (*Acer palmatum*); zones 1–10, 12, 14–24. This delicately scaled deciduous tree comes in many shapes and leaf and bark colors, but most grow slowly and seldom exceed 20 feet in height. For lacy foliage and drooping branches, look for laceleaf Japanese maple (*A.p.* 'Dissectum'); for deep red foliage and upright form, consider *A.p.* 'Burgundy Lace'; and for an upright plant with a rounded crown, try *A.p.* 'Globe'. Give any of them regular water and shelter from intense sunlight.

■ **Southern magnolia** (*M. grandiflora* 'Little Gem'); zones 4–12, 14–24. This small evergreen magnolia grows slowly to 15 to 20 feet. Leaves are glossy, dark green on the top, covered with bright, rust-colored fuzz underneath. Give it full sun and protection from cold winter winds.

■ **Staghorn sumac** (*Rhus typhina*); zones 1–10, 14–17. This deciduous tree with deeply cut, fernlike leaves grows 15 to 20 feet tall in time. Crimson fruit clusters last all winter atop fuzzy branches that resemble deer antlers. Takes full sun; very drought-tolerant.

■ **Vine maple** (*Acer circinatum*); zones 1–6, 14–17. This multitrunked Northwest native adapts well to container culture. Leaves are bright green. Locate it where the sun won't beat down on the trunk.

■ **Windmill palm** (*Trachycarpus fortunei*); zones 4–24. Hardy to 10°, this palm grows slowly in a container (in the ground it eventually reaches 30 feet). Fan-shaped leaves 3 feet across are borne on toothed stalks; the trunk is covered with dark brown, hairy-looking fiber. ◆

AUTUMN arrangement features red chrysanthemums, ornamental peppers, plum-colored nandina leaves, green protea foliage, orange-tinted love-in-a-puff, and rust-colored pin oak leaves. For tips on creating your own basket, see page 296.

November

gardenguide

English cottage style—in Mendocino

Raised beds and billowy plants give this landscape its "cottage garden" appeal

■ "If you have an English garden, you should really have English weather," says seascape artist E. John Robinson. And Mendocino, with its cool, moist climate, is the perfect place for Robinson's English-style cottage garden.

But English-style gardens also demand good soil for abundant flower growth. And that was harder to come by in this area; Robinson's house is in the North Coast's Pygmy Forest, whose trees are stunted by a hardpan layer beneath the soil surface. Before planting, he broke up the hardpan in his garden with a heavy-duty rotary tiller, then added topsoil and amendments. To ensure good drainage, he also formed 2-foot-tall raised beds.

As artists, Robinson and his wife, June, are very particular about color. They chose cool pastels with "bits of burgundy and spots of white."

To keep the plants vigorous, Robinson covers the beds with a 6-inch layer of manure each fall and compost each spring. "And of course the garden wouldn't exist without deer fencing," says Robinson.

— *Lauren Bonar Swezey*

How to create a cottage garden

- Design beds with curving lines.
- Use roses as landscape plants. Fill in around them with billowy companion plants such as catmint and Santa Barbara daisy.
- Arrange plants to create drifts of flower colors.

SINGLE PINK BLOSSOMS cover 'Ballerina' rose like puffs of cotton candy. Across the path, red dianthus, catmint, and scabiosa mingle beside 'Sun Goddess' rose.

House plant accents

■ By enlivening quiet corners with leafy greenery, house plants bring garden freshness to indoor plantings. What they don't always do, however, is add color. Here's a way to have both: Underplant house plants with color.

Interior plantsman Davis Dalbok sets pots of orchids and bromeliads—which hold their blooms for months—around the bases of tall plants.

For the bedroom shown below, Dalbok chose a glossy-leafed New Zealand laurel tree. Around its base he set six orange-flowered bromeliads (*Vriesea splenreit*) with green-and-purple striped leaves, then filled in with living moss (*Tillandsia xerographica*). A *Paphiopedilum* orchid on the side table gives the room "a layer of color," says Dalbok.

Design: Davis Dalbok (Living Green, San Francisco; 415/864-2251).

— *L.B.S.*

Lily culture

■ By using a technique called scaling, you can multiply one lily bulb into enough plants to fill a whole bed. Most lily bulbs are composed of 20 to 60 overlapping scales. Each scale of an Asiatic hybrid lily typically produces one to three pea-size bulblets, while trumpet lilies make three to five marble-size bulblets per scale; both types produce mature plants in two to three years. Oriental lilies also make one to three marble-size bulblets, but take three or four years to mature.

Start the process this fall by selecting whole bulbs, then follow the steps described here. We used this technique to culture the Asiatic lily 'Baronesse', shown above. Shop nurseries for lilies or order from a specialist like B&D Lilies in Port Townsend, Washington (360/385-1738 or www.bdlilies.com; catalog $3).

1. Gently break off each of the bulb's scales (A), discarding any damaged, diseased, or dehydrated ones. Let them dry for two days indoors.

2. Place half of the scales in a 1-gallon plastic freezer bag containing damp vermiculite (B); toss the remaining scales in another bag filled with peat moss as moist as a wrung-out sponge (experts recommend using both cultural mediums to increase chances for success). Label each bag with the variety name and date, punch a few ventilation holes in the plastic, and set the bags on top of the refrigerator. At 70°, most scales will form bulblets in two months.

3. After bulblets form, place the bags in the refrigerator for two months to allow roots to develop (C). Add water as needed to keep the medium slightly damp.

4. In spring, plant the rooted bulblets 1 inch deep in containers filled with potting mix. Place them in sun, feed with a complete fertilizer once, and water regularly. In their first year, bulblets will produce small, leafy plants (D).

5. The following spring, transplant the lilies into rich garden soil; expect substantial growth and a few flowers. By the third year, most lilies reach full size and bloom heavily.

— *Jim McCausland*

JANET DREW

Grow fresh herbs in the kitchen

■ When cold weather puts a damper on your outdoor herb garden, you can still satisfy your craving for fresh herbs by growing them on your kitchen windowsill. Given the proper conditions, a surprising number of perennial herbs thrive indoors. Those listed here grow best near a sunny window where they will get at least five hours of bright light daily.

Chives. *Allium schoenoprasum* has a delicate onion flavor. Chinese chives (*A. tuberosum*) have a mild garlic taste. Cut small bunches of leaves back to the soil level to keep new ones coming.

Mint. Peppermint and spearmint, in particular, grow well in pots.

Oregano. Try pungent Greek oregano (*Origanum vulgare hirtum*), peppery Cretan oregano (*O. onites;* also called pot marjoram),

or Italian oregano (*O. majoricum*), which blends the flavors of oregano and sweet marjoram.

Rosemary. Grow a compact upright variety like 'Taylor's Blue' (trailing types aren't particularly flavorful).

Sage. Try 'Berggarten' or dwarf sage (*Salvia officinalis minimus*). Harvest plants regularly to keep them productive.

Sweet bay. *Laurus nobilis,* the source of bay leaves, can be trained into a topiary.

Thyme. 'English Thyme' and 'Narrow Leaf French' are standard culinary varieties. For distinctive flavors, try caraway thyme (*Thymus herba-barona*) or lemon thyme (*T. citriodorus*).

Many nurseries and some supermarkets sell herbs in 3-inch plastic pots. When you bring the herbs home, set the pots near a window and let plants acclimate for a few weeks. Then transplant

them into individual 6-inch or larger pots filled with a fast-draining potting mix. Allow the soil to dry slightly between waterings. Feed with liquid fertilizer once or twice monthly starting in spring. During the darkest winter months, you may need to supplement sunlight with fluorescent light.

If you can't find the herbs you want locally, try these mail-order sources, which ship potted plants: Goodwin Creek Gardens (Box 83, Williams, OR 97544; 541/846-7357; catalog $1); Mountain Valley Growers (38325 Pepperweed Rd., Squaw Valley, CA 93675; 559/338-2775); Thyme Garden (20546 Alsea Hwy., Alsea, OR 97324; 541/487-8671).

— *Kris Wetherbee*

Foliage that glows in frosty weather

■ The sedum and yucca pictured below display handsome foliage year-round, but they are especially striking in winter, when their colors intensify. When the first frost hits *Sedum spathulifolium,* this Northwest native acquires a rosy blush. The variegated leaves of *Yucca filamentosa* 'Golden Sword' turn richer shades of green and cream.

The bloom bonuses come later. The sedum bears mounds of sulfur yellow flowers in mid- to late spring. In July, the yucca sends up 4- to 5-foot stalks that support spikes of waxy, cream-colored bells.

Both of these plants grow in all *Sunset* climate zones. They need full sun.

If you can't find plants locally, Joy Creek Nursery (503/543-7474) in Scappoose, Oregon, sells several varieties of sedum and yucca.

— *Steven R. Lorton*

RED PINEAPPLE SAGE glows in front of pink roses. Silver foliage plants include 'Powis Castle' artemisia and lamb's ears.

Floral fireworks in San Marino

■ Fire-engine red and rose pink are not often combined. But Shirley Kerins blends them with flair in Robert and Carolyn Volk's garden. "Red and pink work fine together as long as you stick to a true red and not one that veers toward orange or blue," says the Pasadena-based landscape architect, who paired red-flowered *Salvia elegans* with the Volks' pink roses. "No one is surprised to see dark and light blues combined," she adds. "This is exactly the same thing."

Pineapple sage also met many of the Volks' requirements for this highly visible border. The owners wanted color year-round; *S. elegans* starts blooming in summer, peaks in fall, and doesn't stop producing flowers until late winter. They wanted fragrance; the plant's name comes from its fruity-scented leaves. They wanted to attract wildlife; nothing is more inviting to hummingbirds than these nectar-rich scarlet tubes.

The flowers even serve a purpose after dark, when they totally disappear. Since the Volks often use their garden in the evenings, Kerins used lots of silver foliage to glow in the moonlight. "The red flowers create black holes in the garden at night," she says, "and the contrast with the silver is wonderful."

— *Sharon Cohoon*

SPIKY CLUMPS of white Siberian irises and yellow flag irises spring from rocks along the watercourse.

A marriage of water, stone, and plants

■ After construction of an addition left a gaping hole in the backyard of their home in Cherry Hills Village, Colorado, the owners sought help from landscape designer Robert Howard of Boulder. He met the challenge by transforming the unsightly hillside into a lush mountain canyon with a meandering watercourse. Howard's engaging design won a merit award for resi-

dential garden design from the Associated Landscape Contractors of Colorado.

The recirculating stream is punctuated by a series of waterfalls and small pools. Slabs of native red flagstone form steps that lead along the stream, echoing its graceful curves.

Upright spikes of yellow flag irises, white Siberian irises, and ornamental grasses stand in elegant con-

trast to large, round boulders along the streambed. Perennial ground covers scramble around the rocks for an exuberant look that requires little maintenance. In the photo above (taken in mid-June), native bluebells (*Campanula rotundifolia*) brighten the foreground, while patches of pink *Dianthus deltoides* 'Zing Rose' highlight the top of the walk.

All of the plants were set out in autumn. Howard advocates fall planting for several reasons. Plants get partially established before freezing weather arrives, then fill in quicker when the growing season resumes in spring. The cooler temperatures reduce the plants' water needs. Gardeners also get a break from weeding until the following spring.

— *Marcia Tatroe*

Fabulous fremontia

■ This colorful shrub just may be the Madonna of the native plant world—bright, sassy, and a little bit wild. Native to Southern California's dry, sunny slopes, flannel bush (*Fremontodendron*), also called fremontia, covers itself in spring with dazzling blooms that make it hard to miss among gray-green chaparral. It's shapely, too, if you pinch leaf tips and give it a light pruning periodically.

As a garden plant, flannel bush can be finicky. But give it what it needs—full sun, excellent drainage (rocky hillsides are best), and no summer water once established—and the plant will thrive. It looks best in untailored gardens among other natives such as blue-flowered ceanothus and woolly blue curls. Plant flannel bush beyond the reach of sprinklers, and water it by hose through the first dry season only. Shop for plants at well-stocked nurseries and at native plant sales this month. — *Kathleen N. Brenzel*

CLIPPINGS

•**Surf before you shop.** It's not too early to be thinking about ordering bare-root roses by mail. If you like heirlooms, David Austins, and other old garden roses, check out the website of the Victorian Rose Garden at the Arboretum of Los Angeles County (victorian-rose.org) before you order. The ones on this website have proven track records in the Southern California climate.

•**A website for Bay Area gardeners.** The Bay Area Gardener (www.gardens.com) is an informative resource for anyone living in the greater San Francisco Bay Area. Click on "East Bay Nurseries" or one of the other regional nursery guides to find out where to shop for plants. Then go to "Sales/Shows & Events" or "Classes & Talks" to discover what's happening this month or next. You'll also find stories and columns by local garden writers and nursery owners and lists of clubs and societies. Particularly helpful is the resource guide, including a list of cooperative extension offices and local websites.

BACK TO BASICS

JAMIE HADLEY

Dividing clumping perennials

Daylilies and other clumping perennials expand by developing new roots and stems. After three to five years, they need dividing. One way to divide these tough perennials is to insert two spading forks into the center of the clump and pull the roots apart. Or you can use a spade to cut the root mass into sections. Replant the separated clumps as soon as possible. In cold-winter areas, divide plants in spring or late summer.

— *L.B.S.*

Rhapsody in blue

NORMAN A. PLATE

■ There's only one way to describe the fantastic catmint that we planted this past spring around a fountain at *Sunset's* Menlo Park headquarters: A knockout. This beautiful variety of *Nepeta faassenii* (above) is aptly named 'Six Hills Giant'. From its undulating mounds of soft gray-green foliage grow long, upright stems that cover themselves with lavender-blue flowers in late spring and summer. Plants fill out beautifully in just one season.

Good care contributes to the prolific show. This catmint thrives in a sunny, protected courtyard, in a 4½-foot-wide garden bed enriched with compost. We set out plants from 1-gallon nursery cans, spacing them about 1 foot apart. For interest, we added a few plants of pink-flowered 'Apple Blossom' penstemon behind the catmint; it bloomed at the same time.

After the catmint's blooms faded, we cut off flower heads and several inches of foliage to encourage repeat bloom.

You can plant 'Six Hills Giant' this fall. Plants are available at nurseries, or order them from Canyon Creek Nursery in Oroville (530/533-2166).— *L.B.S.*

Persimmon pleasures

■ One of the best (and showiest) trees for many California and Oregon gardens is surely Oriental persimmon (*Diospyros kaki*). This deciduous tree (to 30 ft. tall) with wide-spreading branches bears big, leathery green leaves in spring and summer that turn gold and orange in fall. But it's the fruit that enthusiasts love most: In November, these orange globes dangle like ornaments from bare branches. 'Hachiya', the shapeliest tree for ornamental use, yields big, slightly pointed fruits. 'Fuyu' fruits are flattened like a tomato and firm-fleshed like an apple.

Both trees grow well in *Sunset* climate zones 6–9, 14–16, and 18–23. Plant trees this month in a sunny location with good drainage, away from patios where fruit can drop and splat.

Harvest fruits when they have turned from green to golden orange, then ripen them indoors. You can eat 'Fuyu' fruits when they're still crisp or slightly soft (they won't taste astringent, even when underripe), but 'Hachiya' fruits are best eaten when soft-ripe. — *K.N.B.*

Autumn in a basket

■ The arrangement pictured on page 288 celebrates the many shades of fall—from amber, gold, rust, and red to vibrant orange and lingering apple green. You can put it together in minutes using leaves, prunings, and seed pods from the garden for the framework, and bunches of chrysanthemums, ornamental peppers, and greens such as protea foliage from a florist for the finishing touches.

First, line a basket with a plastic garbage bag. Then put a soaked block of florist's foam inside. Using a hand pruner, make diagonal cuts on the stem ends of branches with leaves still attached—pin oak, liquidambar, and nandina are good choices—so they'll slip more easily into the foam. Arrange tallest branches around the back, center, and sides of the basket. Fill in with shorter branches of foliage, and finish by tucking flowers and berries among the foliage.

If your garden doesn't have deciduous trees whose leaves turn color in fall, you can buy branches with leaves attached at florists and in floral departments at grocery stores in fall. — *K.N.B.*

Pacific Northwest Checklist

PLANTING

☑ **ANNUALS.** Sow seeds of candytuft, clarkia, larkspur, linaria, and wildflowers in well-cultivated, weed-free beds. They'll germinate and flower earlier than the same seeds sown in spring.

☑ **BULBS.** Set out all kinds of spring-flowering bulbs before heavy rains.

☑ **CAMELLIAS.** Zones 4–7: Shop for early-blooming Sasanqua camellias. Set them out now or slip nursery cans into decorative pots to display on a porch or patio, then plant them. Sasanquas are especially attractive when espaliered against a wall under a roof overhang where pelting rains won't shatter the delicate petals.

☑ **CONIFERS.** As deciduous trees drop their leaves, it's easy to appreciate the evergreen beauty of conifers in Northwest landscapes. Unless you have unlimited space, choose garden-scale, dwarf, or prostrate forms of arborvitae, cedar, cryptomeria, firs, junipers, pines, and spruces. Plant immediately.

☑ **GARLIC.** Zones 4–7: Set out cloves for harvest next summer. One good Northwest source is Filaree Farm (509/422-6940 or www.filareefarm. com; catalog $2).

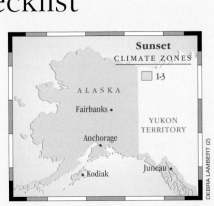

☑ **PEONIES.** Order tuberous roots immediately and get them into the ground as soon as they arrive. In rich, well-drained soil, plant the roots no deeper than 2 inches (make sure the reddish growth buds are pointing upward). These Northwest growers ship roots for fall planting: A&D Nursery (360/668-9690; catalog $2) and Caprice Farm Nursery (503/625-7241 or www.capricefarm.com; catalog $2).

MAINTENANCE

☑ **DIVIDE PERENNIALS.** Zones 4–7: Now is an excellent time to dig and divide perennials, including clumping types (see Back to Basics, page 295).

☑ **CUT BACK MUMS.** When flowers fade, cut plants back to 6 inches. They'll send up vigorous shoots next spring.

☑ **GROOM LAWNS.** Mow, edge, and rake lawns before winter sets in. In zones 4–7, overseed bare spots: Rough up the soil with a rake, sow grass seed, and cover with a thin layer of soil. Keep the seeded area moist until rains take over.

☑ **PRUNE TREES, SHRUBS.** Both deciduous and evergreen plants can be pruned in late fall. First remove dead, diseased, and injured wood, then prune for a graceful shape.

☑ **WINTERIZE BORDERS.** Late in the month, cut back frost-downed perennials, leaving 4- to 6-inch stubs. Rake up leaves and weed the beds. Then spread a 2- to 4-inch layer of organic mulch such as compost or leaf mold. ◆

Northern California Checklist

PLANTING

☑ **BULBS.** Zones 7–9, 14–17: Even though nurseries begin selling bulbs in September, November—when the soil has finally cooled—is one of the best times to plant them in Northern California. If you still need to shop for bulbs, check them carefully; choose only firm ones that aren't sprouting. To get the longest stem lengths on tulips and hyacinths, chill them for six weeks before planting.

☑ **CRAPE MYRTLE.** Zones 7–9, 14–17: These shrubs and trees are particularly attractive for their long summer bloom. Some also produce outstanding fall foliage color. Three of the best for fall color are 'Near East', 'Pecos', and 'Zuni'. If you can't find trees at your nursery, ask the staff to order for you from Monrovia Nursery (wholesale only).

☑ **PLANT FOR PERMANENCE.** Zones 7–9, 14–17: November is one of the best times to plant cold-hardy ground covers, shrubs, trees, and vines. Roots grow through the winter, so by the time spring comes, plants are well established. Wait until spring to set out tender plants, such as bougainvillea, citrus, and princess flower.

Sunset
CLIMATE ZONES
◻ Mountain (1-2)
◻ Valley (7-9)
◻ Inland (14)
◻ Coastal (15-17)

DEBRA LAMBERT

MAINTENANCE

☑ **CLEAN UP DEBRIS.** Pull up what's left of summer annuals and vegetables that have stopped producing. Also rake up leaves and pick up fallen fruit to help eliminate overwintering sites for insects and diseases. Add debris to the compost pile (except diseased plants and any weeds that have gone to seed).

☑ **COMPOST.** Start a simple compost pile by layering greens (grass, plant debris, and weeds without seed heads) with browns (straw, dried leaves). For a more controlled pile, build this simple wire frame: Bend a 4-foot-high piece of 12- to 14-gauge wire fencing into a cylinder about 4 feet across and hook the cut edges together. Chop up composting materials, then put them into the cylinder, alternating a 2- to 8-inch-thick layer

of brown material with a 2- to 8-inch-thick layer of green material (sprinkle each brown layer with water as you go). To help heat up the pile and speed composting, you can also top each brown layer with a shovelful of manure or soil. Keep the pile evenly moist; aerate by turning it every few weeks or so.

☑ **FERTILIZE COOL-SEASON CROPS.** Zones 7–9, 14–17: If you didn't mix a controlled-release fertilizer into the soil at planting time, your annuals and vegetables probably need feeding. You can use an organic fertilizer such as fish emulsion or apply a commercial product in either liquid or dry form.

PEST CONTROL

☑ **SPRAY FRUIT TREES.** Zones 7–9, 14–17: After leaves fall, spray peaches and nectarines with lime sulfur to control peach leaf curl. For brown rot on apricots, spray with a fixed copper spray. (Both sprays are available at local nurseries and home improvement stores.) Spray on dry days when no rain is predicted for at least 36 hours. Cover the branches, stems, and trunk thoroughly. ◆

Southern California Checklist

PLANTING

✔ **GREEN MANURE.** If you don't plan on growing winter vegetables, plant a cover crop like clover, fava bean, vetch, or annual rye in your empty vegetable beds instead. When you turn over the crop in the early spring, you'll be enriching the beds with inexpensive organic material. Legumes—all but the rye—also add nitrogen to the soil.

✔ **WINTER VEGETABLES.** Early November is an excellent time to start cool-season crops in many areas. Sow seeds of beets, carrots, chard, onions, parsley, peas, radishes, and turnips, and set out transplants of broccoli, cabbage, and other cole crops by mid-month in zones 13 and 14–24. Near the coast, continue to plant lettuces and other leafy crops from seed or transplants. Gardeners in the foothills and Central Valley (zones 7–9 and 14) can sow peas and spinach and plant garlic and onions.

✔ **PERMANENT FALL COLOR.** Flowering shrubs that add color to the late fall garden include cape plumbago, Sasanqua camellias, pineapple sage and other salvias, and daisy tree (*Montanoa grandiflora*). Trees or shrubs with colorful fruit, such as persimmon, pomegranate, and strawberry (*Arbutus unedo*), or ones with bright berries, such as toyon, holly, pyracantha, and heavenly bamboo, are other possibilities. Don't forget deciduous

trees. Gold-leafed ginkgo, orange-red Chinese pistache, and liquidambar (various shades) will color up reliably throughout Southern California, even near the coast.

✔ **BIENNIALS.** Cottage-garden favorites—canterbury bells, foxgloves, hollyhocks, and Queen Anne's lace—do best if planted in late fall. They will establish roots now and be ready to bloom on schedule come spring.

MAINTENANCE

✔ **PRUNE CANE BERRIES.** Old canes of blackberry, boysenberry, and loganberry should be cut back to the ground. Leave the new, smooth-barked canes that grew this year to bear fruit next year. Don't cut the canes of low-chill raspberries now; wait until December or January.

✔ **OVERSEED BERMUDA GRASS.** If you don't like the look of dormant grass, overseed with annual rye. Mow lawn short, scatter rye seed (1 lb. per 100 square feet) and compost, and water regularly until seed germinates.

✔ **START A COMPOST PILE.** Don't let your raked leaves and garden prunings go to waste. They're a good beginning for a compost pile in a hidden corner. Build a simple wire bin: Bend a 4-foot-high piece of 12- to 14-gauge wire fencing into a 4-foot cylinder. Alternate greens (grass, weeds, discarded produce) with brown (straw, dry leaves). Keep pile evenly moist and, to speed decomposition, turn every two weeks to aerate.

WEED CONTROL

✔ **STAY AHEAD OF WEEDS.** Pull out annual bluegrass, chickweed, spurge, and other young weeds as they emerge. If they are not allowed to set seed, next year's weeding will be easier. ◆

Mountain Checklist

PLANTING

☑ **BULBS.** Set out spring-flowering bulbs before the ground freezes.

MAINTENANCE

☑ **CONTROL INSECTS ON HOUSE PLANTS.** If scale insects, mites, or aphids trouble any of your house plants, slip a plastic clothing cover (the kind you get from a dry cleaner) over it, then spray insecticidal soap inside. The plastic tent will contain the spray.

☑ **GROOM LAWNS.** Mow the lawn at 2½ inches and edge; rake up fallen leaves before they mat and smother the grass.

☑ **INSULATE ROSES.** In cold-winter areas, lightly prune roses except climbing types, removing only the leggy top third of the canes. After temperatures drop into the 20s for a few nights, mound soil over the plant's bud union (the enlarged knob from which canes emerge). Once the soil surface freezes, set a cylinder of chicken wire or a tomato cage around each plant and fill it with a mulch of leaves, pine boughs, or straw. In spring, lift the mulch and inspect the canes. Remove any dead or damaged wood, then prune for shape.

☑ **MAINTAIN TOOLS.** Sharpen the blades of hoes, spades, and pruning shears, then wipe them down with oil (machine oil for metal parts, linseed oil for handles), and store in a dry place for the winter.

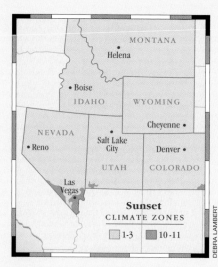

Sunset
CLIMATE ZONES
☐ 1-3   ☐ 10-11

DEBRA LAMBERT

☑ **MAKE COMPOST.** Speed the composting process by grinding up plant waste before you toss it on the compost pile. If you have lots of fallen leaves, go over them with your mower, then dump the bag full of shredded leaves onto the pile. Or rent a shredder for a day and grind up all your garden waste.

☑ **MULCH.** Spread a 3- to 4-inch layer of organic mulch around half-hardy plants, on bulb beds, and under trees and shrubs. If your trees have been damaged during previous winters by rodents burrowing under mulch and chewing on trunks, consider salting the mulch with rodenticide.

☑ **PREPARE PLANTING BEDS.** Before the ground freezes, till a 2- or 3-inch layer of composted steer manure or mushroom compost into planting beds. They'll be ready to plant as soon as soil warms in spring.

☑ **PRUNE TREES, SHRUBS.** After leaves drop, start pruning deciduous trees except stone fruits (wait to prune these in early spring). Work on a mild day when the temperature is above freezing. Remove dead, diseased, and injured branches, water sprouts, and crossing or closely parallel branches. Then prune for shape. Use cut limbs for firewood, and spread smaller boughs over beds that need some frost protection.

☑ **WINTERIZE PERENNIALS.** As you cut back frost-downed perennials to 4- to 6-inch stubs, chop up the prunings and spread them around the plants' crowns as insulation. Then cover beds with a 6-inch layer of loose organic mulch such as shredded leaves, conifer boughs, or straw. ◆

Southwest Checklist

PLANTING

☑ **COOL-SEASON ANNUALS.** Zones 12–13: Plant ageratum, aster, bells-of-Ireland, calendula, candytuft, clarkia, cornflower, foxglove, larkspur, lobelia, painted daisy, petunia, phlox, snapdragon, stock, sweet alyssum, and sweet pea. In shady areas, set out dianthus, English daisy, pansy, primrose, and viola.

☑ **BULBS.** Zones 1–2, 10–11: Plant all spring-blooming bulbs immediately. Zones 12–13: Buy Dutch iris, hyacinth, and long-stemmed varieties of daffodils and tulips; chill their bulbs in the refrigerator for five to six weeks before planting.

☑ **LAWNS.** Zones 12–13: Mow your warm-season lawn at about ½ inch, then overseed it with 10 to 20 pounds of ryegrass per 1,000 square feet. You can use annual or perennial rye; the coarser-leafed annual rye costs less, but stains more and needs more frequent mowing than its perennial cousin. A month after sowing, fertilize the new grass to help it fill in quickly.

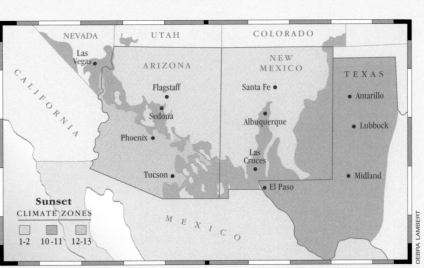

NEVADA · UTAH · COLORADO

CALIFORNIA

Las Vegas

ARIZONA

NEW MEXICO

TEXAS

Flagstaff

Santa Fe

Amarillo

Sedona

Albuquerque

Lubbock

Phoenix

Las Cruces

Tucson

El Paso

Midland

MEXICO

Sunset
CLIMATE ZONES

1-2 10-11 12-13

DEBRA LAMBERT

☑ **TREES AND SHRUBS.** Zones 10–13: This is the best time of year to plant hardy trees and shrubs, including acacia, cassia, *Cordia boissieri*, desert spoon, fairy duster, mesquite, oleander, palo verde, *Salvia greggii*, and Texas ranger. Water them in well.

☑ **VEGETABLES.** Zones 12–13: Sow seeds or set out plants of asparagus, beets, broccoli, brussels sprouts, cabbage, carrots, cauliflower, celery, endive, garlic, kale, kohlrabi, leeks, lettuce, mustard, parsley, peas, radishes, spinach, Swiss chard, and turnips.

MAINTENANCE

☑ **CONTROL APHIDS.** Zones 12–13: Blast them off new growth with a hose every week, or hose them once and follow up with a spray of insecticidal soap.

☑ **CULL SPLIT CITRUS.** Be sure to pick off and discard split fruit, which results from fast growth and water uptake. It attracts fungus and insects to otherwise healthy trees.

☑ **MAINTAIN INDOOR PLANTS.** If house plants start losing leaves and new growth becomes weak and stretched out from low indoor light, consider supplementing daylight with artificial plant lights.

☑ **PRUNE AND FEED ROSES.** Zones 12–13: Remove faded flowers, pruning lightly as you go. Take out dead, diseased, crossing, and injured canes, and prune for shape. Then apply complete fertilizer, watering it in well, to encourage a flush of winter flowers. ◆

Spanish lessons

This Southern California garden is Mediterranean to the core, and it's filled with planting ideas you can use

BY SHARON COHOON

■ A DREAM CLIENT, SAYS SANTA MONICA DESIGNER MARY EFFRON, IS "SOMEONE with a real sense of their home and an appreciation of their climate." And when all elements—from plants and paving to pots—work together to support a property's style, the result is a dream garden.

Take this classic Mediterranean garden, for instance. When its owner bought the Spanish-style house—built in the late 1920s—it was rich in handsome architectural details. But the garden around it was deadly dull. Thirsty turf grass carpeted the front; red bricks paved the back. Though she was not a gardener, the owner knew what she wanted: hardscaping more appropriate for her house, plants better suited to a Mediterranean climate, and beautiful detailing.

Effron and her husband, Javier Valdivia, a contractor, delivered on all counts. Here's what makes the Spanish-style garden they created a perfect marriage with the house and the climate.

• An elevated terrace across the back of the house for outdoor living. The terrace's surface echoes the antique tile flooring inside the house.

• A lap pool that—thanks to its long, narrow shape and cobalt blue tiled surface—recalls the reflecting pools of Moorish-influenced gardens in southern Spain. The frieze along one end complements the '20s-era tiles that decorate the exterior of the house.

• A backyard that feels lush, with planters built into the terrace so plants grow close to the house. Flowering vines scramble up walls, billowy lavenders spill over the pool's edge, and potted plants soften hard surfaces and edges.

• A front yard filled with sculptural plants. Columnar cactus, satiny agave rosettes, and fleshy-fingered *Senecio mandraliscae* have replaced the lawn. Broad paths of decomposed granite between beds let visitors admire the prickly vegetative art from a safe distance. Though this is primarily a foliage garden, it's always splashed with

LEFT: Typical Mediterranean plants—agave, lavender, pride of Madeira, flax—soften the edges of a backyard lap pool. TOP: Antique Mexican doors are used as a rustic garden gate. ABOVE: Mediterranean-style tiles cover the terrace.

STEVEN GUNTHER (2)   FAR LEFT: JERRY HARPUR

STEVEN GUNTHER

some seasonal color; early spring, when pride of Madeira and California poppies are both in bloom, is the showiest period.

Effron is the first to admit that gardens in the late '20s, even those surrounding Spanish-style houses in California, weren't really like this. "This is how you *wish* they'd looked. But it took transplanted Easterners a long time to adjust to the West," she says. The owner doesn't care about any of that. "This garden says Spain," she explains. "It works with the house, it works with the sun, it works with the weather."

Core elements of a Mediterranean garden

A few lavenders and a couple of fan palms do not make a Mediterranean garden. Here are the most important features.

Big patios, small lawn (or no lawn). In Mediterranean gardens, flat, open spaces are more likely to be devoted to people than turf grass, which isn't really at home in arid climates. These spaces are devoted instead to terraces, courtyards, outdoor dining rooms, and patios, and they're paved with level flooring suitable for tables and chairs —flagstone, tile, concrete, or decomposed granite.

Plants with character. Mediterranean weather may be mild, but its light is strong. Plants that look best under harsh sunlight have architectural shapes and heavy textures. Think of the thick leaves of agaves, the starchy blades of flax, and the broad fans of palms. Soft-textured, of-

ten gray-leafed plants such as helichrysum, germander, and lavender are buffers between these bold personalities.

Fearless use of flower color. Forget pastel pink. Orange, red, and sun-drenched gold are more typical Mediterranean colors. Aloes and acacia bloom in early spring; trumpet vines and lion's tail flower in summer. Even the blues are stronger—lapis-lazuli blues—like the dramatic spikes of pride of Madeira.

Aegean foliage colors. The mechanisms that make plants drought-tolerant—such as waxy or hairy leaf surfaces—affect foliage color. Pure greens are rare in Mediterranean plants. Olive greens, gray-greens, and blue-greens are more typical. To accentuate the cobalt and aquamarines in existing tiles and in the new lap pool, the designers

used plants with blue-green foliage extensively in this garden: *Agave attenuata*, *Lavandula heterophylla*, and *Senecio mandraliscae*, for example.

Containers as architecture. Pots, as used in the classic Mediterranean garden, have specific functions. A row of identical containers can act as a wall or room divider. And a solo urn or pot, with or without plants, often substitutes for sculpture. ◆

LEFT: Containers filled with succulents bring the garden closer to the house. Vines, a palm tree, and large accent plants like flax grow in planting beds built into the terrace.
ABOVE: Blue pride of Madeira, contrasted with orange and red California poppies, stops traffic in front of this garden in spring. RIGHT: The same blue is repeated in the backyard's flowers and foliage, as well as in the tiles lining the pool. Design: Mary Effron and Javier Valdivia, Santa Monica.

Desert wildflowers

They're surprisingly easy from seed or seedlings. Plant them now for a riotous show next spring

BY LAUREN BONAR SWEZEY

LEFT: California poppies, desert marigolds, and phacelia light up the ground beneath a large mesquite tree at Arid Zone Trees in Queen Creek, Arizona. Design: Steve Martino (602/957-6150). TOP: Pink and red penstemon mingle with California poppies. ABOVE: Clumps of desert marigolds and phacelia add spots of color to tiered planting beds in Melodie and John Lewis's Paradise Valley, Arizona, garden. Design: Floor & Ten Eyck (602/468-0505 or 395-1295).

■ WHAT'S NOT TO LOVE ABOUT WILDFLOWERS? In the Southwest's deserts in spring, they carpet whole hillsides with brilliant blooms of gold, pink, and blue—especially after a rainy winter.

Some are annuals with willowy stems and crepe paper–thin petals that seem to glow from within when sunlight hits them; others, including coreopsis and penstemons, are tough perennials with thick, voluptuous petals of saturated color.

As the photographs on these pages show, wildflowers don't need a large space in which to flourish; they're perfectly at home in small pockets around a pool, or scattered among agaves, cactus, and other desert plants. Many thrive in light shade beneath native trees such as palo verdes.

In garden beds, wildflowers can reseed year after year, creating a changing color show as the more vigorous plants take over. "What's dominant one year might not be the next," says Phoenix landscape architect Steve Martino, who values this surprise element that wildflowers deliver.

In *Sunset* climate zones 11 through 13, October and November are the best times to sow seeds. Choose a mix that's specifically designed for your climate, or create your own blend by using the list on page 309.

Given regular water, all wildflowers are reliable, easy-care bloomers.

How to plant wildflowers

For a beautiful display next spring, follow these guidelines.

Choose a sunny location. Most wildflowers grow best in full sun.

Prepare the soil. About three weeks before planting, take steps to reduce weeds. Till the soil to 3 to 4 inches deep (if the soil is very heavy or sandy, add an organic soil amendment). Water thoroughly to germinate weed seeds, then pull or hoe them as soon as they appear.

Plant. Broadcast wildflower seeds over the soil according to package directions (you'll need about 1 ounce per 100

ABOVE: Brittlebush, California poppies, California desert bluebells, desert marigolds, and penstemon erupt into bloom in this Phoenix garden, owned by Liz O'Brien and Steve Emrick. Agave, desert spoon, hesperaloe, Mexican bird of paradise, and prickly pear cactus provide the permanent structure.

RIGHT: A dazzling sea of wildflowers colors Sallye Schumacher's Paradise Valley, Arizona, garden at the base of Mummy Mountain. To create the long-blooming show, Schumacher combined a desert mix—from Wild Seed in Tempe, Arizona—containing purple coneflower, yarrow, and other tough beauties.

square feet). Lightly rake the soil to cover the seeds. You can also set out 4-inch or 1-gallon pots of perennial wildflowers, such as penstemon.

Water. To ensure a reliable bloom show, water the planting often enough to keep soil moist. After seedlings appear, continue watering two to three times a week.

Control weeds. As soon as they germinate, pull out weeds that continue to sprout from seeds blown in from surrounding areas. To help you tell the difference between weeds and wildflowers, sow some wildflower seed in a nursery flat at planting time. As soon as

they germinate, compare them with seedlings in the garden bed and pull seedlings from the ground that don't look like those growing in the flat.

Encourage repeat bloom. Stop irrigating annual wildflowers during the summer and allow them to set seed.

When seeds are mature (plants usually turn from green to tan, brown, or black), pull up the plants and then shake them to scatter the seeds. When the blooms have faded, cut the plants back to 4 to 6 inches tall.

For wildflower mixes that include summer bloomers, continue irrigating until all blooms fade. Then, in the fall,

sow fresh seeds of spring bloomers around them.

Where to buy seed

•*Desert Moon Nursery,* Box 600, Veguita, NM 87062; (505) 864-0614. Catalog $1.

•*Plants of the Southwest,* Route 6, Box 11A, Santa Fe, NM 87501; www.plantsofthesouthwest.com or (800) 788-7333. Catalog $3.50.

•*Southwestern Native Seeds,* Box 50503, Tucson, AZ 85703. Catalog $2.

•*Wild Seed,* Box 27751, Tempe, AZ 85285; (602) 276-3536. Catalog free.

Choice wildflowers for desert gardens

■ When combining wildflowers, choose complementary or contrasting colors. Also consider height (refer to catalogs)—place tall varieties in the back of a border, shorter ones in the front. For extended bloom, blend spring- and summer-blooming kinds.

YELLOW: Bahia (*B. absinthifolia*), Bigelow's coreopsis (*C. bigelovii*), chinchweed (*Pectis papposa*), coastal tidytips (*Layia platyglossa*), Cooper's paperflower (*Psilostrophe cooperi*), desert marigold (*Baileya multiradiata*), dyssodia (*D. pentachaeta*), goldfields (*Baeria chrysostoma*), yellow blanket (*Lesquerella gordonii*).

ORANGE: Apricot mallow (*Sphaeralcea ambigua*), California poppy (*Eschscholzia californica*), Mexican gold poppy (*E. mexicana*).

RED: Firecracker penstemon (*P. eatonii*), firewheel (*Gaillardia pulchella*).

PINK: Canyon penstemon (*P. pseudospectabilis*), owl's clover (*Orthocarpus purpurascens*), Parry's penstemon (*P. parryi*).

BLUE: Arroyo lupine (*Lupinus succulentus*), chia (*Salvia columbariae*), Coulter's lupine (*L. sparsiflorus*), desert bell (*Phacelia campanularia*), wild delphinium (*D. scaposum*).

LAVENDER: Arizona lupine (*Lupinus arizonicus*), Bigelow's aster (*Machaeranthera bigelovii*), fleabane (*Erigeron divergens*), Goodding's verbena (*V. gooddingii*).

WHITE: Birdcage evening primrose (*Oenothera deltoides*), blackfoot daisy (*Melampodium leucanthum*), desert chicory (*Rafinesquia neomexicana*), fragrant evening primrose (*O. caespitosa*). — *Judy Mielke* ◆

TERRENCE MOORE

VIREYAS BEAR blossoms ranging from 1 to 5 inches long and ½ to 1 inch across. ABOVE: 'Sunny's Brother'. ABOVE RIGHT: 'Elizabeth Ann Seton'. FAR RIGHT: 'Sweet Wendy'. For details on varieties, see page 313.

Tropical rhodies

Grow colorful Vireya types as indoor-outdoor plants

BY JIM McCAUSLAND • PHOTOGRAPHS BY NORMAN A. PLATE

■ STRUNG OUT OVER THE EQUATOR, THE VAST MALAY ARCHIPELAGO IS THE BIRTHPLACE OF A remarkable group of rhododendrons. These Vireya rhododendrons (also called Malesians) are quite different from their large, spring-blooming cousins that are so popular in the Pacific Northwest. Many Vireyas, with flowers in shades of red, orange, yellow, and white—often intensely fragrant—are small enough to fit in a tabletop pot. They flower heavily in winter, when their color and scent are most welcome, with repeat bloom several times each year.

You can grow Vireyas indoors anywhere, setting plants outside during frost-free months.

Vireyas rise again

Around the mid–19th century, Vireyas were the subject of a big breeding push in England. But most of the early Vireya hybrids were lost during World Wars I and II, when the English directed their resources toward survival. Interest was rekindled in the 1960s when Vireyas came to the United States. Today breeding is scattered across at least three continents, and there are hundreds of named varieties. How do you sort through them all? Our chart on page 313 lists 15 reliable bloomers, with flowers ranging from long trumpets to dainty bells.

Growing tips

•Use a fast-draining potting medium. Or create your own mix by blending 1 part peat moss, 1 part ground bark, and 2 parts perlite. Put plants in terracotta containers that are relatively tall and barely wider than the rootballs (Vireyas grow best when they're slightly rootbound).

•Keep plants in a bright spot indoors during the winter, and move them out into the light shade of a tall tree or covered patio during frost-free months (temperatures below 28° can injure or kill them).

•Most gardeners who have grown Vireyas for a long time chalk up much of their success to careful watering. Water by weight, at least at first. Pick up the pot and feel how much it weighs when the soil is dry. Then drench the soil and pick it up again—it will be much heavier.

ABOVE: 'Mount Kaindi'.
LEFT: *Rhododendron wrightianum*.
ABOVE RIGHT: 'Sirunki Lake'.

This will give you a sense of how light the pot should be before you water again. Water more often when plants are blooming.

•Like rhododendrons in general, Vireyas are light feeders. Twice a year, in spring and fall, apply liquid fertilizer (20-20-20) diluted to half strength.

•Most plants will eventually grow at least 2 feet tall in containers, increasing bloom as they mature. If they get leggy, occasionally pinch new growth tips to force branching.

Sources

Vireyas aren't widely sold at retail nurseries. One excellent mail-order source is Bovees Nursery (1737 S.W.

Coronado St., Portland, OR 97219; 800/435-9250 or www.bovees.com; catalog $2), which sells more than 150 kinds at prices ranging from $7.50 to $35, plus shipping, for one- to five-year-old plants.

The Rhododendron Species Foundation (253/927-6960 or www. halcyon.com/rsf) in Federal Way, Washington, sells Vireya species on-site and by mail. Some of the best include *R. dianthosmum* (pink with peach throat, carnation fragrance), *R. dielsianum* (rose), *R. laetum* (yellow), *R. macgregoriae* (saffron yellow), and *R. wrightianum* (red).

For further reading, check out *Vireyas: A Practical Gardening Guide,* by John Kenyon and Jacqueline Walker (Timber Press, Portland, 1997; $19.95; 800/327-5680).

15 easy-to-grow Vireyas

NAME	FLOWER COLOR	SCENT	COMMENTS
'Aravir'	Large white trumpets	√	Compact growth
'Calavar'	Deep pink outside, creamy yellow inside	√	Robust, open bush with dark green leaves, carnation scent
'Dr. Herman Sleumer'	Reddish pink blooms with creamy yellow throats	√	Large, feltlike leaves
'Elizabeth Ann Seton'	Pale pink tubular blooms	√	Bushy shrub; great in containers
'Hansa Bay'	Red-orange petals fade to gold		Tall, upright plant
'Mount Kaindi'	Pale peach		Bushy, medium to tall plant; long, dark green leaves
'Ne Plus Ultra'	Extra-full clusters of red bells		One of six remaining hybrids from the 19th century; waxy leaves
R. jasminiflorum 'Punctatum'	Pink tubular blooms	√	Compact, small-leafed plant with jasmine scent; good for hanging baskets
R. loranthiflorum	White tubular blooms	√	Well-branched plant; light green leaves
R. wrightianum hybrid (with *R. lochiae*)	Red tubular flowers		Compact, upright plant with shiny dark green leaves; strong repeat bloomer
'Sirunki Lake'	Small, ruffled salmon pink bells		Graceful compact shrub; continuous bloom
'St. Valentine'	Red bells		Small leaves on spreading, slightly dipping branches; good for hanging baskets
'Sunny's Brother'	Yellow flowers with red-orange lobes		Vigorous plant; rounded, dark green leaves
'Sweet Wendy'	Pale yellow blooms flushed with pink	√	Upright plant grows slowly, flowers often
'Vladimir Bukovsky'	Yellow-orange flowers with pale throats		Spreading habit; great in containers ◆

What to plant under oaks and pines?

Some plants get along beautifully with these demanding trees

BY JIM McCAUSLAND

AIRY CLUMPS of ornamental grasses, ground cover shrubs, and red-flowered autumn sage dot a planting under oaks in Pebble Beach, California. Design: Michelle Comeau, Carmel, California.

Although we field all sorts of garden questions at *Sunset,* the query we get most frequently from readers is what they can plant under native oaks and pines. Both trees create tough environments that demand plants capable of tolerating dry shade, slightly acidic soil, and falling leaf litter. Native oaks *must* have dry soil in summer or they risk developing oak root fungus. And the water-hogging roots of pines create dry conditions.

In *Sunset's* gardens, we've been planting under oaks and pines for about 40 years, so we've come to know which plants work. To round out our suggestions (see "Good Companions," on the facing page), we consulted with gardeners, landscape designers, and the California Oak Foundation, a nonprofit group dedicated to protecting and perpetuating California's native oaks.

Under oaks, plant companions that like it dry

Western native oaks love the Mediterranean climate along the coast, with its wet winters and dry summers. Most shade-loving bedding plants, however, need summer water to survive, and if you give it to them, you'll also supply the warm, moist soil that's congenial to oak root fungus (*Armillaria mellea*). This fungus enters the oak's roots and usually kills the tree slowly over many years. Even after you remove the tree, the dis-

ease remains in the soil, attacking other susceptible plants, including elms, grapes, pines, and rhododendrons.

The most at-risk species include coast live oak (*Quercus agrifolia*), canyon oak (*Q. chrysolepis*), mesa oak (*Q. engelmannii*), Oregon white oak (*Q. garryana*), California black oak (*Q. kelloggii*), valley oak (*Q. lobata*), and interior live oak (*Q. wislizenii*).

To reduce the spread of oak root fungus, underplant the tree with drought-tolerant flowering plants and ground covers. Experts recommend that you keep all plantings 4 to 6 feet away from the oak's trunk. You'll need to give the plants a little extra water their first summer, but after that, they should do well on what nature supplies. When you do irrigate, don't water within 4 feet of the

oak's trunk or allow standing water to collect there.

In addition to the plants we describe, you'll find a wide selection of oak-friendly shrubs, ground covers, perennials, grasses, ferns, bulbs, and annuals identified in the booklet *Compatible Plants Under and Around Oaks* (California Oak Foundation, Oakland, CA, 1991; $14.25; 510/763-0282).

Beneath pines, choose plants that "swallow" needles

Pines drive many gardeners to despair. Their roots suck the moisture out of the soil, making life under them difficult for many plants. Their falling needles (pines drop about a fifth of them each year) can smother lawns. Some gardeners just give up and let the needles accumulate,

Good companions

Most of the plants listed here grow well under *both* oaks and pines. We also include a few plants for pines alone (most need extra water).

FLOWERING PERENNIALS, SHRUBS, AND BULBS

Autumn sage (*Salvia greggii; Sunset* climate zones 8–24). Bushy 3- to 4-foot shrub bears red, salmon, or purple flowers from late spring to summer (fall and winter in the desert).

California iris (*I. douglasiana*; zones 4–24). Knee-high plant with purple, blue, white, or cream flowers in spring. Related Pacific Coast hybrids also work well; they need a smattering of summer water.

Catmint (*Nepeta faassenii*; all zones). Lavender-blue flowers make 2-foot mounds in late spring, early summer.

Ceanothus (zones 1–9, 14–24). These native shrubs are most effective around oaks. Low-growing types such as *C. griseus horizontalis* and *C. rigidus* 'Snowball' reach 2 to 6 feet tall. Clusters of lavender-blue or white flowers appear in spring.

Coral bells (*Heuchera*; zones vary by species). Compact perennials with roundish leaves in shades of dark green to purplish red; clusters of coral pink, red, or white flowers in spring or summer.

Daffodil (*Narcissus*; all zones). Flowers from February through April, then dies back and doesn't need water in summer.

Red valerian (*Centranthus ruber*; zones 7–9, 12–24). Perennial 3 feet tall that blooms from spring into summer.

Rosemary (*Rosmarinus officinalis*; zones 4–24). Upright (to 6 feet tall) or prostrate (to 2 feet tall), plants have aromatic dark green leaves, plus lavender-blue flowers in late winter or early spring.

Santa Barbara daisy (*Erigeron karvinskianus*; zones 8–9, 12–24). This 20-inch perennial is covered with pink or white daisies spring into fall. Blooms best with extra light.

Under pines only, add astilbe (zones 2–9, 14–24), azaleas (zones 2–9, 14–24), Japanese anemone (*A. hybrida*; all zones), lilies (all zones), rhododendrons (zones 4–6, 15–17), and *Viburnum davidii* (zones 4–9, 14–24).

GROUND COVERS AND ORNAMENTAL GRASSES

Bamboo (*Sasa veitchii*; hardy to 0°). Dense, 2- to 3-foot-high ground cover; deep green leaves develop white edges in autumn. Needs water only during growth spurts. Can be invasive; contain planting with a plastic bamboo barrier.

Blue fescue (*Festuca ovina* 'Glauca'; all zones). Ankle-high clumps of blue-gray foliage.

Dusty miller (*Senecio cineraria*; all zones). Woolly white leaves grow 2 feet tall.

Fountain grass (*Pennisetum alopecuroides*; zones 3–24). Graceful 3- to 4-foot-high clumps of bright green foliage topped by pinkish flower plumes.

St. Johnswort (*Hypericum calycinum*; zones 2–24). Ground cover with evergreen foliage, yellow summer flowers. ◆

ABOVE: Blue clouds of spring flowers cover ceanothus around live oaks.
TOP: Needles of Japanese red pine are hidden by *Sasa veitchii* bamboo.

but that can create a fire hazard.

There are alternatives. It's hard to go wrong if you plant a skirt of shrubs just inside a tree's drip line; you'll never see the needles that fall behind them. If you choose open shrubs with large leaves, like rhododendrons, most of the needles will drop through their branches and disappear. Avoid planting shrubs with dense, small leaves, which tend to trap the needles.

RED POINSETTIAS and forced white hydrangeas create a festive display on this front porch. A fringe of conifer prunings camouflages the pots. For details, see page 322.

316

December

gardenguide

A DRAGONFLY HOVERS over sunflowers in one illuminated scene from the Garden D'Lights display.

Night-blooming bulbs

Bellevue Botanical Garden glows after dark

■ You might say it's bulb time in Bellevue, Washington. Not daffodils or tulips, but thousands of tiny colored bulbs illuminate Bellevue Botanical Garden during Garden D'Lights, late November until January. Stroll the grounds some evening between 5 and 10 and you'll see electrifying sights: trees and shrubs outlined by white lights, an arbor glowing with purple wisteria blossoms, and borders of flowers—from blue delphiniums to yellow sunflowers—composed entirely of lights.

Arrive about an hour before dusk so you can walk the paths to see the handsome bare branches of deciduous plants etching the winter sky. In addition to the light display, educational programs and musical events are scheduled. The garden, at 12001 Main Street in Bellevue, is open daily from dawn to 10 P.M. during the holidays; the gift shop is open from 5 to 8 P.M. Free admission; donations appreciated. For information or directions, call (425) 452-2750. — *Steven R. Lorton*

Turning lights into flowers

Volunteers use 50-bulb strings of minilights. The bulbs are bunched in clusters of two or three and attached to segments of 22-gauge wire wrapped in florist's tape, then secured to frames of wood stakes.

Bellevue Botanical Garden offers classes on making electric flowers in March and September. For dates and costs, and to register, call (425) 451-3755.

This Christmas tree decorates itself

As perfect as a sheared Douglas fir, this tabletop tree comes with its own ornaments: hundreds of tiny white flowers that make the best natural flocking yet. The blooms and the tiny green and white needles give the plant's real identity away: It's a Christmas heather (*Erica canaliculata*) that's been sheared into a classic Christmas tree shape by the grower. You'll find heather Christmas trees at garden centers, florists, and the floral departments of supermarkets around the West this month.

This South African native loves sun, so give it a spot indoors that gets plenty of light. It's too frost-tender to survive outdoors in cold-winter areas of the Southwest, and this acid-loving plant cannot stand the native alkaline soil.

If you have an exceptionally good indoor environment (like a bright room), try growing it as a container plant, repotting it as it grows. Never let the soil dry out, and feed lightly with acid fertilizer in spring and fall. In fall and winter, expect pink flowers in sun. To make it white for Christmas, the grower allows it to flower under shadecloth. Grow it in light shade and you can achieve the same result. — *Jim McCausland*

NORMAN A. PLATE (2)

Blushing beauty

'Flower Girl', a new shrub from Weeks Roses, is like an ingenue among dowagers. In its presence, other roses look a little stiff and dowdy. Its leaf color—an innocent apple green—has something to do with it. So does the youthful vigor with which it kicks out flowers. Though its soft pink blossoms are small (about 2 inches across), they unfurl in pendulous clusters (30 or more flowers are not uncommon); at times they nearly cover the shrub. The heavy flower clusters on light canes make it weep gracefully.

'Flower Girl' has all the attributes of a great landscaping shrub—attractive habit, disease-resistant foliage, and modest size (about 2½ feet tall). It also comes in 3-foot and 5-foot standards. As for cold-hardiness, 'Flower Girl' stood up to the frigid Minnesota winter in field trials there.

Look for plants in nurseries and garden centers. If you have trouble locating one, try a mail-order source such as Regan Nursery (510/797-3222 or www.regannursery.com) or Michael's Premier Roses (916/369-7673 or michaelsrose.com).
— *Sharon Cohoon*

Ring around the azalea

TWO KINDS of needlepoint ivy surround this pink-flowered azalea.

NORMAN A. PLATE (5)

■ Showy holiday gift plants such as azaleas and chrysanthemums usually come in foil-wrapped plastic pots. They aren't bad-looking but you can improve a gift plant's looks by nesting its plastic pot inside a larger terra-cotta container. For interest around the pot's edges, add a fringe of variegated needlepoint ivy. The ivy conceals the inner pot, and makes a good companion for just about anything that blooms.

DIRECTIONS **1.** Start with a beautiful 15- or 16-inch pot. Fill it partway with potting soil fortified with controlled-release fertilizer, then nest an empty 6-inch plastic pot in the center of the larger container. Fill the space between inner and outer pots with more soil, then plant the space with ivy from 4-inch pots; gently pull apart stems with roots attached (as shown). **2.** Remove the empty inner pot, then drop a 6-inch gift plant (such as the azalea pictured) into the hole, where it will look as though it had been growing forever. You can swap it for a fresh flowering plant any time during the year—or replace it with a fern or flowering indoor plant like spathiphyllum. —*J.M.*

How to condition holiday greens

■ Prunings from many shrubs and trees make wonderful holiday decorations. Conifers (cedar, fir, pine) and shrubs with winter berries (holly, pyracantha, toyon) are obvious choices, but evergreens (citrus, magnolia, osmanthus, pittosporum) and bloomers such as camellias are just as long-lasting.

Before you cut any snippets from the plants, though, try the following conditioning process. It will improve the luster and color of the leaves and help the prunings last longer in arrangements.

A. One week before decorating: Identify the branches you want to cut and tie lengths of ribbon or twine around them as markers. Add 1 or 2 tablespoons of Epsom salts to 1 gallon of water and fill a spray bottle with the solution. Spray the liquid on the chosen branches, leaving them attached to trees or shrubs. The magnesium in the salt will intensify both leaf color and luster.

B. Two days before decorating: Make angled cuts back to side branches or to about 1/4 inch above buds. Pound the stems slightly with a hammer to help them absorb water. To help branches last longer, fill a bathtub with water and soak them overnight. Hang them the next day to straighten and dry. — *S.C.*

Encinitas garden of lights

GLENN CORMIER

■ After dark, strolling through a garden illuminated with 50,000 mini-lights has a salubrious effect. You start downshifting the minute you walk through the gates. You can feel it in your blood and see it in the behavior of your fellow visitors. Adults jettison all their holiday worries, and even the crankiest, over-sugared children become hushed angels. Or at least that's what happens at Quail Botanical Gardens in Encinitas during its Garden of Lights festival.

When outlined by lights, a cycad becomes a giant spider; a thunbergia vine, its web. An angel's trumpet tree looks like a spouting geyser, and a bamboo forest becomes a woodland inhabited by fireflies. Even adults have the good sense to know they've walked into fairyland. The gardens offer additional diversions this month—marshmallow roasting, storytelling, caroling—but everything is deliberately low-key so as not to interfere with the gentling mood. (Don't miss the draft horse–drawn surrey ride through the grounds. Even without snow, the ride makes you feel like you're in a Currier & Ives print.)

Garden of Lights is held during December. The gardens are at 230 Quail Gardens Dr., Encinitas; (760) 436-3036. Call for information about dates, times and admission fees. — *S.C.*

Little spruced coop

■ If it's in Laurie Connable's garden, it has to be pretty. A working chicken coop is no exception. Since Connable, a Poway garden designer, couldn't find a ready-made poultry shed that was good-looking, she dreamed up one. Her custom-made

JEFF LANCASTER

"chicken condo" sports white lattice trim, decorative finials, a faux Dutch door, and a window box.

The coop gets even fancier during the holidays. Connable hangs evergreen wreaths made from garden cuttings along the roof line, and around its perimeter she plants white-flowered plants like cyclamen and pansies that complement the lattice trim. Since regular poinsettias don't survive Poway's temperatures, Connable tucks silk versions into her pots and window box.

The holiday-decorated coop delights all her garden visitors. "My hens even seem to appreciate it," she says. — *S.C.*

CLIPPINGS

•**A book of roses.** *The Rose Bible,* by Rayford Reddell (Chronicle Books, San Francisco, 1998; $24.95; 800/722-6657 or www.chronbooks.com), is filled with expert advice and gorgeous photos, many taken at Reddell's rose nursery, Garden Valley Ranch in Petaluma.

•**Romancing herbs.** *Herbs: Growing & Using the Plants of Romance,* by Bill and Sylvia Varney of Fredericksburg Herb Farm (Ironwood Press, Tucson, 1998; $18.95; 520/579-5319), is informative and beautifully photographed. It earned the 1999 Benjamin Franklin Award for Best Gardening/Agriculture Book.

•**A gift that lasts.** Stumped on what to give a friend, neighbor, or uncle who has everything? Plant a tree in the person's honor and aid TreePeople in its reforestation efforts at the same time. (TreePeople has planted nearly 2 million trees in Southern California over the last 25 years.) For a minimum $20 donation, this nonprofit environmental organization will plant a seedling tree in the mountains surrounding Los Angeles and send the person in whose name it has been planted a personalized card. For a $75 gift, the honoree gets a small grove of five trees and a certificate. For details, call (818) 753-8733.

Hydrangeas as white as snow, in time for the holidays

■ By early fall, hydrangeas have finished blooming in Western gardens and are on their way to dormancy. But this year, a California grower has introduced two hydrangeas that can be forced into bloom for the holidays.

Their snow white flowers, which pair well with all colors, are especially potent companions for red poinsettias. 'Sister Theresa' ('Soeur Therese') has ball-shaped flowers; 'Libelle' (pictured on page 316) is a lace cap type.

Indoors, display them where they'll receive bright, indirect daylight and no drafts. Water whenever the top ½ inch of soil dries out, and mist the leaves daily if the air is especially dry.

In *Sunset* climate zones 3–9 and 14–24), you can successfully transplant these hydrangeas into the garden after the weather warms up in spring. Until then, keep them in a light, protected place like a heated porch and continue to care for them as you would any growing potted plant.

At spring planting time, choose a place that gets part shade, or full sun along the coast, and dig a hole that's three to five times as wide as the hydrangea's rootball and twice as deep.

Add controlled-release fertilizer to the backfill, and plant so the crown of the hydrangea (the place where root meets trunk) is about an inch above the surrounding soil. Allow enough room for it to grow (4 to 6 feet for 'Sister Theresa', 3 to 5 feet for 'Libelle').

You'll find forced white hydrangeas in nurseries and garden centers. — *J.M.*

A Tucson gate with a sunny outlook

■ Rigid, geometric lines are not Kathy Lyle's style. The interior designer prefers free-form shapes. So she didn't bother to shop for a gate for the entry courtyard to her Tucson home. Instead, Lyle sketched her design on paper and took the drawing to a blacksmith to execute. Material and labor for the iron gate cost $1,100—"more than a ready-made gate, but not bad for an original," says Lyle. She has allowed the iron to rust; when it reaches the desired patina, Lyle may apply a clear varnish to arrest the process.

When you work with a blacksmith, you don't have to provide a polished sketch, says Lyle. But if you're timid about your artistry, her design firm can help: Interior Trends Remodel, Tucson; (520) 529-8459. — *S.C.*

BACK TO BASICS

JAMIE HADLEY

Tune-up for tools. Winter is a good time to clean and oil shovels, spades, and other digging tools. Fill a 16-gallon bucket about ¾ full with coarse sand. Mix in 1 quart or more of motor oil (used is fine). Jab your tools into the mixture until the sand has abraded off the dirt and the blades are coated with oil. Brush off sand, then store the tools. Oiled sand can be used indefinitely (discard at a hazardous waste station). Don't use this method on pruners or other crisscrossing blades. — *S.C.*

Pacific Northwest Checklist

PLANTING

☑ **AMARYLLIS.** Pot up bulbs at two-week intervals for a steady show of flowers from Christmas through Valentine's Day. For cultural techniques, see "The Amazing Amaryllis," page 336.

☑ **BUY CAMELLIAS.** Zones 4–7: Sasanquas and other winter-flowering camellias will be blooming at nurseries now (for outstanding varieties, see "Color-Kissed Camellias," page 338). To dress up plants for holiday display, festoon them with ornaments or small lights.

☑ **CONIFERS.** Whether you're shopping for a living Christmas tree or a specimen for your garden, you'll find a wide selection in nurseries this month. Good candidates for living Christmas trees include alpine fir, Douglas fir, and white fir.

MAINTENANCE

☑ **CARE FOR HOUSE PLANTS.** Remove yellowing leaves and faded blooms regularly. If leaves are dusty, rinse plants in the shower under lukewarm water. Fertilize winter-flowering plants, but don't feed others until early spring.

☑ **GLEAN FRAGRANT GREENS.** Prowl your garden for plants with fragrant foliage and cut snippets to scent your house. In addition to pungent cedars, firs, and pines, try native Oregon myrtle (*Umbellularia californica*), sweet bay magnolia (*M. virginiana*), and rosemary.

☑ **GROUND-LAYER EVERGREENS.** Use this technique to propagate new plants from evergreens. Select a low-hanging branch and scrape a patch of bark the size of a fingernail off the underside. Dust the bare patch with rooting hormone. Push the nicked portion of the branch to the ground, scratch a shallow hole in the soil, and fill around the branch with soil, leaving the tip exposed. Lay a stone or brick atop the branch to hold it firmly to the ground. To encourage rooting, keep the soil around it moist. Late next fall, sever the branch from its parent plant and you'll have a rooted shoot to transplant.

☑ **PRUNE CONIFERS, HOLLY.** Prune evergreen conifers and use the boughs for holiday wreaths and swags. If you prune holly now, you can use the berry-laden sprigs for decoration.

☑ **TEND GIFT PLANTS.** To prolong the bloom of Christmas cactus, cyclamen, kalanchoe, and poinsettias, remove decorative foil or wrap from pots so water won't pool up inside.

☑ **WATER.** Don't overlook plants growing under house eaves. Sheltered from the rain, they need regular irrigation. Well-watered plants are less susceptible to frost damage. ◆

Northern California Checklist

PLANTING, DECORATING

☑ **BARE-ROOT PLANTS. Zones 7–9, 14–17:** Late this month, nurseries begin selling bare-root cane berries, fruit trees, grapes, and roses. You'll also find perennial vegetables, such as asparagus, horseradish, and rhubarb. Ask nursery personnel to recommend varieties suitable for your climate. Plant as soon as possible after bringing them home. If soil is too wet to plant, temporarily cover roots with moistened mulch or plant in containers.

☑ **BULBS. Zones 7–9, 14–17:** If you still have tulips and other bulbs stored in the refrigerator or the garage, December is a good time to plant them. Toss out soft or molding bulbs.

☑ **GIVE A LIVING GIFT.** Bypass the hectic shopping center this year and give your gardening friends a gift that will continue to live on well after the holidays. For an edible surprise, pot up your favorite dwarf citrus or a handful of strawberry plants. If it's a blooming present you need, choose a camellia, Christmas cactus, or orchid.

☑ **INSTANT COLOR. Zones 7–9, 14–17:** Most nurseries have a good supply of 4- and 6-inch pots of color in stock now. Add several foliage plants to the mix (ferns, for instance) to create a colorful container for the front porch. Some choices include azaleas,

Sunset
CLIMATE ZONES
■ Mountain (1-2)
□ Valley (7-9)
■ Inland (14)
□ Coastal (15-17)

DEBRA LAMBERT

calendulas, Christmas cactus, cineraria, cyclamen, English primroses, fairy primroses, kalanchoe, pansies, *Primula obconica*, and snapdragons. Protect Christmas cactus and kalanchoe from frost.

☑ **MAKE A WREATH OR SWAG.** Nurseries are stocked with plenty of greenery for adorning a door and draping on a mantel. Staff at Yamagami's Nursery in Cupertino spray their wreaths and garlands with fire retardant. You can also spray untreated greens with an antitranspirant to help delay the drying process.

MAINTENANCE

☑ **FILL HUMMINGBIRD FEEDERS. Zones 7–9, 14–17:** These birds stay in Northern California through winter. Since flowers are scarce in most gardens now, it's important to keep your feeder filled; clean and refill it every few days.

☑ **USE WARM WATER ON HOUSE PLANTS.** Most house plants come from tropical climates. For that reason, cooperative extension researchers recommend watering them with lukewarm water (or room temperature water) to avoid shocking them. The researchers found that irrigating with cold water can cause plants—particularly ficus—to drop leaves. Before filling your watering can, test the temperature of the water by flicking a few drops on your wrist as you would milk from a baby's bottle.

PEST CONTROL

☑ **APPLY DORMANT SPRAY. Zones 7–9, 14–17:** To smother overwintering insect eggs and pests such as aphids, mites, and scale, spray deciduous flowering and fruit trees as well as roses with dormant oil after leaves have fallen. For complete coverage, spray the branches, branch crotches, trunk, and ground beneath the drip line. Also rake up and destroy any remaining fallen fruit and leaves. ◆

Southern California Checklist

PLANTING

✔ **BARE-ROOT PLANTS.** For the best selection in bare-root roses, visit nurseries soon—current favorites tend to disappear quickly. Deciduous fruit trees, cane berries, grapes, and perennial vegetables like artichokes and asparagus will arrive later this month and next. Plant anything bare-root as soon after purchase as possible. If the soil is too soggy for immediate planting, cover roots with soil or plant temporarily in containers.

✔ **WINTER-FLOWERING SHRUBS.** Sasanqua camellias provide great winter color and are versatile plants (see the article on page 338 for details). Other reliable winter bloomers include breath of heaven (*Coleonema*), Geraldton waxflower, giant daisy tree (*Montanoa grandiflora*), New Zealand tea tree (*Leptospermum scoparium*), pink powder puff (*Calliandra*), and spotted emu bush (*Eremophila maculata*).

✔ **WINTER VEGETABLES.** If there are bare spots in your vegetable beds, sow arugula, collard, chard, kale, leaf lettuces, mustard, peas, radishes, or spinach from seed or plant sets of onion and garlic. Nursery broccoli, cabbage, and cauliflower seedlings can also be transplanted.

✔ **BULBS.** Coastal, inland, and low-desert gardeners can continue to plant spring-blooming bulbs. Tulip and hyacinth bulbs that have been chilled for at least six weeks can go into the ground too.

MAINTENANCE

✔ **APPLY DORMANT OIL.** As soon as their leaves fall, spray deciduous flowering and fruit trees with dormant oil to smother overwintering aphids, mites, and scale. If you haven't already done so, treat susceptible trees for peach leaf curl. Add lime sulfur or fixed copper to the dormant oil. (Don't use lime on apricots.) Spray branches, crotches, and trunk, as well as the ground beneath the tree's drip line. If it rains within 48 hours of spraying, repeat treatment. Spray again at the height of dormancy and at first bud swell.

✔ **CARE FOR CHRISTMAS TREES.** To prolong the freshness of a cut tree, saw an inch off the bottom of the trunk, then store the tree in a bucket of water in a shady area outdoors. When ready to bring in, saw off another inch of trunk before setting the tree in a stand. Use a stand that holds water and keep the reservoir full (check daily the first week). Keep living trees outdoors until shortly before the holidays—don't leave indoors more than two weeks.

✔ **PREPARE FOR FROST.** Move tender container plants under the eaves or indoors when cold weather is predicted. Cover frost-tender plants—such as banana, bougainvillea, citrus, and *Mandevillea* 'Alice du Pont'—in the ground with perforated plastic or burlap supported by a frame (four tall stakes, for example) that will keep the cover from touching the foliage.

✔ **FERTILIZE FALL PLANTINGS.** Feed actively growing winter vegetables and annuals to promote steady growth. ◆

Mountain Checklist

PLANTING AND SHOPPING

☑ **AMARYLLIS.** Pot up amaryllis bulbs at two-week intervals for a steady show of flowers Christmas through Valentine's Day. For techniques, see "The Amazing Amaryllis," page 336.

☑ **LIVING CHRISTMAS TREES.** Buy a tree you can plant in the garden later. Good choices include Colorado blue spruce (*Picea pungens* 'Glauca'), alpine fir (*Abies lasiocarpa*), Douglas fir (*Pseudotsuga menziesii*), and white fir (*Abies concolor*). During the tree's indoor stay, keep its roots cool and moist by covering the soil surface with two trays of ice cubes daily.

MAINTENANCE

☑ **BUILD A BRUSH PILE.** Use pruned branches to start a brush pile. Brush provides shelter for small birds, who often nest in it.

☑ **CARE FOR GIFT PLANTS.** To prolong the bloom of azaleas, Christmas cactus, cyclamen, kalanchoe, paper white narcissus, and poinsettias, remove decorative foil or wrap from pots so water won't pool inside.

Sunset
CLIMATE ZONES
☐ 1-3   ■ 10-11

DEBRA LAMBERT

☑ **HARVEST HOLIDAY GREENS.** Prune evergreen conifers and use the boughs for holiday wreaths and swags. Don't leave stubs; cut just above side branches that you want to grow. While you're at it, remove dead, diseased, and injured branches. Then prune for shape, working from the bottom of the tree to the top, and from the inside out.

☑ **MULCH.** It's not too late to spread a 3- to 4-inch layer of mulch over beds of perennials, bulbs, and shrubs.

☑ **PREPARE INDOOR CACTUS FOR BLOOM.** Hold off watering springflowering indoor cactus from midDecember through February, then water. Apply a dilute solution of fertilizer every second watering. If the cactus is in a bright spot, buds and blooms should follow.

☑ **PROPAGATE HOUSE PLANTS.** Chinese evergreen, dracaena, philodendron, and other plants can become leggy in winter. To start new plants, snip off elongated stems and immerse the cut ends in water until roots form, then transplant rooted cuttings in potting soil.

☑ **PROTECT YOUNG TREES.** Young trees with trunks less than 4 inches in diameter are subject to sunscald when the low winter sun shines on their bark. Shield them with commercial tree wrap. Or make a protective collar using corrugated plastic drainpipe with a diameter slightly larger than the trunk; split pipe lengthwise and fit it around the trunk.

☑ **SPRAY DORMANT PLANTS.** To control overwintering insects and diseases on deciduous ornamental and fruit-bearing trees and shrubs, including roses, apply dormant oil mixed with lime sulfur or fixed copper. Spray on a clear day when the temperature is above freezing.

☑ **WATER.** When temperatures stay above freezing, water dry spots in the garden, especially plants in containers and under house eaves. ◆

Southwest Checklist

PLANTING

☑ **BULBS.** Early in the month, set out daffodil, Dutch iris, hyacinth, ranunculus, and tulip bulbs that have been chilled in the refrigerator for at least six weeks.

☑ **COOL-SEASON FLOWERS.** Zones 12–13: Set out calendulas, candytuft, cyclamen, dianthus, Iceland poppies, larkspur, pansies, petunias, primroses, snapdragons, stock, sweet alyssum, and violas. In zone 13, you can also plant bedding begonias and cineraria.

☑ **NATIVE PLANTS.** Zones 10–13: Take advantage of cool air and soil temperatures by planting hardy native trees and shrubs now. Water regularly during the first year until roots become established.

☑ **PEPPERS AND TOMATOES.** Zones 12–13: Sow seeds of peppers and tomatoes indoors in containers of sterile potting soil. Moisten the soil thoroughly and put the containers in a warm place (70° to 80°) until seeds germinate. When seedlings emerge, move them into bright light. Plants should be ready to set out in late February after frost danger is past.

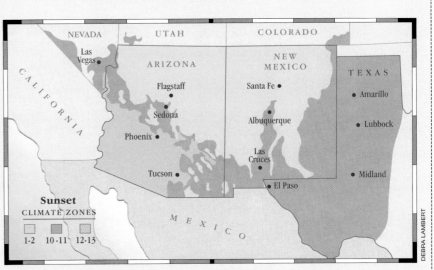

☑ **LIVING CHRISTMAS TREES.** Buy a living tree that you can plant in the garden later. Choices vary by climate. Zones 11–13: Try Afghan pine (*P. eldarica*), aleppo pine (*P. halepensis*), or, in zones 11 and 12, deodar cedar (*Cedrus deodara*). Zone 10 (Albuquerque): Try Colorado blue spruce (*Picea pungens* 'Glauca'), deodar cedar, or Douglas fir (*Pseudotsuga menziesii*). During the tree's indoor stay, keep roots cool and moist by covering the soil surface with two trays of ice cubes daily.

MAINTENANCE

☑ **FEED DORMANT FRUIT TREES.** For established trees (those at least four years old), spread 9 pounds of 10-10-10 fertilizer under the drip line now. After harvest, apply 3 more pounds of the same fertilizer.

☑ **HARVEST HOLIDAY GREENS.** Prune evergreens and use the boughs for swags and wreaths. Don't leave stubs; cut just beyond side branches you want to grow.

☑ **PREPARE INDOOR CACTUS FOR BLOOM.** Hold off watering spring-flowering indoor cactus from mid-December through February, then water. Fertilize lightly every second watering.

☑ **WATER.** When temperatures stay above freezing, water dry spots in the garden, especially plants in containers and under house eaves. ◆

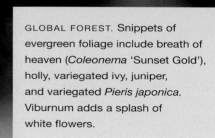

GLOBAL FOREST. Snippets of
evergreen foliage include breath of
heaven (*Coleonema* 'Sunset Gold'),
holly, variegated ivy, juniper,
and variegated *Pieris japonica*.
Viburnum adds a splash of
white flowers.

Garden-fresh hanging bouquets

These ornaments are easy to make: Just tuck cut flowers and greenery into foam-filled berry baskets

BY KATHLEEN N. BRENZEL • PHOTOGRAPHS BY NORMAN A. PLATE

■ IN MANY PARTS OF THE WEST, WINTER flowers are as much a part of holiday decorating as holly and mistletoe—much to the delight of Bud Stuckey, *Sunset's* test garden coordinator, who never misses a chance to celebrate with flowers. After planting many hanging baskets with annuals and perennials last spring and summer, he wondered if he could adapt the hanging bouquet idea to form indoor arrangements for the holidays. He experimented, using cut flowers and florist's foam, and came up with the three creations pictured here and on page 330. Each one measures about 8 inches in diameter.

Garden globes like these are easy to make. Cut sprigs of small-leafed greenery such as fir, ivy, rosemary, spruce, and viburnum, and poke the stems into

PRETTY IN PINK. Flowers carry the show: azaleas (deep clear pink), cyclamen (pale pink), heather (tiny lavender pink blooms), and *Grevillea* 'Noellii' (rosy pink tubes). Silvery gray dusty miller foliage adds accents.

BLOOMS AND BERRIES. Red 'Yuletide' Sasanqua camellias and red holly berries are finishing touches among variegated ivy, Douglas fir, rosemary (flecked with blue flowers), and white fir.

moist florist's foam. Brighten them with winter flowers from your garden or a florist, festoon them with gold or silver cord, then hang them over a doorway or in front of a window outlined with little white lights. For a holiday table centerpiece, poke one on top of a wood candleholder (you can secure the foam on a nail in the top of the holder).

Kept moist, these ornaments can last a week or more. Every day or two, hold the basket under running water over a sink, or spritz the foam with water from a plastic spray bottle.

Step-by-step

TIME: 1 hour
COST: $5 to $6 (not including plants)

MATERIALS
- 1 block florist's foam, 3 inches high, 4 inches wide, and 9 inches long (enough for three ornaments)
- Sharp knife for cutting foam
- Plastic mesh berry basket, 1-pint size
- Scissors
- 1 roll decorative gold or silver cord, about 1/8 inch wide (one basket needs about 8 to 10 feet)
- Hand pruners
- Foliage branches and flowers from your garden or a florist

DIRECTIONS
1. Soak the foam block in a basin of water until thoroughly saturated (about 30 minutes). Set it on paper towels to drain.
2. Using a sharp knife, cut the foam into three equal pieces. Put one foam piece into the plastic berry basket.
3. Using scissors, cut four equal lengths of gold or silver cord, each at least 1½ feet long (or longer, depending on where you want to hang the ornament). Fasten one length at each corner of the basket's rim. Set the basket atop a can, letting the cords dangle free, or hang the basket by tying the tops of the cords to an overhead kitchen cupboard handle.
4. With pruners, cut branches of foliage into snippets about 4 inches long. Strip off lowest foliage, leaving 1 to 2 inches of stem. Cut the base of the stem on a diagonal. Poke snippets into the foam, spacing them evenly around the basket as shown below to create a framework. Fill in with more foliage, then add flowers until the foam is completely covered.
5. Gather ends of the four cords and tie them together with a strong knot. Hang the ornament away from heat sources. ◆

TUCKER & HOSSLER

VOTIVE CANDLES on metal holders glow between planters filled with white mums, red kalanchoe, ferns, and trailing ivy.

Plant a living centerpiece

Decorate your holiday table with festive "shoe box" planters

BY PETER O. WHITELEY

Creating a centerpiece scaled for a big holiday dinner is a real challenge, especially if you've extended your dining table to seat Aunt Sadie and her brood. But small bouquets get lost on a crowded tabletop and oversize arrangements can end up blocking views and spilling over plates.

What you need are long, narrow containers you can fill with greenery and flowers that stay well below eye level. Finding such vessels can be difficult, but making them is easy—with shoe box–size plastic storage containers. Something wonderful happens when you fill them with living plants and trim the boxes with festive ribbon. Instantly, you have a centerpiece elegant enough to grace any table, and you can make it as long as you want simply by adding more boxes.

For the arrangement shown here, we used three boxes and filled them with indoor plants readily available at nurseries and floral shops: florist's chrysanthemum, kalanchoe, 'Ocean Spray' maidenhair fern, and variegated ivy. In mild-winter areas, you can substitute cool-season flowers such as primroses, pansies, and Johnny-jump-ups. Since the boxes are relatively shallow, plants should be no larger than 4-inch size. Once planted, the centerpiece can be displayed for a week or two. Water sparingly to keep soil evenly moist, not soggy. After the parties are over, repot the plants individually for indoor display; cool-season flowers can be set out in the garden.

Shoe box–size plastic containers cost less than $2 each at most home supply centers. You can mask the boxes with any variety of materials, from rice paper to satin ribbon. Coordinate the color with the flowers and your tablecloth.

TIME: 1 hour or less

COST: About $35 as shown

MATERIALS

- Three plastic storage boxes, each at least $12\frac{1}{2}$ inches long, 7 inches wide, and $3\frac{1}{2}$ inches deep
- Potting soil
- Three plants each of florist's mum, kalanchoe, and fern from 4-inch pots (or substitute cyclamen, *Primula obconica,* or Rieger begonia)
- 18 plants of variegated ivy from sixpacks (optional)
- Satin ribbon or other trimming material, $3\frac{1}{2}$ inches wide
- Candles (optional)

DIRECTIONS

1. Fill each box with potting soil.

2. In each box, set three 4-inch plants and firm soil around them. Fill in around the sides with trailing ivy, if desired.

3. Lightly water the soil and wipe the sides of the boxes.

4. Set the boxes on a tabletop, all together or spaced a few inches apart to make room for candles, if desired. Wrap a length of ribbon around each box to cover the sides. ◆

BOW OF CHILIES
and "rose" of desert
spoon petals
embellish this
prickly pear wreath.

Deck the halls in desert style

Make wreaths and arrangements from Southwest flora

BY SHARON COHOON • PHOTOGRAPHS BY NORMAN A. PLATE

■ The Southwest has such strength of character that it leaves its stamp on everything within its embrace. Witness its cooking, writing, painting, and architecture—all instantly recognizable as desert born and bred. Holiday decorations used to be the exception. Come December, people turned to colder climates for inspiration: They decked their halls with holly and Scotch pine, just as if they lived in Portland or Seattle.

But that's changing, thanks to local artists whose work is pictured here. The forms these Tucsonans employ are traditional—wreaths and centerpieces—but the materials come from local foothills, farmlands, and backyards. They've linked the holiday to their landscape; they've stamped it unquestionably Southwest. Following are three projects you can copy.

Southwestern simplicity

Glenda Pierce of Glenda's Custom Desert Designs uses prickly pear cactus pads and dried chili pods to create wreaths that are as dramatic and quintessentially Southwest as a saguaro backlit by a sunset. (If you're intimidated by all those spines and would rather buy than make a wreath, contact Pierce at 520/322-9350; prices are $38 to $200.)

TIME: 2½ hours

COST: $25–$30 (plus prickly pear pads)

MATERIALS

• Wreath hanger or hook
• Straw wreath base, available at craft stores
• Wood florist's picks, 4 inches long
• 8 to 10 prickly pear pads of similar size, sold in produce sections of many markets (if you use ones from your garden, cut the pads from the plant with a saw or hand pruners, holding on to the stems with tongs;

don't bother with gloves, as these spines can pierce the thickest leather)
• Dried desert spoon petals or cornhusks to make a "rose," or raffia for a bow
• Glue gun and glue sticks
• 4-inch-long wood stem or ¼-inch-diameter dowel
• 22-gauge wire
• Several dozen dried red chili pods
• Clear polyurethane spray paint

DIRECTIONS

1. Attach hanger or hook to the back of wreath base according to product instructions.
2. Using florist's picks, attach prickly pear pads securely to the wreath, round side up. Place the picks through the base of each pad, then overlap the pad bases slightly

RED-HOT CHILI BOUQUET
Guests at the Arizona Inn in Tucson expect traditions to be honored, and the hotel's director of design, Bill Dillon, meets their expectations. But he finds clever ways to work in references to the surrounding desert. The bouquet shown here, for example, fills a burnished gourd. First arrange fir and pine prunings in the gourd or another container. Then add berried branches of pyracantha and photinia prunings. Embellish the arrangement with dried chili pods, white winterberries, and green eucalyptus pods.

as you go. Use three or four florist's picks for each pad, and push them completely through pad, well into the straw base. Do not use glue, as it will blister the pads, causing them to rot. Leave a 6-inch opening at the top center of the wreath for the rose/chilies detail.

3. Make a rose out of desert spoon petals. Trim the edges to round them, then glue them around the wood stem or dowel. Attach the rose to the opening in the wreath's top center by applying glue to the stem end, then poking it into the straw base. You can substitute a fat bow of raffia pieces for the rose; to attach it, twist a length of wire around the bow's center, then poke the ends into the straw base.

4. Clean the chilies with a damp cloth and cut off stems. Cut a 6-inch piece of wire for each chili. Dip the wire into the glue, then insert the wire partway though the stem end. Dip the other end of the wire into the glue, then poke it into the straw base, on one side of the rose. Continue adding chilies, creating a generous cascade on each side of the rose.

5. Spray the entire wreath (*except the raffia bow,* if you use one) with clear polyurethane to intensify the color of the cactus pads and strengthen the chilies. (Do not use polyurethane on Santa Rita prickly pears, however, as it changes their wonderful deep lavender coloring to dull green.)

Della Robbia

I n the desert, shapes are strong and colors are subtle. For this wreath, Ruth Hamilton uses yucca pods to carry the show, adding other seed pods as color accents. The mauve pinks, violets, and gray-blues are reminiscent of hues reflected off desert hills in the late afternoon.

Hamilton teaches classes in wreath making at botanical gardens in Tucson (materials are provided at the classes). For details, call (520) 297-0954.

TIME: Six hours
COST: $15–$20

MATERIALS
• A beveled polystyrene wreath base
• Dark brown water-base spray paint
• Wreath hanger or hook
• Corrugated cardboard
• Construction-grade adhesive (such as Liquid Nails)
• Bleached yucca pods, about 125 pods to cover a 12-inch-diameter wreath (300 pods for a 24-inch wreath), with $\frac{1}{2}$-inch stems. (To bleach pods, soak them in a solution of $\frac{1}{2}$ gallon bleach to 3 gallons water for 10 minutes, then put in the sun to dry.) You could substitute bottle tree or milkweed pods, which don't need bleaching
• Other dried material for accents: desert spoon petals, deodar cedar "roses," dried pomegranates, coyote melons, mesquite, cotton and poppy pods, and devil's claws
• Wood florist's picks with attached wire

DIRECTIONS
1. Spray the front side of the wreath base with dark brown paint so the base will disappear into shadow.
2. Attach hanger or hook to the back of wreath.
3. To strengthen the wreath, cut out a doughnut-shaped piece of corrugated cardboard the same size as the wreath base, spread adhesive over it as if you were icing a cake, and press it onto back of the wreath base.
4. Cull your largest pods for the outer ring of the wreath. Dip their stems into the adhesive and poke them into the foam. Continue adding pods until the outer row is complete. Repeat, using slightly smaller pods for the next row.
5. Add pods to cover the inside of the wreath frame.
6. Fill in the face of the wreath with remaining pods and add accents, attaching each piece separately with a florist's pick. Dip pick into glue first for extra security, if desired.
Note: It is illegal to harvest many native plants from the wild. Some dry seed pods are excluded from this rule, depending on the plant. The safest course is to gather material only from private land *with permission.* Other options: Many botanical gardens sell dried plant materials during the holidays. Native-plant nurseries may too. Also check with craft stores; Ben Franklin Crafts in Tucson, for instance, usually carries dried native-plant material during the holidays. ◆

Watering cans to covet

Heirloom-quality watering cans make perfect gifts for avid gardeners

BY SHARON COHOON

Sources

Traditional English brass-trimmed galvanized steel can and classic red powder-coated steel can: **Kinsman Company;** *(800) 733-4146 or www.kinsmangarden.com.* Copper can with brass oval rose: **Smith & Hawken;** *(800) 776-3336 or www.smithandhawken.com.*

DECKED FOR HOLIDAY GIVING: From left, 2¼-gallon red powder-coated can ($32), 3-pint copper can ($69), and 1.9-gallon galvanized steel can with brass trim ($69).

I bet there's not a gardener on your holiday shopping list who doesn't secretly long for a traditional English watering can with double handles and a twist of wire bracing the spout just like the one Mr. McGregor uses in Beatrix Potter's *The Tale of Peter Rabbit.* Actually, we wouldn't mind watering our creeping Charlie with that sleek polished copper can shown above, too. And wouldn't that fire engine red one be fun?

Not that we'd dream of buying any of these luxury cans for ourselves, mind you. We may know that a well-crafted watering can is a joy to use as well as behold. And that a metal can not only will outlive a plastic one but will outlast us and our heirs too, making it an outstanding value. But somehow we still feel guilty spending extra dollars for a top-of-

the-line model. Though we dearly want the real McGregor, we're not likely to get it unless it's a gift. (That's a hint, honey.)

Of the many watering cans available today, some—including the three pictured above—have features that set them apart from the rest of the pack.

Anatomy of a perfect watering can

There's a reason the traditional metal watering can remains popular, and it isn't nostalgia. The design is hard to improve upon. Here are some key features.

■ Enduring material. Metal is heavier and more expensive than plastic, but it ages beautifully. **Copper** oxidizes over time, developing a verdigris finish, but is otherwise impervious to the elements. Because copper is a rather soft metal

that dents easily, however, these cans are best for indoor use. **Steel** is very strong but also rust-prone. A coating of zinc solves that problem. (Look for the words "galvanized" or "dipped in zinc" in product literature.)

■ Double handles. They make balancing easy. You support most of the weight of the filled can with the top handle and tip and pour with the side one. Rolled edges or tubular handles increase comfort—they don't press into your palms when you lift the filled container.

■ Spout support. Structural support, whether twisted wires or a welded brace, keeps the spout from bending and developing leaks at the base.

■ Removable brass rose. Small holes in the rose soften water flow so it's gentle enough for tender seedlings. (Inverted oval roses, like the one on the copper can above, produce a particularly fine spray.) Brass is the favored material because it won't corrode and it resists mineral deposits, keeping the tiny perforations clear. When you want a lot of water quickly, remove the rose and pour a direct stream. ◆

The amazing amaryllis

Each bulb produces huge, trumpet-shaped blooms

BY LAUREN BONAR SWEZEY

Amaryllis bulbs carry lots of surprises inside. Just weeks after planting, a dramatic 1- to 1½-foot-tall stalk emerges from each large brown bulb, then unfurls a cluster of four or five perfect trumpet-shaped blooms as large as 9 inches across. Over a period of several weeks, each bulb produces one or two additional stalks topped with equally beautiful blooms in delicious candy colors—from cherry red to peppermint pink and white, depending on variety.

Flower colors have changed dramatically in recent years. Reds have been the standard fare and are still some of the most striking colors available. But breeders have developed a stunning array of pastel shades, including pink, salmon, yellow, and striped and feathered bicolors.

Although the classic amaryllis flower is shaped like a single trumpet, a range of double-flowered types—including one with voluptuous blooms reminiscent of peonies, and a multipetaled bloom with ruffled edges—are now available.

In spite of their hothouse look, amaryllis are easy to grow. All you need is a pot, a saucer, and a small amount of potting soil. Plant several amaryllis pots to chase away the winter doldrums or to give as gifts. In six to eight weeks, even nongardeners will be delighted by the beautiful blooms that grow from those humble brown bulbs.

WHAT TO BUY
•Large, firm bulbs that aren't sprouting.
•A pot that's wide enough to allow a 1-inch gap between the pot rim and the bulbs—6 inches wide for one bulb, 10 to 12 inches wide for three bulbs.

HOW TO PLANT
•Fill the pot halfway with potting mix. Set each bulb in pot, stem end up, as shown at left. Cover it with potting mix, leaving the top third showing above soil.
•Water the newly planted bulbs well. Do not get water on the bulb noses (the thickened tops), or they may rot.

GROWING TIPS
•Place the pot in a room where the temperature always stays between 65° and 70°.

Sources

Bulbs are available at many nurseries. But for wide selections, try these sources. **Garden.com,** 3301 Steck Ave., Austin, TX 78757; (800) 466-8142 or www. garden.com. **Wayside Gardens,** 1 Garden Lane, Hodges, SC 29695; (800) 845-1124 or www.waysidegardens.com.

•Water sparingly until growth emerges don't let the soil dry out.
•When growth emerges, give the plan bright, indirect light.
•Keep the soil moist but not wet.
•Stake the stems, if necessary (weak leggy stems indicate too little light)
•When buds open, move the pot to a cooler place, since temperatures of 60° or so prolong flower life.

AFTER-BLOOM CARE

• Cut off the old bloom stalks about ½ inch from the top of the bulb. Foliage will soon appear.

• Keep the plant in a bright location.

• After the last freeze, move the pot outdoors where it will get morning sun and afternoon shade.

• Continue to water and fertilize regularly.

• To initiate bloom in fall, plants need a cooling period (48° to 55°) for 10 weeks starting in October or November—a natural occurrence outdoors (protect from freezes in cold climates). Stop fertilizing during the cooling period.

• After the cooling period, cut the leaves back to 4 inches above the bulb neck and bring the pot back inside.

• Repot every other year right after the cooling period. ◆

HERALDING the holidays are, from left, double 'Red Peacock', soft pink-and-white 'Apple Blossom', coral-and-white 'Vera', and peony-flowered 'Nymph'.

'NAVAJO'

'CHANSONETTE'

'APPLE BLOSSOM'

'TANYA'

'SHOWA-NO-SAKAE'

'POLAR ICE'

'WINTER'S CHARM'

'SETSUGEKKA'

'SNOW FLURRY'

'YULETIDE'

'FROSTED STAR'

Color-kissed camellias

Early-flowering Sasanquas brighten the holidays

BY JIM McCAUSLAND

PHOTOGRAPHS BY
DEIDRA WALPOLE

■ DURING THE HOLIDAY SEASON, NURSERIES from San Diego to Seattle showcase Sasanqua camellias—and with good reason. Sasanquas are one of the earliest and showiest winter-flowering shrubs in mild areas of the West. In fact, they produce more flowers than their spring-blooming cousins—the Japonica camellias—and since Sasanquas bloom during cool weather, the blossoms tend to keep coming for a long time (up to two months). Even when they are out of bloom, their shiny evergreen leaves add elegance to the landscape.

Sold in 1-, 2-, or 5-gallon containers, Sasanquas start flowering young. Plant them right away, or slip the nursery can into a decorative container for display on a patio or porch until blooms are past, then plant in spring. Many nurseries also offer young espaliered plants ($50 to $80); plant them against an east-facing wall with overhanging eaves so their delicate flowers will be protected from rain.

Sasanquas are hardy in *Sunset* climate zones 4–9 and 14–27. They thrive in the filtered shade of large trees or in a spot protected from hot midday sun. In mild-summer areas along the coast, they can tolerate full sun. They like well-drained soil amended with plenty of peat moss or leaf mold.

At planting time, water them well and spread a 2-inch layer of organic mulch around plants. Thereafter, water to keep the soil constantly moist, but not soggy.

When new leaves emerge in spring, feed plants with half-strength fish emulsion. Then feed every six weeks: If your garden soil is neutral or alkaline (typical in Southern California), give each plant a half-strength application of liquid acid fertilizer. If your soil is acidic (common in the Northwest), apply a complete fertilizer at half strength.

Although Sasanquas will grow into small trees if you let them, few plants take better to pruning. Right after flowering, prune to get the form you want, removing dead or weak wood and thin-

After bloom, prune dense growth to make room for next year's flowers.

'RAINBOW'

ning dense growth so flowers will have room to open fully.

Sasanquas seem to have less trouble with camellia petal blight—a disease that causes blossoms to turn an ugly brown—than Japonica types.

But if aphids or scale insects appear, you'll notice black sooty mold coating the leaves beneath the infestations. Start by spraying with insecticidal soap, which will help wash off the sooty mold and smother the aphids. To control scale, follow up by spraying horticultural oil right after bloom is finished. Apply horticultural oil only when the temperature is expected to remain between 40° and 85° for a few days.

The same strategy—insecticidal soap followed by horticultural oil—can also help with mite infestations, which make camellia leaves look dusty and gray. Mites are more of a problem in Southern California. Hose dust and tiny mite webs off leaves every couple of weeks.

Sasanquas and friends: Pick your favorite flower colors, forms

■ Flowers come in single and double forms, ranging from 1½ to 5 inches across, often with a big yellow brush of anthers in the center. When choosing between single or double flowers, remember that singles shed rain better—a good trait in the Northwest. Nurseries often sell plants of related Hiemalis and Vernalis camellias as part of the Sasanqua group.

Sasanquas
Rose to red: 'Cleopatra' (semidouble), 'Hiryu' (double with curled edges), 'Rosette' (loose peony form with golden-tipped white stamens), 'Tanya' (small single flowers), and 'Yuletide' (single, bright red

with yellow anthers). **Pink:** 'Chansonette' (double), 'Frosted Star' (semidouble), 'Himekoki' (rose form), 'Jean May' (double), and 'Rosea' (single, yellow anthers; light fragrance). **White:** 'Setsugekka' (big semidouble), 'White Doves' (double; also sold as 'Mine-No-Yuki'). **Apple-blossom types** (white with pink or red blush): 'Apple Blossom', 'Hana Jiman', 'Navajo', 'Rainbow' (single, white with red fringe), 'Taishuhai' (single to semidouble), 'Yae Arare'.

Hiemalis and Vernalis
Both of these types are probably crosses of *C. sasanqua* and *C. japonica*.

More cold-hardy than most Sasanquas, Hiemalis types flower well in fall and winter, while most Vernalis bloom in spring. **Rose:** 'Bonanza' (peony-like flowers with yellow stamens), 'Dazzler' (semidouble), 'Kanjiro' (single to semidouble), 'Shishi-Gashira' (semidouble to double; can bloom continuously for five months). **Pink:** 'Showa-no-sakae' and its offspring 'Showa Supreme' spread so effectively that they can be used as ground covers.

Hardy hybrids
These varieties are hybrids between *C. japonica* and *C. sasanqua* or *C. hiemalis*. Hardy to -10°, they need

overhead protection (like a tree canopy that screens them from open sky) and shelter from cold, drying winds. **Purplish red:** 'Winter's Star'. **Pink:** 'Winter's Beauty', 'Winter's Charm', 'Winter's Dream', 'Winter's Fire', 'Winter's Interlude', 'Winter's Peony', 'Winter's Rose'. **White:** 'Polar Ice', 'Snow Flurry', 'Winter's Hope', 'Winter's Waterlily'.

SOURCES
Camellias are widely sold in nurseries and garden centers. You can also shop for plants by mail from the West's leading camellia breeder: Nuccio's Nurseries in Altadena, California; (626) 794-3383; free catalog. ◆

Article Titles Index

Renee's Garden
Jewel-Toned Bell Peppers
Crimson, Gold & Orange

"Set a table in the garden"
—Renee Shepherd

W. D. A. STEPHENS

W. D. A. STEPHENS

NORMAN A. PLATE

General Subject Index

NORMAN A. PLATE

Bulbs (cont'd)
    South African, 190
    tulip, 99, 272–277
Butterflies, attracting, 48, 163
Butterfly bush, 81, 88

Caesalpinia pulcherrima, 89
Calibrachoa, 190
California poppy, 82
Calla, new colors of, 90
Calluna vulgaris, 284
Camellias, Sasanqua, 338–340
Campsis radicans, 85
Cape fuchsia, 157
Cape plumbago, 88–89
Carthamus tinctorius, 208
Catananche caerulea, 208
Catharanthus roseus, 88
Catmint, 78, 86, 157, 296, 315
Ceanothus, 315
Centaurea rothrockii, 64
Centranthus ruber, 76, 80, 84, 88, 315
Cerinthe major purpurascens, 74
Chamelaucium uncinatum, 63
Chinese foxglove, 80
Chrysanthemum parthenium, 192
Clematis
    dioscoreifolia, 77, 85, 235
    jackmanii, 77
    montana 'Rubens', 77, 97
    suitable for containers, 116, 119
Color
    champions for western regions,
        74–89
    combinations using tulips, 272–277
    for containers, 166, 180–181
    daring combinations of, 265, 293
    fall, 260, 284–285, 296
    from foliage plants, 65, 237
    in harsh climates, 62, 166
    for Mediterranean gardens,
        304–305
    shades of green, 255
    from wildflowers, 309
Colorado gardening, book about, 30
Common sneezeweed, 84
Common trumpet creeper, 83, 85
Concrete, new ways of using, 44, 48,
    49, 142, 143, 146, 206
Conifers, dwarf, 237
Container gardening
    clematis for, 119
    foliage color for, 65, 189
    grasses suitable for, 32
    high-altitude techniques for, 166
    instant "bouquets" from, 91–93
    for parties, 180–181

Container gardening (cont'd)
    planting tips for, 192, 248–250
    in a strawberry pot, 56–57
    trees suitable for, 287
    for tropical effects, 212
    watering tips for, 191
    wildflowers for, 286
    See also Pots
Coral bells, 315
Coreopsis, 157
Cornflower, 64
Cosmos bipinnatus, 78
Courtyards, 143, 166, 230–231, 236
Cover crops, 240
Creeping zinnia, 74
Crocosmia, 84, 285
Cupid's dart, 208
Curcuma alistmatifolia, 97
Cytisus purgans, 266

Daffodil, 66, 251–253, 315
Dahlberg daisy, 82
Dahlias, storing for winter, 263
Daylily, 78–80, 86, 122–123
Decks, ideas for, 142, 152–153, 226
Deer damage, coping with, 191
Delosperma, 83, 84
Desert gardening. See Dry-climate
    gardening; Southwest, garden
    ideas and information for
Diascia, 76, 157, 266
Diospyros kaki, 296
Diseases, plant
    late blight on tomatoes, 101
    neem used for, 133
    rust on hollyhocks, 31
    See also specific plant listings
Dried flowers, 208, 213
Driveways, ideas for, 34, 44
Dry-climate gardening
    book about, 66, 163
    border for, 282
    in Hawaii, 237
    under oaks, 141, 314–315
    wildflowers for, 306–309
    See also Southwest, garden ideas
    and information for
Dusty miller, 315
Dwarf cup flower, 82
Dyssodia tenuiloba, 82

Echinacea purpurea, 76, 77
English garden style, 131, 290
Entertaining, outdoor, 44–45, 50, 142,
    152–153, 177–179, 180–181

W. D. A. STEPHENS

The Golden Poppy
State Flower of California

Theodore Payne Foundation
10459 Tuxford Street
Sun Valley, CA 91352

Entryway ideas, 51, 53, 230–231, 236
Erica canaliculata, 319
Erigeron karvinskianus, 80, 81, 157,
    315
Eryngium amethystinum, 208
Erysimum, 80
Eschscholzia californica, 82
Espalier, 36
Eulalia grass, 81, 285
Eupatorium maculatum, 76
Evergreens
    care of, for holidays, 320
    island of coniferous, 237
Everlasting arrrangements. See Dried
    flowers

Fall color, 260, 284–285, 296
Fallugia paradoxa, 85
Fences, ideas for, 53, 225
Fertilizers, natural, 240
Festuca ovina 'Glauca', 315
Feverfew, 192
Firecracker penstemon, 86–88
Flannel bush, 295
Foliage plants
    border of, 280
    for color and texture, 65, 96, 189,
        237, 304–305
    design principles for using, 254–255
    for late-year interest, 285, 292
    suitable for containers, 65, 189
Fountain grass, 81, 315
Fountains, 43, 51, 131, 143, 146, 206
Fremontia, 295
Frost damage, 66

NORMAN A. PLATE

NORMAN A. PLATE

New Mexico gardening, book about, 163

New Zealand tea tree, 63

Nierembergia hippomanica violacea, 82

Northern California, garden ideas and information for

best plant choices for summer color, 78–81

coastal scrub garden reflects nature, 286

cottage-garden style suits coastal climate (Mendocino), 290

entryway dilemma solved (Cameron Park), 51

garden checklists. *See* Article Titles Index

Mediterranean adaptation (Saratoga), 51

minimalist marriage with nature (Philo), 50

parking strip abloom (Fort Bragg), 34

redefined entryway for a small space (Los Altos), 53

rich colors, sculptural forms (Berkeley), 211

sculpture gallery garden (Berkeley), 49

serene foliage garden (Sonoma), 254–255

sixties style perfected (Sacramento), 53

small-space makeover (San Jose), 46–47

softened driveway approach (Los Altos), 44

Sonoma County nurseries, book about, 265

Nurseries, specialty

book about, 265

for daffodils, 66

for Japanese iris, 166

for lavender, 187

for orchids, 63

for sweet peas, 168

for tillandsias, 27

See also other specific plant listings; Gardens, public, and display nurseries

Oaks, underplanting, 141, 314–315

Oenothera berlandieri, 88

Oleander, 81, 89

Orange globe mallow, 88

Orchids, 63

Mountain states, garden ideas and information for *(cont'd)*

climate-adapted color (Denver), 62

Colorado gardens, book about, 30

deer-country solutions (Boulder), 191

garden checklists. *See* Article Titles Index

from lawn to crazy-quilt terrace (Denver), 207

narrow side-yard water garden (Vail), 164

Plant Select winners for 2000, 266

prize-winning container garden (Denver area), 166

Mountain states, garden ideas and information for *(cont'd)*

state-specific garden notebooks, 190

streambed transforms problem slope (Cherry Hills Village, CO), 294

Mulch, 229, 238

Narcissus, 250, 252–253, 315

Nasturtium, 76

Native plants, using, 35, 48, 50, 101, 145, 286

Neem, pros and cons of, 133

Nemesia fruticans, 157

Nepeta faassenii, 78, 86, 157, 296, 315

Nerium oleander, 81, 89

NORMAN A. PLATE

NORMAN A. PLATE

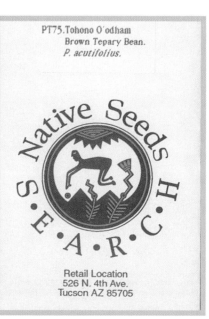

PT75.Tohono O'odham
Brown Tepary Bean.
P. acutifolius.

Native Seeds S·E·A·R·C·H

Retail Location
526 N. 4th Ave.
Tucson AZ 85705

Oriental Vegetable Seeds

Chinese Kale (Kailaan)

长青

NET WT.
2 G

芥　藍　*Cái Ró*

EVERGREEN Y.H. ENTERPRISES

W. D. A. STEPHENS (2)